THE
KOVELS'
Illustrated Price Guide to
ROYAL DOULTON

BOOKS BY RALPH AND TERRY KOVEL

Dictionary of Marks—Pottery and Porcelain

A Directory of American Silver, Pewter and Silver Plate

American Country Furniture 1780–1875

Kovels' Know Your Antiques,® Revised

The Kovels' Antiques & Collectibles Price List

The Kovels' Bottle Price List

The Kovels' Collector's Guide to American Art Pottery

Kovels' Organizer for Collectors

The Kovels' Price Guide for Collector Plates, Figurines, Paperweights, and Other Limited Editions

The Kovels' Illustrated Price Guide to Depression Glass and American Dinnerware

The Kovels' Collectors' Source Book

Kovels' Know Your Collectibles

The Kovels' Book of Antique Labels

THE
KOVELS'
Illustrated Price Guide to
ROYAL DOULTON

Second Edition

Ralph and Terry Kovel

CROWN PUBLISHERS, INC.   NEW YORK

Published by Crown Publishers, Inc., One Park Avenue, New York, New York 10016, and simultaneously in Canada by General Publishing Company Limited

Manufactured in the United States of America

Library of Congress Cataloging in Publication Data

Kovel, Ralph M.
    The Kovels' Illustrated price guide to Royal Doulton.

    Bibliography: p.
    1. Doulton and Company—Catalogs. 2. Royal Doulton
figurines—Catalogs. 3. Toby jugs—Catalogs.
4. Character jugs—Catalogs. 5. Plates (Tableware)—
Catalogs. I. Kovel, Terry H. II. Title. III. Title:
Illustrated price guide to Royal Doulton.
NK4660.K68   1984   738'.09424'63   83–26221
ISBN: 0–517–55044–X
10 9 8 7 6 5 4 3 2 1
Second Edition

Contents

Authors' Note to Readers

Writing a book can be full of hazards, mysteries, and discoveries. This is a report of the Royal Doulton market in the United States from September 1982 to July 1983. Prices that are included are for pieces that have actually been offered for sale during that period. A few rare pieces have been appraised and the price is in italics. Doulton and Company, Inc., was helpful in offering information and pictures, but no information was given on prices. During the time the prices were reported, the Canadian dollar was worth about $.87 in U.S. currency and the English pound was worth from $1.55 to $1.70 in U.S. currency. Prices from these countries are not included, but they should be comparable.

We are researchers and collectors, and we have tried to read every book and article available about the Royal Doulton wares (see Bibliography for complete list of books). There are several important books with much information, and these books have been credited in their proper chapter. Other books were also helpful and we would be remiss not to thank and credit the authors of all of them.

Many of the pictures used in this book have been reproduced from old catalogs and literature of Doulton and Co., Inc. These are reproduced by permission of Royal Doulton. The prices and opinions stated in the book are those of the authors and are not necessarily endorsed by Royal Doulton.

Many of the special bits of information about some of the Royal Doulton wares have been located through the help of the Royal Doulton International Collectors Club. With the help of their publications and staff, especially Louise Irvine and Marguerita Trevelyan-Clark, we have been able to fill in gaps such as missing HN numbers, original issue prices, special marks, and other problems. Collectors interested in Royal Doulton should contact the American branch of the club at P.O. Box 1815, Somerset, New Jersey 08873, for membership information. The cost is $15.00 per year, and the membership includes a quarterly newsletter and the rights to purchase special club figurines and other pieces.

Special thanks also to Fred S. Dearden, Jr., Pascoe & Solomon of New York, Jenny Cox of Pick Kwik Discount Wines & Spirits, and Royal

Doulton Company in New Jersey—especially Laura M. Burk and Nancy E. Oliver-Clarke—and in England—especially David Allen and Eve Mountford.

There are many things still unsolved. The series ware, rouge flambé, and miscellaneous pieces are included in spite of the obvious omissions. We thought it better to "light one little candle" and show a bit of the path to many collectors. Dealers and collectors from all over the world have helped us to compile the many lists and histories. If you have any information that can be added, please write to us in care of Crown Publishers, Inc., One Park Avenue, New York, New York 10016.

Ralph M. Kovel—American Society of Appraisers, Senior Member International Society of Appraisers

Terry H. Kovel—American Society of Appraisers, Senior Member International Society of Appraisers

Acknowledgments

Many, many people helped us with this book. Thank you to all those listed here. Each bit of information, large or small, added to the jigsaw puzzle that became this book. Thank you also to the authors of the other books on this subject. It is only proper to include both the authors and the titles, with complete information about finding the books. Please see the bibliography for this list. David Allen; Ashtabula Antiques Importing Company, Inc., P.O. Box 338, Ashtabula, Ohio 44004; B & J Collectibles, 4540 State Road, Cleveland, Ohio 44109; Lester Barrett Antiques, 153 East 85th Street, Apt. 4, New York, New York 10028; Mrs. Vance Bartlett, Reynoldsburg, Ohio; Beach Antiques, P.O. Box 5391, Virginia Beach, Virginia 23455; Mary Bloomquist; Diane Braun; Frances Breshears; Laura M. Burk; Charlton Press, 299 Queen Street West, Toronto, Ontario M5V 1Z9, Canada; Lillian V. Christensen; John Clark; Collectors Cabinet, 2826 Tonawanda Drive, Rocky River, Ohio 44116; Collector's Den, P.O. Box 1876, Rockville, Maryland 20850; Colonial Corner Antiques, 504 Main Street, Wareham, Massachusetts 02571; Jenny Cox; Jerry J. Cranor; Curiosity Shop, 7835 Broadview Road, Cleveland, Ohio 44131; Cynthia's, 419½ Chillicothe Street, Portsmouth, Ohio 45662; Mary L. Dahl, P.O. Box 2308, San Bernardino, California 92406; T. M. Davies; Fred S. Dearden, Jr.; Richard Dennis, 144 Kensington Church Street, London, England; Veneka Downer; E & J Antiques, 2958 Merrick Road, Bellmore, New York 11710; Steve Eabry; Helen Eyles; Jan Fetterly; Bob and Helen Fortune, P.O. Box 188, Ashtabula, Ohio 44004; Adele Geary; Mary Gerstner; Adriana Goheski; Gourmet Antiques, 1313 South Main Street, Mansfield, Ohio 44907; H. E. Guenther; Barbara Guffroy; Harllo Antiques, 2970 Merrick Road, Bellmore, New York 11710; Margaret Helvey, 3259 Village Drive, Mishawaka, Indiana 46545; Hershy's, 8642 20th Avenue, Brooklyn, New York 11214; L. P. Hibbard; The Hillmans, Swampscott, Massachusetts; Hither & Yon, Ltd., P.O. Box 1042, Williamsburg, Virginia 23185; Bruce A. A. Hitman; Marilyn Hollis; Karen Inglis; Louise Irvine; Jamens Collectibles, 2982 Cheryl Road, Merrick, New York 11566; Jantiques, Hamden, Connecticut; John Jenkins and Stephen Nunn, 64 Fulham High Street, London SW6, England; Charles E. Johnson; Kay Antiques & Gifts, 2248 Route 6, Swansea, Massachusetts 02777; The Kichlines, Easton, Pennsylvania; Wayne B. Kielsmeier; Don Knight; The Laughing Dog Antiques, 4030 Dado Court, Ellicott City, Maryland 21043; Rita Leiter, P.O. Box 154, Little Neck,

New York 11363; Jocelyn Lukins, 14 Keith Grove, London W12 9EZ, England; John W. Mack, Jr.; Doris McIntire; Merric Collectables, P.O. Box 1298, Madison Square Station, New York, New York 10159; Pearl & Harry Morris, Unit 21, The Mall, Camden Passage, Islington, London, England; Eve Mountford; Meg Nathan; Old Towne Colonial Corner, 16960 North Meadows Lane, Strongsville, Ohio 44136; Nancy E. Oliver-Clarke; Pascoe & Solomon, Inc., 1122 Madison Avenue, New York, New York 10028; Mary Petersen; Diane Peterson, P.O. Box 2544, Atherton, California 94025; D. A. Philabaum, Seven Acres, 5840 Horning Road, Kent, Ohio 44240; Phillips, 406 East 79th Street, New York, New York 10021; Pick Kwik Discount Wines and Spirits; Sue Pingley; Michael Pithouse Enterprises, 26 Chapel Lane, Horrabridge, Yelverton, Devon PL20 7SP, England; The Plate Rack, 13399 Old Pleasant Valley Road, Middleburg Heights, Ohio 44130; The Plate Rail, 12570 Beacon Hill Road, Plymouth, Michigan 48170; Porcelain Products Limited, Box 892, Devon, Pennsylvania 19333; Ed Pry, P.O. Box 2655, Fort Myers, Florida 33902; Queens Things, Forest Hills, New York; John F. Re, P.O. Box 124, Pittsburgh, Pennsylvania 15230; Red Door, 516 E. Washington Street, Chagrin Falls, Ohio 44022; Mrs. E. A. Retzloff; Harry D. Richey; Rogers de Rin Antiques, 76 Royal Hospital Road, Paradise Walk, Chelsea SW3, England; Royal Antiques, P.O. Box 1546, St. Charles, Missouri 63302; Royal Doulton International Collectors Club, U.S. Branch, Box 1815, Somerset, New Jersey 08873; Royal Doulton International Collectors Club, 5, Egmont House, 116 Shaftesbury Avenue, London W1V 7DJ, England; Madeleine S. Samuels; Scadms Collectibles, Box 239, Smallwood, New York 12778; Vernon & Vesper Schneider; Art Schuenaman; Norman Spurgeon; Stairway to Collectables, 375 Garafraxa Street North, P.O. Box 130, Durham, Ontario, Canada NOG 1RO; Dorothy V. Strike; Patricia A. Sullivan; T & C Antiques, P.O. Box 240, Oxford, Michigan 48051; The Teachers, Dennis & Helen Clifton, Box 202, LaVerne, California 91750; Stanley Tessel, 301 East 47th Street, New York, New York 10017; D. L. Thomas, Orlando, Florida; William Throop; Mrs. Michael Todd; Jean-Marie Turrell, 6 Van Dyke Place, Summit, New Jersey 07901; Nick Tzimes, London, England; VIP Antiques, P.O. Box 14244, Atlanta, Georgia 30324; Arthur Weiner, Chicago, Illinois; Barry Weinrebe; S. Jean Wensink; S. Elizabeth Whipple; Lyle Williams; Stan Worrey, 6618 Newbury Lane, Parma Heights, Ohio 44130; Ye Olde Shoppe, 15022 Claymoor Court #8, Chesterfield, Missouri 63017; Yesterdays, P.O. Box 296, New City, New York 10956; Frank H. Boos Gallery, 1137 S. Adams, Birmingham, Michigan 48011.

Special thanks are due to Harriet Goldner for her tireless checking of the manuscript.

Investing in Royal Doulton

Dealers invest, but collectors should buy for sheer enjoyment and beauty. Fortunately, most buyers of Royal Doulton have been able to resell their collections at a price that has not only kept up with inflation but has also given them a profit. What the future holds is just a guess. The final result will depend on many factors, including inflation, the economy, the talent of the buyer, the continued interest in old Royal Doulton, and, finally, the structure of the retail market for new Royal Doulton pieces.

There are a few general rules that have held in the past. Old, out-of-production figurines have gone up in value. Sometimes, the less desirable the figurine was when it was new or the more unattractive in the eyes of the buyer of its day, the fewer that were made. Consequently, some of them are rarer and more expensive today.

The mark on the bottom has some influence on the price, especially the "A mark" found on jugs and "potted" on figurines.

There are known color variations on pieces and they frequently add little or nothing extra to the value.

The collector who wishes to invest must remember several things. You usually buy at retail from a store or dealer. If you wish to sell your collection, you must become a dealer or sell it at wholesale, which can be from 30 percent to 50 percent less than retail. If you own the collection, you must care for it, keep it from breakage and loss, etc. This can mean the added expenses of a burglar alarm, insurance, and record keeping. Keep careful records of your expenses so that if you eventually sell or give your collection to your heirs, you will have the proper accounting for tax purposes.

New Royal Doulton wares have gone up in price each year as the cost of production and inflation has increased. Older pieces are compared to the new ones in price and so they have also gone up in actual dollars. Owners of Royal Doulton have had years of enjoyment from owning a collection; and, if the market continues as it has, they may have a profit in actual dollars when the collection is sold. The "investment" return can be the fun of searching for the collection, the joy of living with the collection, and the money to be realized when the collection is finally sold.

Care, Repair, and Other Factors That Determine Value

The prices listed in this book are for pieces of Royal Doulton that are in mint, unrepaired, and undamaged condition. There were a few special limited edition pieces that were sold with a presentation box and certificate and were priced to include the box and certificate. Any type of damage will lower the value. A minor, clean break in a figurine's arm or leg that can be easily glued and remain almost invisible will lower the value one-third or less. Always be very careful when buying figurines. House sales, local ads, going-out-of-business sales often offer bargains; but there are usually no return privileges and breaks can be hard to find. If it is possible, place the Royal Doulton figurine or jug under an ultraviolet or black light. It will help to locate the breaks that have been repaired. But be very careful. If you don't have a black light, examine the piece carefully. Run your hands over the glaze to try to locate any break. This is a good idea anyway as there is a new method of repair that is black-light proof.

Royal Doulton should be treated like any fine china. It may be washed in warm water with a mild detergent or soap. Never store it in very hot or very cold locations. Never take a pitcher from the refrigerator to be washed in hot water. Any sudden change of temperature may crack the glaze or even the piece.

If you look at a collection of Royal Doulton figurines, you may notice a difference in the look of the glaze colors. Earlier pieces have a softer shine and the colors are usually less harsh. Decorating fashions influenced the factory's choice of shades, so pastel pinks are often from the 1930s, green and blue from the 1940s, and turquoise and orange in the 1950s, etc. Now it is the pale "Laura Ashley" palette.

History of the Doulton Factory

The Royal Doulton porcelains that are so popular with today's collectors are made by a company with a long history of ceramic production.

John Doulton was born at Fulham, England, on November 17, 1793. He apprenticed at the Fulham Pottery of London, England, from 1805 to 1812. He was a "thrower" who threw the lump of clay on the wheel and manipulated it until a vessel was shaped. He left in 1815 to become a partner of John Watts and Mrs. John Jones (widow of a potter who owned the house) in a pothouse in Vauxhall Walk, Lambeth, England.

Jones, Watts, and Doulton made stoneware bottles, jugs, figural flasks, whistles, rushlight holders, inkstands, pitchers, candlesticks, money boxes, and other domestic pottery. They also made Toby jugs.

Mrs. Jones left the partnership in 1820 and Doulton and Watts continued the business. The pothouse prospered and by 1826 it moved to High Street, Lambeth, where their location gave room for further expansion. A new kiln was build and over a two-year period the firm gradually moved from the old Vauxhall Walk buildings. By 1827 the company began making stoneware water pipes and water filters and continued making domestic wares and tiles. They also began experimenting with special containers for use in the chemical industry. By the 1830s they were making blacking bottles, jam jars, and ink bottles.

Henry Doulton, John's second son, was born in 1820. He was only fifteen when he chose to become a potter. The factory continued expanding and made a variety of chemical and domestic wares. Henry Doulton, who was trained as a potter, took some chemistry courses, worked with engineers, and learned basics needed to develop new products. He experimented to produce a cream-colored opaque-glazed ware. He also developed an airtight covered jar for food storage and a screw-stoppered bottle, and he received many patents for improvements to kilns, jars, vases, and tanks. The company developed improvements in sewer pipes, including an important special self-adjusting joint that was popular with the industry.

In 1846 Henry Doulton founded a sewer pipeworks called "Henry Doulton and Company," with his father, John Doulton, and his younger brother, Frederick Doulton. John Doulton, Jr., started his own factory in 1847 and continued with his business until 1853. John Watts decided to retire in 1853, and the three companies, Doulton and Watts, Henry Doulton and Company, and John Doulton, Junior, all dissolved and the new firm of Doulton and Company was formed. Henry Doulton's pipe business had been the most valuable, so when the new company was formed he became the largest shareholder. A series of Doulton brothers and sons entered and left the company, shares changed hands, and the firm grew and prospered. John Doulton, Sr., died in 1873.

Doulton and Company continued the family tradition of innovation, research, and successful management. The last half of the 1800s produced many new types of pottery and porcelain with varied glazes and designs.

The company worked with John Sparkes and the Lambeth School of Art after 1863. This association led to the hiring of several artists, including George Tinsworth and Hannah Barlow, and to the eventual development of salt-glazed stonewares. The company developed many other new ceramic bodies and glazes, including Lambeth faïence, Crown Lambeth, impasto ware, silicon ware, carrara ware, marqueterie ware, ciné ware, natural foliage ware, cipper ware, majolica, Persian ware, velluma ware, and others. The factory also made many commemorative pieces, jugs, and Toby jugs.

In 1877 the firm bought an interest in a Burslem pottery factory that was called Pinder, Bourne and Company. The entire company became part of Doulton and Company in 1882. They only made earthenwares at first but chinaware was soon made. They made earthenware and porcelain tablewares, art wares, and lamps, as well as sanitary wares. Henry Doulton died in 1897. His son Lewis became head of the company. It became Doulton and Company, Limited, in 1899. The words "Royal Doulton" were used after 1902.

Charles John Noke joined Doulton in 1889. He modeled vases and by 1893 was making Parian figures up to 20 inches in height. He developed Lactolian ware, Holbein ware, Rembrandt ware, and Titanian ware. In 1914 he became the art director, and he was succeeded by his son Cecil J. Noke in 1936. With the help of other artists and chemists, the factory continued producing new products and glazes, including Sung, Chang, sang de boeuf, and rouge flambé.

The factory continued making sanitary wares, pipes, and other money-making but unglamorous products; however, the part of the history of the Doulton Company that is important to this book is the development of the art wares and tablewares made after 1900. The figurines, Toby jugs, character jugs, animals, limited editions, commemorative wares, and series wares produced during this time are all part of that story.

Users of this book should note that a single asterisk (*) following a descriptive entry indicates that the piece is illustrated in black and white, and that double asterisks (**) indicate that the piece is illustrated in the color insert found after page 136.

Bibliography

The Charlton Standard Catalogue of Royal Doulton Figurines. Toronto, Canada: Charlton Press, 1981.

Dennis, Richard. *Doulton Character Jugs.* London, England: Malvern Press, 1976.

_____. *Royal Doulton Limited Edition Loving-Cups and Jugs.* Privately printed, 1981 (144 Kensington Church St., London W8 4BN, England).

Eyles, Desmond. *The Doulton Burslem Wares.* London, England: Barrie & Jenkins, Ltd., 1980.

_____. *The Doulton Lambeth Wares.* London, England: Hutchinson & Co., 1975.

_____. *Royal Doulton Character & Toby Jugs.* Stoke-on-Trent, England: Royal Doulton Tableware Ltd., 1979.

_____. *Royal Doulton 1815–1965.* London, England: Hutchinson & Co., 1965.

Eyles, Desmond, and Richard Dennis. *Royal Doulton Figures Produced at Burslem c. 1890–1978.* Stoke-on-Trent, England: Royal Doulton Tableware Ltd., 1978.

Irvine, Louise. *Royal Doulton Series Ware,* vol. 1. Privately printed, 1980 (144 Kensington Church St., London W8 4BN, England).

Irvine, Louise, and Richard Dennis. *Royal Doulton Figures Supplement No. 1: 1979–1982.* Stoke-on-Trent, England: Royal Doulton Tableware Ltd., 1981.

Kovel, Ralph and Terry. *The Kovels' Illustrated Price Guide to Royal Doulton.* New York: Crown Publishers, 1980.

Lukins, Jocelyn. *Doulton Flambé Animals.* Privately printed (14 Keith Grove, London, W12 9EZ, England).

Lynch, Rebecca and Robert. *1979 Supplement to First Edition of "A Price Guide to Royal Doulton Figurines."* Privately printed, 1979 (P.O. Box 18233, East Hartford, Connecticut 06118).

_____. *A Price Guide to Royal Doulton Figurines.* Privately printed, 1978 (P.O. Box 18233, East Hartford, Connecticut 06118).

McClinton, Katharine Morrison. *Royal Doulton Figurines and Character Jugs.* Des Moines, Iowa: Wallace Homestead Book Co., 1978.

Mills, Arthur H. *Royal Doulton Figurines Old and New.* Privately printed, 1975 (P.O. Box 8742, Detroit, Michigan 48224).

Weiss, Princess and Barry. *Royal Doulton Discontinued Character Jugs,* 4th edition. Privately printed, 1983 (P.O. Box 296, New City, New York 10956).
Yaeger, Mary Lou. *The Price Guide to the Complete Royal Doulton Figurine Collection.* Privately printed, 1978 (P.O. Box 1042, Williamsburg, Virginia 23185).

Catalogs and Pamphlets by Doulton and Company, Inc.

Champions by Royal Doulton (c. 1945)

Character and Toby Jugs by Royal Doulton (nos. 1–5 and 1978–1981)

Character Jugs by Royal Doulton (c. 1939, c. 1945, c. 1950)

Figurines by Royal Doulton (c. 1950)

Haute Ensemble (1974)

Lady Musicians (1970)

Nursery Rhymes and Lines (c. 1948)

Period Figures in English History (c. 1948)

Royal Doulton Art Sculptures by Robert Jefferson

Royal Doulton Figurines (nos. 1–18)

Royal Doulton Fine Art on China

Assorted pamphlets on Royal Doulton figurines

Numerous Royal Doulton Price Lists

Clubs and Publications

The IGC Doulton Collectors' Newsletter
P.O. Box 2644
Ft. Myers, Florida 33902

Royal Doulton International Collectors Club

British Branch:
5 Egmont House
116 Shaftesbury Avenue
London W1V 7DJ, England

Canadian Branch:
Doulton Canada, Inc.
850 Progress Ave.
Scarborough
Ontario M1H 3C4, Canada

Australian Branch:
Doulton Tableware Pty Ltd.
P.O. Box 47
17–23 Merriwa Street
Gordon NSW 2072, Australia

U.S.A. Branch:
Doulton & Co., Inc.
P.O. Box 1815
Somerset, New Jersey 08873

Marks

The Doulton factory used a series of backstamps, which included a lion, crown, the words "Doulton" or "Royal Doulton," and other symbols (see chart below).

The company was first called Doulton and Company, and in 1899 it became Doulton and Company, Limited. The Royal Warrant of Appointment was given to the factory in 1901. They were permitted to add the word "Royal" to their products. The mark with the words "Royal Doulton" was first used in 1902. Another company name that has been used since 1972 is Royal Doulton Tableware Limited.

Many pieces include a copyright date, written "Copr.," and the numeral representing the year. These dates represent the year the design was listed, but the piece was usually not offered for sale until at least one year later. A copyright date of 1957 on a piece in current production merely means that the first time that particular piece was made was in 1957. It may have been made anytime from 1957 to the present time.

The HN mark was first used in 1913. The initials HN were for Harry Nixon, the artist in charge of painting the figures. The numbers were more or less in chronological order until about 1940. After that time, groups of numbers have been held to be used by a single modeler over a period of time. Some numbers have never been used for production figures. Some numbers were given to a figurine that was not produced for several years after being numbered.

The style of type used as part of the backstamp on Royal Doulton figurines, character jugs, and other pieces changed slightly through the years. The name of the figurine, such as "Boy with Turban," was handwritten from 1902 to 1932. The name of the figurine was handwritten on M figures from 1932 to 1949. These names were enclosed in quotation marks. The marks from the 1960s used a type style that resembled Darling. The marks from the 1970s were modernized to a type style that resembled DARLING.

The M numbers were given to miniature figures starting in 1932. The M numbers were stopped in 1949, although some of the miniature Dickens figures are still being made without the number. More recent figurines of this group were made with slight color changes. Early figures were marked "Doulton" or "Doulton England," and they usually had an impressed number. Later ones had the full Royal Doulton mark.

The words "Potted by Doulton and Co." or "Potted by Royal Doulton" were sometimes handwritten on figurines before 1939. Impressed dates are sometimes found on figures, but these are often the date that the mold was made and not the date of production of the figure. These dates were not used after the 1930s. Occasionally, after 1927, a printed number can be found to the right of the crown on the base of a figurine. Add 1927 to the number and that will give the year of manufacture. Thus, if you see "12" on a figurine, add 1927 and find that it was made in the year 1939. The words "Bone China" were added to some marks about 1932. Registration dates appear about 1945.

It is also said that pieces with printed names in quotation marks date from the A mark period, probably before the late 1950s.

Doulton and Company, Limited
Burslem, England, 1882–

Impressed or printed mark on decorated stoneware, 1879–1902; china after 1884.
The word "England" was added after 1891.

Impressed or printed mark, 1885–1902.
The word "England" was added after 1891.

Royal Doulton Marks
Burslem, England, 1902–
Lambeth, England, 1902–1956

First "Royal" Doulton mark.
Printed or impressed mark,
1902–1922, 1927–1932.
The words "Made in England" added after
1930.

Printed or impressed on Lambeth pieces, 1922–
1956.

Printed on Burslem pieces, 1922–1927.

Printed on Burslem earthenware pieces, 1932–
present. The words "Bone China" are added
underneath, 1932–1959.
The words "English Fine Bone China" are
added underneath, 1959–present.
The words "English Translucent China" are
added underneath, 1960–present.

Current mark
(notice shortened lines between the words
"Royal Doulton" and "England"), since
1959.

REGISTRY MARK:

Royal Doulton pieces since the 1940s have had a registry number in one of a variety of forms or type styles. The date is for the registration of the design and is up to one year earlier than the actual production date.

1940s—large R, small underlined d, variety of numeral styles.

Rᵈ Nº 791566.

Rᵈ Nº 846731

Rᵈ Nº 821265.

after 1959

Rᵈ Nº 787812

1960s—present

Rd Nu 926655

Rd. Registered mark in type style used before 1970s.

Rᵈ Nº 549.784

"Registered in Australia" mark.

Regᵈ in Australia

Regᵈ in
Australia
0942

HN TYPE STYLE:

The HN number was assigned when the piece was first designed. If the piece remained in production for a long period of time, a new type style may have been used for the old number. Hand-painted numbers were used prior to 1959.

1920s—1930s

H.N.527

1940s–1960   *H.N. 1991*

1940s (notice H.N.)   H.N. 2041.

1966 }
         more modern style 1960s–1970s–1980s   H N 2312
1974 }
                                                       H N 2705

FIGURINE NAMES:

   It would seem logical that the type style used for the figurine names
changed in some predictable manner. So far, we have had limited suc-
cess with that theory. Below are some pieces we have dated from the
actual purchase date, the copyright, HN number, or factory mark. Hand
lettered names were used on early figurines, dating from 1910 to 1930
or even 1940. The lettering is italicized.

1910–1930   *Lady of the Fair*

                                 The Parson's Daughter.

                                    " An Arab "

Quotation marks and a printed style similar to the earlier hand-painted
lettering was used in the 1930s–1940s.

pre–1940s   "Biddy"

1946   `` Market Day ''

1946   Dainty May

A variety of styles appeared in the 1940s and 1950s.

1940s   Sweet & Twenty

1946   Belle J The Ball

1951   ` Lord Nelson `

1954   The Balloon Man

1960s type styles:

1958–1960   ''Griselda ''

1960s   Southern Belle

1966   Soiree

1968   Tuppence A Bag

1970s type styles:

1970s	**HENRY VIII**
1974	**JULIA**
1975	**"The Balloon Man"**
1979	The Rag Doll.

We are confused by the use of quotation marks. It would seem that after the 1940s, quotes were used only on figurines that had already been registered. Even if the type style changed, the quotation marks were kept for older figurines.

OTHER

A Mark:

Internal factory mark in use about 1939 to 1955. See Character Jug chapter for a full explanation.

"Potted" mark used in the 1930s. Probably discontinued in early 1940s.

Some pieces have a special date stamp. A small number appears to the right of the crown in the factory mark. Add this number to 1927 to determine the date.

The number 14 indicates the year. Add 1927 to determine actual year of dating. This jug was made in 1941.

Modelers signature:

   Sometimes a modeler's name is hand-painted on a figurine from 1913 to the present.

Michael Doulton's signature has been added to pieces during in-store promotions from 1978 to the present. He signs the piece over the glaze, then seals it with a clear liquid coat of glaze.

The words "Doulton & Co. Limited" appear on pieces from 1946 to 1972.

DOULTON & CO LIMITED

The words "© Royal Doulton Tableware Ltd." appear since 1972.

© ROYAL DOULTON
TABLEWARE LTD 1975

IMPRESSED MARKS:

From 1913 to the 1930s, an impressed date-number system was used to indicate when the mold was made. The first numerals are the day, next the month, then the year. So, 4–3–29 means the fourth of March 1929. If two numbers were used, it indicates month and year. So, 10–27 means October 1927.

DICKENS FIGURINES:

Small-size Dickens figures were renumbered from HN numbers to M figurines in the 1930s. The early versions with HN numbers are marked "Doulton, England," and the name of the figurine, such as Sairey Gamp. The M figurines are marked with the lion-crown-circle mark and the figurine name.

THE
KOVELS'
Illustrated Price Guide to
ROYAL DOULTON

Figurines

Charles John Noke joined the Doulton Company in 1889 as the chief modeler for the firm. It was customary for companies that exhibited at the large national and international exhibitions to make exceptional, often unique, large works as special display pieces. Noke made several pieces for the Chicago Exhibition in 1893. Several large vases, one of which was almost 6 feet high, were shown. A few figures were also made, but there was apparently no mention of them in the newspaper accounts of the time. He made "Jack Point," "Moorish Minstrel," "Lady Jester," "A Jester" (seated), "Mirth and Melancholy," and an unnamed figure of a double-sided jester. From 1893 to 1897 he made a few figures, including "A Jester" (standing), "Pierrot," "Shylock," "A Geisha," "Ellen Terry as Queen Catherine," "Henry Irving as Cardinal Wolsey," the double figure "Mephistopheles and Marguerite," and the double figure "Oh Law!" These figures, ranging from 8 to 20 inches high, were larger than the later ones made with the HN markings. They were made of a Parian porcelain, tinted ivory and mainly decorated in pink and green. Very few of these pastel figures appear to have been sold.

It was not until 1909 that Charles Noke decided to try again to make a commercial line of figurines. He invited several sculptors to design small figures. In 1913, twenty models were introduced and modeled by Charles Noke, George Lambert, Phoebe Stabler, F. C. Stone, Charles Vyse, or William White. The figurines were eventually given HN numbers, but the first group had not been numbered when Queen Mary visited the factory in 1913. She commented on a figure that was called "Bedtime." She called it "a darling." The name was changed and "Darling" became HN1. Several figures modeled in earlier years by Noke were included in the series of figurines after 1913 and given numbers that might suggest a later date. Some figurines were slightly modified or changed in color or decoration and given new HN numbers. The figurines did not seem to sell well, and the records show that only 680 were made from 1913 to September of 1917.

Many other artists and decorators worked on the figurines. The production appeared to be small into the 1920s. Many of the earlier figures were discontinued from 1941 to 1949. Desmond Eyles, in his book *Royal Doulton Figures Produced at Burslem,* says that "of those figures which had been withdrawn by 1949, it is unlikely that as many as 2,000 of any one had been made—probably far fewer of many of them." After the war

1

the figurine line was expanded and the numbers grew. Over 2,000 models have been made and less than 200 are in current production.

Some problems remain in the discussion of figurines. We have seen a figurine that appeared to have the HN number 1 although it was a figurine that should have been marked 1354. The Doulton factory has assured us that there might have been an error of some sort at the factory and the number decal was probably torn or damaged before the firing.

A "prototype" figure occasionally appears on the market. These were usually made for consumer-testing panels and were never put into general production. We have seen some of these prototypes offered for sale, so we have included their prices and titles. We understand that they were not commercially produced figurines and were probably removed from exhibitions and still might legally be property of the Doulton factory; consequently they should never be offered for sale.

A few Royal Doulton figurines have been made as limited editions. These are included in this list.

The description of each figurine used in this listing includes the most obvious features and any color variation or changes that distinguishes it from a similar figure. There is a full listing by name, another by HN number immediately after the alphabetical list. Figures marked with one asterisk (*) are pictured in black and white, (**) means a color picture is in the center color section.

Many figurines were made in limited editions or special groupings and these are listed here. Issue price is included if known.

These prices are reports of actual offerings in the marketplace. In order to give a complete list of figurines, we have included some pieces with an estimated value or N.A., meaning the price is not available because so few pieces were made. Estimates, printed in italicized numerals, are based on a knowledge of the general market and sales of past years.

Although wall masks are included in the listing of HN numbers, the prices will be found in the chapter titled Miscellaneous.

LIMITED EDITION FIGURINES
Current Prices in Main List
This list only shows first time issue prices.

Figurine	HN Number	Date	Issue Price	Edition Limit
Duke of Edinburgh	2386	1981-	$750.00	1500
General Washington at Prayer	2861	1977-1977	$875.00	750
Henry VIII	1792	1933-1939		200
Her Majesty Queen Elizabeth II	2878	1983-		2500
Indian Brave	2376	1967-1978	$2500.00	500
Marriage of Art and Industry	2261	1958-1958		12

LIMITED EDITION FIGURINES

Figurine	HN Number	Date	Issue Price	Edition Limit
Palio	2428	1971–	$2500.00	100
Prince of Wales	2883	1981–	$750.00	1500
Prince of Wales	2884	1981–	$1200.00	1500
Princess of Wales	2885	1982–	$750.00	1500
Princess of Wales	2887	1982–	$1200.00	1500
Queen Elizabeth II	2502	1973–1978		750
Queen Mother	2882	1980–	$650.00	1500
Royal Canadian Mounted Police	2547	1973–		1500
Royal Canadian Mounted Police, 1973	2555	1973–1973		1500

AGE OF CHIVALRY

Figurine	HN Number	Date	Issue Price	Edition Limit
Sir Edward	2370	1979–		500
Sir Ralph	2371	1979–		500
Sir Thomas	2372	1979–		500

DANCERS OF THE WORLD

Figurine	HN Number	Date	Issue Price	Edition Limit
Balinese Dancer	2808	1982–	$950.00	750
Breton Dancer	2383	1981–	$850.00	750
Chinese Dancer	2840	1980–	$750.00	750
Indian Temple Dancer	2830	1977–	$400.00	750
Kurdish Dancer	2867	1979–	$500.00	750
Mexican Dancer	2866	1979–	$500.00	750
North American Indian Dancer	2809	1982–	$950.00	750
Philippine Dancer	2439	1978–	$450.00	750
Polish Dancer	2836	1980–	$750.00	750
Scottish Highland Dancer	2436	1978–	$450.00	750
Spanish Flamenco Dancer	2831	1977–	$400.00	750
West Indian Dancer	2384	1981–	$850.00	750

FEMMES FATALES

Figurine	HN Number	Date	Issue Price	Edition Limit
Cleopatra	2868	1979–	$750.00	750
Helen of Troy	2387	1981–	$1250.00	750
Queen of Sheba	2328	1982–	$1250.00	750
Tz'u-Hsi Empress Dowager	2391	1983–	$1250.00	750

GARBE

Figurine	HN Number	Date	Issue Price	Edition Limit
Beethoven	1778	1933–1939		25
Cloud	1831	1933–1939		25
Lady of the Snows	1780	1933–1939		25
Macaw	1779	1933–1939		25
Macaw	1829	1933–1939		
Salome	1775	1933–1939		100
Spirit of the Wind	1777	1933–1939		50
Spring	1774	1933–1939		100
West Wind	1776	1933–1939		25

LADY MUSICIANS

Figurine	HN Number	Date	Issue Price	Edition Limit
Cello	2331	1970–1978	$250.00	750
Chitarrone	2700	1974–1978	$350.00	750

Figurine	HN Number	Date	Issue Price	Edition Limit
Cymbals	2699	1974-1978	$325.00	750
Dulcimer	2798	1975-1978	$375.00	750
Flute	2483	1973-1978	$250.00	750
French Horn	2795	1976-1978	$400.00	750
Harp	2482	1973-1978	$275.00	750
Hurdy Gurdy	2796	1975-1978	$375.00	750
Lute	2431	1972-1978	$250.00	750
Viola d'Amore	2797	1976-1978	$400.00	750
Violin	2432	1972-1978	$250.00	750
Virginals	2427	1971-1978	$250.00	750

MYTHS AND MAIDENS

Figurine	HN Number	Date	Issue Price	Edition Limit
Lady and the Unicorn	2825	1982-	$2500.00	300
Leda and the Swan	2826	1983-	$2500.00	300

SHIPS' FIGUREHEADS

Figurine	HN Number	Date	Issue Price	Edition Limit
Ajax	2908	1980-	$750.00	950
Benmore	2909	1980-	$750.00	950
Chieftain	2929	1982-	$950.00	950
Hibernia	2932	1983-	$950.00	950
Lalla Rookh	2910	1981-	$950.00	950
Mary Queen of Scots	2931	1983-	$950.00	950
Nelson	2928	1981-	$950.00	950
Pocahontas	2930	1982-	$950.00	950

SOLDIERS OF REVOLUTION

Figurine	HN Number	Date	Issue Price	Edition Limit
Captain, 2nd New York Regiment, 1775	2755	1976-1977	$750.00	350
Corporal, 1st New Hampshire Regiment, 1778	2780	1975-1976	$750.00	350
Major, 3rd New Jersey Regiment, 1776	2752	1975-1976	$750.00	350
Private, Connecticut Regiment, 1777	2845	1978-1980	$750.00	350
Private, Delaware Regiment, 1776	2761	1977-1978	$750.00	350
Private, 1st Georgia Regiment, 1777	2779	1975-1976	$750.00	350
Private, Massachusetts Regiment, 1778	2760	1977-1978	$750.00	350
Private, Pennsylvania Rifle Battalion, 1776	2846	1978-1980	$750.00	350
Private, Rhode Island Regiment, 1781	2759	1975-1978	$750.00	350
Private, 2nd South Carolina Regiment	2717	1975-1976	$750.00	350
Private, 3rd North Carolina Regiment	2754	1976-1977	$750.00	350
Sergeant, 6th Maryland Regiment, 1777	2815	1976-1977	$750.00	350
Sergeant, 1st Regiment Continental Light Dragoons, Virginia, 1779	2844	1978-1980	$1500.00	350

SWEET AND TWENTIES

Figurine	HN Number	Date	Issue Price	Edition Limit
Deauville	2344	1982-	$195.00	1500
Monte Carlo	2332	1982-	$195.00	1500

Unlimited Series

CHARACTERS FROM CHILDREN'S LITERATURE

Figurine	HN Number	Date	Issue Price	Edition Limit
Heidi	2975	1983-	$50.00	
Huckleberry Finn	2927	1982-	$50.00	

Figurine	HN Number	Date	Issue Price	Edition Limit
Little Lord Fauntleroy	2972	1982–	$50.00	
Pollyanna	2965	1982–	$50.00	
Tom Brown	2941	1983–	$50.00	
Tom Sawyer	2926	1982–	$50.00	

CHILDHOOD DAYS

And One for You	2970	1983–	$75.00	
And So to Bed	2966	1982–	$75.00	
As Good as New	2971	1982–	$75.00	
Dressing Up	2964	1982–	$75.00	
It Won't Hurt	2963	1982–	$75.00	
Please Keep Still	2967	1983–	$75.00	
Save Some for Me	2959	1983–	$75.00	

ENCHANTMENT COLLECTION

April Shower	3024	1983–	$75.00	
Fairyspell	2979	1983–	$65.00	
Lyric	2757	1983–	$95.00	
Magic Dragon	2977	1983–	$75.00	
Magpie Ring	2978	1983–	$95.00	
Musicale	2756	1983–	$95.00	
Queen of the Dawn	2437	1983–	$125.00	
Queen of the Ice	2435	1983–	$125.00	
Rumpelstiltskin	3025	1983–	$125.00	
Serenade	2753	1983–	$95.00	
Sonata	2438	1983–	$95.00	

FIGURES OF WILLIAMSBURG

Blacksmith of Williamsburg	2240	1960	$50.00	
Boy from Williamsburg	2183	1969–	$30.00	
Child from Williamsburg	2154	1964–	$25.00	
Gentleman from Williamsburg	2227	1960–	$45.00	
Hostess of Williamsburg	2209	1960–	$38.50	
Lady from Williamsburg	2228	1960–	$45.00	
Royal Governor's Cook	2233	1960–	$45.00	
Silversmith of Williamsburg	2208	1960–	$50.00	
Wigmaker of Williamsburg	2239	1960–	$50.00	

GILBERT AND SULLIVAN

Colonel Fairfax	2903	1982–	$750.00	
Elsie Maynard	2902	1982–	$750.00	
Ko-Ko	2898	1980–	$650.00	
Pirate King	2901	1981–	$750.00	
Ruth the Pirate Maid	2900	1981–	$750.00	
Yum-Yum	2899	1980–	$650.00	

HAUTE ENSEMBLE

A la Mode	2544	1974–1978	$135.00	
Boudoir	2542	1974–1978	$135.00	
Carmen	2545	1974–1978	$135.00	
Eliza	2543	1974–1978	$135.00	

Figurine	HN Number	Date	Issue Price	Edition Limit
Eliza	2543A	1974–1978	$135.00	
Mantilla	2712	1974–1978	$135.00	

IMAGES

Figurine	HN Number	Date	Issue Price	Edition Limit
Awakening	2837	1980–	$65.00	
Awakening	2875	1980–	$65.00	
Contemplation	2241	1983–	$75.00	
Contemplation	2213	1983–	$75.00	
Family	2721	1978–	$125.00	
Family	2720	1978–	$125.00	
Lovers	2763	1980–	$125.00	
Lovers	2762	1980–	$125.00	
Mother and Daughter	2843	1980–	$125.00	
Mother and Daughter	2841	1980–	$125.00	
Peace	2433	1980–	$65.00	
Peace	2470	1980–	$65.00	
Sympathy	2838	1980–	$95.00	
Sympathy	2876	1980–	$95.00	
Tenderness	2714	1983	$75.00	
Tenderness	2713	1983–	$75.00	
Tranquility	2426	1978–	$95.00	
Tranquility	2469	1978–	$95.00	
Yearning	2921	1983–	$75.00	
Yearning	2920	1983–	$75.00	

IMAGES OF NATURE

Figurine	HN Number	Date	Issue Price	Edition Limit
Capricorn	3523	1983–	$50.00	
Courtship	3525	1983–	$250.00	
Gift of Life	3524	1983–	$175.00	
Going Home	3527	1983–	$50.00	
Leap	3522	1983–	$75.00	
Shadowplay	3526	1983–	$75.00	

KATE GREENAWAY

Figurine	HN Number	Date	Issue Price	Edition Limit
Amy	3958	1982–	$100.00	
Anna	2802	1976–	$50.00	
Beth	2870	1979–	$85.00	
Carrie	2800	1976–1981	$50.00	
Edith	2957	1982–	$100.00	
Emma	2834	1977–1981	$50.00	
Georgina	2377	1981–	$100.00	
James	3013	1983–	$100.00	
Kathy	2346	1981–	$100.00	
Lori	2801	1976–	$50.00	
Louise	2869	1979–	$85.00	
Lucy	2863	1980–	$85.00	
Nell	3014	1983–	$100.00	
Ruth	2799	1976–1981	$50.00	
Sophie	2833	1977–	$50.00	
Tess	2865	1978–	$55.00	
Tom	2864	1978–1981	$55.00	

Figurine	HN Number	Date	Issue Price	Edition Limit
LADIES OF COVENT GARDEN				
Catherine	2395	1983-	$210.00	
Deborah	2701	1983-	$210.00	
Juliet	2968	1983-	$210.00	
Kimberly	2969	1983-	$210.00	
PRESTIGE FIGURES				
Columbine	2738	1982	$750.00	
Fighter Elepant	2640	1961-	$250.00	
Fox, sitting	2634	1957-	$140.00	
Harlequin	2737	1982-	$750.00	
Jack Point	2080	1953-	$300.00	
King Charles	2084	1952-	$275.00	
Leopard on Rock	2638	1953-	$225.00	
Lion on Rock	2641	1957-	$225.00	
Matador and Bull	2324	1964-	$2900.00	
Moor	2082	1952-	$190.00	
Pheasant	2632	1954-	$52.50	
Princess Badoura	2081	1952-	$1400.00	
St. George and the Dragon	2856	1978-	$3500.00	
Tiger	2646	1961-	$125.00	
Tiger on Rock	2639	1953-	$225.00	
TOLKIEN				
Aragorn	2916	1981-	$45.00	
Barliman Butterbur	2923	1982-	$45.00	
Bilbo	2914	1980-	$35.00	
Boromir	2918	1981-	$50.00	
Frodo	2912	1980-	$35.00	
Galadriel	2915	1981-	$45.00	
Gandalf	2911	1980-	$45.00	
Gimli	2922	1981-	$45.00	
Gollum	2913	1980-	$35.00	
Legolas	2917	1981-	$45.00	
Samwise	2925	1982-	$35.00	
Tom Bombadil	2924	1982-	$50.00	
VANITY FAIR				
Angela	2389	1983-	$95.00	
Ann	2739	1983-	$95.00	
Barbara	2962	1982-	$95.00	
Carol	2961	1982-	$95.00	
Heather	2956	1982-	$95.00	
Jean	2710	1983-	$95.00	
Joanne	2373	1983-	$95.00	
Margaret	2397	1982-	$95.00	
Nancy	2955	1982-	$95.00	
Patricia	2715	1983-	$95.00	
Samantha	2954	1982-	$95.00	
Tracy	2736	1983-	$95.00	

Complete Alphabetical Figurine List Including Descriptions and Prices

A LA MODE **HN 2544** 1974-1978   175.00 to 240.00
    Haute Ensemble series; olive green dress.

A 'COURTING **HN 2004** 1947-1953   495.00 to 550.00
    Rose dress.

ABDULLAH **HN 1410** 1930-1938   920.00
    Blue cushions, green turban.

   HN 2104 1953-1962   475.00 to 675.00
    Yellow chair, orange turban.

ADRIENNE **HN 2152** 1954-1976   135.00
    Rose red dress.

   HN 2304 1964-   83.00 to 156.00
    Blue dress.

AFFECTION **HN 2236** 1962-   52.50 to 104.00
    Brown-purple dress. *

AFTERNOON CALL **HN 82** 1918-1938   *2000.00*
    Lavender coat, fur muff and collar, blue hat, beige
    print dress.

AFTERNOON TEA **HN 1747** 1935-1982   175.00 to 325.00
    Pink dress.

   HN 1748 1935-1949   *500.00*
    Green dress.

AILEEN **HN 1645** 1934-1938   *650.00*
    Green dress.

   HN 1664 1934-1938   600.00
    Pink skirt.

   HN 1803 1937-1949   *600.00*
    Cream dress, blue shawl.

AJAX **HN 2908** 1980-   300.00 to 760.00
    One of Ships' Figureheads series limited to 950. Red,
    green, blue, and gold costume.

ALCHEMIST **HN 1259** 1927-1938   *1400.00*
    Mottled robe, red hat.

   HN 1282 1928-1938   1280.00
    Brown hat, red scarf.

ALEXANDRA **HN 2398** 1970-1976   135.00 to 220.00
    Olive green dress, yellow cape.

ALFRED JINGLE **HN 541** 1922-1932   *60.00*
    Black jacket, tan trousers, 3 3/4 in.

   M 52 1932-1982   25.00 to 30.00
    Black jacket, tan pants.

ALICE **HN 2158** 1960-1980   80.00 to 110.00
    Pale green dress.

ALISON **HN 2336** 1966-   155.00 to 156.00
    Blue overdress. *

ALL ABOARD **HN 2940** 1982-   110.00 to 175.00
    Blue shirt, tan pants, black boots and cap.

Affection HN 2236

Alison HN 2336

ALL-A-BLOOMING **HN 1466** 1931-1938   *800.00*
  Red dress.
AMY **HN 2958** 1982-   58.00 to 100.00
  One of Kate Greenaway series; white dress, blue
  trim, white cap.
AND ONE FOR YOU **HN 2970** 1983-   47.00 to 75.00
  One of Childhood Days series; girl feeding teddy
  bear.
AND SO TO BED **HN 2966** 1982-   47.00 to 75.00
  One of Childhood Days series; white nightgown,
  teddy bear.
ANGELA **HN 1204** 1926-1938   680.00
  Red and purple costume.
  HN 1303 1928-1938   *800.00*
  Blue fan, spotted costume.
  HN 2389 1983-   67.00 to 95.00
  One of Vanity Fair series; white dress, tiara.
ANGELINA **HN 2013** 1948-1951   600.00
  Red dress.
ANN **HN 2739** 1983-   95.00
  One of Vanity Fair series; sleeveless dress.
ANNA **HN 2802** 1976-1982   65.00 to 100.00
  One of the Kate Greenaway series. Purple dress,
  white apron.
ANNABELLA **HN 1871** 1938-1949   400.00
  Peach skirt, green bodice.
  HN 1872 1938-1949   400.00 to 675.00
  Green skirt.
ANNABELLA **HN 1875** 1938-1949   *450.00*
  Red dress.
ANNETTE **HN 1471** 1931-1938   360.00
  Blue dress.

**Users of this book should note that a single asterisk
(*) following a descriptive entry indicates that the piece
is illustrated in black and white, and that double asterisks (**) indicate that the piece is illustrated in the
color insert found after page 136.**

HN 1472   1931-1949   400.00
  Green dress.
HN 1550   1933-1949   295.00 to 350.00
  Red blouse, green underskirt.
ANTHEA   HN 1526   1932-1938   500.00
  Green dress.
HN 1527   1932-1969   540.00
  Purple dress, red umbrella.
HN 1669   1934-1938   500.00
  Pink skirt, red jacket.
ANTOINETTE   HN 1850   1938-1949   *700.00*
  Red and white dress.
HN 1851   1938-1949   *700.00*
  Blue and pink dress.
HN 2326   1967-1978   180.00
  White dress. *
APPLE MAID   HN 2160   1957-1962   275.00 to 395.00
  Green blouse, black skirt.
APRIL SHOWER   HN 3024   1983-   75.00
  One of the Fantasy group from the Enchantment
  Collection. Ivory body, burnished gold trim.
ARAB   HN 33   1913-1938   1600.00
  Green robe, blue cloak.
HN 343   1919-1938   *1400.00 to 1750.00*
  Striped yellow and purple cloak.
HN 378   1920-1938   *1600.00 to 1750.00*
  Green and yellow costume, dark cloak.
ARAGORN   HN 2916   1981-   23.00 to 48.00
  One of Tolkien series; brown costume, black cape.
ARTFUL DODGER   HN 546   1922-1932   18.00 to 30.00
  Red vest, blue tie, 3 3/4 in.
M 55   1932-   30.00 to 32.00
  Red vest, black coat.
AS GOOD AS NEW   HN 2971   1982-   47.00 to 75.00
  One of Childhood Days series; boy painting dog-
  house.
ASCOT   HN 2356   1968-   89.00 to 185.00
  Gray-green dress.
AT EASE   HN 2473   1973-1978   135.00 to 200.00
  Yellow dress.
AUTUMN   HN 2087   1952-1959   400.00
  Red dress.
AUTUMN BREEZES   HN 1911   1939-1976   120.00 to 260.00
  Peach dress, green jacket.
HN 1913   1939-1971   165.00 to 250.00
  Green dress, blue jacket.
HN 1934   1940-   100.00 to 240.00
  Red dress.
HN 2147   1955-1971   140.00 to 325.00
  White dress, black jacket. *

Antoinette HN 2326

Autumn Breezes HN 2147

AUTUMN, THE SEASONS **HN 314** 1918-1938		*1100.00*
Pink dress.		
HN 474 1921-1938		*1100.00*
Patterned robe.		
AWAKENING **HN 1927** 1940-1949		*1400.00 to 1750.00*
White draped figure.		
HN 2837 1980-		35.00 to 75.00
One of Images collection; black.		
HN 2875 1980-		39.00 to 75.00
One of Images collection; white.		
BABA **HN 1230** 1927-1938		*500.00*
Yellow and purple striped trousers.		
HN 1243 1927-1937		*500.00*
Orange pants.		
HN 1244 1927-1938		*500.00*
Yellow and green pants.		
HN 1245 1927-1938		*500.00*
Black, white, and blue pants.		
HN 1246 1927-1938		*500.00*
Green pants.		
HN 1247 1928-1938		*500.00*
White and black pants.		
HN 1248 1927-1938		*500.00*
Green and red pants.		
BABETTE **HN 1423** 1930-1938		*500.00*
Yellow and red striped clothes, multicolored cloak.		
HN 1424 1930-1938		520.00
Blue cloak and shorts.		
BABIE **HN 1679** 1935-		75.00 to 76.00
Green bodice, light skirt. *		

HN 1842 1938-1949   *150.00*
   Pink dress, green umbrella and hat.
HN 2121 1983-   52.50 to 75.00
   Floral print skirt, white flowers on pink background.
BABY HN 12 1913-1938   *1800.00*
   Blue-gray cloak.
BABY BUNTING HN 2108 1953-1959   *250.00*
   Brown and white bunny suit.
BACHELOR HN 2319 1964-1975   195.00 to 260.00
   Black vest, beige trousers.
BALINESE DANCER HN 2808 1982-   950.00
   One of Dancers of the World series, limited to 750.
   Red, yellow, and green costume.
BALLAD SELLER HN 2266 1968-1973   225.00 to 320.00
   Pink dress.
BALLERINA HN 2116 1953-1973   200.00 to 325.00
   White costume, red shoes. *
BALLOON GIRL HN 2818 1982-   80.00 to 125.00
   Yellow blouse, gray skirt, white apron, gray and red
   shawl.
BALLOON MAN HN 1954 1940-   70.00 to 180.00
   Dark jacket, green pants.
BALLOON SELLER HN 479 1921-1938   *1000.00*
   Blue dress, white spots.
HN 486 1921-1938   *1000.00 to 1200.00*
   Blue dress, no hat.
HN 548 1922-1938   *600.00 to 800.00*
   Black shawl, blue dress.
HN 583 1923-1949   300.00 to 500.00
   Green shawl, cream dress.
HN 697 1925-1938   *600.00 to 800.00*
   Striped red shawl, blue dress.
BALLOON SELLER WITH CHILD, see Balloon Seller
BALLOON WOMAN, see Balloon Seller
BARBARA HN 1421 1930-1938   *600.00*
   Flowered skirt.
HN 1432 1930-1938   *600.00*
   Multicolored dress.
HN 1432 1930-1938   875.00
   Potted.
HN 1461 1931-1938   *550.00*
   Green dress.
HN 2962 1982-   60.00 to 95.00
   One of Vanity Fair series; white dress.
BARLIMAN BUTTERBUR HN 2923 1982-   28.00 to 45.00
   One of Tolkien series; brown, white, and beige
   costume.
BASKET WEAVER HN 2245 1959-1962   395.00 to 450.00
   Green dress.

Babie HN 1679

Ballerina HN 2116

BATHER **HN 597** 1924-1938 *600.00*
   Mottled gray robes, blue base.
   HN 687 1924-1949 675.00
   Purple and blue robe.
   HN 773 1925-1938 *700.00*
   Pink robe.
   HN 774 1925-1938 *700.00*
   Purple, red, and black robe.
   HN 781 1926-1938 *650.00*
   Blue and green robe.
   HN 782 1926-1938 *650.00*
   Purple robe, black lining.
   HN 1227 1927-1938 *750.00*
   Flowered pink robe.
   HN 1238 1927-1938 *750.00*
   Red and black robe.
   HN 1708 1935-1938 *850.00*
   Black bathing suit added, green and red robe.
BEACHCOMBER **HN 2487** 1973-1976 135.00 to 200.00
   Purple shirt.
BEAT YOU TO IT **HN 2871** 1980- 150.00 to 360.00
   Girl in pink dress, dog on blue cushion.
BEDTIME **HN 1978** 1945- 40.00 to 55.00
   White nightgown. *
BEDTIME STORY **HN 2059** 1950- 97.00 to 225.00
   Rose dress. Mother.
BEETHOVEN **HN 1778** 1933-1939 N.A.
   Matt ivory. One of the Garbe figurines.
   Production limited to 25.
BEGGAR **HN 526** 1921-1949 495.00
   Blue trousers, red sash.
   HN 591 1924-1949 600.00
   Different glaze.
   HN 2175 1956-1962 380.00 to 575.00
   Black coat, orange sash.
BELLE **HN 754** 1925-1938 *1000.00*
   Pastel multicolored dress.

Bedtime HN 1978

Belle O' The Ball HN 1997

HN 776 1925-1938		*1050.00*
Color unknown.		
HN 2340 1968-		45.00 to 68.00
Green dress.		
BELLE O' THE BALL **HN 1997** 1947-1978		175.00 to 280.00
Red dress, white underskirt. *		
BENMORE **HN 2909** 1980-		300.00 to 760.00
One of Ships' Figureheads series; limited to 950.		
Flag costume.		
BERNICE **HN 2071** 1951-1953		700.00 to 800.00
Pink dress.		
BESS **HN 2002** 1947-1969		220.00 to 295.00
Red cloak.		
HN 2003 1947-1950		*350.00*
Purple cloak.		
BETH **HN 2870** 1979-		45.00 to 100.00
One of the Kate Greenaway series. Pink dress,		
white apron and hat.		
BETSY **HN 2111** 1953-1959		340.00
Lilac dress.		
BETTY **HN 402** 1920-1938		*1750.00*
Pink dress.		
HN 403 1920-1938		*1750.00*
Green skirt, blue, yellow, white border.		
HN 435 1921-1938		*1750.00*
Blue skirt, yellow spots.		
HN 438 1921-1938		*2100.00*
Green skirt.		
HN 477 1921-1938		*2100.00*
Spotted green skirt.		
HN 478 1921-1938		*2100.00*
White spotted skirt.		
HN 1404 1930-1938		400.00
Pink and white dress.		
HN 1405 1930-1938		*400.00*
Green dress.		
HN 1435 1930-1938		*400.00*
Multicolored dress.		

HN 1436 1930-1938 *400.00*
Patterned green dress.
BIDDY **HN 1445** 1931-1938 165.00 to 300.00
Green-yellow dress, blue shawl.
HN 1500 1932-1938 *300.00*
Yellow dress.
HN 1513 1932-1951 150.00 to 240.00
Red dress, blue shawl.
BIDDY PENNY FARTHING **HN 1843** 1938- 70.00 to 180.00
Cream skirt, gray shawl. *
BILBO **HN 2914** 1980- 23.00 to 40.00
One of Tolkien series; brown, yellow, and white
costume.
BILL SYKES **HN 537** 1922-1932 80.00
Brown vest, black jacket, 3 3/4 in.
M 54 1932-1982 29.95
Orange vest, black coat, pants and hat.
BIRD **HN 1779** 1933-1939 N.A.
Macaw, one of the Garbe figurines. Production
limited to 25.
HN 1829 1933-1939 N.A.
Macaw, one of Garbe figurines.
BLACKSMITH OF WILLIAMSBURG **HN 2240** 1960- 99.00 to 200.00
White skirt, brown hat. One of Figures of
Williamsburg.
BLIGHTY **HN 323** 1918-1938 1208.00
British uniform, mottled green.
BLITHE MORNING **HN 2021** 1949-1971 140.00 to 240.00
Blue and pink dress.
HN 2065 1950-1973 150.00 to 225.00
Red dress.
BLOSSOM **HN 1667** 1934-1949 *600.00*
Orange multicolored shawl.
BLUE BIRD **HN 1280** 1928-1938 *500.00*
Nude child on red-pink base.
BLUEBEARD **HN 75** 1917-1938 *2250.00*
Pale blue coat, red hat, white skirt.
HN 410 1920-1938 *2000.00 to 3000.00*
Blue costume
HN 1528 1932-1949 720.00
Red robe.
HN 2105 1953- 365.00 to 380.00
Dark cloak, orange and green costume. *
BO-PEEP **HN 777** 1926-1938 *1000.00*
Purple dress.
HN 1202 1926-1938 *900.00*
Purple skirt, green, pink, and black trim.
HN 1327 1929-1938 *900.00*
Multicolored flowered dress.

Biddy Penny Farthing HN 1843

Bluebeard HN 2105

Bo-Peep HN 1811

HN 1328 1929-1938		*900.00*
Pink dress, black and lilac squares.		
HN 1810 1937-1949		*250.00*
Blue dress.		
HN 1811 1937-		45.00 to 100.00
Orange dress, green hat. *		
M 82 1939-1949		*500.00*
Pink skirt, red overdress, blue bonnet.		
M 83 1939-1949		*400.00*
Blue skirt and overdress, red bonnet.		
BOATMAN **HN 2417** 1971-		75.00 to 185.00
Yellow slicker.		
BON APPETIT **HN 2444** 1972-1976		145.00 to 225.00
Gray coat.		
BON JOUR **HN 1879** 1938-1949		*600.00*
Green dress.		
HN 1888 1938-1949		540.00
Red dress.		
BONNIE LASSIE **HN 1626** 1934-1953		225.00 to 310.00
Red plaid shawl.		
BOROMIR **HN 2918** 1981-		23.00 to 56.00
One of Tolkien series; brown and tan costume.		
BOUDOIR **HN 2542** 1974-1978		300.00 to 375.00
Haute Ensemble series; white dress.		
BOUQUET **HN 406** 1920-1938		*120.00*
No details available.		
HN 414 1920-1938		*1300.00*
Pink and yellow shawl.		
HN 422 1920-1938		*1300.00*
Yellow and pink striped skirt.		

HN 428 1921-1938   *1300.00*
  Blue dress.
HN 429 1921-1938   *1300.00*
  Multicolored dress.
HN 567 1923-1938   1000.00
  Cream shawl, green and red spots.
HN 794 1926-1938   *1300.00*
  Blue shawl, red and green spots.
BOY FROM WILLIAMSBURG **HN 2183** 1969-   56.50 to 115.00
  Purple jacket, red vest. One of Figures of
  Williamsburg. *
BOY ON CROCODILE **HN 373** 1920-1938   4000.00
  White figure, brown crocodile.
BOY ON PIG **HN 1369** 1930-1938   *850.00*
  Nude child, dark mottled pig.
BOY WITH TURBAN **HN 586** 1923-1938   *475.00*
  Green skirt, blue pants.
HN 587 1923-1938   *475.00*
  Red shirt, green pants.
HN 661 1924-1938   *450.00*
  Blue costume.
HN 662 1924-1938   *450.00*
  Black and white costume.
HN 1210 1926-1938   *450.00*
  Black and red turban.
HN 1212 1926-1938   385.00 to 450.00
  Pink-purple and green pants.
HN 1213 1926-1938   *450.00*
  White costume, black squares.
HN 1214 1926-1938   *450.00*
  White costume, black and green markings.
HN 1225 1927-1938   *450.00*
  Yellow pants, blue spots.
BRETON DANCER **HN 2383** 1981-   595.00 to 850.00
  One of Dancers of the World series; limited to
  750. Purple dress, white apron and hat.
BRIDE **HN 1588** 1933-1938   *600.00*
  White flowers.
HN 1600 1933-1949   425.00
  Yellow roses.
HN 1762 1936-1949   495.00
  Cream dress.
HN 1841 1938-1949   700.00
  Blue dress.
HN 2166 1956-1976   225.00 to 240.00
  Pale pink dress. *
HN 2873 1980-   93.00 to 172.00
  White dress and veil, gold trim. Third version.
BRIDESMAID **HN 2148** 1955-1959   140.00 to 225.00
  Cream dress.

Boy From Williamsburg
HN 2183

Bride HN 2166

Bridesmaid
HN 2196

HN 2196 1960-1976 White dress, pink trim. *	88.00 to 115.00
HN 2874 1980- Child in white dress and cap, gold trim. Fourth version.	65.00 to 100.00
M 11 1932-1938 Pink ruffled dress.	280.00
M 12 1932-1945 Multicolored ruffled dress.	235.00 to 280.00
M 30 1932-1945 Lavender and red ruffled dress.	280.00 to 285.00
BRIDGET **HN 2070** 1951-1973 Peach shawl, green skirt.	175.00 to 300.00
BROKEN LANCE **HN 2041** 1949-1975 White horse, blue blanket.	550.00 to 695.00
BUDDIES **HN 2546** 1973-1976 Blue skirt.	175.00 to 220.00
BUMBLE **M 76** 1939-1982 Red vest, green coat, black hat.	19.00 to 32.00
BUNNY **HN 2214** 1960-1975 Blue-green dress. **	100.00 to 160.00
BUTTERCUP **HN 2309** 1964- Pale yellow dress, green bodice.	85.00 to 156.00
HN 2399 1983- Red dress.	98.00 to 145.00
BUTTERFLY **HN 719** 1925-1938 Pink and apricot costume.	680.00
HN 720 1925-1938 Black and red costume.	*700.00*
HN 730 1925-1938 Blue-black wings, yellow dress.	*700.00*
HN 1203 1926-1938 Gold wings.	*700.00*
HN 1456 1931-1938 Purple-pink cloak.	*675.00*

BUZ FUZ   **HN 538**   1922-1932   *60.00*
   Brown vest, black robe, 3 3/4 in. **
  M 53   1932-   21.00 to 32.00
   Black cloak.
CALLED LOVE, A LITTLE BOY   **HN 1545**   1933-1949   *300.00*
   Nude child, tan base, red and blue pail.
CALUMET   **HN 1428**   1930-1949   1020.00
   Striped rug.
  HN 1689   1935-1949   600.00 to 880.00
   Green costume, blue pot.
  HN 2068   1950-1953   480.00 to 700.00
   Glaze differences.
CAMELLIA   **HN 2222**   1960-1971   200.00 to 260.00
   Pink dress. *
CAMILLA   **HN 1710**   1935-1949   *600.00*
   Pink dress.
  HN 1711   1935-1949   *600.00*
   Green dress.
CAMILLE   **HN 1586**   1933-1949   *500.00*
   Red bodice and overskirt.
  HN 1648   1934-1949   *475.00*
   Light skirt, green bodice and hat.
  HN 1736   1935-1949   *550.00*
   Red and white dress.
CAPRICORN   **HN 3523**   1982-   50.00
   One of Images of Nature series; mountain goat.
CAPTAIN   **HN 778**   1926-1938   *1200.00*
   Red and white uniform.
  HN 2260   1965-1982   129.00 to 365.00
   Black, white, and gold uniform. *

Camellia HN 2222

Captain HN 2260

CAPTAIN COOK **HN 2889** 1980-   199.00 to 380.00
　　Black coat, white vest and breeches, gray socks.
CAPTAIN CUTTLE **M 77** 1939-1982   21.00 to 32.00
　　Yellow vest, tan pants and hat, black coat.
CAPTAIN MACHEATH **HN 464** 1921-1949   600.00 to 750.00
　　Red jacket.
　HN 590 1924-1949   *600.00 to 750.00*
　　Yellow cravat.
　HN 1256 1927-1938   *700.00*
　　Earthenware.
CAPTAIN, 2ND N.Y. REG., 1775 **HN 2755** 1975-1977   840.00
　　One of Soldiers of Revolution series, edition
　　limited to 350; brown and blue uniform.
CARMEN **HN 1267** 1928-1938   680.00
　　Red dress, black shawl.
　HN 1300 1928-1938   700.00
　　Light dress, green shoes.
　HN 2545 1974-1978   159.00 to 240.00
　　Haute Ensemble series; white blouse, blue skirt.
CARNIVAL **HN 1260** 1927-1938   *1100.00*
　　Pink tights.
　HN 1278 1928-1938   *1000.00*
　　Pale green tights.
CAROL **HN 2961** 1982-   60.00 to 95.00
　　One of Vanity Fair series; white dress, pink trim.
CAROLYN **HN 2112** 1953-1965   250.00 to 360.00
　　White floral print dress. *
　HN 2974 1983-   108.00 to 155.00
　　Green dress.
CARPET SELLER **HN 1464** 1931-?   200.00 to 325.00
　　Gray-green robe, open hand.
　HN 1464A ?-1969   255.00
　　Hand closed.
CARPET VENDOR **HN 38** 1914-1938   *1500.00 to 2500.00*
　　Yellow and red shirt, blue and red turban, blue
　　pants, blue striped carpet.
　HN 38A 1914-1938   *1500.00 to 2500.00*
　　Persian-style carpet.
　HN 76 1917-1938   1720.00
　　Blue costume, green hat, orange patterned carpet.
　HN 348 1919-1938   *1800.00 to 2000.00*
　　Blue-green costume, checkered base.
　HN 350 1919-1938   *1800.00 to 3000.00*
　　Blue costume, green and brown floral carpet.
CARRIE **HN 2800** 1976-1981   45.00 to 105.00
　　One of the Kate Greenaway series. Blue coat.
CASSIM **HN 1231** 1927-1938   *500.00*
　　Blue hat and pants.
　HN 1232 1927-1938   *500.00*
　　Brown vest, orange and white pants.

HN 1311 1929-1938   *600.00*
  Mounted on lid of pink bowl.
HN 1312 1929-1938   *600.00*
  Mounted on lid of green bowl.
CATHERINE HN 2395 1983-   210.00
  Second in the Ladies of Covent Garden series;
  originally available only from American Express.
  Red dress.
CAVALIER HN 369 1920-1938   *2000.00*
  Blue pants, green waistcoat, dark coat.
HN 2716 1976-1982   99.00 to 200.00
  Dark costume, apricot cape.
CAVALLINI, see Doris Keene As Cavallini
CELESTE HN 2237 1959-1971   200.00 to 225.00
  Green dress.
CELIA HN 1726 1935-1949   800.00
  Pink dress.
HN 1727 1935-1949   700.00 to 850.00
  Green dress.
CELLIST HN 2226 1960-1967   335.00 to 475.00
  Black suit. *
CELLO HN 2331 1970-1978   800.00 to 1400.00
  One of Lady Musicians series; limited to 750.
  Yellow dress.
CENTURION HN 2726 1982-   150.00 to 250.00
  Gray armor, red and chartreuse costume.
CERISE HN 1607 1933-1949   260.00
  Pink dress with flowers, pink sash.
CHARACTER FROM ISLE OF MAN HN 2366   1000.00
  Experimental model, not issued.
CHARLEY'S AUNT HN 35 1914-1938   450.00 to 700.00
  Black dress. *
HN 640 1924-1938   *800.00*
  Green and mauve spotted dress.

Carolyn HN 2112   *Cellist HN 2226*   *Charley's Aunt HN 35*

HN 1411   1930-1938   *1200.00*
  Black dress.
HN 1554   1933-1938   *950.00*
  Purple dress.
HN 1703   1935-1938   *750.00*
  White dress, no base.
CHARLOTTE   **HN 2421**   1972-   95.00 to 185.00
  Rose dress.
CHARMIAN   **HN 1568**   1933-1938   *450.00*
  Red and white dress.
HN 1569   1933-1938   400.00 to 700.00
  Light green-blue skirt.
HN 1651   1934-1938   *575.00*
  Red bodice, green skirt.
CHELSEA PAIR   **HN 577**   1923-1938   495.00
  Woman, white flowered dress.
HN 578   1923-1938   *600.00*
  Woman, red blouse, yellow flowers.
HN 579   1923-1938   *650.00*
  Man, red jacket, yellow flowers.
HN 580   1923-1938   *650.00*
  Man, blue flowers.
CHELSEA PENSIONER   **HN 689**   1924-1938   *1100.00*
  Red uniform.
CHERIE   **HN 2341**   1966-   51.00 to 100.00
  Blue-gray dress. **
CHIEF   **HN 2892**   1979-   95.00 to 220.00
  Buckskin costume, eagle feather bonnet.
CHIEFTAIN   **HN 2929**   1982-   950.00
  One of Ships' Figureheads series; limited to 950.
  Blue costume, black tam.
CHILD AND CRAB   **HN 32**   1913-1938   *1700.00*
  Light blue robe.
CHILD FROM WILLIAMSBURG   **HN 2154**   1964-   62.50 to 115.00
  Blue dress. One of Figures of Williamsburg. *
CHILD STUDY   **HN 603A**   1924-1938   *300.00*
  Primroses on base. White figure kneeling on one
  knee, other leg extended.
HN 603B   1924-1938   *300.00*
  Kingcups on base. White figure kneeling on one
  knee, other leg extended.
HN 604A   1924-1938   *300.00*
  Primroses on base. White figure kneeling in
  crouched position.
HN 604B   1924-1938   *300.00*
  Kingcups on base. White figure kneeling in
  crouched position.
HN 605A   1924-1938   *300.00*
  Primroses on base. White figure standing.

HN 605B   1924-1938   *300.00*
   Kingcups on base. White figure standing.
HN 606A   1924-1938   *300.00*
   Primroses on base. White figure bending.
HN 606B   1924-1938   *300.00*
   Kingcups on base. White figure bending.
HN 1441   1931-1938   *350.00*
   Blonde hair; figure kneeling on one knee, other
   leg extended; green base with flowers.
HN 1442   1931-1938   *350.00*
   Blonde figure bending; green base with flowers; 6 1/4 in.
HN 1443   1931-1938   *350.00*
   Blonde figure bending; green base with flowers; 5 in.
CHILD'S GRACE   **HN 62**   1916-1938   *1450.00*
   Green coat, black pattern.
HN 62A   1916-1938   *1600.00*
   Without black patterning on coat.
HN 510   1921-1938   *1500.00*
   Checkered dress, green base.
CHINA REPAIRER   **HN 2943**   1983-   124.00 to 130.00
   Gray-haired man mending figurines. *
CHINESE DANCER   **HN 2840**   1980-   525.00 to 750.00
   One of Dancers of the World series limited to
   750. Red, green, and purple costume.
CHITARRONE   **HN 2700**   1974-1978   725.00 to 880.00
   One of Lady Musicians series, limited to 750.
   Blue overdress.
CHLOE   **HN 1470**   1931-1949   280.00
   Yellow dress.
HN 1476   1931-1938   280.00 to 285.00
   Blue-white dress.
HN 1479   1931-1949   *270.00*
   Pink-blue dress.

Child From Williamsburg
HN 2154

China Repairer HN 2943

HN 1498 1932-1938   *300.00*
Yellow dress.
HN 1765 1936-1950   240.00 to 275.00
White-blue dress.
HN 1956 1940-1949   320.00
Red skirt, green ribbon.
M 91 1932-1945   215.00 to 280.00
Pink ruffled dress.
M 10 1932-1945   280.00 to 300.00
Blue ruffled dress.
M 29 1932-1945   280.00 to 285.00
Red and cream ruffled gown.
CHOICE **HN 1959** 1941-1949   *700.00*
Red dress.
HN 1960 1941-1949   700.00 to 720.00
Purple-pink dress.
CHOIR BOY **HN 2141** 1954-1975   70.00 to 100.00
Red and white robe.
CHORUS GIRL **HN 1401** 1930-1938   *1400.00*
Red and yellow costume.
CHRISTINE **HN 1839** 1938-1949   *700.00*
Lilac dress, blue shawl.
HN 1840 1938-1949   740.00
Pink dress, blue shawl.
HN 2792 1978-   125.00 to 250.00
Blue flowered overdress.
CHRISTMAS MORN **HN 1992** 1947-   77.50 to 156.00
Red dress.
CHRISTMAS PARCELS **HN 2851** 1978-1982   109.50 to 220.00
Dark green dress. *
CHRISTMAS TIME **HN 2110** 1953-1967   300.00 to 385.00
Red dress.
CICELY **HN 1516** 1932-1949   *800.00*
Blue and white dress.
CIRCE **HN 1249** 1927-1938   *1100.00*
Pink and green robe.
HN 1250 1927-1938   *1100.00*
Orange and black robe.
HN 1254 1927-1938   *1100.00*
Orange and red robe.
HN 1255 1927-1938   *1100.00*
Blue robe.
CISSIE **HN 1808** 1937-1951   220.00
Green dress.
HN 1809 1937-   50.00 to 100.00
Red dress. *
CLARE **HN 2793** 1980-   125.00 to 250.00
Pale floral print dress, yellow shawl and bonnet.
CLARIBEL **HN 1950** 1940-1949   380.00
Blue dress.

Christmas Parcels
HN 2851

Cissie HN 1809

Clockmaker HN 2279

HN 1951 1940-1949		375.00
Red dress.		
CLARINDA **HN 2724** 1975-1980		115.00 to 200.00
Blue dress.		
CLARISSA **HN 1525** 1932-1938		495.00 to 520.00
Green dress, red shawl.		
HN 1687 1935-1949		680.00
Light blue dress, green shawl.		
HN 2345 1968-1981		125.00 to 140.00
Olive green dress.		
CLEMENCY **HN 1633** 1934-1938		*550.00*
Lavender bodice.		
HN 1634 1934-1949		*650.00*
Cream dress, pink trim.		
HN 1643 1934-1938		560.00
Green trim on dress, red top.		
CLEOPATRA **HN 2868** 1979-		895.00 to 1200.00
One of Femmes Fatales series; limited to 750.		
White costume and fan.		
CLOCKMAKER **HN 2279** 1961-1975		185.00 to 320.00
Dark green shirt. *		
CLOTHILDE **HN 1598** 1933-1949		495.00
Cream dress, red cape.		
HN 1599 1933-1949		*500.00*
Flowered dress, red and blue cape.		
CLOUD **HN 1831** 1933-1939		*3000.00*
Ivory and gold. One of Garbe figurines,		
production limited to 25.		
CLOWN **HN 2890** 1979-		145.00 to 300.00
Orange coat, blue-gray pants, orange and white		
polka dot bow.		
COACHMAN **HN 2282** 1963-1971		440.00 to 500.00
Purple coat.		
COBBLER **HN 542** 1922-1939		*900.00*
Yellow shirt, dark green robe.		

HN 543   1922-1938   *900.00*
  Special firing.
HN 681   1924-1938   *550.00*
  Green costume, red skirt.
HN 682   1924-1938   *650.00*
  Red skirt, green robe.
HN 1251   1927-1938   *600.00*
  Black pants, red shirt.
HN 1283   1928-1949   *600.00*
  Green robe, yellow and red shirt.
HN 1705   1935-1949   240.00 to 540.00
  Blue and red costume.
HN 1706   1935-1969   225.00 to 295.00
  Green and blue striped shirt and hat with
  yellow.*
COLLINETTE   HN 1998   1947-1949   420.00
  Green robe.
HN 1999   1947-1949   275.00 to 420.00
  Red robe.
COLONEL FAIRFAX   HN 2903   1982-   435.00 to 750.00
  One of Gilbert and Sullivan series. Red uniform,
  black hat.
COLUMBINE   HN 1296   1928-1938   *600.00*
  Purple line border on orange and purple dress.
HN 1297   1928-1938   600.00 to 660.00
  White line border on dress.
HN 1439   1930-1938   *600.00*
  Red multicolored dress.
HN 2185   1957-1969   240.00
  Pale pink dress. *
HN 2738   1982-   750.00
  Prestige figure; pink floral dress.
COMING OF SPRING   HN 1722   1935-1949   *1100.00*
  Pink dress.
HN 1723   1935-1949   *1100.00*
  Light green dress.
CONSTANCE   HN 1510   1932-1938   *800.00*
  Purple and yellow dress.
HN 1511   1932-1938   *800.00*
  Pink dress, red purse.
CONTEMPLATION   HN 2213   1983-   60.00 to 75.00
  One of Images collection. White.
HN 2241   1983-   60.00 to 75.00
  One of Images collection. Black.
CONTENTMENT   HN 395   1920-1938   *1500.00*
  Yellow skirt, blue blouse.
HN 396   1920-1938   *1500.00*
  Yellow and pink striped chair.
HN 421   1920-1938   *1350.00*
  Pale blue costume.

Cobbler HN 1706

Columbine HN 2185

Coppelia HN 2115

HN 468 1921-1938	*1350.00*
Green spotted dress.	
HN 572 1923-1938	*1400.00*
Pink blouse, spotted, cream skirt, spotted.	
HN 685 1923-1938	*1400.00*
Black and white floral dress.	
HN 686 1924-1938	*1400.00*
Black and white striped chair.	
HN 1323 1929-1938	1560.00
Red dress, blue chair.	
COOKIE **HN 2218** 1958-1975	125.00 to 160.00
Pink dress.	
COPPELIA **HN 2115** 1953-1959	540.00 to 795.00
Blue and red tutu. *	
COQUETTE **HN 20** 1913-1938	2300.00
Two versions: yellow-green costume, blue	
costume.	
HN 37 1914-1938	*2300.00*
Green costume with flower sprays.	
CORALIE **HN 2307** 1964-	78.00 to 156.00
Yellow dress. **	
CORINTHIAN **HN 1973** 1941-1949	*950.00*
Beige trousers, black and red cape.	
CORPORAL, 1ST N.H. REG., 1778 **HN 2780** 1975-1976	840.00
One of Soldiers of Revolution series; production	
limited to 350. Gray-green and red uniform.	
COUNTRY LASS **HN 1991A** 1975-1981	105.00 to 148.00
Renamed version of Market Day.	
COURT SHOEMAKER **HN 1755** 1936-1949	*1000.00*
Red coat, lavender dress.	
COURTIER **HN 1338** 1929-1938	*1100.00*
Rose-red costume.	
COURTSHIP **HN 3525** 1982-	250.00
One of Images of Nature series; two terns.	
COVENT GARDEN **HN 1339** 1929-1938	*900.00*
Green dress, lavender apron.	
CRADLE SONG **HN 2246** 1959-1962	395.00 to 400.00
Green dress. *	

Cradle Song HN 2246

CRAFTSMAN **HN 2284** 1961-1965   400.00
 Blue shirt.
CRINOLINE   780.00
 Lambeth, early experimental, c. 1900.
 HN 8 1913-1938   *1200.00*
 Pale lilac dress.
 HN 9 1913-1938   1200.00
 Pale green skirt with flower sprays.
 HN 9A 1913-1938   *1200.00*
 Pale green skirt, no flower sprays.
 HN 21 1913-1938   1200.00
 Yellow skirt with rosebuds.
 HN 21A 1913-1938   *1200.00*
 Yellow skirt, no rosebuds.
 HN 413 1920-1938   *1700.00*
 White and blue dress.
 HN 566 1923-1938   *1250.00*
 Cream skirt, green spots, green blouse.
 HN 628 1924-1938   *1350.00*
 Yellow and blue bodice.
CRINOLINE LADY **HN 650** 1924-1938   *500.00*
 Green overdress, white patterned skirt. Miniature.
 HN 651 1924-1938   *500.00*
 Orange trim, green flowers. Miniature.
 HN 652 1924-1938   *500.00*
 Purple dress. Miniature.
 HN 653 1924-1938   *500.00*
 Gray and white striped dress. Miniature.
 HN 654 1924-1938   *500.00*
 Orange and green mottled dress. Miniature.
 HN 655 1924-1938   *500.00*
 Blue dress. Miniature.
CROUCHING NUDE **HN 457** 1921-1938   475.00
 Ivory, blue-green base.
CUP OF TEA **HN 2322** 1964-   85.00 to 155.00
 Black dress, gray sweater. **

CURLY KNOB **HN 1627** 1934-1949 *500.00*
    Blue and red striped shawl.
CURLY LOCKS **HN 2049** 1949-1953 250.00 to 280.00
    Pink flowered dress.
CURTSEY **HN 57A** 1916-1938 *1500.00*
    Orange lustre dress.
  HN 57B 1916-1938 *1500.00*
    Lilac dress.
  HN 66A 1916-1938 *1500.00*
    Lilac dress.
  HN 327 1918-1938 *1500.00*
    Blue dress.
  HN 334 1918-1938 *1450.00*
    Lilac dress, brown pattern, green trim.
  HN 363 1919-1938 *1500.00*
    Lilac and peach dress.
  HN 371 1920-1938 *1500.00*
    Yellow dress.
  HN 518 1921-1938 *1600.00*
    Lilac skirt, orange spots.
  HN 547 1922-1938 *1300.00*
    Green and yellow skirt, blue bodice.
  HN 629 1924-1938 *1300.00*
    Green dress, black trim.
  HN 670 1924-1938 *1300.00*
    Pink and yellow spotted dress.
CYMBALS **HN 2699** 1974-1978 625.00 to 880.00
    One of Lady Musicians series, limited to 750.
    Green overdress.
CYNTHIA **HN 1685** 1935-1949 *600.00*
    Pink and green dress.
  HN 1686 1935-1949 595.00
    Blue and red dress.
DAFFY DOWN DILLY **HN 1712** 1935-1975 250.00 to 350.00
    Green dress and hat. *
  HN 1713 1935-1949 285.00
    White and red hat, green-purple dress.
DAINTY MAY **HN 1639** 1934-1949 250.00 to 320.00
    Red dress, green underskirt.
  HN 1656 1934-1949 265.00
    White flowered dress, purple hat.
  M 67 1935-1949 275.00 to 300.00
    Pink skirt, blue overdress.
  M 73 1936-1949 *350.00*
    Pale green, pink overdress.
DAISY **HN 1575** 1933-1949 545.00
    Blue dress.
  HN 1961 1941-1949 260.00
    Pink dress.

Daphne HN 2268

Daffy Down Dilly HN 1712

Darling HN 1985

DAMARIS **HN 2079** 1951-1952   720.00
  Green dress, purple cape.
DANCERS OF THE WORLD SERIES, see individual figurines
DANCING EYES AND SUNNY HAIR **HN 1543** 1933-1949   *300.00*
  Nude child sitting on blue base, brown hair.
DANCING FIGURE **HN 311** 1918-1938   *3200.00 to 3500.00*
  Pink gown.
DANCING YEARS **HN 2235** 1965-1971   250.00 to 360.00
  Lilac to peach dress. **
DANDY **HN 753** 1925-1938   *900.00 to 1100.00*
  Red jacket, purple sash.
DAPHNE **HN 2268** 1963-1975   145.00 to 225.00
  Pink dress. *
DARBY **HN 1427** 1930-1949   380.00
  Mottled pink coat.
  HN 2024 1949-1959   225.00 to 300.00
  Glaze differences.
DARLING **HN 1** 1913-1928   1040.00
  White nightshirt.
  HN 1319 1929-1959   110.00 to 160.00
  Black base.
  HN 1371 1930-1938   *300.00*
  Green nightshirt.
  HN 1372 1930-1938   *300.00*
  Pink nightshirt.
  HN 1985 1946-   30.00 to 55.00
  White nightshirt. *
DAVID COPPERFIELD **M 88** 1949-   18.00 to 55.00
  Black coat, tan pants.
DAWN **HN 1858** 1938-?   *950.00*
  Green drape headdress.
  HN 1858A ?-1949   710.00
  No headdress.

DAYDREAMS **HN 1731** 1935-?   85.00 to 156.00
    Pink bodice, light skirt.
  HN 1732 1935-1949   *300.00*
    Light blue dress, pink trim.
  HN 1944 1940-1949   400.00
    Red dress, blue hat.
DEAUVILLE **HN 2344** 1983-   195.00
    One of the Sweet and Twenties series, limited to
    1500. Yellow and white tennis dress.
DEBBIE **HN 2385** 1969-1982   100.00
    Blue overdress.
  HN 2400 1983-   53.00 to 75.00
    Pink overdress.
DEBORAH **HN 2701** 1983-   210.00
    Third in the Ladies of Covent Garden series;
    originally available only from American Express.
    White flowered dress, green flounce.
DEBUTANTE **HN 2210** 1963-1967   300.00 to 360.00
    Pale blue dress.
DEIDRE **HN 2020** 1949-1955   275.00 to 350.00
    Blue dress, red underskirt.
DELICIA **HN 1662** 1934-1938   460.00
    Pale pink and purple dress.
  HN 1663 1935-1938   550.00
    Purple, green, and yellow flowered skirt.
  HN 1681 1935-1938   *550.00*
    Green and purple dress.
DELIGHT **HN 1772** 1936-1967   125.00 to 200.00
    Red dress.
  HN 1773 1936-1949   200.00
    Green dress.
DELPHINE **HN 2136** 1954-1967   250.00 to 265.00
    Blue overdress, pink skirt. *
DENISE **HN 2273** 1964-1971   225.00 to 260.00
    Red dress.
  M 34 1933-1945   *350.00*
    Green dress, blue bodice, red overskirt.
  M 35 1933-1945   *350.00*
    Pink dress, light blue overskirt.
DERRICK **HN 1398** 1930-1938   500.00
    Blue costume, red hat.
DESPAIR **HN 596** 1924-1938   1400.00
    Mottled blue.
DETECTIVE **HN 2359** 1977-   82.50 to 168.00
    Brown coat.
DIANA **HN 1716** 1935-1949   *250.00*
    Pink top, blue skirt.
  HN 1717 1935-1949   240.00
    Green dress, red hat.

HN 1986   1946-1975   90.00 to 135.00
Red dress, purple hat ties. **
DICK SWIVELLER   **M 90**   1949-1982   22.00 to 32.00
Black coat and top hat, tan pants.
DIGGER   **HN 321**   1918-1938   *1000.00*
New Zealand uniform, mottled green.
HN 322   1918-1938   700.00 to 900.00
Australian uniform, brown.
HN 353   1919-1938   *900.00 to 1200.00*
Australian uniform, natural colors.
DILIGENT SCHOLAR   **HN 26**   1913-1938   1760.00
Brown and green costume.
DIMITY   **HN 2169**   1956-1959   295.00 to 320.00
White skirt, green bodice.
DINKY DO   **HN 1678**   1934-   33.00 to 68.00
Blue bodice, light skirt. *
HN 2120   1983-   46.00 to 65.00
Red and pink costume.
DO YOU WONDER WHERE   **HN 1544**   1933-1949   *300.00*
Child in lavender shorts, beige base.
DOCTOR   **HN 2858**   1979-   99.00 to 220.00
Gray pants and vest, black coat.
DOLLY   **HN 355**   1919-1938   1140.00
Pale blue nightgown.
DOLLY VARDON   **HN 1514**   1932-1938   *650.00*
Flowered cape.
HN 1515   1932-1949   *700.00*
Red cape.
DORCAS   **HN 1490**   1932-1938   *450.00*
Beige dress.
HN 1491   1932-1938   460.00
Light green-blue dress.
HN 1558   1933-1952   210.00 to 425.00
Red dress.
DOREEN   **HN 1363**   1929-1938   *500.00 to 700.00*
Pink dress.

Delphine HN 2136   *Dinky Do HN 1678*

HN **1389** 1930–1938   *700.00*
  Green dress.
HN **1390** 1929–1938   475.00
  Lilac dress.
DORIS KEENE AS CAVALLINI HN **90** 1918–1936   *1600.00 to 2000.00*
  Black dress.
HN **96** 1918–1938   1800.00
  Black dress, white shawl.
HN **345** 1919–1949   *1800.00 to 2500.00*
  Dark fur color, striped muff.
HN **467** 1921–1936   *1500.00 to 2000.00*
  Gold jewelry.
DOUBLE JESTER HN **365** 1920–1938   *1500.00 to 2000.00*
  Multicolored costume.
DREAMLAND HN **1473** 1931–1938   *1400.00*
  Purple and red robe.
HN **1481** 1931–1938   *1400.00*
  Red-yellow nightgown, dark couch.
DREAMWEAVER HN **2283** 1972–1976   200.00 to 240.00
  Blue shirt.
DRESSING UP HN **2964** 1982–   47.00 to 75.00
  One of Childhood Days series; white dress, blue
  trim. *
DRUMMER BOY HN **2679** 1976–1981   246.00 to 380.00
  Red uniform.
DRYAD OF THE PINES HN **1869** 1938–1949   *2300.00*
  Ivory and gold.
DUKE OF EDINBURGH HN **2386** 1981–   325.00 to 700.00
  Admiral of the Fleet uniform; limited to 1500.
DULCIE HN **2305** 1981–   92.50 to 185.00
  Blue dress.
DULCIMER HN **2798** 1975–1978   880.00 to 1650.00
  One of Lady Musicians series, limited to 750.
  Pink overdress.
DULCINEA HN **1343** 1929–1938   *850.00*
  Red and black dress, black shoes.

Dressing Up HN 2964

HN 1419   1930-1938   625.00 to 1200.00
   Red and pink dress, green shoes.
DUNCE   HN 6   1913-1938   *1800.00 to 2500.00*
   Gray gown and dunce cap.
HN 310   1918-1938   *1700.00 to 2500.00*
   Black and white costume, green base.
HN 357   1919-1938   *1800.00 to 2500.00*
   Gray costume, black pattern.
EASTER DAY   HN 1976   1945-1951   360.00 to 600.00
   White dress, blue flowers.
HN 2039   1949-1969   235.00 to 300.00
   Multicolored dress, green hat. **
EDITH   HN 2957   1982-   58.00 to 100.00
   One of Kate Greenaway series; chartreuse dress,
   white pinafore, hat.
ELAINE   HN 2791   1980-   90.00 to 185.00
   Blue dress.
ELEANOR OF PROVENCE   HN 2009   1948-1953   600.00 to 850.00
   Purple dress, red print, red cape.
ELEANORE   HN 1753   1936-1949   *600.00*
   Blue bodice, green and pink skirt.
HN 1754   1936-1949   600.00
   Orange dress, white bodice with flowers.
ELEGANCE   HN 2264   1961-   125.00 to 220.00
   Beige and green dress. *
ELFREDA   HN 2078   1951-1955   480.00 to 645.00
   Red overdress, blue skirt.
ELIZA   HN 2543   1974-1978   150.00 to 225.00
   Haute Ensemble series; rust dress, 11 1/4 in.
HN 2543A   1974-1978   240.00
   Haute Ensemble series; rust dress, 11 3/4 in.
ELIZABETH   HN 2946   1982-   135.00 to 225.00
   Green and yellow dress, bonnet.
ELIZABETH FRY   HN 2   1913-1938   4000.00
   Blue-gray costume, green base.
HN 2A   1913-1938   *4000.00*
   Blue-gray costume, blue base.
ELLEN TERRY, QUEEN CATHERINE   HN 379   1920-1949 *2100.00 to 2500.00*
   Blue and lilac dress.
ELSIE MAYNARD   HN 639   1924-1949   *700.00*
   Predominantly white dress, blue wrap.
HN 2902   1982-   600.00 to 750.00
   One of Gilbert and Sullivan series. Green skirt,
   white blouse, blue hat.
ELYSE   HN 2429   1972-   185.00
   Blue dress.
EMBROIDERING   HN 2855   1980-   100.00 to 220.00
   Blue-green dress.

Elegance HN 2264

*Enchantment
HN 2178*

EMIR **HN 1604** 1933-1949	*700.00*
Orange and green scarf.	
HN 1605 1933-1949	680.00
Orange and purple scarf.	
EMMA **HN 2834** 1977-1981	45.00 to 100.00
Pink dress, white apron.	
ENCHANTMENT **HN 2178** 1957-1982	78.00 to 156.00
Green dress. *	
ERMINE **M 40** 1933-1945	360.00
Pink dress and shoes, white spotted cloak.	
ERMINE COAT **HN 1981** 1945-1967	220.00 to 320.00
Red dress under coat.	
ERMINE MUFF, see Lady Ermine	
ESMERALDA **HN 2168** 1956-1959	300.00 to 325.00
Cream dress, red shawl.	
ESTELLE **HN 1566** 1933-1938	*700.00*
Lavender and white dress.	
HN 1802 1937-1949	*600.00*
Pink dress.	
EUGENE **HN 1520** 1932-1938	*600.00*
Green and pink dress.	
HN 1521 1932-1938	*600.00*
Red and white dress.	
EUROPA AND THE BULL **HN 95** 1918-1938	*2750.00 to 3000.00*
Lavender dress.	
EVELYN **HN 1622** 1934-1949	500.00
Red bodice, red hat.	
HN 1637 1934-1938	*650.00*
Light multicolored dress.	
EVENTIDE **HN 2814** 1977-	81.00 to 168.00
Pale blue dress.	
FAGIN **HN 534** 1922-1932	*60.00*
Black coat, 4 in.	
M 49 1932-	18.00 to 32.00
Black coat.	
FAIR LADY **HN 2193** 1963-	80.00 to 156.00
Green dress. *	

Fair Lady HN 2193

Fair Maiden HN 2211

HN 2832 1977– Red dress.	79.00 to 156.00
HN 2835 1977– Orange dress.	77.00 to 170.00
FAIR MAIDEN **HN 2211** 1967– Green dress. *	51.00 to 100.00
HN 2434 1983– Red gown.	67.00 to 95.00
FAIRY **HN 1324** 1929–1938 Several related figures. Multicolored.	*600.00 to 800.00*
HN 1374 1930–1938 Yellow flowers.	310.00
HN 1375 1930–1938 Purple hat.	*700.00 to 800.00*
HN 1376 1930–1938 Smaller than HN 1532, no mushroom.	*500.00 to 650.00*
HN 1378 1930–1938 Orange flowers.	*400.00 to 550.00*
HN 1379 1930–1939 Blue flowers, leaves overhead.	*500.00 to 650.00*
HN 1380 1930–1938 Dark mottled mushroom.	800.00
HN 1393 1930–1938 Yellow flowers.	*450.00 to 550.00*
HN 1394 1930–1938 Yellow flowers.	*450.00 to 550.00*
HN 1395 1930–1938 Blue flowers.	*450.00 to 550.00*
HN 1396 1930–1938 White flowers with blue edge.	*400.00 to 550.00*
HN 1532 1932–1938 Yellow mushroom.	*400.00*
HN 1533 1932–1938 Multicolored flowers.	*400.00*
HN 1534 1932–1938 Large yellow flowers.	*400.00*

HN 1535 1932-1938 *400.00*
  Yellow and blue flowers.
HN 1536 1932-1938 360.00
  Light green base.
FAIRYSPELL **HN 2979** 1983- 65.00
  One of the Fantasy group from the Enchantment
  Collection. Ivory body, burnished gold trim.
FALL-A-BLOOMING **HN 1457** 1931- *800.00*
  Blue dress.
FALSTAFF **HN 571** 1923-1938 *700.00*
  Rust coat, green patterned cloth.
HN 575 1923-1938 *700.00*
  Brown coat, yellow spotted cloth on base.
HN 608 1924-1938 *700.00*
  Red coat, red cloth.
HN 609 1924-1938 *700.00*
  Green coat, green cloth.
HN 618 1924-1938 *700.00*
  Black collar, lilac blanket, green base.
HN 619 1924-1938 *700.00*
  Brown coat, green collar, yellow cloth.
HN 638 1924-1938 *700.00*
  Red coat, spotted cream cloth.
HN 1216 1926-1949 *700.00*
  Multicolored costume.
HN 1606 1933-1949 *700.00*
  Green cloth with red circles.
HN 2054 1950- 70.00 to 148.00
  Red jacket, brown belt and boots.
FAMILY **HN 2720** 1978- 95.00 to 145.00
  One of Images collection, white.
HN 2721 1978- 70.00 to 145.00
  One of Images collection, black.
FAMILY ALBUM **HN 2321** 1966-1973 325.00 to 380.00
  Green skirt, green and black striped shawl.
FANNY, see Angela
FARAWAY **HN 2133** 1958-1962 225.00 to 340.00
  White dress, blue trim. *

Faraway HN 2133

FARMER'S BOY **HN 2520** 1938-1960   700.00 to 960.00
   Farmer on horse.
FARMER'S WIFE **HN 2069** 1951-1955   469.00 to 520.00
   Red jacket, green skirt.
FAT BOY **HN 530** 1922-1932   *60.00*
   Blue jacket, white pants, 3 1/2 in.
   HN 555 1923-1939   300.00 to 500.00
   Blue jacket, white scarf, 7 in.
   HN 1893 1938-1952   260.00 to 340.00
   Color changes.
   HN 2096 1952-1967   240.00 to 320.00
   Blue jacket, yellow scarf.
   M 44 1932-   19.00 to 32.00
   Gray shirt, tan pants.
FAVOURITE **HN 2249** 1960-   83.00 to 165.00
   Blue dress. *
FIDDLER **HN 2171** 1956-1962   600.00 to 1100.00
   Green and cream striped jacket.
FIGHTER ELEPHANT **HN 2640** 1961-   1080.00 to 1450.00
   Prestige figure; open mouth; long white tusks.
FIONA **HN 1924** 1940-1949   680.00
   Pink skirt.
   HN 1925 1940-1949   555.00 to 585.00
   Green skirt.
   HN 1933 1940-1949   760.00
   Multicolored dress.
   HN 2694 1974-1980   105.00 to 160.00
   Red and white dress.
FIRST DANCE **HN 2803** 1977-   85.00 to 172.00
   White dress.
FIRST STEPS **HN 2242** 1959-1965   400.00 to 450.00
   Blue dress. *

Favourite HN 2249

First Steps HN 2242

FIRST WALTZ   **HN 2862**   1979-   109.00 to 295.00
   Red print dress, white fan.
FISHERWOMEN   **HN 80**   1917-1938   N.A.
   Pink shawl.
   HN 349   1919-1968   N.A.
   Middle woman with yellow shawl.
   HN 359   1919-1938   N.A.
   Middle woman with red shawl.
   HN 631   1924-1938   *2400.00*
   Middle woman with green shawl.
FLEUR   **HN 2368**   1968-   95.00 to 185.00
   Green dress.
   HN 2369   1983-   185.00
   Orange dress; pale blue jacket.
FLEURETTE   **HN 1587**   1933-1949   395.00 to 500.00
   Red and white dress.
FLORA   **HN 2349**   1966-1973   260.00
   Brown dress, white apron.
FLOUNCED SKIRT   **HN 57A**   1916-1938   *1400.00 to 1600.00*
   Orange lustre dress.
   HN 66   1916-1938   1360.00
   Lilac dress.
   HN 77   1917-1938   *1400.00 to 1600.00*
   Lemon yellow dress, black trimmings.
   HN 78   1917-1938   *1400.00 to 1600.00*
   Flowered yellow luster dress.
   HN 333   1918-1938   *1400.00 to 1600.00*
   Brown mottled dress.
FLOWER SELLER   **HN 789**   1926-1938   800.00
   Green cape, cream skirt.
FLOWER SELLER'S CHILDREN   **HN 525**   1921-1949   *600.00*
   Boy in green, girl in blue costume.
   HN 551   1922-1949   *500.00*
   Boy in blue costume, girl in orange and yellow.
   HN 1206   1926-1949   *500.00*
   Dark blue skirt.
   HN 1342   1929-   197.50 to 395.00
   Red and yellow roses.
   HN 1406   1930-1938   *500.00*
   Yellow dress, dark blue cloth over basket.
FLUTE   **HN 2483**   1973-1978   800.00 to 1300.00
   One of Lady Musicians series, limited to 750. Red
   dress.
FOAMING QUART   **HN 2162**   1955-   82.00 to 168.00
   Orange and brown costume. *
FOLLY   **HN 1335**   1929-1938   950.00
   Green hat, pink dress.
   HN 1750   1936-1949   1200.00
   Brown hat, white muff, earthenware.

Foaming Quart HN 2162   Fortune Teller HN 2159

FORGET-ME-NOT   **HN 1812**   1937-1949   *500.00*
    Pink dress, green ribbon.
    HN 1813   1937-1949   400.00
    Red dress, blue hat.
FORTUNE TELLER   **HN 2159**   1955-1967   365.00 to 475.00
    Orange dress, green shawl. *
FORTY THIEVES   **HN 417**   1920-1938   *1000.00*
    Forty Thieves, or One of the Forty, is a group of
    small figures, each about 5 inches high, that is an
    unending source of confusion for collectors. The
    thieves pictured are from the Oriental story of "Ali
    Baba and the Forty Thieves," adapted for an oper-
    etta, "Chu Chum Chow." More than 40 different
    thief models were made, and there were sometimes
    color variations for a model. At least 13 versions
    were made. See HN 418, 423, 427, 480, 481, 482, 483,
    484, 490, 491, 492, 493, 494, 495, 496, 497, 498, 499,
    500, 501, 528, 645, 646, 647, 648, 649, 663, 664, 665,
    666, 667, 677, 704, 712, 713, 714, 1336, 1350, 1351,
    1352, 1353, 1354. HN 417 is the first version, model
    289, and is green and blue. See HN 490, 495, 501,
    528, 648, 677, 1351, 1352.
    HN 418   1920-1938   *1000.00*
    Striped green robes. Second version, model 298, see
    HN 494, 498, 647, 666, 704, 1353.
    HN 423   1921-1938   300.00
    Made in a variety of colors. Third–eight versions,
    models 291, 295, 296, 299, 300, 301.
    HN 427   1921-1938   *1000.00*
    Brown costume. Ninth version.
    HN 480   1921-1938   *1000.00*
    Mottled green robe, yellow pants with black stripes,
    blue hat. Tenth version, model 328. See HN 493,
    497, 499, 664, 714.
    HN 481   1921-1938   *1000.00*
    Eleventh version, model 319. See HN 483, 491, 646,
    667, 712, 1336, 1350.

HN 482 1921-1938   *1000.00*
Spotted waistband. Twelfth version, model 327. See HN 484, 492, 645, 663, 713.

HN 483 1921-1938   *1000.00*
Brown hat, green striped robes. See HN 481.

HN 484 1921-1938   *1000.00*
Mottled green robes. See HN 482.

HN 490 1921-1938   *1000.00*
Blue and brown checkered coat. See HN 417.

HN 491 1921-1938   875.00
White robe, green turban. See HN 481.

HN 492 1921-1938   *1000.00*
Cream costume, yellow sash and turban. See HN 482.

HN 493 1921-1938   *1000.00*
Blue hat and waistband. See HN 480.

HN 494 1921-1938   *1000.00*
White costume, blue sash and turban. See HN 418.

HN 495 1921-1938   *1000.00*
Blue hat and waistband. See HN 417.

HN 496 1921-1938   *1000.00*
Thirteenth version, model 313. See HN 500, 649, 665, 1354.

HN 497 1921-1938   *1000.00*
Brown hat, checkered pants. See HN 480.

HN 498 1921-1938   *1000.00*
Dark striped coat, pale striped pants. See HN 418.

HN 499 1921-1938   *1000.00*
Cream costume, green hat. See HN 480.

HN 500 1921-1938   *1000.00*
Checkered coat, red hat. See HN 496.

HN 501 1921-1938   *1000.00*
Green striped coat. See HN 417.

HN 528 1921-1938   *1000.00*
Brown costume, multicolored turban. See HN 417.

HN 645 1924-1938   *1000.00*
Blue, black, and white robes. See HN 482.

HN 646 1924-1938   *1000.00*
Blue, black, and white robes. See HN 481.

HN 647 1924-1938   *1000.00*
Blue, black, and white robes. See HN 418.

HN 648 1924-1938   *1000.00*
Blue, black, and white robes. See HN 417.

HN 649 1924-1938   *1000.00*
Blue, black, and white robes. See HN 496.

HN 663 1924-1938   *1000.00*
Checkered yellow robes. See HN 482.

HN 664 1924-1938   800.00 to 950.00
Yellow patterned robes. See HN 480.

HN 665 1924-1938 *1000.00*
  Yellow patterned robes. See HN 496.
HN 666 1924-1938 940.00
  Yellow patterned robes. See HN 418.
HN 667 1924-1938 *1000.00*
  Yellow patterned robes. See HN 481.
HN 677 1924-1938 *1000.00*
  Orange, green, and red striped robes. See HN 417.
HN 704 1925-1938 950.00
  Red checkered robe. See HN 418.
HN 712 1925-1938 *1000.00*
  Red checkered robes. See HN 481.
HN 713 1925-1938 *1000.00*
  Red checkered robes. See HN 482.
HN 714 1925-1938 *1000.00*
  Red patterned robe. See HN 480.
HN 1336 1929-1938 *1000.00*
  Red, orange, and blue robes. See HN 481.
HN 1350 1929-1949 *1000.00*
  Multicolored robes. See HN 481.
HN 1351 1920-1949 1120.00
  Red, gold, and blue costume. See HN 417.
HN 1352 1920-1949 *1000.00*
  Multicolored robes. See HN 417.
HN 1353 1929-1949 *1000.00*
  Multicolored robes. See HN 418.
HN 1354 1929-1949 *1000.00*
  Multicolored robes. See HN 496.
FORTY WINKS **HN 1974** 1945-1973 165.00 to 280.00
  Dark dress, white apron.
FOUR O'CLOCK **HN 1760** 1936-1949 *500.00*
  Lavender dress.
FOX, SITTING **HN 2634** 1957- 350.00 to 750.00
  Prestige figure; 10 1/2 in.
FRAGRANCE **HN 2334** 1966- 85.00 to 172.00
  Blue dress.
FRANCINE **HN 2422** 1972-1980 55.00 to 85.00
  Green dress.
FRANGCON **HN 1720** 1935-1949 *600.00*
  Floral print dress.
HN 1721 1935-1949 560.00
  Green dress.
FRENCH HORN **HN 2795** 1976-1978 725.00 to 800.00
  One of Lady Musicians series, limited to 750; purple
  overdress.
FRENCH PEASANT **HN 2075** 1951-1955 375.00 to 520.00
  Gray-green jacket, peach skirt.
FRIAR TUCK **HN 2143** 1954-1965 385.00 to 550.00
  Brown robe. *

Friar Tuck HN 2143

FRODO   **HN 2912**   1980-   18.00 to 40.00
   One of Tolkien series; black and white costume.
FRUIT GATHERING   **HN 449**   1921-1938   *2300.00*
   Blue striped blouse, blue skirt.
   HN 476   1921-1938   *2300.00*
   Green checkered blouse.
   HN 503   1921-1938   *2300.00*
   Brown and blue checkered dress.
   HN 561   1923-1938   *2300.00*
   Green blouse.
   HN 562   1923-1938   *2300.00*
   Pink blouse, spotted skirt.
   HN 706   1925-1938   *2185.00*
   Purple blouse, yellow skirt.
   HN 707   1925-1938   *2300.00*
   Spotted skirt, red blouse.
GAFFER   **HN 2053**   1950-1959   310.00 to 350.00
   Dark jacket, yellow plaid scarf.
GAINSBOROUGH   **HN 453**   1921-1938   *1100.00*
   Red, blue, and green dress.
GAINSBOROUGH HAT   **HN 46**   1915-1938   *1100.00*
   Lilac dress.
   HN 46A   1915-1938   *1100.00*
   Black patterned collar.
   HN 47   1915-1938   1200.00
   Light green dress.
   HN 329   1918-1938   *1100.00*
   Patterned blue dress.
   HN 352   1919-1938   *1200.00*
   Yellow dress, purple hat.
   HN 383   1920-1938   *1100.00*
   Striped dress.
   HN 675   1924-1938   *1100.00*
   Purple-blue dress, red and yellow spots.
   HN 705   1925-1938   1030.00
   Multicolored dress.
GALADRIEL   **HN 2915**   1981-   23.00 to 48.00
   One of Tolkien series; white dress and cape.

GANDALF **HN 2911** 1980-   34.00 to 56.00
    One of Tolkien series; black, white and gray robes,
    black hat.
GAY MORNING **HN 2135** 1954-1967   225.00 to 300.00
    Pale peach dress. *
GEISHA **HN 354** 1919-1938   *2000.00*
    Yellow kimono.
   HN 376 1920-1938   2200.00
    Blue and yellow mottled kimono.
   HN 387 1920-1938   *2000.00*
    Blue kimono, yellow sleeves.
   HN 634 1924-1938   1600.00
    Black and white kimono.
   HN 741 1925-1938   *2000.00*
    Dark multicolored kimono, black trim.
   HN 779 1926-1938   *2000.00*
    Red dress, purple spots. **
   HN 1223 1927-1938   825.00
    Purple and red multicolored kimono.
   HN 1234 1927-1938   850.00
    Green, red, yellow multicolored kimono.
   HN 1292 1928-1938   *800.00*
    Blue-green collar, orange-pink kimono.
   HN 1310 1929-1938   *750.00*
    Multicolored spotted kimono.
   HN 1321 1929-1938   *2000.00*
    Green kimono.
   HN 1322 1929-1938   *2000.00*
    Pink and blue kimono.
GENERAL WASHINGTON AT PRAYER **HN 2861** 1977   1200.00 to 1500.00
    Blue and beige uniform; red-lined cape. Designed
    by Laszlo Ispanky for the Limited Editions Collec-
    tors Society of America. Edition limited to 750; issue
    price $75.00.
GENEVIEVE **HN 1962** 1941-1975   160.00 to 240.00
    Red dress.
GENIE **HN 2989** 1983-   57.00 to 75.00
    Deep blue cloak. *
GENTLEMAN FROM WILLIAMSBURG **HN 2227** 1960-   99.00 to 200.00
    Green jacket. One of Figures of Williamsburg.
GENTLEWOMAN **HN 1632** 1934-1949   500.00 to 700.00
    Lavender dress.
GEORGIANA **HN 2093** 1952-1955   400.00 to 950.00
    Rust overdress, blue skirt.
GEORGINA **HN 2377** 1981-   100.00
    One of the Kate Greenaway series; red cloak, white
    bonnet.
GERALDINE **HN 2348** 1972-1976   135.00 to 185.00
    Brown dress.

Gay Morning HN 2135   *Genie HN 2989*

GIFT OF LIFE **HN 3524** 1982-   175.00
    One of Images of Nature series; mare and foal.
GILLIAN **HN 1670** 1934-1949   *500.00*
    Dark pink dress.
  HN 1670A dates unknown   560.00
    Floral dress.
GIMLI **HN 2922** 1981-   23.00 to 48.00
    One of Tolkien series; brown, white and beige cos-
    tume.
GIRL WITH YELLOW FROCK **HN 588** 1923-1938   1100.00
    Yellow dress.
GISELLE **HN 2139** 1954-1969   325.00
    Blue dress.
GISELLE, FOREST GLADE **HN 2140** 1954-1965   352.00 to 380.00
    White dress.
GLADYS **HN 1740** 1935-1949   *500.00*
    Green blouse.
  HN 1741 1935-1938   *500.00*
    Pink blouse.
GLEANER **HN 1302** 1928-1938   *1500.00 to 2000.00*
    Red jacket, cream and green striped skirt; sometimes
    called Gypsy Girl with Flowers.
GLORIA **HN 1488** 1932-1938   620.00
    Gray-blue cape and dress.
  HN 1700 1935-1938   *700.00*
    Green dress, dark cloak.
GNOME **HN 319** 1918-1938   *900.00*
    Pale blue costume.
  HN 380 1920-1938   *950.00*
    Lilac costume.
  HN 381 1920-1938   *950.00*
    Green costume.
GOING HOME **HN 3527** 1982-   50.00
    One of Images of Nature series; flying geese.

GOLDEN DAYS **HN 2274** 1964-1973   125.00 to 145.00
  White dress. **

GOLLUM **HN 2913** 1980-   23.00 to 40.00
  One of Tolkien series; brown.

GOLLYWOG **HN 1979** 1945-1959   280.00
  White overalls.

  HN 2040 1949-1959   220.00
  Blue overalls, green hat.

GOOD CATCH **HN 2258** 1966-   75.00 to 168.00
  Dark green suit. *

GOOD KING WENCESLAS **HN 2118** 1953-1976   280.00 to 325.00
  Peach robe, brown cloak.

GOOD MORNING **HN 2671** 1974-1976   110.00 to 200.00
  Apricot dress, white apron.

GOODY TWO SHOES **HN 1889** 1938-1949   *250.00*
  Green dress.

  HN 1905 1939-1949   *200.00*
  Pink skirt, red overdress.

  HN 2037 1949-   50.00 to 100.00
  Red dress.

  M 80 1939-1949   *500.00*
  Blue skirt, red overdress.

  M 81 1939-1949   320.00 to 450.00
  Pink skirt, blue and red shaded overdress.

GOOSEGIRL **HN 425** 1921-1938   N.A.
  Blue skirt, striped blue blouse.

  HN 436 1921-1938   N.A.
  Green skirt, blue spots, spotted blouse.

  HN 437 1921-1938   N.A.
  Checkered brown and blue dress.

  HN 448 1921-1938   N.A.
  Blue striped dress, blue hat.

  HN 559 1923-1938   N.A.
  Pink spotted dress.

  HN 560 1923-1938   N.A.
  Red blouse.

GOSSIPS **HN 1426** 1930-1949   *450.00*
  Blue and red dresses.

  HN 1429 1930-1949   440.00
  Red dress, white dress.

  HN 2025 1949-1967   295.00 to 395.00
  Glaze differences.

GRACE **HN 2318** 1966-1980   84.00 to 160.00
  Green dress. **

GRAND MANNER **HN 2723** 1975-1981   159.00 to 236.00
  Pale blue dress.

GRANDMA **HN 2052** 1950-1959   250.00 to 350.00
  Predominantly blue shawl.

  HN 2052A 1950-1959   340.00
  Red multicolored shawl.

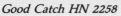
Good Catch HN 2258

Granny's Heritage HN 2031

GRANNY **HN 1804** 1937-1949	*700.00*
Gray dress.	
HN 1832 1937-1949	*700.00*
Yellow dress, red shawl.	
GRANNY'S HERITAGE **HN 1873** 1938-1949	*450.00*
Red shawl.	
HN 1874 1938-1949	*450.00*
Blue shawl, green skirt.	
HN 2031 1949-1969	*400.00*
Green skirt, light multicolored shawl. *	
GRANNY'S SHAWL **HN 1642** 1934-1949	*375.00*
Blue cape.	
HN 1647 1934-1949	225.00 to 390.00
Red cape.	
GRETA **HN 1485** 1931-1953	175.00 to 240.00
Off-white dress, red shawl.	
GRETCHEN **HN 1397** 1930-1938	500.00
Blue and white dress.	
HN 1562 1933-1938	*650.00*
Red and purple dress.	
GRIEF **HN 595** 1924-1938	*850.00*
Pale off-white.	
GRISELDA **HN 1993** 1947-1953	335.00 to 400.00
Lilac dress, white floral underskirt.	
GRIZEL **HN 1629** 1934-1938	460.00
Red multicolored bodice, light skirt.	
GROSSMITH'S TSANG IHANG **HN 582** 1923-?	460.00
Yellow and blue multicolored costume.	
GUY FAWKES **HN 98** 1918-1949	1200.00
Red cloak.	
HN 347 1919-1938	*1050.00 to 1200.00*
Brown cloak.	
HN 445 1921-1938	*1050.00 to 1200.00*
Green cloak.	
GWENDOLEN **HN 1494** 1932-1938	495.00
Green and pink dress.	
HN 1503 1932-1949	*650.00*
Orange-yellow dress.	

HN 1570 1933-1949   *600.00*
　Pink dress.
GWYNNETH **HN 1980** 1945-1952   220.00 to 300.00
　Red dress.
GYPSY DANCE **HN 2157** 1955-1957   400.00
　Purple and white dress.
　HN 2230 1959-1971   245.00 to 320.00
　Purple and white dress. *
GYPSY GIRL WITH FLOWERS, see Gleaner
GYPSY WOMAN WITH CHILD **HN 1301** 1928-1938 *1500.00 to 2000.00*
　Green shawl, blue skirt.
H.M. QUEEN ELIZABETH II, see Queen Elizabeth II
HAPPY JOY, BABY BOY **HN 1541** 1933-1949   *300.00*
　Blonde child with drape.
HARLEQUIN **HN 2186** 1957-1969   180.00 to 240.00
　Pale blue costume. *
　HN 2737 1982-   750.00
　Prestige figure; multicolored suit, black hat.
HARLEQUINADE **HN 585** 1923-1938   *750.00*
　Purple and green costume.
　HN 635 1924-1938   800.00 to 1200.00
　Gold costume.
　HN 711 1925-1938   *750.00*
　Black and white costume.
　HN 780 1926-1938   *750.00*
　Pink dress, blue, black, and orange markings.
HARLEQUINADE MASKED **HN 768** 1925-1938   *1000.00 to 1200.00*
　Black, red, green checkered costume.
　HN 769 1925-1938   *1000.00 to 1200.00*
　Blue, red, and yellow costume.
　HN 1274 1928-1938   *900.00 to 1000.00*
　Red and black costume.
　HN 1304 1928-1938   *900.00 to 1000.00*
　Black spotted costume.
HARMONY **HN 2824** 1978-   85.00 to 172.00
　Gray dress.
HARP **HN 2482** 1973-1978   1200.00
　One of Lady Musicians series, limited to 750.
　Brown dress.
HARRIETTE **HN 2083** 1943-1949   *400.00*
　Curly hair.
HAZEL **HN 1796** 1936-1949   *300.00*
　Green dress.
　HN 1797 1936-1949   *300.00*
　Orange and green dress.
HE LOVES ME **HN 2046** 1949-1962   *175.00*
　Pink dress.
HEART TO HEART **HN 2276** 1961-1971   300.00 to 325.00
　Lavender dress. White and green dress. **

Harlequin HN 2186

Gypsy Dance HN 2230

Her Ladyship HN 1977

HEATHER **HN 2956** 1982-	60.00 to 95.00
One of Vanity Fair series; white dress, fan on wrist.	
HEIDI **HN 2975** 1983-	34.00 to 50.00
One of characters from Children's Literature series; green dress, white smock.	
HELEN **HN 1508** 1932-1938	*550.00*
Green dress.	
HN 1509 1932-1938	*550.00*
White, blue, and red dress.	
HN 1572 1933-1938	550.00 to 560.00
Red dress.	
HELEN OF TROY **HN 2387** 1981-	695.00 to 1250.00
One of Femmes Fatales series; limited to 750. Pink and green costume, peacock.	
HELMSMAN **HN 2499** 1974-	200.00
Cream coat.	
HENRIETTA MARIA **HN 2005** 1949-1953	450.00 to 600.00
Cream mottled dress, red underskirt.	
HENRY IRVING, CARDINAL WOLSEY **HN 344** 1919-1949	*2000.00*
Red robe.	
HENRY LYTTON AS JACK POINT **HN 610** 1924-1949	*750.00*
Black and gold striped costume.	
HENRY VIII **HN 370** 1920-1938	*2300.00*
Multicolored costume.	
HN 673 1924-1938	*2300.00*
Brown and lilac robe.	
HN 1792 1933-1939	*2000.00*
Ermine-trimmed cape. Limited to 200.	
HER LADYSHIP **HN 1977** 1945-1959	225.00 to 310.00
Cream dress, red shawl. *	
HERE A LITTLE CHILD I STAND **HN 1546** 1933-1949	225.00 to 320.00
Child in pale lavender dress, green base.	
HERMINIA **HN 1644** 1934-1938	*800.00*
White flower-print dress.	

HN 1646   1934-1938   620.00
   Red dress, white stripes.
HN 1704   1935-1938   850.00 to 950.00
   Red dress, green purse.
HERMIONE   **HN 2058**   1950-1952   640.00
   Purple overdress.
HIBERNIA   **HN 2932**   1983-   950.00
   One of Ships' Figureheads series; limited to 950.
   Black, white, and gold.
HIGHWAYMAN   **HN 527**   1921-1949   *650.00*
   Red costume, dark coat.
HN 592   1924-1949   *650.00*
   Different glaze.
HN 1257   1927-1949   *650.00*
   Earthenware.
HILARY   **HN 2335**   1967-1980   96.00 to 150.00
   Blue dress.
HINGED PARASOL   **HN 1578**   1933-1949   300.00
   Blue-dotted skirt.
HN 1579   1933-1949   *400.00*
   Red dress, purple ruffles.
HOME AGAIN   **HN 2167**   1956-   69.00 to 125.00
   Orange-red dress. *
HONEY   **HN 1909**   1939-1949   325.00 to 345.00
   Pink dress.
HN 1910   1939-1949   *350.00*
   Green dress, blue jacket.
HN 1963   1941-1949   *350.00*
   Red dress, blue hat, and shawl.
HORNPIPE   **HN 2161**   1955-1962   560.00 to 750.00
   Blue jacket, blue and white striped trousers.
HOSTESS OF WILLIAMSBURG   **HN 2209**   1960-   99.00 to 200.00
   Pink dress. One of Figures of Williamsburg. *
HUCKLEBERRY FINN   **HN 2927**   1982-   32.00 to 50.00
   One of characters from Children's Literature
   series; yellow shirt, brown pants, straw hat.

Hostess Of Williamsburg
HN 2209

Home Again HN 2167

HUNTING SQUIRE   **HN 1409**   1930-1938   *2250.00*
   Red jacket, dappled gray horse.
HUNTS LADY   **HN 1201**   1926-1938   *1000.00*
   Gray jacket, rust boots.
HUNTSMAN   **HN 1226**   1927-1938   *1400.00*
   Red jacket, black hat.
  HN 1815   1937-1949   3000.00
   Earthenware. Renamed version of John Peel, HN
   1408
  HN 2492   1974-1978   125.00 to 200.00
   Gray-green jacket.
HURDY GURDY   **HN 2796**   1975-1978   880.00
   One of Lady Musicians series, limited to 750.
   Blue overdress.
IBRAHIM   **HN 2095**   1952-1955   560.00 to 750.00
   Earthenware. Renamed.
IN GRANDMA'S DAYS   **HN 339**   1919-1938   *1200.00*
   Renamed version of Lilac Shawl. Yellow gown,
   brown shawl.
  HN 340   1919-1938   *1200.00*
   Yellow and lilac dress.
  HN 362   1919-1938   1000.00
   Blue patterned dress.
  HN 388   1920-1938   *1400.00*
   Blue patterned dress.
  HN 442   1921-1938   *1400.00*
   White spotted skirt, green shawl.
IN THE STOCKS   **HN 1474**   1931-1938   *900.00 to 1200.00*
   Red dress.
  HN 1475   1931-1938   *1000.00*
   Green dress.
  HN 2163   1955-1959   540.00 to 700.00
   Rust jacket.
INDIAN BRAVE   **HN 2376**   1967-1978   5200.00
   Limited to 500; black and white horse,
   multicolored costume.
INDIAN TEMPLE DANCER   **HN 2830**   1977-   560.00
   One of Dancers of the World series; limited to
   750. Yellow sari.
INNOCENCE   **HN 2842**   1979-   80.00 to 156.00
   Red dress.
INVITATION   **HN 2170**   1956-1975   100.00 to 160.00
   Pink dress. *
IONA   **HN 1346**   1929-1938   *1500.00 to 2000.00*
   Green hat, white costume.
IRENE   **HN 1621**   1934-1951   285.00 to 425.00
   Pale yellow dress.
  HN 1697   1935-1949   *450.00*
   Pink dress, green hat.

Invitation HN 2170

Ivy HN 1768

HN 1952 1940-1950   *550.00*
Red dress.
IRISH COLLEEN **HN 766** 1925-1938   *1300.00 to 1500.00*
Red jacket.
HN 767 1925-1938   *1200.00*
Green skirt, black jacket.
IRISHMAN **HN 1307** 1928-1938   *1000.00*
Green jacket and hat.
IT WON'T HURT **HN 2963** 1982-   47.00 to 75.00
One of Childhood Days series; blue dress, white
apron, and hat with Red Cross symbol.
IVY **HN 1768** 1936-1978   74.00 to 80.00
Pink hat, lavender dress. *
HN 1769 1936-1938   *300.00*
Color not recorded.
JACK **HN 2060** 1950-1971   150.00 to 170.00
Green jacket.
JACK POINT **HN 85** 1918-1938   *2200.00 to 2500.00*
Red checkered costume.
HN 91 1918-1938   *2200.00 to 2500.00*
Green and black costume.
HN 99 1918-1938   1600.00 to 1650.00
Heraldic tunic.
HN 2080 1952-   1350.00 to 1600.00
Prestige figure; red tights, red and purple
costume.
JACQUELINE **HN 2000** 1947-1951   340.00
Lilac dress.
HN 2001 1947-1951   380.00
Rose dress.
HN 2333 1983-   100.00 to 145.00
Lilac dress, yellow sash and flower.
JAMES **HN 3013** 1983-   100.00
White smock, gray pants, straw hat. One of Kate
Greenaway figures.
JANE **HN 2014** 1948-1951   600.00
Red-rose dress.

HN 2806 1983-   95.00 to 135.00
  Yellow dress, multicolored parasol.
JANET HN 1537 1932-   120.00
  Red dress. *
  HN 1538 1932-1949   *300.00*
  Blue-red dress.
  HN 1652 1934-1949   *325.00*
  Red bodice, pink flowered skirt.
  HN 1737 1935-1949   285.00 to 300.00
  Green and white dress.
  HN 1916 1939-1949   150.00 to 280.00
  Blue bodice, pink skirt. Reduced size of HN 1537.
  HN 1964 1941-1949   320.00
  Pink dress.
  M 69 1936-1949   320.00
  Pale green skirt, green overdress.
  M 75 1936-1949   300.00
  White skirt, rose shaded overdress.
JANICE HN 2022 1949-1955   285.00 to 540.00
  Green dress.
  HN 2165 1955-1965   440.00 to 550.00
  Dark overdress.
JANINE HN 2461 1971-   170.00 to 172.00
  Green overdress.
JAPANESE FAN HN 399 1920-1938   *1000.00 to 1400.00*
  Purple and dark multicolored costume.
  HN 405 1920-1938   *1000.00 to 1200.00*
  Pale yellow dress.
  HN 439 1921-1938   *1400.00*
  Blue dress, green spots.
  HN 440 1921-1938   *1400.00*
  Yellow dress, orange spots.
JASMINE HN 1862 1938-1949   *600.00*
  Floral jacket with lavender trim.
  HN 1863 1938-1949   *600.00*
  White dress, floral jacket with green trim.
  HN 1876 1938-1949   640.00
  Blue floral jacket, pink trim.
JEAN HN 1877 1938-1949   275.00
  Pink dress, blue shawl.
  HN 1878 1938-1949   400.00
  Green dress, red shawl.
  HN 2032 1949-1959   210.00 to 340.00
  Green dress, red cloak. *
  HN 2710 1983-   95.00
  One of Vanity Fair series; hair brush and ribbon
  lying on lap.
JENNIFER HN 1484 1931-1949   360.00
  Cream-colored dress, yellow flowers, blue cloak.

Janet HN 1537

Jester HN 2016

Jean HN 2032

HN 1484 1931-1949		425.00
Potted.		
HN 2392 1982-		40.00 to 150.00
Blue and white dress. Second version.		
JERSEY MILKMAID **HN 2057** 1950-1959		200.00 to 325.00
Red bodice, blue skirt.		
JERSEY MILKMAID, see also Milkmaid		
JESTER		1600.00
Early experimental, Burslem, designed Noke, c. 1895.		
HN 45 1915-1938		*1200.00*
Black and white checkered costume.		
HN 45A 1915-1938		*1200.00*
Green and white checkered costume.		
HN 45B 1915-1938		*1200.00*
Red and white checkered costume.		
HN 55 1916-1938		*1200.00 to 1400.00*
Black and lilac costume.		
HN 71 1917-1938		1140.00
Black, green, and red costume.		
HN 71A 1917-1938		1140.00
Dark green costume.		
HN 308 1918-1938		*1200.00 to 1400.00*
Black and lilac costume.		
HN 320 1918-1938		*1200.00 to 1400.00*
Green and black costume.		
HN 367 1920-1938		*1300.00 to 1500.00*
Green, red, and yellow costume.		
HN 412 1920-1938		*1300.00*
Green and red striped tights.		

HN 426   1921-1938   *1200.00*
   Costume with pink pattern, black tights.
HN 446   1921-1938   *1300.00*
   Green sleeves, blue base.
HN 552   1922-1938   *1300.00*
   Black and red costume.
HN 616   1924-1938   *1300.00*
   Quartered heraldic tunic.
HN 627   1924-1938   1295.00
   Brown checkered costume.
HN 630   1924-1938   *1300.00*
   Brown striped tights.
HN 1295   1928-1949   780.00
   Black, orange, and blue shirt.
HN 1333   1929-1949   *1300.00*
   Blue tunic, yellow and black stripes.
HN 1702   1935-1949   740.00
   Brown, purple, red costume.
HN 2016   1949-   100.00 to 200.00
   Pink, purple, and orange costume. *
JILL   **HN 2061**   1950-1971   150.00 to 160.00
   Red dress.
JOAN   **HN 1422**   1930-1949   535.00
   Blue dress.
   HN 2023   1949-1959   300.00 to 535.00
   Glaze differences.
JOANNE   **HN 2373**   1983-   67.00 to 95.00
   One of the Vanity Fair series; white gown.
JOHN PEEL   **HN 1408**   1930-1937   *2600.00*
   Red jacket, brown horse. Renamed Huntsman,
   HN 1815.
JOLLY SAILOR   **HN 2172**   1956-1965   560.00 to 625.00
   Blue and white striped shirt. *
JOVIAL MONK   **HN 2144**   1954-1967   155.00 to 240.00
   Brown robe.
JUDGE   **HN 2443**   1972-1976   225.00
   Red robe; glossy finish.

Jolly Sailor HN 2172

HN 2443A   1976-   180.00
   Matte finish.

JUDGE AND JURY   HN 1264   1927-1938   *2000.00 to 2500.00*
   Red, ermine-trimmed robe.

JUDITH   HN 2089   1952-1959   235.00 to 380.00
   Rose dress, lilac bodice.

JULIA   HN 2705   1975-   78.00 to 156.00
   Deep apricot dress.

JULIET   HN 2968   1983-   210.00
   First in the Ladies of Covent Garden series;
   originally available only from American Express.
   White dress, blue trim.

JUNE   HN 1690   1935-1949   *400.00*
   Green dress.

HN 1691   1935-1949   300.00 to 400.00
   Pink shoes, light floral dress.

HN 1947   1940-1949   *400.00*
   Red-purple dress.

HN 2027   1949-1952   340.00
   Glaze differences.

M 65   1935-1949   *350.00*
   Blue skirt, pink overdress, blue bonnet.

M 71   1936-1949   320.00 to 375.00
   Pale blue dress and parasol.

KAREN   HN 1994   1947-1955   350.00
   Red dress.

HN 2388   1982-   105.00 to 175.00
   White blouse, red skirt.

KATE   HN 2789   1978-   98.00 to 156.00
   White dress.

KATE HARDCASTLE   HN 1718   1935-1949   425.00 to 535.00
   Pink dress, green underskirt.

HN 1719   1935-1949   475.00 to 680.00
   Green dress, pink underskirt.

HN 1734   1935-1949   *700.00*
   White and green dress, pink flower.

HN 1861   1938-1949   475.00 to 720.00
   Red, blue, and green dress.

HN 1919   1939-1949   *750.00*
   Green dress, black base, red overskirt.

HN 2028   1949-1952   580.00
   Glaze differences.

KATHARINE   HN 61   1916-1938   *1300.00 to 1500.00*
   Green dress.

HN 74   1917-1938   *1400.00 to 1600.00*
   Pale blue dress, green spots.

HN 341   1919-1938   *1300.00*
   Red dress.

HN 471   1921-1938   *1600.00 to 1800.00*
   Spotted blouse and dress.

HN 615   1924-1938   *1200.00 to 1400.00*
Pink skirt, green spots.
HN 793   1926-1938   *1500.00*
Lilac dress, green spots.
KATHLEEN   **HN 1252**   1927-1938   680.00
Pale pink skirt.
HN 1253   1927-1938   *700.00*
Orange-red skirt.
HN 1275   1928-1938   *700.00*
Black floral shawl.
HN 1279   1928-1938   *700.00*
Pink-red skirt, red-orange shawl.
HN 1291   1928-1938   *700.00*
Red shawl, yellow dress.
HN 1357   1929-1938   *700.00*
Pink, orange, and yellow skirt.
HN 1512   1932-1938   *700.00*
Lilac dress, blue hat.
KATHY   **HN 2346**   1981-   45.00 to 100.00
One of the Kate Greenaway series; white dress
with red flowers, white bonnet, red shoes.
KATRINA   **HN 2327**   1965-1969   255.00 to 295.00
Red dress. *
KIMBERLY   **HN 2969**   1983-   210.00
Fourth in the Ladies of Covent Garden series;
originally available only from American Express.
Yellow dress.
KING CHARLES   **HN 404**   1920-1951   500.00 to 850.00
Dark costume, pink base.
HN 2084   1952-   625.00 to 1500.00
Prestige figure; black clothing; 16 3/4 in.
KING WENCESLAS,   See Good King Wenceslas
KIRSTY   **HN 2381**   1971-
Apricot dress. 4 93.00 to 185.00
KITTY   **HN 1367**   1930-1938   *850.00*
White skirt, purple stripes.
KO-KO   **HN 1266**   1928-1949   *700.00*
Black and white costume.
HN 1286   1938-1949   640.00
Red robe.
HN 2898   1980-   300.00 to 750.00
One of Gilbert and Sullivan series; yellow
kimono, black and green design, blue jacket.
KURDISH DANCER   **HN 2867**   1979-   500.00 to 750.00
One of Dancers of the World series; limited to
750. Blue and purple costume.
LA SYLPHIDE   **HN 2138**   1956-1965   325.00 to 450.00
White costume.
LADY & BLACKAMOOR   **HN 374**   1920-1938   *2300.00 to 2600.00*
Blue and green dress.

Katrina HN 2327

Lady April HN 1958

HN 375 1920-1938	*2300.00 to 2600.00*
Yellow dress.	
HN 377 1920-1938	*2300.00 to 2600.00*
Pink and green dress.	
HN 470 1921-1938	*2300.00 to 2600.00*
Green and lilac dress.	
LADY & THE UNICORN **HN 2825** 1982-	2500.00
One of Myths and Maidens series; limited to 300.	
Purple and gold dress, white unicorn.	
LADY ANNE **HN 83** 1918-1938	*2500.00 to 2700.00*
Yellow dress.	
HN 87 1918-1938	*2500.00 to 2700.00*
Green dress.	
HN 93 1918-1938	*2500.00 to 2700.00*
Blue dress.	
LADY ANNE NEVILL **HN 2006** 1948-1953	600.00 to 950.00
Purple dress, ermine-trim.	
LADY APRIL **HN 1958** 1940-1959	195.00 to 350.00
Red dress. *	
HN 1965 1941-1949	475.00
Green dress.	
LADY BETTY **HN 1967** 1941-1951	275.00 to 375.00
Red dress.	
LADY CHARMIAN **HN 1948** 1940-1973	175.00 to 200.00
Green dress, red shawl.	
HN 1949 1940-1975	175.00 to 240.00
Red dress, green shawl.	
LADY CLARE **HN 1465** 1931-1938	680.00
Pink dress.	
LADY CLOWN **HN 717** 1925-1938	*1000.00 to 1300.00*
White, red, and black costume.	
HN 718 1925-1938	*1000.00 to 1300.00*
White costume, red stripes, black spots.	
HN 738 1925-1938	*1000.00 to 1300.00*
Black and white pants, red spots.	
HN 770 1925-1938	*1000.00 to 1300.00*
Green masks and streamers painted on costume.	
HN 1263 1927-1938	800.00
Blue and red pants.	

LADY ERMINE **HN 54** 1916-1938 · · · · · · · · · · · · · · 1200.00
  Blue coat.
  HN 332 1918-1938 · · · · · · · · · · · · · · *1200.00 to 1400.00*
  Red coat and hat, green and yellow patterned
  skirt.
  HN 671 1924-1938 · · · · · · · · · · · · · · *400.00 to 1600.00*
  Green coat, yellow skirt.
LADY FAYRE **HN 1265** 1928-1938 · · · · · · · · · · · · · · *500.00*
  Purple and red dress.
  HN 1557 1933-1938 · · · · · · · · · · · · · · 325.00 to 675.00
  Pink dress.
LADY FROM WILLIAMSBURG **HN 2228** 1960- · · · · · · 99.00 to 200.00
  Green dress. One of Figures of Williamsburg. *
LADY JESTER **HN 1221** 1927-1938 · · · · · · · · · · *950.00 to 1100.00*
  Pink and black costume.
  HN 1222 1927-1938 · · · · · · · · · · · · · · 960.00
  Black and white costume.
  HN 1284 1928-1938 · · · · · · · · · · · · · · 720.00
  Blue vest, red tights.
  HN 1285 1928-1938 · · · · · · · · · · · · · · 720.00 to 900.00
  Red vest, blue and red tights.
  HN 1332 1929-1938 · · · · · · · · · · · · · · *950.00 to 1100.00*
  Red, blue and black skirt.
LADY MUSICIANS SERIES, see individual figurines
LADY OF THE ELIZABETHAN PERIOD
  HN 40 1914-1938 · · · · · · · · · · · · · · *1600.00 to 1800.00*
  Orange and brown patterned dress.
  HN 40A 1914-1938 · · · · · · · · · · · · · · *1600.00 to 1800.00*
  Plain dress.
  HN 73 1917-1938 · · · · · · · · · · · · · · *1700.00 to 2000.00*
  Dark blue-green costume.
  HN 309 1918-1938 · · · · · · · · · · · · · · *1600.00 to 2000.00*
  Raised pattern on dress.
  HN 411 1920-1938 · · · · · · · · · · · · · · *1800.00 to 2000.00*
  Brown mottled dress.
LADY OF THE FAN **HN 48** 1916-1938 · · · · · · · · · *1400.00 to 1700.00*
  Lilac dress.
  HN 52 1916-1938 · · · · · · · · · · · · · · *1400.00 to 1700.00*
  Yellow dress.
  HN 53 1916-1938 · · · · · · · · · · · · · · *1450.00 to 1700.00*
  Dark blue dress.
  HN 53A 1916-1938 · · · · · · · · · · · · · · *1450.00 to 1700.00*
  Green-blue dress.
  HN 335 1919-1938 · · · · · · · · · · · · · · *1400.00 to 1700.00*
  Blue dress.
  HN 509 1921-1938 · · · · · · · · · · · · · · *1400.00 to 1700.00*
  Green, lilac, and blue spotted dress.
LADY OF THE GEORGIAN PERIOD **HN 41** 1914-1938 *1800.00 to 2100.00*
  Rust overdress.

Lady From Williamsburg HN 2228

Lady Pamela HN 2718

HN 331 1918-1938   *1800.00 to 2100.00*
  Brown and yellow dress.
HN 444 1921-1938   *1800.00 to 2100.00*
  Green-blue spotted dress.
HN 690 1925-1938   *1800.00*
  Colors unknown.
HN 702 1625-1938   *1800.00 to 2000.00*
  Striped pink skirt, green overdress.
LADY OF THE SNOWS **HN 1780** 1933-1939   N.A.
  One of the Garbe figurines. Production limited to
  25.
HN 1830 1937-1949   N.A.
  Tinted finish.
LADY PAMELA **HN 2718** 1974-1980   110.00 to 160.00
  Pink dress. *
LADY WITH PARASOL, see Miss Demure
LADY WITH ROSE **HN 48A** 1916-1938   1900.00
  Cream dress.
HN 52A 1916-1938   *1500.00 to 1700.00*
  Yellow dress.
HN 68 1916-1938   *1500.00 to 1700.00*
  Green and yellow dress.
HN 304 1918-1938   *1500.00 to 1700.00*
  Gray-lilac dress, brown pattern.
HN 336 1919-1938   *1500.00 to 1700.00*
  Multicolored dress, brown pattern.
HN 515 1921-1938   *1500.00 to 1700.00*
  Green dress, lilac stripes.
HN 517 1921-1938   *1500.00 to 1700.00*
  Lilac dress, orange spots.
HN 584 1923-1938   *1500.00 to 1700.00*
  Green and pink dress.
HN 624 1924-1938   *1500.00 to 1700.00*
  Green-blue skirt, pink and black cuffs.
LADY WITH SHAWL **HN 447** 1921-1938   *2200.00*
  Pale blue and white striped dress.
HN 458 1921-1938   *2200.00*
  Multicolored shawl, pink dress.

HN 626   1924-1938   *2200.00 to 2800.00*
  Yellow shawl, pink spots, white dress, green
  spots.
HN 678   1924-1938   *2200.00 to 2800.00*
  Black and white shawl, yellow and white dress.
HN 679   1924-1938   *2200.00 to 2800.00*
  Black, yellow, and blue shawl, black and white
  dress.
LADY WITHOUT BOUQUET   **HN 393**   1920-1938   *1400.00 to 1700.00*
  Peach and blue dress.
  HN 394   1920-1938   *1400.00 to 1700.00*
  Blue and yellow dress.
LADYBIRD   **HN 1638**   1934-1949   *750.00 to 900.00*
  Pink costume.
  HN 1640   1934-1938   *750.00 to 900.00*
  Light blue costume.
LAIRD   **HN 2361**   1969-   86.00 to 180.00
  Green and white plaid kilt, brown jacket.
LALLA ROOKH   **HN 2910**   1981-   425.00 to 950.00
  One of Ships' Figureheads series; limited to 950.
  Costume trimmed in red and gold, turban.
LAMBETH WALK   **HN 1880**   1938-1949   1200.00
  Blue dress.
  HN 1881   1938-1949   *1200.00*
  Pink dress, green hat.
LAMBING TIME   **HN 1890**   1938-1980   105.00 to 175.00
  Light orange smock.
LAND OF NOD   **HN 56**   1916-1938   1600.00
  Ivory nightshirt.
  HN 56A   1916-1938   *1600.00 to 1800.00*
  Pale gray nightshirt, green candlestick.
  HN 56B   1916-1938   *1600.00 to 1800.00*
  Pale gray nightshirt, red candlestick.
LAST WALTZ   **HN 2315**   1967-   93.00 to 185.00
  Apricot dress. *

Last Waltz HN 2315

LAURA **HN 2960** 1983-   98.00 to 145.00
   Peach flowers on white gown, blue underskirt.
LAURIANNE **HN 2719** 1974-1978   125.00
   Dark blue overdress.
LAVENDER WOMAN **HN 22** 1913-1938   *1600.00 to 1800.00*
   Pale aqua dress.
  HN 23 1913-1938   *1600.00 to 1800.00*
   Green dress.
  HN 23A 1913-1938   *1600.00 to 1800.00*
   Blue and green dress.
  HN 342 1919-1938   *1600.00 to 1800.00*
   Patterned dress, lilac shawl.
  HN 569 1924-1938   *1300.00 to 1600.00*
   Red striped shawl.
  HN 744 1925-1938   *1300.00 to 1600.00*
   Blue spotted dress, striped shawl.
LAVINIA **HN 1955** 1940-1978   90.00 to 120.00
   Red dress.
LEADING LADY **HN 2269** 1965-1976   145.00 to 200.00
   Lavender overdress. **
LEAP **HN 3522** 1982-   75.00
   One of Images of Nature series; dolphin.
LEDA & THE SWAN **HN 2826** 1983-   2500.00
   One of Myths and Maidens series; limited to 300.
   Gown of brown and gold; white swan. *
LEGOLAS **HN 2917** 1981-   23.00 to 48.00
   One of Tolkien series; white and beige costume.
LEISURE HOUR **HN 2055** 1950-1965   350.00 to 475.00
   Mottled green and peach dress.
LEOPARD ON ROCK **HN 2638** 1953-   1200.00 to 1650.00
   Prestige figure; 8 1/2 x 16 in.
LIDO LADY **HN 1220** 1927-1938   700.00
   Flowered blue costume.
  HN 1229 1927-1938   *700.00*
   Flowered pink costume.
LIGHTS OUT **HN 2262** 1965-1969   150.00 to 215.00
   Yellow polka-dot top. **
LILAC SHAWL **HN 44** 1915-1938   1280.00
   Also produced under the names In Grandma's
   Days and Poke Bonnet. Lilac shawl with roses,
   cream skirt.
  HN 44A 1915-1938   1040.00
   Printed pattern on shawl.
LILAC TIME **HN 2137** 1954-1969   265.00 to 280.00
   Red dress. *
LILY **HN 1798** 1936-1949   95.00 to 145.00
   White shawl, pink dress. **
  HN 1799 1936-1949   *125.00*
   Blue shawl, green dress.

Leda & The Swan HN 2826

Lilac Time HN 2137

LINDA **HN 2106** 1953-1976	120.00
Red cloak.	
LION ON ROCK **HN 2641** 1957-	907.00 to 1650.00
Prestige figure; 10 1/2 x 18 in.	
LISA **HN 2310** 1969-1982	85.00 to 172.00
Violet and white dress.	
HN 2394 1983-	88.00 to 125.00
Yellow and lilac costume.	
LISETTE **HN 1523** 1932-1938	*700.00 to 800.00*
White and red dress.	
HN 1524 1932-1938	*700.00*
Multicolored dress.	
HN 1684 1935-1938	*700.00*
Pink dress. Green trim.	
LITTLE BOY BLUE **HN 2062** 1950-1973	110.00 to 160.00
Blue smock.	
LITTLE BRIDESMAID **HN 1433** 1930-1951	125.00 to 160.00
Pale yellow dress.	
HN 1433 1930-1951	210.00
Potted.	
HN 1434 1930-1949	95.00 to 200.00
Yellow dress.	
HN 1530 1932-1938	*200.00*
Yellow and green dress.	
LITTLE CHILD RARE AND SWEET **HN 1540** 1933-1949	*350.00*
Nude child, standing on green base.	
HN 1542 1933-1949	320.00
Nude child sitting on blue base, brown hair.	
LITTLE JACK HORNER **HN 2063** 1950-1953	240.00
Red jacket.	
LITTLE LADY MAKE BELIEVE **HN 1870** 1938-1949	350.00
Red cape.	
LITTLE LAND **HN 63** 1916-1938	*1700.00 to 1900.00*
Green and yellow dress.	
HN 67 1916-1938	1400.00 to 1750.00
Blue costume.	

LITTLE LORD FAUNTLEROY   **HN 2972** 1982-   32.00 to 50.00
One of characters from Children's Literature
series; blue suit, white collar and stockings.

LITTLE MISTRESS   **HN 1449** 1931-1949   295.00 to 460.00
Pale green dress, lavender-gray shawl.

LITTLE MOTHER   **HN 389** 1920-1938   N.A.
Pink dress, blonde hair.

HN 390 1920-1938   N.A.
Pink dress, dark hair.

HN 469 1921-1938   1800.00 to 2000.00
White dress, brown hair.

HN 1418 1930-1938   900.00 to 1100.00
Dark-colored basket. Renamed version of Young
Widow, HN 1399.

HN 1641 1934-1949   900.00
Light skirt, green shawl. Renamed version of
Young Widow, HN 1399.

LITTLE NELL   **HN 540** 1922-1932   60.00
Pink dress, 4 in.

M 51 1932-   19.00 to 32.00
White dress.

LIZANA   **HN 1756** 1936-1949   600.00
Pink dress, green cloak.

HN 1761 1936-1938   700.00 to 800.00
Green dress, leopard cloak.

LOBSTER MAN   **HN 2317** 1964-   83.00 to 168.00
Blue sweater. *

LONDON CRY, STRAWBERRIES   **HN 749** 1925-1938   700.00
Cream overdress, red skirt.

HN 772 1925-1938   750.00
Multicolored dress.

LONDON CRY, TURNIPS AND CARROTS   **HN 752** 1925-1938   650.00
Red bodice, purple skirt.

HN 771 1925-1938   700.00
Multicolored dress and blouse.

LONG JOHN SILVER   **HN 2204** 1957-1965   420.00 to 575.00
Dark uniform.

LORETTA   **HN 2337** 1966-1980   84.00 to 140.00
Rose-red dress, yellow shawl. **

LORI   **HN 2801** 1976-   45.00 to 100.00
One of the Kate Greenaway series. White dress.

LORNA   **HN 2311** 1965-   65.00 to 125.00
Green dress, apricot shawl.

LOUISE   **HN 2869** 1979-   50.00 to 100.00
One of the Kate Greeenaway series. Brown dress,
white collar and cuffs, brown bonnet.

LOVE LETTER   **HN 2149** 1958-1976   280.00 to 300.00
Pink and white dress, blue dress.

Lobster Man HN 2317

Lucy Lockett HN 524

LOVERS **HN 2762** 1980-	70.00 to 145.00
One of Images collection, white.	
HN 2763 1980-	95.00 to 145.00
One of Images collection, black.	
LUCY **HN 2863** 1980-	55.00 to 100.00
One of Kate Greenaway series; white and blue dress and bonnet.	
LUCY ANN **HN 1502** 1932-1951	200.00 to 260.00
Pale pink dress.	
HN 1565 1933-1938	*350.00*
Light green dress.	
LUCY LOCKETT **HN 485** 1921-1949	*600.00*
Green dress.	
HN 524 1921-1949	475.00 to 600.00
Yellow dress. *	
HN 695 1925-1949	*600.00*
Gold dress.	
HN 696 1925-1949	*600.00*
Light blue dress.	
LUNCHTIME **HN 2485** 1973-1980	140.00 to 200.00
Beige coat.	
LUTE **HN 2431** 1972-1978	880.00 to 1300.00
One of Lady Musicians series; limited to 750. Blue and white dress.	
LYDIA **HN 1906** 1939-1949	*325.00*
Orange-pink dress.	
HN 1907 1939-1949	*325.00*
Green dress.	
HN 1908 1939-	68.00 to 79.00
Red dress. *	
LYNNE **HN 2329** 1971-	81.00 to 172.00
Olive green dress.	
LYRIC **HN 2757** 1983-	95.00
One of the musicians group from the Enchantment Collection. Ivory body, burnished gold trim.	
M'LADY'S MAID **HN 1795** 1936-1949	*1200.00 to 1300.00*
Red dress.	

Lydia HN 1908

HN 1822 1937-1949		*800.00 to 1000.00*
Multicolored dress.		
MADONNA OF THE SQUARE **HN 10** 1913-1938		1040.00
Lilac dress.		
HN 10A 1913-1938		1500.00
Blue dress.		
HN 11 1913-1938		*1400.00 to 1500.00*
Gray dress.		
HN 14 1913-1938		*1400.00 to 1500.00*
Renumbered version of HN 10A.		
HN 27 1913-1938		*1400.00 to 1500.00*
Mottled green and blue costume.		
HN 326 1918-1938		*1300.00 to 1400.00*
Earthenware, gray-blue costume.		
HN 573 1913-1938		*1400.00 to 1500.00*
Orange skirt.		
HN 576 1923-1938		*1100.00 to 1200.00*
Green skirt, black patterned shawl.		
HN 594 1924-1938		*1000.00 to 1100.00*
Green skirt, brown patterned shawl.		
HN 613 1924-1938		*1000.00 to 1100.00*
Striped pink skirt, orange spotted shawl.		
HN 764 1925-1938		*1100.00 to 1200.00*
Blue and purple striped shawl, yellow skirt.		
HN 1968 1941-1949		*800.00*
Light green dress.		
HN 1969 1941-1949		*800.00*
Lilac dress.		
HN 2034 1949-1951		650.00 to 775.00
Light green-blue costume.		
MAGIC DRAGON **HN 2977** 1983-		75.00
One of the Fantasy group from the Enchantment		
Collection. Ivory body, burnished gold trim.		
MAGPIE RING **HN 2978** 1983-		95.00
One of the Fantasy group from the Enchantment		
Collection. Ivory body, burnished gold trim.		
MAISIE **HN 1618** 1934-1949		375.00
White dress.		

HN 1619   1934-1949   320.00
  Pink dress.
MAJOR, 3RD N.J. REG., 1776   **HN 2752**   1975-1976   840.00
  One of Soldiers of Revolution series, limited to
  350; pale blue uniform.
MAKE BELIEVE   **HN 2225**   1962-   50.00 to 100.00
  White dress. **
MAM'SELLE   **HN 658**   1924-1938   *750.00*
  White and black dress.
  HN 659   1924-1938   *800.00*
  Purple and red dress.
  HN 724   1925-1938   *800.00*
  Pink skirt.
  HN 786   1926-1938   *800.00*
  Pink and black dress.
MAN IN TUDOR COSTUME   **HN 563**   1923-1938   1400.00
  Orange striped costume, green tights, dark cloak.
MANDARIN   **HN 84**   1918-1938   *2000.00 to 2200.00*
  Mauve shirt, green cloak.
  HN 316   1918-1938   *2000.00 to 2200.00*
  Black and yellow costume.
  HN 318   1918-1938   *2000.00 to 2200.00*
  Gold and black costume.
  HN 366   1920-1938   *1450.00 to 1600.00*
  Yellow and blue costume.
  HN 382   1920-1938   *1900.00 to 2100.00*
  Blue and yellow costume.
  HN 450   1921-1938   *1400.00 to 1500.00*
  Red robe.
  HN 455   1921-1938   *1400.00 to 1500.00*
  Green costume.
  HN 460   1921-1938   *1400.00 to 1500.00*
  Blue costume.
  HN 461   1921-1938   *1400.00 to 1500.00*
  Red costume.
  HN 601   1924-1938   *1300.00 to 1400.00*
  Blue costume.
  HN 611   1924-1938   *1300.00 to 1400.00*
  Yellow patterned tunic.
  HN 641   1924-1938   *1300.00 to 1400.00*
  Onyx color.
  HN 746   1925-1938   *1800.00 to 2000.00*
  Black costume with green dragons.
  HN 787   1926-1938   *1700.00 to 1800.00*
  Pink and orange tunic, black flowers.
  HN 791   1926-1938   *1700.00 to 1800.00*
  Yellow tunic, green and red markings.
MANDY   **HN 2476**   1982-   45.00 to 65.00
  Cream, colored ground. *

Mandy HN 2476

Marguerite HN 1928

MANTILLA **HN 2712** 1974-1978 Red dress, black lace mantilla; one of Haute Ensemble series.	250.00 to 325.00
MARGARET **HN 1989** 1947-1959 Red coat, green dress.	320.00
HN 2397 1982- One of Vanity Fair series; white dress and hat, blue sash and bow. Second version.	67.00 to 95.00
MARGARET OF ANJOU **HN 2012** 1948-1953 Green dress.	475.00 to 700.00
MARGERY **HN 1413** 1930-1949 Red dress.	315.00 to 400.00
MARGOT **HN 1628** 1934-1938 Blue bodice.	540.00
HN 1636 1934-1938 Red bodice, yellow and pink skirt.	*600.00*
HN 1653 1934-1938 White and red dress, red hat.	*600.00*
MARGUERITE **HN 1928** 1940-1959 Pink dress. *	265.00 to 310.00
HN 1929 1940-1949 Pink to yellow trim on dress.	*400.00*
HN 1930 1940-1949 Blue dress with purple stripes.	*400.00*
HN 1946 1940-1949 Red dress, green hat.	*400.00*
MARIANNE **HN 2074** 1951-1953 Red-rose dress.	460.00
MARIE **HN 401** 1920-1938 Pink dress, white, yellow, blue skirt.	*1800.00 to 2000.00*
HN 434 1921-1938 Yellow skirt, orange stripes.	*1800.00 to 2000.00*
HN 502 1921-1938 White dress, red and blue bodice.	*1800.00 to 2000.00*
HN 504 1921-1938 Green and blue dress, red spots.	*1800.00 to 2000.00*
HN 505 1921-1938 Green and lilac skirt, blue spotted bodice.	*1800.00 to 2000.00*

HN 506   1921-1938   *1800.00 to 2000.00*
Blue and green striped bodice, spotted lilac skirt.
HN 1370   1930-   45.00 to 68.00
Lavender-purple dress. **
HN 1388   1930-1938   *300.00*
Red and blue flowered dress.
HN 1417   1930-1949   *300.00*
Orange dress.
HN 1489   1932-1949   320.00
Yellow-green dress.
HN 1531   1932-1938   *300.00*
Yellow-green dress.
HN 1635   1934-1949   326.00
Pink flowered skirt.
HN 1655   1934-1938   300.00
Pink bodice, flowered white skirt.
MARIETTA   **HN 1341**   1929-1949   375.00
Black costume, red cape.
HN 1446   1931-1949   600.00
Lilac costume, green cape.
HN 1699   1935-1949   *650.00*
Green dress, red cape.
MARIGOLD   **HN 1447**   1931-1949   *400.00*
White and purple dress.
HN 1451   1931-1938   *400.00*
Yellow dress.
HN 1555   1933-1949   *400.00*
Pink dress, blue bow.
MARION   **HN 1582**   1933-1938   *650.00*
Pink skirt.
HN 1583   1933-1938   *650.00*
Blue skirt.
MARIQUITA   **HN 1837**   1938-1949   *900.00*
Red and lavender dress.
MARJORIE   **HN 2788**   1980-   83.00 to 185.00
Blue and white dress.
MARKET DAY   **HN 1991**   1947-1955   215.00 to 325.00
Red flowered shawl, white apron.
MARRIAGE OF ART AND INDUSTRY   **HN 2261**   1958   N.A.
Bronze color. Edition limited to 12.
MARY HAD A LITTLE LAMB   **HN 2048**   1949-   50.00 to 100.00
Lilac dress. *

Mary Had A Little Lamb HN 2048

MARY JANE **HN 1990** 1947-1959   350.00 to 475.00
    Pink dress.
MARY MARY **HN 2044** 1949-1973   135.00 to 160.00
    Pink dress.
MARY QUEEN OF SCOTS **HN 2931** 1983-   950.00
    One of Ships' Figureheads series; limited to 950.
    Red, white, and green.
MASK **HN 656** 1924-1938   500.00 to 796.00
    Blue and purple costume.
  HN 657 1924-1938   *800.00 to 900.00*
    Black and white costume.
  HN 729 1925-1938   *800.00*
    Red and black costume.
  HN 733 1925-1938   *800.00*
    White and black costume.
  HN 785 1926-1938   *800.00*
    Blue costume, pink striped skirt.
  HN 1271 1928-1938   *800.00*
    Multicolored spotted costume.
MASK SELLER **HN 1361** 1929-1938   250.00
    Black cape, red hat.
  HN 2103 1953-   90.00 to 180.00
    Green coat, black hat. *
MASQUE **HN 2554** 1973-1982   85.00 to 180.00
    Dark blue cape.
MASQUERADE **HN 599** 1924-1949   *650.00*
    Man. Red jacket.
  HN 600 1924-1949   350.00
    Woman. Pink dress.
  HN 636 1924-1938   *700.00*
    Man. Gold costume.
  HN 637 1924-1938   *700.00*
    Woman. Gold dress.
  HN 674 1924-1938   *600.00*
    Woman. Orange and yellow checkered dress.
  HN 683 1924-1938   560.00
    Man. Green coat.
  HN 2251 1960-1965   240.00 to 395.00
    Blue-green overskirt.
  HN 2259 1960-1965   360.00
    Red dress.
MASTER **HN 2325** 1967-   91.00 to 168.00
    Gray-green jacket.
MASTER SWEEP **HN 2205** 1957-1962   540.00 to 575.00
    Green shirt.
MATADOR & BULL **HN 2324** 1964-   1150.00
    Prestige figure. Black and gold costume.
MATILDA **HN 2011** 1948-1953   520.00 to 600.00
    Purple dress, red print, red cape.

Mask Seller HN 2103   *Mayor HN 2280*   *Mendicant HN 1365*

MAUREEN **HN 1770** 1936-1959   170.00 to 310.00
  Red dress.
  HN 1771 1936-1949   *550.00*
  Lilac dress.
  M 84 1939-1949   300.00 to 400.00
  Orange jacket, shaded orange skirt, black hat and
  gloves.
  M 85 1939-1949   320.00 to 360.00
  Red and blue shaded jacket, pale skirt, black hat
  and gloves.
MAYOR **HN 2280** 1963-1971   380.00 to 425.00
  Red cape. *
MAYTIME **HN 2113** 1953-1967   230.00 to 320.00
  Rose-pink dress.
MEDITATION **HN 2330** 1971-   125.00 to 236.00
  Peach and white dress.
MELANIE **HN 2271** 1965-1980   95.00 to 160.00
  Blue dress. **
MELISSA **HN 2467** 1981-   94.00 to 172.00
  Red dress, white underskirt.
MELODY **HN 2202** 1957-1962   300.00
  Green top, beige skirt.
MEMORIES **HN 1855** 1938-1949   325.00
  Green bodice, red skirt.
  HN 1856 1938-1949   *400.00*
  White and blue dress, green book.
  HN 1857 1938-1949   *400.00*
  Red bodice, red and lilac skirt.
  HN 2030 1949-1959   300.00 to 420.00
  Green and red dress.
MENDICANT **HN 1355** 1929-1938   *375.00*
  Black and brown robe.
  HN 1365 1929-1969   225.00 to 300.00
  Different glaze effects. *

MEPHISTO **HN 722** 1925-1938   *1200.00 to 1300.00*
  Black blouse.
HN 723 1925-1938   *1100.00 to 1300.00*
  Red blouse.
MEPHISTOPHELES AND MARGUERITE
  HN 755 1925-1949   *1000.00 to 1100.00*
  Orange dress, purple cloak.
HN 775 1925-1949   880.00 to 900.00
  Red cloaks.
MERIEL **HN 1931** 1940-1949   760.00 to 965.00
  Pink dress.
HN 1932 1940-1949   *800.00*
  Green dress.
MERMAID **HN 97** 1918-1936   400.00 to 600.00
  Green seaweed in hair, beige base.
HN 300 1918-1936   *800.00 to 900.00*
  Red berries in hair, dark base.
MERYLL **HN 1917** 1939-1940   *1000.00*
  Red jacket, green skirt.
MERYLL, see also Toinette
MEXICAN DANCER **HN 2866** 1979-   500.00 to 750.00
  One of Dancers of the World series; limited to
  750. Gold dress and hat, white petticoat and
  scarf.
MICAWBER, see Mr. Micawber
MICHELLE **HN 2234** 1967-   77.50 to 156.00
  Green dress.
MIDINETTE **HN 1289** 1928-1938   *1100.00 to 1200.00*
  Peach skirt.
HN 1306 1928-1938   *1000.00 to 1100.00*
  Red blouse, green skirt.
HN 2090 1952-1965   255.00 to 325.00
  Blue dress. *
MIDSUMMER NOON **HN 1899** 1939-1949   550.00
  Red dress.
HN 1900 1939-1949   500.00
  Blue dress.
HN 2033 1949-1955   295.00 to 675.00
  Color change.
MILADY **HN 1970** 1941-1949   520.00 to 700.00
  Rust dress, black hat.
MILKING TIME **HN 3** 1913-1938   *1500.00 to 1700.00*
  Light blue dress, white apron.
HN 306 1913-1938   *1500.00 to 1700.00*
  Pale costume, black markings.
MILKMAID **HN 2057A** 1975-1981   85.00 to 150.00
  Incorrectly numbered 2100 at first. Green dress,
  white hat. Renamed version of Jersey Milkmaid.
MILKMAID, see also Jersey Milkmaid

MILLICENT **HN 1714** 1935-1949   960.00
   Pink shawl.
   HN 1715 1935-1949   895.00
   Purple dress, flowered shawl.
   HN 1860 1938-1949   *850.00*
   No details available.
MINUET **HN 2019** 1949-1971   200.00 to 325.00
   White dress, floral print. *
   HN 2066 1950-1955   340.00
   Red dress.
MIRABEL **HN 1743** 1935-1949   *650.00 to 750.00*
   Pale blue-green dress.
   HN 1744 1935-1949   *650.00*
   Pink dress.
   M 68 1936-1949   *200.00 to 300.00*
   Pink skirt, green cloak.
   M 74 1936-1949   *200.00 to 300.00*
   Blue dress, red cloak.
MIRANDA **HN 1818** 1937-1949   *650.00*
   Red skirt.
   HN 1819 1937-1949   *650.00*
   Green skirt.
MIRROR **HN 1852** 1938-1949   *750.00*
   Pink robe.
   HN 1853 1938-1949   *750.00*
   Blue robe.
MISS DEMURE **HN 1402** 1930-1975   150.00 to 250.00
   Pale pink dress. *
   HN 1440 1930-1949   *300.00*
   Pale blue dress.
   HN 1463 1931-1949   *300.00*
   Green dress.
   HN 1499 1932-1938   *350.00*
   Pink dress, yellow hat.

Midinette HN 2090

Miss Demure HN 1402

Minuet HN 2019

HN 1560 1933-1949   *300.00*
Purple bow, red shawl.
MISS FORTUNE **HN 1897** 1938-1949   460.00
Blue and white shawl, pink dress.
HN 1898 1938-1949   *450.00*
Green and yellow shawl, blue dress.
MISS MUFFET **HN 1936** 1940-1967   100.00 to 180.00
Red coat. **
HN 1937 1940-1952   155.00 to 320.00
Green coat.
MISS WINSOME **HN 1665** 1934-1949   480.00
Pale lavender dress.
HN 1666 1934-1949   530.00
Green dress.
MISS 1926 **HN 1205** 1926-1938   1600.00
Ermine trimmed coat.
HN 1207 1926-1938   *1600.00 to 1700.00*
Black fur collar.
MODENA **HN 1845** 1938-1949   *700.00*
Blue dress.
HN 1846 1938-1949   *700.00*
Red dress.
MODERN PIPER **HN 756** 1925-1938   1395.00 to 1660.00
Pale green cape, lavender jacket.
MOIRA **HN 1347** 1929-1938   1800.00 to 2000.00
Green hat, blue costume.
MOLLY MALONE **HN 1455** 1931-1938   *1100.00 to 1200.00*
Black skirt, red overdress, white apron.
MONICA **HN 1458** 1931-1949   200.00
White flower-print dress.
HN 1459 1931-   *200.00*
Lilac dress.
HN 1467 1931-   50.00 to 100.00
Red hat. *

Monica HN 1467

M 66 1935-1949   300.00
Pink shaded skirt, blue blouse.
M 72 1936-1949   *300.00*
Dress shaded blue to white, pink hat.
MONTE CARLO **HN 2332** 1983-   195.00
One of the Sweet and Twenties series; limited to
1500. Green dress, multicolored wrap.
MOOR **HN 1308** 1929-1938   *1500.00*
Blue costume, red cloak.
HN 1366 1930-1949   *1200.00 to 1300.00*
Red costume.
HN 1425 1930-1949   *1200.00*
Dark multicolored costume.
HN 1657 1934-1949   *1300.00 to 1400.00*
Striped waistband, black cloak.
HN 2082 1952-   798.00 to 1450.00
Prestige figure; red costume, dark cloak.
MOORISH MINSTREL **HN 34** 1913-1938   1050.00 to 1750.00
Dark blue robe.
HN 364 1920-1938   *2200.00 to 2500.00*
Blue, green, and orange striped costume.
HN 415 1920-1938   *2200.00 to 2500.00*
Green and yellow striped costume.
HN 797 1926-1949   *1500.00*
Purple costume.
MOORISH PIPER MINSTREL **HN 301** 1918-1938   1750.00
Dark blue robe, red hat.
HN 328 1918-1938   *2000.00 to 2200.00*
Green and brown striped robe.
HN 416 1920-1938   *2000.00 to 2200.00*
Green and yellow striped robe.
MOTHER & DAUGHTER **HN 2841** 1980-   70.00 to 145.00
One of Images collection; white.
HN 2843 1981-   70.00 to 145.00
One of Images collection; black.
MOTHER'S HELP **HN 2151** 1962-1969   190.00
Black dress, white apron. **
MOTHERHOOD **HN 28** 1913-1938   *2300.00 to 2500.00*
Gray dress.
HN 30 1913-1938   *2300.00 to 2500.00*
Patterned dress, white apron with blue designs.
HN 303 1918-1938   *2300.00 to 2500.00*
White dress, black pattern.
MR. MICAWBER **HN 532** 1922-1932   *60.00*
Yellow vest, red dotted tie, 3 1/2 in.
HN 557 1923-1939   *400.00*
Brown jacket, black trousers, 7 in.
HN 1895 1938-1952   *350.00*
Color changes.

HN 2097   1952-1967   275.00 to 310.00
   Black jacket, beige trousers.
   M 42   1932-   30.00 to 32.00
   Yellow vest, orange trousers, black coat.
MR. MICAWBER BOOKEND   HN 1615   300.00
   Large bust mounted on wood.
MR. PECKSNIFF   M 43   1932-1982   30.00 to 32.00
   Black suit.
MR. PICKWICK   HN 529   1922-1932   60.00
   Yellow vest, black jacket, 3 3/4 in.
   HN 556   1923-1939   195.00 to 310.00
   Blue jacket, yellow trousers, 7 in.
   HN 1894   1938-1952   240.00
   Color changes.
   HN 2099   1952-1967   225.00 to 350.00
   Black jacket, beige trousers. *
   M 41   1932-   30.00 to 32.00
   Yellow vest, orange trousers, black coat.
MR. PICKWICK BOOKEND   HN 1623   300.00
   Large bust mounted on wood. **
MRS. BARDELL   M 86   1949-1982   21.00 to 32.00
   Gray dress, white collar. *
MRS. FITZHERBERT   HN 2007   1948-1953   520.00 to 725.00
   Cream mottled dress, apricot bodice.
MUSICALE   HN 2756   1983-   95.00
   One of the Musicians group from the
   Enchantment Collection. Ivory body, burnished
   gold trim.
MY LOVE   HN 2339   1969-   82.00 to 185.00
   White dress, gold trim.
MY PET   HN 2238   1962-1975   115.00 to 120.00
   White blouse, blue skirt.
MY PRETTY MAID   HN 2064   1950-1954   225.00 to 300.00
   Green dress.
MY TEDDY   HN 2177   1962-1967   280.00
   Pale green dress. *

Mr. Pickwick HN 2099   *Mrs. Bardell M 86*   *My Teddy HN 2177*

NADINE **HN 1885** 1938-1949   *550.00*
    Green dress.
  HN 1886 1938-1949   480.00 to 695.00
    Orange dress, blue trim, purple ribbon.
NANA **HN 1766** 1936-1949   240.00
    Red dress.
  HN 1767 1936-1949   240.00
    Lilac dress.
NANCY **HN 2955** 1982-   60.00 to 95.00
    One of Vanity Fair series; white dress, long white
    gloves.
NANNY **HN 2221** 1958-   88.00 to 180.00
    Blue dress. **
NEGLIGEE **HN 1219** 1927-1938   *850.00*
    Dark blue hairband.
  HN 1228 1927-1938   *850.00 to 950.00*
    Rust hairband.
  HN 1272 1928-1938   *850.00*
    Red and yellow mottled negligee.
  HN 1273 1928-1938   *850.00*
    White negligee.
  HN 1454 1931-1938   *850.00*
    Pink negligee, red base.
NELL **HN 3014** 1983-   100.00
    Pink dress, white pinafore. One of Kate
    Greenaway figures.
NELL GWYNN **HN 1882** 1938-1949   500.00 to 650.00
    Blue skirt.
  HN 1887 1938-1949   475.00 to 540.00
    Orange skirt, green bodice.
NELSON **HN 2928** 1981-   425.00 to 950.00
    One of Ships' Figureheads series; limited to 950.
    Blue jacket, red sash, black hat.
NEW BONNET **HN 1728** 1935-1949   *550.00*
    Pink dress, green hat.
  HN 1957 1940-1949   480.00
    Red dress, red flowers.
NEW COMPANIONS **HN 2770** 1982-   110.00 to 175.00
    Red blouse, blue shawl, dark striped skirt.
NEWHAVEN FISHWIFE **HN 1480** 1931-1938   *1100.00 to 1200.00*
    Red and white striped skirt.
NEWSBOY **HN 2244** 1959-1965   470.00 to 625.00
    Dark jacket, plaid hat. *
NICOLA **HN 2839** 1978-   125.00 to 250.00
    Lavender dress, yellow flowers.
NINA **HN 2347** 1969-1976   165.00 to 185.00
    Blue dress.
NINETTE **HN 2379** 1971-   93.00 to 185.00
    Yellow dress.

Newsboy HN 2244

Old Balloon Seller HN 1315

NOELLE **HN 2179** 1957-1967	350.00 to 385.00
Red, ermine-trimmed coat.	
NORMA **M 36** 1933-1945	320.00
Shaded red dress, light green shawl.	
M 37 1933-1945	*320.00*
Red print dress, blue sleeves, green shawl.	
NORTH AMERICAN INDIAN DANCER **HN 2809** 1982-	950.00
One of Dancers of the World series, limited to 750. Yellow costume.	
NUDE ON ROCK **HN 593** 1924-1938	*800.00*
Pale blue-green glaze.	
ODDS AND ENDS **HN 1844** 1938-1949	620.00 to 725.00
Striped dress, yellow apron.	
OFFICER OF THE LINE **HN 2733** 1983-	136.50
Red coat, fawn breeches and waistcoat.	
OLD BALLOON SELLER **HN 1315** 1929-	82.00 to 175.00
Green skirt and shawl, red jacket. *	
OLD BALLOON SELLER AND BULLDOG	
HN 1791 1932-1938	*1000.00 to 1100.00*
On mahogany stand.	
HN 1912 1939-1949	N.A.
No details available.	
OLD KING **HN 358** 1919-1938	*1200.00 to 1400.00*
Red, purple, green costume.	
HN 623 1924-1938	*1400.00 to 1600.00*
Gray, red and green robe.	
HN 1801 1937-1954	N.A.
No details available.	
HN 2134 1954-	220.00 to 475.00
Red shirt, green and purple robe.	
OLD KING COLE **HN 2217** 1963-1967	560.00 to 700.00
Ermine-lined robe.	
OLD LAVENDER SELLER **HN 1492** 1932-1949	560.00 to 625.00
Green and orange cape.	
HN 1571 1933-1949	*600.00*
Orange patterned cape.	

OLD MAN   **HN 451**   1921-1938   N.A.
  No examples found.
OLD MEG   **HN 2494**   1974-1976   165.00 to 250.00
  Blue dress, purple shawl. *
OLD MOTHER HUBBARD   **HN 2314**   1964-1975   300.00
  Green dress, polka dot apron.
OLGA   **HN 2463**   1972-1975   179.00 to 200.00
  Green overdress.
OLIVER TWIST   **M 89**   1949-   30.00 to 32.00
  Black coat, red tie, tan pants.
OLIVIA   **HN 1995**   1947-1951   375.00
  Red and green dress.
OMAR KHAYYAM   **HN 408**   1920-1938   *1800.00 to 2000.00*
  Dark blue-green robe.
  HN 409   1920-1938   *1800.00 to 2000.00*
  Black robe, yellow pants.
  HN 2247   1965-   80.00 to 168.00
  Red turban, brown and black costume.
OMAR KHAYYAM AND THE BELOVED
  HN 407   1920-1938   *2800.00 to 3000.00*
  Colors unrecorded.
  HN 419   1920-1938   *2800.00 to 3000.00*
  Blue-green costumes.
  HN 459   1921-1938   *2800.00 to 3000.00*
  Multicolored costumes.
  HN 598   1924-1938   *2800.00 to 3000.00*
  Pink cloak, striped, blue dress, striped.
ONCE UPON A TIME   **HN 2047**   1949-1955   *200.00*
  Pink dotted dress.
ONE OF FORTY,   see Forty Thieves
ONE THAT GOT AWAY   **HN 2153**   1955-1959   *250.00*
  Brown slicker.
ORANGE LADY   **HN 1759**   1936-1975   175.00 to 240.00
  Pink skirt.
  HN 1953   1940-1975   175.00 to 240.00
  Yellow dress, green shawl.

Old Meg HN 2494

ORANGE SELLER   **HN 1325**   1929-1949   475.00
   Lavender jacket, green skirt.
ORANGE VENDOR   **HN 72**   1917-1938   *1050.00*
   Green coat.
  HN 508   1921-1938   *950.00*
   Purple coat.
  HN 521   1921-1938   *950.00*
   Pale blue costume, black collar, purple hood.
  HN 1966   1941-1949   540.00 to 850.00
   Black cloak, red robe.
ORGAN GRINDER   **HN 2173**   1956-1965   595.00 to 695.00
   Green jacket. *
OUT FOR A WALK   **HN 86**   1918-1936   *2100.00 to 2200.00*
   Pink and gray dress.
  HN 443   1921-1936   *2000.00 to 2200.00*
   Pink and gray.
  HN 748   1925-1936   *2000.00 to 2100.00*
   Dark multicolored dress, white muff.
OWD WILLUM   **HN 2042**   1949-1973   200.00 to 280.00
   Brown jacket.
PAISLEY SHAWL   **HN 1391**   1930-1949   *300.00*
   White dress, red shawl.
  HN 1460   1931-1949   265.00 to 400.00
   Green dress and shawl, pink trim.
  HN 1707   1935-1949   540.00
   Purple shawl, green hat.
  HN 1739   1935-1949   380.00
   Green-white dress, red-yellow and green shawl.
  HN 1914   1939-1949   165.00 to 225.00
   Yellow-green skirt and hat.
  HN 1987   1946-1959   200.00 to 300.00
   Cream dress, red shawl. *
  HN 1988   1946-1975   120.00 to 220.00
   Cream and yellow skirt, red hat.
  M 3   1932-1938   245.00
   Blue dress, lavender shawl.

Organ Grinder
HN 2173

Paisley Shawl
HN 1987

M 4   1932-1945   215.00 to 280.00
  Yellow-green dress, rose-colored shawl.
M 26   1932-1945   225.00 to 300.00
  Light green dress, green shawl.
PALIO   **HN 2428**   1971-1975   6600.00
  Limited edition figurine; planned production was
  500; broken mold caused edition of only 100.
  Brown horse, multicolored costume.
PAMELA   **HN 1468**   1931-1938   495.00 to 500.00
  Blue dress, red sash.
HN 1469   1931-1938   475.00
  Yellow dress.
HN 1564   1933-1938   *600.00*
  Pink dress.
PAN ON ROCK   **HN 621**   1924-1938   *900.00*
  Brown base.
HN 622   1924-1938   *900.00*
  Black base.
PANTALETTES   **HN 1362**   1929-1938   300.00 to 380.00
  Green skirt, red tie on hat.
HN 1412   1930-1949   *350.00*
  Pink skirt, green tie on hat.
HN 1507   1932-1949   *450.00*
  Yellow dress.
HN 1709   1935-1938   *500.00*
  Red dress and hat.
M 15   1932-1945   *275.00*
  Dress in two shades of blue, red hat.
M 16   1932-1945   250.00 to 280.00
  Pink skirt, red top, black bonnet.
M 31   1932-1945   *275.00*
  Light blue skirt, blue jacket, light-colored bonnet.
PARISIAN   **HN 2445**   1972-1975   125.00 to 225.00
  Blue shirt.
PARSON'S DAUGHTER   **HN 337**   1919-1938   *700.00*
  Lilac dress, brown flowered pattern.
HN 338   1919-1938   *700.00 to 800.00*
  Blue patterned dress, red cap and shawl.
HN 441   1921-1938   *650.00*
  Yellow dress, orange spots.
HN 564   1923-1949   350.00 to 425.00
  Multicolored skirt.
HN 790   1926-1938   *600.00*
  Patchwork skirt, dark multicolored shawl.
HN 1242   1927-1938   *600.00*
  Lilac shawl, patchwork skirt.
HN 1356   1929-1938   *550.00*
  Red, blue, and purple striped border on dress.
HN 2018   1949-1953   400.00
  Patchwork skirt, purple hat and cloak.

PAST GLORY   **HN 2484**   1973-1978   150.00 to 200.00
   Red uniform.
PATCHWORK QUILT   **HN 1984**   1945-1959   200.00 to 480.00
   Green dress. *
PATRICIA   **HN 1414**   1930-1949   400.00 to 520.00
   Yellow dress.
   HN 1431   1930-1949   400.00 to 680.00
   Pink and blue dress.
   HN 1462   1931-1938   *600.00*
   Green-yellow dress, pink hat.
   HN 1567   1933-1949   *650.00*
   Red dress.
   HN 2715   1983-   67.00 to 95.00
   One of Vanity Fair series; white gown.
   M 7   1932-1945   325.00
   Pastel skirt, red top.
   M 8   1932-1938   *325.00*
   Yellow-orange dress.
   M 28   1932-1945   225.00 to 285.00
   Blue top, pink and blue skirt.
PAULA   **HN 2880**   1980-   185.00
   Yellow-green dress, dark green trim.
   HN 2906   1980-   180.00 to 185.00
   Yellow dress.
PAULINE   **HN 1444**   1931-1938   *400.00*
   Blue dress, green hat.
PAVLOVA   **HN 487**   1921-1938   1200.00
   White tutu, black base.
   HN 676   1924-1938   *1200.00 to 1400.00*
   Green base.
PEACE   **HN 2433**   1980-   35.00 to 75.00
   One of Images collection. Black.
   HN 2470   1980-   39.00 to 75.00
   One of Images collection. White.
PEARLY BOY   **HN 1482**   1931-1949   280.00
   Red jacket.
   HN 1547   1933-1949   *300.00*
   Green coat, purple pants.
   HN 2035   1949-1959   240.00
   Red jacket. *
PEARLY GIRL   **HN 1483**   1931-1949   *350.00*
   Red jacket.
   HN 1548   1933-1949   *350.00*
   Purple bodice, green skirt.
   HN 2036   1949-1959   *250.00*
   Red jacket.
PECKSNIFF   **HN 535**   1922-1932   *60.00*
   Red vest, black coat, 3 3/4 in.
   HN 553   1922-1939   *400.00*
   Tan vest, black trousers, 7 in.

Patchwork Quilt HN 1984   *Pearly Boy HN 2035*

HN 1891 1938-1952	*350.00*
Color changes.	
HN 2098 1952-1967	285.00 to 350.00
Black jacket, brown trousers.	
M 43 1932-1982	30.00 to 32.00
Black suit.	
PEDLAR WOLF **HN 7** 1913-1938	1980.00
Black wolf in blue-gray robe.	
PEGGY **HN 1941** 1940-1949	155.00
Red dress, green trim.	
HN 2038 1949-1978	55.00 to 90.00
Red dress, green trim.	
PENELOPE **HN 1901** 1939-1975	265.00 to 500.00
Red dress. *	
HN 1902 1939-1949	560.00
Green petticoat, blue bodice and skirt.	

Penelope HN 1901

PENNY **HN 2338** 1968-   40.00 to 68.00
  Green overdress.
  HN 2424 1983-   45.50 to 65.00
  Yellow costume.
PENSIVE MOMENTS **HN 2704** 1975-1981   105.00 to 185.00
  Blue dress.
PERFECT PAIR **HN 581** 1923-1938   *850.00 to 950.00*
  Pink dress, red jacket.
PHEASANT, COCK **HN 2632** 1954-   229.00 to 495.00
  Prestige figure.
PHILIPPINE DANCER **HN 2439** 1978-   450.00 to 650.00
  One of Dancers of the World series; limited to
  750. Pale blue-green dress.
PHILLIPPA OF HAINAULT **HN 2008** 1948-1953   480.00
  Blue dress, orange print.
PHYLLIS **HN 1420** 1930-1949   545.00 to 575.00
  Flowered overskirt and shawl.
  HN 1430 1930-1938   *650.00*
  Pink skirt, dark blue shawl.
  HN 1486 1931-1949   575.00
  Blue shawl, pink skirt.
  HN 1698 1935-1949   *700.00*
  Green dress and hat.
PICARDY PEASANT, FEMALE **HN 4** 1913-1938   1320.00
  White hat, blue skirt.
  HN 5 1913-1938   *1400.00 to 1600.00*
  Dove gray costume.
  HN 17A 1913-1938   1400.00 to 1600.00
  Green costume.
  HN 351 1919-1938   *1500.00 to 2000.00*
  Pale blue hat and costume.
  HN 513 1921-1938   *1600.00 to 1800.00*
  Blue blouse, spotted skirt.
PICARDY PEASANT, MALE **HN 13** 1913-1938   1320.00
  Blue costume.
  HN 17 1913-1938   *1400.00 to 1600.00*
  Green hat and green trousers.
  HN 19 1913-1938   *1400.00 to 1600.00*
  Green costume.
PICNIC **HN 2308** 1965-   52.50 to 104.00
  Yellow dress. **
PIED PIPER **HN 1215** 1926-1938   *700.00*
  Red hat and cape.
  HN 2102 1953-1976   225.00 to 260.00
  Black with red trim, gray-green hat. *
PIERRETTE **HN 642** 1924-1938   *650.00*
  Red dress.
  HN 643 1924-1938   *650.00*
  Black and red dress.

HN 644   1924-1938   525.00 to 760.00
White and black dress.
HN 691   1925-1938   *900.00*
Gold costume.
HN 721   1925-1938   *900.00*
Black and white striped costume.
HN 731   1925-1938   *900.00*
Spotted black and white shirt.
HN 732   1925-1938   925.00
Black and white dress.
HN 784   1926-1938   *900.00*
Pink costume, black ruff.
HN 795   1926-1938   *600.00*
Pink roses on skirt, 3 1/2 in.
HN 796   1926-1938   *600.00*
White skirt, silver spots, 3 1/2 in.
HN 1391   1930-1938   720.00
Red costume.
HN 1749   1936-1949   1080.00
Pink and blue costume with playing cards.
PILLOW FIGHT   **HN 2270**   1965-1969   200.00
Pink nightgown. **
PINKIE   **HN 1552**   1933-1938   *400.00*
Pink dress.
HN 1553   1933-1938   *400.00 to 500.00*
Yellow and blue dress.
PIPER   **HN 2907**   1980-   125.00 to 252.00
Blue kilt, white shirt, bagpipes.
PIRATE KING   **HN 2901**   1981-   299.00 to 760.00
One of Gilbert and Sullivan series. Green shirt,
tan pants, dark jacket, pirate's hat.
PIROUETTE   **HN 2216**   1959-1967   200.00 to 260.00
White dress. *

Pied Piper HN 2102   *Pirouette HN 2216*

PLEASE KEEP STILL **HN 2967** 1982-   47.00 to 75.00
    One of Childhood Days series; boy bathing dog.
POACHER **HN 2043** 1949-1959   275.00 to 340.00
    Dark gray jacket.
POCAHONTAS **HN 2930** 1982-   950.00
    One of Ships' Figureheads series; limited to 950.
    White dress, red wrap, feathered headpiece.
POKE BONNET **HN 612** 1924-1938   1200.00
    Yellow skirt, green plaid shawl. Renamed version
    Lilac Shawl, HN 44.
    HN 765 1925-1938   *1200.00 to 1400.00*
    Dark green, blue and purple mottled skirt.
POLISH DANCER **HN 2836** 1980-   550.00 to 750.00
    One of Dancers of the World series; limited to
    750. White blouse, blue floral print skirt, dark
    vest, apron.
POLKA **HN 2156** 1955-1969   185.00 to 260.00
    Pale pink dress. *

Polka HN 2156

POLLY PEACHUM **HN 463** 1921-1949   *650.00*
    White dress.
    HN 465 1921-1949   *550.00*
    Red dress.
    HN 489 1921-1938   *500.00*
    Green dress.
    HN 549 1922-1949   175.00 to 360.00
    Red dress, deep curtsey.
    HN 550 1922-1949   275.00 to 480.00
    Red dress.
    HN 589 1924-1949   350.00
    Pink dress, yellow underskirt.
    HN 614 1924-1949   *500.00*
    Pale pink dress, blue bows.
    HN 620 1924-1938   *450.00*
    Pink dress, cream underskirt.
    HN 680 1924-1949   *600.00*
    White dress, black, yellow, and blue spots.

HN 693 1925-1949   *600.00*
First version, standing. Rose-pink dress, green
bows.
HN 694 1925-1949   *450.00*
Second version, curtsying. Rose-pink dress, green
bows.
HN 698 1925-1949   340.00
Pink dress. Miniature.
HN 699 1925-1949   340.00
Blue dress. Miniature.
HN 734 1925-1949   *350.00*
White skirt, black spots and bodice.
HN 757 1925-1949   *350.00*
Red bodice, spotted skirt, miniature.
HN 758 1925-1949   *350.00*
Pink skirt, orange stripes, miniature.
HN 759 1925-1949   *350.00*
Yellow and white skirt, black spots, miniature.
HN 760 1925-1949   *350.00*
Multicolored mottled skirt, miniature.
HN 761 1925-1949   *350.00*
Blue and purple skirt.
HN 762 1925-1949   *350.00*
Pink roses on skirt.
M 21 1932-1945   275.00 to 300.00
Rose-colored dress.
M 22 1932-1938   *300.00*
Red and blue dress.
M 23 1932-1938   *300.00*
White skirt, red dotted overskirt.
POLLYANNA **HN 2965** 1982-   32.00 to 50.00
One of characters from Children's Literature
series; gray dress, white pinafore.
POPE JOHN PAUL II **HN 2888** 1982-   88.00 to 150.00
White robe.
POTTER **HN 1493** 1932-   185.00 to 350.00
Dark red-brown cloak. *

Potter HN 1493

HN 1518 1932-1949   550.00
Green cloak.
HN 1522 1932-1949   *400.00*
Dark blue and green cloak.
PREMIERE **HN 2343** 1969-1978   185.00
White dress, green cape.
PRETTY LADY **HN 69** 1916-1938   *1300.00 to 1400.00*
Flowered blue dress.
HN 70 1916-1938   *1300.00 to 1400.00*
Pale blue dress.
HN 302 1918-1938   *1400.00 to 1600.00*
Patterned lilac dress.
HN 330 1918-1938   *1400.00 to 1600.00*
Patterned lilac dress.
HN 361 1919-1938   *1400.00 to 1600.00*
Blue-green dress.
HN 384 1920-1938   *1400.00 to 1600.00*
Red dress, striped skirt.
HN 565 1923-1938   880.00
Orange dress, green spots.
HN 700 1925-1938   *1300.00 to 1400.00*
Yellow dress, black spots.
HN 763 1925-1938   *1300.00 to 1400.00*
Orange dress.
HN 783 1926-1938   *1300.00 to 1400.00*
Blue dress.
PRIMROSES **HN 1617** 1934-1949   475.00 to 650.00
Red dress, gray shawl.
PRINCE OF WALES **HN 1217** 1926-1938   *1100.00 to 1300.00*
Red jacket, black hat.
HN 2883 1981-   350.00 to 750.00
Limited to 1500. Ermine-trimmed robe, black suit.
HN 2884 1981-   600.00
Uniform of the Welsh Guards, red jacket, black
pants. Second version. Limited to 1500.
PRINCESS **HN 391** 1920-1938   *2100.00 to 2400.00*
Green cloak, lilac skirt.
HN 392 1920-1938   *2100.00 to 2400.00*
Multicolored costume, striped skirt.
HN 420 1920-1938   *2100.00 to 2400.00*
Pink and green striped skirt, blue cloak.
HN 430 1921-1938   *2100.00 to 2400.00*
Green flowered dress, blue-green striped cloak.
HN 431 1921-1938   *2100.00 to 2400.00*
Pink dress, blue-green cloak.
HN 633 1924-1938   *2100.00 to 2400.00*
Black and white dress.
PRINCESS BADOURA **HN 2081** 1952-   6700.00
Prestige figure; pink-gowned figure atop elephant.

PRINCESS OF WALES   **HN 2885**   1982-   350.00 to 760.00
   Evening dress. Limited to 1500.
   HN 2887   1982-   600.00
   Wedding dress, veil, yellow and white flowers.
   Limited to 1500.
PRISCILLA   **HN 1337**   1929-1938   360.00
   Pale lavender and yellow dress.
   HN 1340   1929-1949   250.00 to 315.00
   Red dress, purple collar.
   HN 1495   1932-1949   *450.00*
   Blue dress, green hat, and umbrella.
   HN 1501   1932-1938   460.00
   Yellow dress.
   HN 1559   1933-1949   *450.00*
   Pink and yellow skirt.
   M 13   1932-1938   *450.00*
   Yellow and green ruffled dress.
   M 14   1932-1945   200.00 to 300.00
   Blue ruffled dress.
   M 24   1932-1945   280.00
   Red ruffled dress, green bonnet.
PRIVATE, CONN. REG., 1777   **HN 2845**   1975-1980   840.00
   One of Soldiers of Revolution series, production
   limited to 350; brown and beige uniform.
PRIVATE, DELAWARE REG., 1776   **HN 2761**   1975-1980   840.00
   One of the Soldiers of Revolution series, limited
   to 350: beige trousers, blue coat.
PRIVATE, MASS. REG., 1778   **HN 2760**   1975-1978   840.00
   One of Soldiers of Revolution series, limited to
   350; white uniform.
PRIVATE, PA. RIFLE BAT., 1776   **HN 2846**   1975-1980   840.00
   One of Soldiers of Revolution series, limited to
   350.
PRIVATE, RHODE IS. REG., 1781   **HN 2759**   1975-1978   840.00
   One of Soldiers of Revolution series, limited to
   350; beige, blue, and red uniform.
PRIVATE, 1ST GEORGIA REG., 1777   **HN 2779**   1975-1976   840.00
   One of Soldiers of Revolution series, limited to
   350; olive green uniform.
PRIVATE, 2ND S.C. REG., 1781   **HN 2717**   1975-1976   840.00
   One of Soldiers of Revolution series, limited to
   350; blue, red, beige uniform.
PRIVATE, 3RD N.C. REG., 1778   **HN 2754**   1975-1977   840.00
   One of Soldiers of Revolution series, limited to
   350. Beige buckskin uniform.
PRIZED POSSESSIONS   **HN 2942**   1982-1982   125.00
   Woman in chair holding book and looking at
   figurine. Limited to year of production. Originally
   available only to members of Royal Doulton
   International Collectors Club.

Professor HN 2281

PROFESSOR **HN 2281** 1965-1980	160.00
Rust suit, dark robe. *	
PROMENADE **HN 2076** 1951-1953	1600.00
Blue overdress, peach skirt.	
PROPOSAL **HN 715** 1925-1938	*850.00*
Woman. Red dress.	
HN 716 1925-1938	*850.00*
Woman. Cream dress, black squares.	
HN 725 1925-1938	*850.00*
Man. Red coat.	
HN 788 1926-1938	*850.00 to 900.00*
Woman. Pink dress.	
HN 1209 1926-1938	*850.00 to 900.00*
Man. Blue coat, pink waistcoat.	
PRUDENCE **HN 1883** 1938-1949	760.00
Blue dress.	
HN 1884 1938-1949	*750.00*
Pink dress.	
PRUE **HN 1996** 1947-1955	310.00 to 320.00
Red dress, black bodice.	
PUFF AND POWDER **HN 397** 1920-1938	*1800.00 to 2000.00*
Yellow skirt, brown bodice.	
HN 398 1920-1938	*1800.00 to 2000.00*
Pale blue skirt.	
HN 400 1920-1938	*1800.00 to 2000.00*
Green and blue bodice, yellow skirt.	
HN 432 1921-1938	*1800.00 to 2000.00*
Lilac skirt, orange spots.	
HN 433 1921-1938	*1800.00 to 2000.00*
Yellow skirt, blue spots.	

PUNCH AND JUDY MAN **HN 2765** 1981- 165.00 to 300.00
Green shirt, yellow pants.
PUPPETMAKER **HN 2253** 1962-1973 425.00 to 475.00
Green vest, brown trousers.
PUSSY **HN 18** 1913-1938 2000.00 to 3500.00
Gray dress.
HN 325 1918-1938 *2500.00 to 2700.00*
White dress, black pattern.
HN 507 1921-1938 *2500.00 to 2700.00*
Spotted blue dress.
PYJAMS **HN 1942** 1940-1949 *300.00*
Pink pajamas.
QUALITY STREET **HN 1211** 1926-1938 750.00
Rose-red dress.
QUEEN ELIZABETH, see Miscellaneous chapter, busts
QUEEN ELIZABETH II **HN 2502** 1973-1976 1260.00
Pale blue dress. Limited to 750.
HN 2878 1983- 520.00
Blue and crimson robes, white gown; Royal
Portrait Figures series; limited to 2500.
QUEEN MOTHER **HN 2882** 1980- 1095.00 to 1900.00
Limited to 1500. Pink dress.
QUEEN OF SHEBA **HN 2328** 1982- 525.00 to 1250.00
One of Femmes Fatales series; limited to 750.
Purple robe, tiger.
QUEEN OF THE DAWN **HN 2437** 1983- 125.00
One of the Queens group from the Enchantment
Collection. Ivory body, burnished gold trim.
QUEEN OF THE ICE **HN 2435** 1983 125.00
One of the Queens group from the Enchantment
Collection. Ivory body, burnished gold trim.
RACHEL **HN 2919** 1981- 102.00 to 185.00
Yellow fur-trimmed coat.
RAG DOLL **HN 2142** 1954- 39.00 to 76.00
Blue dress, white apron. *

Rag Doll HN 2142

REBECCA **HN 2805** 1980-   165.00 to 325.00
   Pale blue and pink costume.
REFLECTIONS **HN 1820** 1937-1938   *850.00*
   Red dress, lilac couch.
  HN 1821 1937-1938   *850.00*
   Green dress, red couch.
  HN 1847 1938-1949   650.00 to 800.00
   Red dress, green couch.
  HN 1848 1938-1949   *750.00*
   Green skirt.
REGAL LADY **HN 2709** 1975-   87.00 to 172.00
   Blue overdress.
REGENCY **HN 1752** 1936-1949   560.00
   Purple and green costume.
REGENCY BEAU **HN 1972** 1941-1949   800.00
   Red suit, green cape.
RENDEZVOUS **HN 2212** 1962-1971   300.00 to 420.00
   Red to pink dress.
REPOSE **HN 2272** 1972-1978   165.00 to 220.00
   Pink dress.
REST AWHILE **HN 2728** 1981-   110.00 to 200.00
   Gray dress, white apron, blue bonnet.
RETURN OF PERSEPHONE **HN 31** 1913-1938   *3500.00 to 3800.00*
   Gray and ivory costumes.
REVERIE **HN 2306** 1964-1981   120.00 to 250.00
   Peach dress.
RHAPSODY **HN 2267** 1961-1973   175.00 to 245.00
   Green dress. *
RHODA **HN 1573** 1933-1949   *550.00*
   Yellow-beige skirt.
  HN 1574 1933-1938   560.00
   Orange shawl, dark skirt.
  HN 1688 1935-1949   540.00
   Orange dress, red shawl.
RHYTHM **HN 1903** 1939-1949   1000.00
   Pink dress.

Rhapsody HN 2267

HN 1904   1939-1949   *800.00*
  Pale green dress.
RITA   **HN 1448**   1931-1938   700.00
  Yellow and pink dress.
  HN 1450   1931-1938   500.00
  Blue dress.
RIVER BOY   **HN 2128**   1962-1975   125.00 to 160.00
  Blue trousers, white shirt.
ROBERT BURNS   **HN 42**   1914-1938   *2800.00 to 3200.00*
  Brown, black, rust, yellow plaid costume.
ROBIN   **M 38**   1933-1945   *320.00*
  Red shirt, blue pants.
  M 39   1933-1945   320.00
  Blue shirt, green pants.
ROCKING HORSE   **HN 2072**   1951-1953   960.00 to 1700.00
  White horse, blue suit.
ROMANCE   **HN 2430**   1972-1980   85.00 to 145.00
  Apricot dress. *
ROMANY SUE   **HN 1757**   1936-1949   540.00 to 675.00
  Green dress, red shawl.
  HN 1758   1936-1949   *600.00*
  Purple dress.
ROSABELL   **HN 1620**   1934-1938   640.00
  Pink flowered shawl.
ROSALIND   **HN 2393**   1970-1975   200.00
  Blue dress.
ROSAMUND   **HN 1320**   1929-1938   *1400.00 to 1600.00*
  Pink jacket, pale green skirt.
  HN 1497   1932-1938   550.00 to 975.00
  Red dress.
  HN 1551   1933-1938   *650.00*
  Blue dress.
  M 32   1932-1945   355.00
  Yellow dress tinged with blue.
  M 33   1932-1945   325.00 to 420.00
  Shaded red dress.
ROSE   **HN 1368**   1930-   37.50 to 75.00
  Pink-red dress. *
  HN 1387   1930-1938   *250.00*
  Blue and pink flowered dress, orange flowers.
  HN 1416   1930-1949   110.00 to 255.00
  Blue-purple dress.
  HN 1506   1932-1938   *250.00*
  Yellow dress.
  HN 1654   1934-1938   *250.00*
  Green bodice, flowered skirt.
  HN 2123   1983-   45.50 to 65.00
  Lilac dress.

Romance HN 2430   *Rose HN 1368*   *Rosemary HN 2091*

ROSEANNA **HN 1921** 1940-1949	*350.00*
Green dress.	
HN 1926 1940-1959	250.00 to 400.00
Red dress.	
ROSEBUD **HN 1580** 1933-1938	*600.00*
Pink dress.	
HN 1581 1933-1938	*600.00*
Light dress, flower sprays.	
HN 1983 1945-1952	225.00 to 460.00
Red shawl.	
ROSEMARY **HN 2091** 1952-1959	295.00 to 325.00
Red dress, blue shawl. *	
ROSINA **HN 1358** 1929-1938	*650.00*
Red dress, ermine trim.	
HN 1364 1929-1938	*650.00*
Red, purple, and pink dress and shawl.	
HN 1556 1933-1938	740.00
Light-colored dress.	
ROWENA **HN 2077** 1951-1955	455.00 to 520.00
Red overdress, green skirt.	
ROYAL CAN. MTD. POLICE **HN 2547** 1973-	120.00
Red uniform, black hat, edition limited to 1500.	
Same HN number appears on bird model	
Budgerigars; see Animal and Bird list, page 199.	
ROYAL CAN. MTD. POLICE, 1873 **HN 2555** 1973-	40.00
Limited edition of 1500; HN number duplicates 6	
in. Drake Mallard, see Animal and Bird list, page	
199.	
ROYAL GOVERNOR'S COOK **HN 2233** 1960-	99.00 to 200.00
Black dress, white apron. One of Figures of	
Williamsburg.	
RUBY **HN 1724** 1935-1949	*300.00*
Pink and white dress.	

HN 1725   1935-1949   *300.00*
Blue and white dress.

RUMPLESTILTSKIN   **HN 3025**   1983-   125.00
One of the Fantasy group from the Enchantment
Collection. Ivory body, burnished gold trim.

RUSTIC SWAIN   **HN 1745**   1935-1949   *1300.00 to 1400.00*
Red suit.

HN 1746   1935-1949   *1300.00 to 1400.00*
Green suit.

RUTH   **HN 2799**   1976-1981   50.00 to 100.00
One of the Kate Greenaway series. Olive green
dress.

RUTH THE PIRATE MAID   **HN 2900**   1981-   299.00 to 760.00
One of Gilbert and Sullivan series. Red skirt, blue
jacket, white apron, pirate's hat.

SABBATH MORN   **HN 1982**   1945-1959   195.00 to 320.00
Red dress, green-yellow shawl.

SAILOR'S HOLIDAY   **HN 2442**   1972-1978   125.00 to 200.00
Apricot jacket.

SAIREY GAMP   **HN 533**   1922-1932   *60.00*
Green dress, black cape, 4 in.

HN 558   1923-1939   *400.00*
Black dress and cape, 7 in.

HN 1896   1938-1952   *350.00*
Color changes.

HN 2100   1952-1967   260.00 to 320.00
White dress, green cape. *

M 46   1932-   19.00 to 32.00
Light green dress, darker cape.

SAIREY GAMP BOOKEND   **HN 1625**   *300.00*
Large bust mounted on wood. **

Sairey Gamp HN 2100

SALOME **HN 1775** 1933-1939   N.A.
   Matte ivory finish. One of the Garbe figurines.
   Production limited to 100.
   HN 1828 1937-1949   *1500.00 to 1800.00*
   Tinted finish.
SAM WELLER **HN 531** 1922-1932   *60.00*
   Striped yellow vest, 4 in.
   M 48 1932-1982   25.00 to 32.00
   Orange vest, black hat and trousers.
SAMANTHA **HN 2954** 1982-   60.00 to 95.00
   One of Vanity Fair series; white dress and hat.
SAMWISE **HN 2925** 1982-   22.00 to 35.00
   One of Tolkien series; brown and black costume,
   black cape.
SANDRA **HN 2275** 1969-   78.00 to 156.00
   Apricot dress.
   HN 2401 1983-   155.00
   Dress in shades of green.
SANTA CLAUS **HN 2725** 1982-1982   49.00 to 195.00
   Red and white suit, pack of toys. *

Santa Claus HN 2725

SARA **HN 2265** 1981-   108.00 to 220.00
   White dress, red overdress.
SAUCY NYMPH **HN 1539** 1933-1949   *275.00*
   Nude child, green base.
SAVE SOME FOR ME **HN 2959** 1982-   47.00 to 75.00
   Childhood Days series; blue dress and long white
   apron.
SCHOOLMARM **HN 2223** 1958-1980   125.00 to 180.00
   Gray dress, brown shawl.
SCOTCH GIRL **HN 1269** 1928-1938   *1000.00 to 1200.00*
   Red plaid costume.
SCOTTIES **HN 1281** 1928-1938   675.00 to 680.00
   Red dress.

Sea Sprite HN 2191

HN 1349 1929-1949   *650.00*
  Light multicolored dress, white scotties.
SCOTTISH HIGHLAND DANCER **HN 2436** 1978-   450.00 to 600.00
  One of Dancers of the World series; limited to
  750. Red plaid dress.
SCRIBE **HN 305** 1918-1936   *1000.00 to 1200.00*
  Olive green robe.
  HN 324 1918-1938   *1000.00 to 1200.00*
  Green hat, brown costume.
  HN 1235 1927-1938   *900.00*
  Brown coat, blue hat.
SCROOGE **M 87** 1949-1982   18.00 to 32.00
  Dark coat, white cap.
SEA HARVEST **HN 2257** 1969-1976   165.00 to 184.00
  Blue jacket.
SEA SPRITE **HN 1261** 1927-1938   *500.00*
  Red and purple drape.
  HN 2191 1958-1962   220.00 to 300.00
  Pink dress. *
SEAFARER **HN 2455** 1972-1976   200.00 to 225.00
  Beige sweater.
SEASHORE **HN 2263** 1961-1965   180.00 to 250.00
  Red shorts.
SECRET THOUGHTS **HN 2382** 1971-   108.00 to 220.00
  Green dress.
SENTIMENTAL PIERROT **HN 36** 1914-1938   *1500.00 to 1700.00*
  Black and white costume.
  HN 307 1918-1938   *1500.00 to 1700.00*
  Black and white costume.
SENTINEL **HN 523** 1921-1938   5000.00
  Reported as red and gray.
SERENA **HN 1868** 1938-1949   720.00
  Blue, red, pink dress.
SERENADE **HN 2753** 1983-   95.00
  One of Musicians group from the Enchantment
  Collection. Ivory body, burnished gold trim.
SERGEANT, 1ST VA. REG., 1777 **HN 2844** 1975-1980 1440.00 to 1750.00
  Continental Light Dragoons. One of Soldiers of

She Loves Me Not
HN 2045

Revolution series, edition of 350. Brown horse,
brown and green uniform.

SERGEANT, 6TH MD. REG., 1777 **HN 2815** 1975-1977   840.00
One of Soldiers of Revolution series, production
limited to 350. White uniform, green and red
trim.

SHADOWPLAY **HN 3526** 1982-   75.00
One of Images of Nature series; cat.

SHE LOVES ME NOT **HN 2045** 1949-1962   110.00 to 160.00
Blue shorts and shirt. *

SHEPHERD **HN 81** 1918-1938   *2200.00*
Earthenware. Tan coat.

  HN 617 1924-1938   *1600.00 to 1800.00*
China body, purple-blue pants and coat.

  HN 632 1924-1938   *1600.00 to 1800.00*
China body, white smock, blue pants.

  HN 709 1925-1938   *500.00*
Green jacket, miniature.

  HN 751 1925-1938   *1000.00 to 1300.00*
Green jacket, red cap.

  HN 1975 1945-1975   140.00 to 220.00
Orange smock.

  M 17 1932-1938   280.00
Blue coat, red cloak, black pants.

  M 19 1932-1938   *450.00*
Blue cloak, brown pants.

SHEPHERDESS **HN 708** 1925-1948   *550.00*
Red overskirt, miniature.

  HN 735 1925-1938   *1000.00 to 1300.00*
Purple overdress, blue and red skirt.

  HN 750 1925-1938   *1000.00 to 1300.00*
Pink bodice, yellow skirt.

  M 18 1932-1938   420.00
Light green skirt, pink overskirt.

  M 20 1932-1938   *450.00*
Yellow skirt.

SHORE LEAVE **HN 2254** 1965-1978   165.00 to 200.00
Dark uniform.

SHY ANNE **HN 60**   1916-1938   *1300.00 to 1500.00*
   Flowered blue dress.
   HN 64   1916-1938   800.00
   White dress.
   HN 65   1916-1938   1400.00
   Blue spotted dress, dark blue hem.
   HN 568   1923-1938   1120.00
   Green dress.
SHYLOCK **HN 79**   1917-1938   *1800.00 to 2000.00*
   Multicolored cloak, yellow sleeves.
   HN 317   1918-1938   *1800.00 to 2000.00*
   Dark multicolored cloak.
SIBELL **HN 1668**   1934-1949   *600.00*
   Red dress, green underskirt.
   HN 1695   1935-1949   *600.00*
   Dark green dress, lilac trim.
   HN 1735   1935-1949   375.00 to 520.00
   Blue and green dress.
SIESTA **HN 1305**   1928-1938   900.00
   Pink and lavender drape.
SILKS AND RIBBONS **HN 2017**   1949-   75.00 to 150.00
   Green dress. *

Silks And Ribbons HN 2017

SILVERSMITH OF WILLIAMSBURG **HN 2208**   1960-   90.00 to 200.00
   Green jerkin. One of Figures of Williamsburg.
SIMONE **HN 2378**   1971-1981   119.00 to 185.00
   Olive green dress.
SIR EDWARD **HN 2370**   1979-   400.00 to 500.00
   One of Age of Chivalry series; limited to 500.
   Gray armor, red garment.
SIR RALPH **HN 2371**   1979-   400.00 to 500.00
   One of Age of Chivalry series; limited to 500.
   Gray armor, blue garment.
SIR THOMAS **HN 2372**   1979-   400.00 to 500.00
   One of Age of Chivalry series; limited to 500.
   Black armor, red and white checked underskirt.

SIR THOMAS LOVELL **HN 356** 1919-1938   1200.00
   Red, green, and black costume.
SIR WALTER RALEIGH **HN 1742** 1935-1949   *600.00*
   Green cape.
  HN 1751 1936-1949   450.00 to 750.00
   Earthenware, purple-red mottled cape.
  HN 2015 1948-1955   350.00 to 695.00
   Orange costume, dark cloak.
SKATER **HN 2117** 1953-1971   300.00 to 350.00
   Red and white dress. *
SLEEP **HN 24** 1913-1938   1200.00
   Pale blue-green dress.
  HN 24A 1913-1938   *1200.00 to 1400.00*
   Dark blue dress.
  HN 25 1913-1938   *1200.00 to 1400.00*
   Blue-green dress.
  HN 25A 1913-1938   *1200.00 to 1400.00*
   Blue-green dress; fewer firings.
  HN 424 1921-1938   *1000.00 to 1100.00*
   Blue, 6 in.
  HN 692 1925-1938   *1000.00 to 1200.00*
   Gold dress.
  HN 710 1925-1938   *1000.00 to 1200.00*
   Matte vellum finish.
SLEEPY DARLING **HN 2953** 1981-1981   100.00
   Gray pajamas, white blanket, pink trim. Limited
   to year of issue. Originally available only to
   members of Royal Doulton International
   Collectors Club.
SLEEPY SCHOLAR **HN 15** 1913-1938   *1400.00 to 1600.00*
   Blue dress.
  HN 16 1913-1938   1500.00 to 1520.00
   Yellow dress.
  HN 29 1913-1939   *1400.00 to 1600.00*
   Brown costume.

Skater HN 2117

SLEEPYHEAD **HN 2114** 1953-1955   680.00 to 850.00
   White dress, orange mottled chair.
SMILING BUDDHA **HN 454** 1921-1938   *1200.00*
   Blue-green robe.
SNAKE CHARMER **HN 1317** 1929-1938   *950.00*
   Green and black turban and robe.
SOIREE **HN 2312** 1967-   85.00 to 175.00
   Green overskirt. *
SOLDIERS OF REVOLUTION,   see individual figures
SOLITUDE **HN 2810** 1977-   107.00 to 220.00
   White dress, multicolored flowers.
SONATA **HN 2438** 1983-   95.00
   One of Musicians group from the Enchantment
   Collection. Ivory body, burnished gold trim.
SONG OF THE SEA **HN 2729** 1983-   105.00
   Blue sweater, denim pants, black boots. *
SONIA **HN 1692** 1935-1949   *650.00*
   Pink bodice, white skirt.
  HN 1738 1935-1949   *650.00*
   Green dress.
SONNY **HN 1313** 1929-1938   *700.00*
   Pink clothes.
  HN 1314 1929-1938   680.00
   Purple clothes.
SOPHIE **HN 2833** 1977-   50.00 to 100.00
   Pink dress, white apron.
SOUTHERN BELLE **HN 2229** 1958-   92.50 to 185.00
   Red and cream dress.
  HN 2425 1983-   185.00
   Pale blue and pink dress.

Song Of The Sea
HN 2729

Soiree HN 2312

SPANISH FLAMENCO DANCER **HN 2831** 1977-   560.00
     One of Dancers of the World series; limited to
     750. Red and white dress.
SPANISH LADY **HN 1262** 1927-1938   800.00
     Black dress, red flowers.
     HN 1290 1928-1938   *800.00*
     Yellow dress.
     HN 1293 1928-1938   *800.00*
     Black dress, orange and red flowers.
     HN 1294 1928-1938   *800.00 to 900.00*
     Red mottled dress.
     HN 1309 1929-1938   *800.00*
     Multicolored skirt, black bodice.
SPIRIT OF THE WIND **HN 1777** 1933-1939   4675.00
     Matte ivory finish. One of the Garbe figurines.
     Production limited to 50.
     HN 1825 1937-1949   N.A.
     Green and white.
SPOOK **HN 50** 1916-1938   900.00
     Blue-green robe, dark green cap.
     HN 51 1916-1938   *900.00*
     Red cap.
     HN 51A 1916-1938   *900.00*
     Black cap.
     HN 51B 1916-1938   *900.00*
     Blue cloak.
     HN 58 1916-1938   N.A.
     Color not recorded.
     HN 512 1921-1938   *900.00*
     Blue spotted costume.
     HN 625 1924-1938   *900.00*
     Yellow robe.
     HN 1218 1926-1938   *900.00*
     Multicolored costume, blue cap.
SPOOKS **HN 88** 1918-1936   *1200.00*
     Pale blue-green robes, dark green caps.
     HN 89 1918-1936   *1200.00*
     Red caps.
     HN 372 1920-1936   *1200.00*
     Patterned green costume. Brown cap.
SPRING **HN 1774** 1933-1939   N.A.
     Matte ivory finish. One of the Garbe figurines.
     Production limited to 100.
     HN 1827 1937-1949   *2200.00 to 2500.00*
     Tinted finish.
     HN 2085 1952-1959   400.00
     Lavender dress. *
SPRING FLOWERS **HN 1807** 1937-1959   200.00 to 325.00
     Green skirt, gray-blue overskirt.

Spring HN 2085   *Stayed At Home HN 2207*

HN 1945 1940-1949	600.00
Green skirt, pink overskirt.	
SPRING MORNING **HN 1922** 1940-1973	160.00 to 200.00
Green coat.	
HN 1923 1940-1949	245.00 to 400.00
Orange coat.	
SPRING, THE SEASONS **HN 312** 1918-1938	*1100.00 to 1300.00*
Pale yellow dress.	
HN 472 1921-1938	1080.00
Patterned robe.	
SPRINGTIME **HN 1971** 1941-1949	*700.00*
Blue dress, pink coat, green hat.	
SQUIRE **HN 1814** 1937-1949	*2000.00*
Earthenware.	
ST. GEORGE **HN 385** 1920-1938	*4500.00 to 5000.00*
Dapple gray horse, blue-green costume; model one.	
HN 386 1920-1938	*4500.00 to 5000.00*
Dark horse, blue and white costume; model one.	
HN 1800 1934-1950	2860.00
Crosses on green cloak, red robe; model one.	
HN 2051 1950-	240.00 to 475.00
White horse and costume; model two.	
HN 2067 1950-1976	2000.00 to 2500.00
Purple, red, and orange blanket; model one.	
ST. GEORGE AND THE DRAGON **HN 2856** 1978-	5200.00 to 7000.00
Prestige figure; white horse, cream robe with red lining.	
STAYED AT HOME **HN 2207** 1958-1969	160.00
Green dress. *	
STEPHANIE **HN 2807** 1977-1982	87.00 to 172.00
Dark yellow dress.	
HN 2811 1983-	114.00 to 170.00
Red dress, autumn leaf motif.	

STIGGINS   **HN 536**   1922-1932   *60.00*
   Black vest and coat, 3 3/4 in.
  M 50   1932-1982   25.00 to 32.00
   Black suit.
STITCH IN TIME   **HN 2352**   1966-1980   100.00 to 160.00
   Purple dress, apricot shawl.
STOP PRESS   **HN 2683**   1977-1980   99.00 to 180.00
   Brown jacket.
SUITOR   **HN 2132**   1962-1971   375.00 to 400.00
   Blue-gray overskirt, brown jacket. **
SUMMER   **HN 2086**   1952-1959   340.00 to 400.00
   Rose dress.
SUMMER, THE SEASONS   **HN 313**   1918-1938   *1100.00*
   Pale green dress.
  HN 473   1921-1938   *1100.00*
   Patterned robe.
SUMMER'S DAY   **HN 2181**   1957-1962   360.00
   White dress.
SUNDAY BEST   **HN 2206**   1979-   150.00 to 295.00
   Yellow dress.
SUNDAY MORNING   **HN 2184**   1963-1969   250.00 to 280.00
   Rose-red dress. *
SUNSHINE GIRL   **HN 1344**   1929-1938   *1100.00*
   Green and black bathing suit.
  HN 1344   1929-1938   2300.00
   Potted.
  HN 1348   1929-1938   *1100.00*
   Black and orange bathing suit.
SUSAN   **HN 2056**   1950-1959   *375.00*
   Purple dress.
  HN 2952   1982-   105.00 to 185.00
   Orange dress, blue ruffled overskirt, black vest.
   Second version.

Sunday Morning HN 2184

Sweet And Twenty HN 1298

SUSANNA **HN 1233** 1927-1938   *900.00*
   Pink robe.
  HN 1288 1928-1938   *900.00*
   Dark red robe.
  HN 1299 1928-1938   *900.00*
   Black, red, and blue robe.
SUZETTE **HN 1487** 1931-1950   300.00
   Pink dress.
  HN 1577 1933-1949   *400.00*
   Blue dress, red underskirt.
  HN 1585 1933-1938   *400.00*
   Green and yellow dress.
  HN 1696 1935-1949   400.00
   Green dress and hat.
  HN 2026 1949-1959   245.00 to 300.00
   Glaze differences.
SWEET AND FAIR **HN 1864** 1938-1949   *650.00*
   Blue shawl, pink dress.
  HN 1865 1938-1949   580.00 to 940.00
   Green dress.
SWEET AND TWENTY **HN 1298** 1928-1969   225.00 to 240.00
   Red and pink dress. *
  HN 1360 1929-1938   *300.00*
   Blue-pink-purple dress, blue-green couch.
  HN 1437 1930-1938   250.00
   Red dress, dark couch.
  HN 1438 1930-1938   *300.00*
   Multicolored dress.
  HN 1549 1933-1949   *300.00*
   Multicolored dress and couch.
  HN 1563 1933-1938   *300.00*
   Light pink dress, black couch.

HN 1589 1933-1949   250.00
  Red-blue dress, green couch
HN 1610 1933-1938   250.00 to 320.00
  Red dress, yellow couch.
HN 1649 1934-1949   *300.00*
  Green shirt, orange couch.
SWEET ANNE **HN 1318** 1929-1949   190.00 to 220.00
  Blue jacket, pale green skirt.
HN 1330 1929-1949   *300.00*
  Red, pink, and yellow skirt.
HN 1331 1929-1949   300.00
  Blue and yellow skirt.
HN 1453 1931-1949   *300.00*
  Green dress, blue hat.
HN 1496 1932-1967   200.00
  Pink and purple dress and hat. *

Sweet Anne HN 1496

HN 1631 1934-1938   *300.00 to 400.00*
  Pink and yellow flowered dress, blue trim.
HN 1701 1935-1938   *300.00*
  Yellow and pink flowered dress, blue trim.
M 5 1932-1945   240.00 to 280.00
  Red-tinged dress, blue jacket.
M 6 1932-1945   255.00
  Light blue dress, blue jacket.
M 27 1932-1945   215.00 to 290.00
  Red jacket and bonnet, light-colored skirt.
SWEET APRIL **HN 2215** 1965-1967   275.00 to 400.00
  Pink dress.
SWEET DREAMS **HN 2380** 1971-   75.00 to 150.00
  Cream chair, green trim, multicolored clothes.
SWEET LAVENDER **HN 1373** 1930-1949   540.00 to 850.00
  Red and green plaid shawl, cream skirt.
SWEET MAID **HN 1504** 1932-1938   *800.00*
  Blue dress.

HN 1505 1932-1938   *800.00*
 Pink-red dress.
HN 2092 1952-1955   460.00
 Pale lavender dress.
SWEET SEVENTEEN **HN 2734** 1975-   92.00 to 185.00
 White dress.
SWEET SIXTEEN **HN 2231** 1958-1965   165.00 to 300.00
 White blouse, pale blue skirt. *
SWEET SUZY **HN 1918** 1939-1949   *600.00*
 Peach dress, green underskirt.
SWEETING **HN 1935** 1940-1973   110.00 to 200.00
 Pink dress.
HN 1938 1940-1949   *300.00*
 Blue multicolored dress.
SWIMMER **HN 1270** 1928-1938   1000.00
 Black, floral print bathing suit.
HN 1326 1929-1938   *1000.00 to 1200.00*
 Orange and lilac costume.
HN 1329 1929-1938   *1000.00 to 1200.00*
 Pink costume.
SYLVIA **HN 1478** 1931-1938   500.00
 Yellow-orange dress, blue-gray coat.
SYMPATHY **HN 2838** 1980-   56.00 to 110.00
 One of Images collection; black.
HN 2876 1980-   56.00 to 110.00
 One of Images collection; white.
SYMPHONY **HN 2287** 1961-1965   340.00 to 520.00
 Brown top, yellow-green skirt.
TAILOR **HN 2174** 1956-1959   600.00 to 625.00
 Orange vest.
TAKING THINGS EASY **HN 2677** 1975-   99.00 to 220.00
 Blue jacket.
TALL STORY **HN 2248** 1968-1975   165.00 to 220.00
 Green sweater and trousers.
TEATIME **HN 2255** 1972-   82.50 to 168.00
 Red dress.

Sweet Sixteen HN 2231

Teenager HN 2203

TEENAGER **HN 2203** 1957-1962	235.00 to 280.00
Red shawl, white skirt. *	
TENDERNESS **HN 2713** 1982-	60.00 to 75.00
One of Images collection. White.	
HN 2714 1982-	60.00 to 75.00
One of Images collection. Black.	
TERESA **HN 1682** 1935-1949	*800.00*
Red dress.	
HN 1683 1935-1938	*800.00*
Light blue dress.	
TESS **HN 2865** 1978-	56.00 to 100.00
One of Kate Greenaway series; green dress.	
TETE-A-TETE **HN 798** 1926-1938	1150.00
Mottled pink and blue dress.	
HN 799 1926-1938	800.00
Purple and pink dress.	
HN 1236 1927-1938	*600.00*
Purple and pink dress. Miniature of HN 798.	
HN 1237 1927-1938	*600.00*
Pink dress.	
THANK YOU **HN 2732** 1983-	101.50
Pink floral blouse.	
THANKS DOC **HN 2731** 1975-	100.00 to 200.00
White coat.	
THANKSGIVING **HN 2446** 1972-1976	165.00 to 225.00
Blue overalls.	
THIS LITTLE PIG **HN 1793** 1936-	37.50 to 80.00
Red blanket. *	
HN 1794 1936-1949	220.00
Purple and blue striped blanket.	
TIGER **HN 2646** 1961-	850.00 to 950.00
Prestige figure; 5 3/4 x 16 in.	
TIGER ON ROCK **HN 2639** 1953-	1200.00 to 1650.00
Prestige figure; 11 1/2 x 14 in.	
TILDY **HN 1576** 1933-1938	400.00 to 545.00
Red bodice, light skirt.	

This Little Pig HN 1793

HN 1859 1938-1949	N.A.
No details available.	
TINKLE BELL **HN 1677** 1935-	42.00 to 76.00
Pink dress. **	
TINSMITH **HN 2146** 1962-1967	460.00 to 495.00
Brown shirt, black vest.	
TINY TIM **HN 539** 1922-1932	*60.00*
Blue scarf and socks, 3 1/2 in. **	
M 56 1932-	21.00 to 32.00
Black jacket, red pants.	
TO BED **HN 1805** 1937-1949	180.00
Green shirt and shorts.	
HN 1806 1937-1949	280.00
Light shirt and shorts.	
TOINETTE **HN 1940** 1940-1949	*1000.00*
Red dress.	
TOINETTE, see also Meryll	
TOM **HN 2864** 1978-1981	56.00 to 100.00
One of Kate Greenaway series; cream shirt, blue trousers.	
TOM BOMBADIL **HN 2924** 1982-	32.00 to 50.00
One of Tolkien series; black coat, yellow boots, brown hat, blue feather.	
TOM BROWN **HN 2941** 1983-	34.00 to 50.00
One of characters from Children's Literature series. Blue jacket, cream pants. *	
TOM SAWYER **HN 2926** 1982-	32.00 to 50.00
One of characters from Children's Literature series; blue shirt, blue jeans, straw hat.	
TONY WELLER **HN 346** 1919-1938	*1200.00 to 1400.00*
Green coat, blue rug.	
HN 368 1920-1938	*1200.00 to 1400.00*
Blue coat, brown blanket.	

Tom Brown HN 2941   *Top O' The Hill HN 1834*   *Town Crier HN 2119*

HN 544 1922-1932	*60.00*
Red vest, yellow dotted tie, 3 1/2 in.	
HN 684 1924-1938	950.00
Green coat, plaid rug.	
M 47 1932-1982	30.00 to 32.00
Red vest, yellow tie with spots, dark green coat.	
TONY WELLER BOOKEND **HN 1616**	*300.00*
Large bust mounted on wood.	
TOOTLES **HN 1680** 1935-1975	45.00 to 115.00
Pink bodice.	
TOP O' THE HILL **HN 1833** 1937-1971	145.00 to 200.00
Green dress.	
HN 1834 1937-	68.00 to 175.00
Red dress. *	
HN 1849 1938-1975	175.00
Orange dress, green and red scarf.	
TOWN CRIER **HN 2119** 1953-1976	185.00 to 280.00
Orange jacket, green weskit. *	
TOYMAKER **HN 2250** 1959-1973	350.00 to 450.00
Green shirt, brown trousers.	
TOYS **HN 1316** 1929-1938	*1500.00 to 1700.00*
Red jacket, green skirt.	
TRACY **HN 2736** 1983-	67.00 to 95.00
One of Vanity Fair series; white dress and	
petticoats, rose.	
TRANQUILITY **HN 2426** 1978-	56.00 to 110.00
One of Images collection. Black.	
HN 2469 1978-	56.00 to 110.00
One of Images collection. White.	
TREASURE ISLAND **HN 2243** 1962-1975	160.00 to 200.00
Blue shorts, beige skirt.	
TROTTY VECK **M 91** 1949-1982	30.00 to 32.00
Black coat, pants and top hat, white apron.	

TULIPS **HN 466** 1921-1938   *1200.00 to 1400.00*
  Green dress.
  HN 488 1921-1938   *1200.00 to 1400.00*
  Ivory dress.
  HN 672 1927-1938   *1200.00 to 1400.00*
  Green shawl, cream dress.
  HN 747 1925-1938   *1200.00 to 1400.00*
  Purple dress, green shawl.
  HN 1334 1929-1938   *1200.00 to 1400.00*
  Green dress, blue and pink shawl.
TUPPENCE A BAG **HN 2320** 1968-   83.00 to 168.00
  Green dress, blue shawl.
TWILIGHT **HN 2256** 1971-1976   155.00 to 220.00
  Dark green dress.
TWO-A-PENNY **HN 1359** 1929-1938   820.00
  Red blouse, yellow-green skirt, yellow and green
  striped shawl.
TZ'U-HSI EMPRESS DOWAGER **HN 2391** 1983-   999.00 to 1250.00
  One of Femmes Fatales series; limited to 750; red
  coat, blue cloak, floral dress. *
UNCLE NED **HN 2094** 1952-1965   320.00 to 600.00
  Brown jacket.
UNDER THE GOOSEBERRY BUSH **HN 49** 1916-1938   1140.00
  Nude child, green bush.
UPON HER CHEEKS SHE WEPT **HN 59** 1916-1938   *1400.00 to 1600.00*
  Pale blue dress.
  HN 511 1921-1938   *1300.00*
  Lilac dress.
  HN 522 1921-1938   *1300.00*
  Lilac dress, spots.

Tz'u-Hsi Empress Dowager
HN 2391

URIAH HEEP **HN 545** 1922-1932   *60.00*
  Yellow vest, black suit, 4 in.
  HN 554 1923-1939   275.00 to 400.00
  Black jacket, black trousers, 7 1/4 in.
  HN 1892 1938-1952   340.00
  Color changes.
  HN 2101 1952-1967   299.00 to 320.00
  Black jacket, green trousers. **
  M 45 1932-   30.00
  Black suit.
VALERIE **HN 2107** 1953-   52.50 to 100.00
  Red overdress, pink skirt. *

Valerie HN 2107

VANESSA **HN 1836** 1938-1949   250.00 to 450.00
  Purple bodice, green skirt.
  HN 1838 1938-1949   *450.00*
  Green bodice, red skirt.
VANITY **HN 2475** 1973-   52.50 to 100.00
  Deep pink dress.
VENETA **HN 2722** 1974-1980   85.00 to 159.50
  Olive green overdress.
VERA **HN 1729** 1935-1938   460.00
  Pink blouse.
  HN 1730 1935-1938   *500.00*
  Green blouse.
VERENA **HN 1835** 1938-1949   *600.00*
  Rose and green dress.
  HN 1854 1938-1949   600.00
  Green dress.
VERONICA **HN 1517** 1932-1951   265.00 to 325.00
  Red and white dress.

HN 1519   1932-1938   440.00
Blue-white dress, red hat.
HN 1650   1934-1949   *450.00*
Green dress.
HN 1915   1939-1949   300.00 to 450.00
Red and white dress, blue hat. Reduced size of
HN 1517.
HN 1943   1940-1949   *450.00*
Blue hat, pink dress.
M 64   1934-1949   280.00
Dress with red top, white skirt shaded with red,
blue hat.
M 70   1934-1949   *280.00*
Green dress.
VICTORIA   HN 2471   1973-   94.00 to 172.00
Pink dress.
VICTORIAN LADY   HN 726   1925-1938   380.00
Purple and pink multicolored dress.
HN 727   1925-1938   235.00 to 320.00
Yellow skirt, red shawl.
HN 728   1925-1952   250.00 to 295.00
Red skirt, purple shawl.
HN 736   1925-1938   *350.00*
Purple dress, light blue border design, red shawl.
HN 739   1925-1938   350.00
Blue and yellow skirt, yellow scarf, mottled red.
HN 740   1925-1938   360.00
Red dress, red and yellow shawl.
HN 742   1925-1938   *350.00*
Black and white checkered shawl, white dress,
blue spots.
HN 745   1925-1938   *350.00*
Pink rose-patterned dress.
HN 1208   1926-1938   *350.00*
Red shawl, green dress.
HN 1258   1927-1938   *350.00*
Blue dress, purple shawl.
HN 1276   1928-1938   460.00
Red, green and yellow skirt, purple shawl.
HN 1277   1928-1938   *350.00*
Red, green, and yellow skirt, purple shawl.
HN 1345   1929-1949   *250.00*
Blue-green skirt, purple shawl.
HN 1452   1931-1949   350.00
Green dress and shawl.
HN 1529   1932-1938   *350.00*
Orange-yellow dress, green shawl.
M 1   1932-1945   280.00 to 295.00
Red-tinged dress, light green shawl.

M 2   1932-1945   *300.00*
  Blue dress, purple shawl.
M 25   1932-1945   *300.00*
  Red ruffled skirt, blue shawl.
VIKING   **HN 2375**   1973-1976   `,` 260.00
  Blue and brown costume.
VIOLA D'AMORE   **HN 2797**   1976-1978   800.00
  One of Lady Musicians series, limited to 750;
  pale blue flowered overdress.
VIOLIN   **HN 2432**   1972-1978   720.00 to 1400.00
  One of Lady Musicians series; limited to 750.
  Brown overdress.
VIRGINALS   **HN 2427**   1971-1978   *1000.00*
  One of Lady Musicians series; limited to 750.
  Green overdress.
VIRGINIA   **HN 1693**   1935-1949   *600.00*
  Yellow dress.
  HN 1694   1935-1949   *600.00*
  Green dress.
VIVIENNE   **HN 2073**   1951-1967   220.00 to 300.00
  Red dress. *

Vivienne HN 2073

VOTES FOR WOMEN   **HN 2816**   1978-1981   140.00 to 236.00
  Rust coat.
WANDERING MINSTREL   **HN 1224**   1927-1938   620.00 to 980.00
  Purple, pink, and red costume.
WARDROBE MISTRESS   **HN 2145**   1954-1967   400.00 to 450.00
  White dress. *
WAYFARER   **HN 2362**   1970-1976   150.00 to 200.00
  Green jacket, gray trousers.
WEDDING MORN   **HN 1866**   1938-1949   *900.00 to 1000.00*
  Cream dress.
  HN 1867   1938-1949   *900.00 to 1000.00*
  Red dress.
WEE WILLIE WINKIE   **HN 2050**   1949-1953   179.00 to 375.00
  Blue nightshirt.

Wardrobe Mistress
HN 2145

WELSH GIRL **HN 39** 1914-1938	2220.00
Brown, purple, red costume.	
HN 92 1918-1938	*2000.00 to 2300.00*
Blue-gray costume.	
HN 456 1921-1938	*1900.00 to 2100.00*
Green blouse, brown skirt.	
HN 514 1921-1938	*1900.00 to 2100.00*
Green skirt, spotted apron.	
HN 516 1921-1938	*1900.00 to 2100.00*
Checkered lilac dress, black spotted cloak.	
HN 519 1921-1938	*1900.00 to 2100.00*
Blue and lilac skirt.	
HN 520 1921-1938	*1900.00 to 2100.00*
Spotted lilac dress.	
HN 660 1924-1938	*1900.00 to 2100.00*
Spotted white costume, blue-lined cloak.	
HN 668 1924-1938	*1900.00 to 2100.00*
Yellow checkered costume, pink-lined cloak.	
HN 669 1924-1938	*1900.00 to 2100.00*
Yellow spotted costume, checkered green lined cloak.	
HN 701 1925-1938	*1900.00 to 2100.00*
Striped costume, checkered blue-lined coat.	
HN 792 1926-1938	*1900.00 to 2100.00*
Pink checkered costume, blue cloak.	
WENDY **HN 2109** 1953-	75.00 to 80.00
White dress.	
WEST INDIAN DANCER **HN 2384** 1981-	625.00 to 850.00
One of Dancers of the World series; limited to 750. White skirt, yellow and red overdress, purple scarf.	
WEST WIND **HN 1776** 1933-1939	N.A.
Matte ivory finish. One of the Garbe figurines. Production limited to 25.	
HN 1826 1937-1949	*3000.00 to 3400.00*
Tinted finish.	

Wigmaker Of Williamsburg
HN 2239

Winsome HN 2220

WIGMAKER OF WILLIAMSBURG **HN 2239** 1960- Beige jerkin. One of Figures of Williamsburg. *	95.00 to 200.00
WILLY-WON'T HE **HN 1561** 1933-1949 Blue jacket.	*400.00*
HN 1584 1933-1949 Red jacket, blue hat.	*400.00*
HN 2150 1955-1959 Glaze differences.	275.00 to 320.00
WINDFLOWER **HN 1763** 1936-1949 Red flowered dress.	360.00
HN 1764 1936-1949 Blue flowered dress.	420.00
HN 1920 1939-1949 Multicolored skirt.	*500.00*
HN 1939 1940-1949 Blue hat and gloves, pink skirt.	*500.00*
HN 2029 1949-1952 Red blouse, pale skirt with red flowers. First version, model 926. Slightly larger version of HN 1763.	420.00
M 78 1939-1949 Girl looking to her left. Green skirt, blue blouse, green hat.	*400.00*
M 79 1939-1949 Girl looking straight ahead. Green skirt, blue blouse, green hat.	320.00 to 450.00
WINDMILL LADY **HN 1400** 1930-1938 Green and orange plaid shawl, green skirt.	320.00 to 1000.00
WINNER **HN 1407** 1930-1938 Jockey wears white pants, blue and white striped shirt, red vest.	*2400.00 to 2600.00*
WINSOME **HN 2220** 1960- Red dress. *	77.50 to 166.00
WINTER **HN 2088** 1952-1959 Green and red cape.	175.00 to 400.00

WINTER, THE SEASONS **HN 315** 1918-1938   *1000.00 to 1100.00*
    Pale blue dress.
    HN 475 1921-1938   *1000.00 to 1100.00*
    Patterned robe.
WISTFUL **HN 2396** 1979-   163.00 to 325.00
    Orange dress, white underskirt, floral decorations.
WIZARD **HN 2877** 1979-   108.00 to 215.00
    Blue costume, black and white hat, owl, cat.
WOMAN HOLDING CHILD **HN 462** 1921-1938   *1500.00*
    Green dress, white apron.
    HN 570 1923-1938   *1500.00*
    Pink and green striped skirt, red striped blanket.
    HN 703 1925-1938   *1500.00*
    Purple cloak, black and red skirt.
    HN 743 1925-1938   *1500.00*
    Blue and yellow striped apron.
WOMAN OF THE TIME OF HENRY VI **HN 43** 1914-1938   *2500.00*
    Yellow, green overdress, green head covering.
WOOD NYMPH **HN 2192** 1958-1962   *300.00*
    Blue-green dress. *

Wood Nymph HN 2192

YEARNING **HN 2920** 1982-   60.00 to 75.00
    One of Images collection, white.
    HN 2921 1982-   60.00 to 75.00
    One of Images collection, black.
YEOMAN OF THE GUARD **HN 688** 1924-1938   715.00 to 960.00
    Red uniform
    HN 2122 1954-1959   600.00 to 695.00
    Minor glaze differences. **
YOUNG KNIGHT **HN 94** 1918-1936   650.00
    Maroon robe, dark cloak, helmet and sword.
YOUNG LOVE **HN 2735** 1975-   350.00 to 695.00
    White dress, brown jacket.

Young Master HN 2872

YOUNG MASTER **HN 2872** 1980-		163.00 to 360.00
Boy in red jacket, gray pants. *		
YOUNG MISS NIGHTINGALE **HN 2010** 1948-1953		520.00 to 725.00
Green dress, red surcoat.		
YOUNG WIDOW **HN 1399** 1930-1930		*1300.00*
Light-colored basket. Renamed Little Mother, HN 1418, HN 1641.		
YUM-YUM **HN 1268** 1928-1938		*650.00*
White kimono, blue and pink pattern.		
HN 1287 1928-1939		640.00
Red, yellow, and orange kimono.		
HN 2899 1980-		760.00
One of Gilbert and Sullivan series. Green kimono, yellow triangles.		

Complete HN Number Figurine List Including Prices

Descriptions of Figurines Included in Alphabetical Price List

HN 1	Darling	1040.00
HN 2	Elizabeth Fry	4000.00
HN 2A	Elizabeth Fry	*4000.00*
HN 3	Milking Time	*1500.00 to 1700.00*
HN 4	Picardy Peasant, Female	1320.00
HN 5	Picardy Peasant, Female	*1400.00 to 1600.00*
HN 6	Dunce	*1800.00 to 2500.00*
HN 7	Pedlar Wolf	1980.00
HN 8	Crinoline	*1200.00*
HN 9	Crinoline	1200.00
HN 9A	Crinoline	*1200.00*

HN 10	Madonna Of The Square	1040.00
HN 10A	Madonna Of The Square	1500.00
HN 11	Madonna Of The Square	*1400.00 to 1500.00*
HN 12	Baby	*1800.00*
HN 13	Picardy Peasant, Male	1320.00
HN 14	Madonna Of The Square	*1400.00 to 1500.00*
HN 15	Sleepy Scholar	*1400.00 to 1600.00*
HN 16	Sleepy Scholar	1500.00 to 1520.00
HN 17	Picardy Peasant, Male	*1400.00 to 1600.00*
HN 17A	Picardy Peasant, Female	1400.00 to 1600.00
HN 18	Pussy	2000.00 to 3500.00
HN 19	Picardy Peasant, Male	*1400.00 to 1600.00*
HN 20	Coquette	2300.00
HN 21	Crinoline	1200.00
HN 21A	Crinoline	*1200.00*
HN 22	Lavender Woman	*1600.00 to 1800.00*
HN 23	Lavender Woman	*1600.00 to 1800.00*
HN 23A	Lavender Woman	*1600.00 to 1800.00*
HN 24	Sleep	1200.00
HN 24A	Sleep	*1200.00 to 1400.00*
HN 25	Sleep	*1200.00 to 1400.00*
HN 25A	Sleep	*1200.00 to 1400.00*
HN 26	Diligent Scholar	1760.00
HN 27	Madonna Of The Square	*1400.00 to 1500.00*
HN 28	Motherhood	*2300.00 to 2500.00*
HN 29	Sleepy Scholar	*1400.00 to 1600.00*
HN 30	Motherhood	*2300.00 to 2500.00*
HN 31	Return Of Persephone	*3500.00 to 3800.00*
HN 32	Child And Crab	*1700.00*
HN 33	Arab	1600.00
HN 34	Moorish Minstrel	1050.00 to 1750.00
HN 35	Charley's Aunt	450.00 to 700.00
HN 36	Sentimental Pierrot	*1500.00 to 1700.00*
HN 37	Coquette	*2300.00*
HN 38	Carpet Vendor	*1500.00 to 2500.00*
HN 38A	Carpet Vendor	*1500.00 to 2500.00*
HN 39	Welsh Girl	2220.00
HN 40	Lady Of The Elizabethan Period	*1600.00 to 1800.00*
HN 40A	Lady Of The Elizabethan Period	*1600.00 to 1800.00*
HN 41	Lady Of The Georgian Period	*1800.00 to 2100.00*
HN 42	Robert Burns	*2800.00 to 3200.00*
HN 43	Woman Of The Time Of Henry VI	*2500.00*
HN 44	Lilac Shawl	1280.00
HN 44A	Lilac Shawl	1040.00
HN 45	Jester	*1200.00*
HN 45A	Jester	*1200.00*
HN 45B	Jester	*1200.00*
HN 46	Gainsborough Hat	*1100.00*
HN 46A	Gainsborough Hat	*1100.00*
HN 47	Gainsborough Hat	1200.00

HN 48	Lady Of The Fan	1400.00 to 1700.00
HN 48A	Lady With Rose	1900.00
HN 49	Under The Gooseberry Bush	1140.00
HN 50	Spook, Potted	900.00
HN 51	Spook	900.00
HN 51A	Spook	900.00
HN 51B	Spook	900.00
HN 52	Lady Of The Fan	1400.00 to 1700.00
HN 52A	Lady With Rose	1500.00 to 1700.00
HN 53	Lady Of The Fan	1450.00 to 1700.00
HN 53A	Lady Of The Fan	1450.00 to 1700.00
HN 54	Lady Ermine	1200.00
HN 55	Jester	1200.00 to 1400.00
HN 56	Land Of Nod	1600.00
HN 56A	Land Of Nod	1600.00 to 1800.00
HN 56B	Land Of Nod	1600.00 to 1800.00
HN 57	Curtsey	1500.00
HN 57A	Flounced Skirt	1400.00 to 1600.00
HN 57B	Curtsey	1500.00
HN 58	Spook	N.A.
HN 59	Upon Her Cheeks She Wept	1400.00 to 1600.00
HN 60	Shy Anne	1300.00 to 1500.00
HN 61	Katharine	1300.00 to 1500.00
HN 62	Child's Grace	1450.00
HN 62A	Child's Grace	1600.00
HN 63	Little Land	1700.00 to 1900.00
HN 64	Shy Anne	800.00
HN 65	Shy Anne	1400.00
HN 66	Flounced Skirt	1360.00
HN 66A	Curtsey	1500.00
HN 67	Little Land	1400.00 to 1750.00
HN 68	Lady With Rose	1500.00 to 1700.00
HN 69	Pretty Lady	1300.00 to 1400.00
HN 70	Pretty Lady	1300.00 to 1400.00
HN 71	Jester	1140.00
HN 71A	Jester	1140.00
HN 72	Orange Vendor	1050.00
HN 73	Lady Of The Elizabethan Period	1700.00 to 2000.00
HN 74	Katharine	1400.00 to 1600.00
HN 75	Blue Beard	2250.00
HN 76	Carpet Vendor	1720.00
HN 77	Flounced Skirt	1400.00 to 1600.00
HN 78	Flounced Skirt	1400.00 to 1600.00
HN 79	Shylock	1800.00 to 2000.00
HN 80	Fisherwomen	N.A.
HN 81	Shepherd	2200.00
HN 82	Afternoon Call	2000.00
HN 83	Lady Anne	2500.00 to 2700.00
HN 84	Mandarin	2000.00 to 2200.00
HN 85	Jack Point	2200.00 to 2500.00

HN 86	Out For A Walk	2100.00 to 2200.00
HN 87	Lady Anne	2500.00 to 2700.00
HN 88	Spooks	1200.00
HN 89	Spooks	1200.00
HN 90	Doris Keene As Cavallini	1600.00 to 2000.00
HN 91	Jack Point	2200.00 to 2500.00
HN 92	Welsh Girl	2000.00 to 2300.00
HN 93	Lady Anne	2500.00 to 2700.00
HN 94	Young Knight	650.00
HN 95	Europa And The Bull	2750.00 to 3000.00
HN 96	Doris Keene As Cavallini	1800.00
HN 97	Mermaid	400.00 to 600.00
HN 98	Guy Fawkes	1200.00
HN 99	Jack Point	1600.00 to 1650.00
HN 100-299	Animals And Birds. See Pages 182-194.	
HN 300	Mermaid	800.00 to 900.00
HN 301	Moorish Piper Minstrel	1750.00
HN 302	Pretty Lady	1400.00 to 1600.00
HN 303	Motherhood	2300.00 to 2500.00
HN 304	Lady With Rose	1500.00 to 1700.00
HN 305	Scribe	1000.00 to 1200.00
HN 306	Milking Time	1500.00 to 1700.00
HN 307	Sentimental Pierrot	1500.00 to 1700.00
HN 308	Jester	1200.00 to 1400.00
HN 309	Lady Of The Elizabethan Period	1600.00 to 2000.00
HN 310	Dunce	1700.00 to 2500.00
HN 311	Dancing Figure	3200.00 to 3500.00
HN 312	Spring, The Seasons	1100.00 to 1300.00
HN 313	Summer, The Seasons	1100.00
HN 314	Autumn, The Seasons	960.00
HN 315	Winter, The Seasons	1000.00 to 1100.00
HN 316	Mandarin	2000.00 to 2200.00
HN 317	Shylock	1800.00 to 2000.00
HN 318	Mandarin	2000.00 to 2200.00
HN 319	Gnome	900.00
HN 320	Jester	1200.00 to 1400.00
HN 321	Digger	1000.00
HN 322	Digger	700.00 to 900.00
HN 323	Blighty	1208.00
HN 324	Scribe	1000.00 to 1200.00
HN 325	Pussy	2500.00 to 2700.00
HN 326	Madonna Of The Square	1300.00 to 1400.00
HN 327	Curtsey	1500.00
HN 328	Moorish Piper Minstrel	2000.00 to 2200.00
HN 329	Gainsborough Hat	1100.00
HN 330	Pretty Lady	1400.00 to 1600.00
HN 331	Lady Of The Georgian Period	1800.00 to 2100.00
HN 332	Lady Ermine	1200.00 to 1400.00
HN 333	Flounced Skirt	1400.00 to 1600.00
HN 334	Curtsey	1450.00

HN 335	Lady Of The Fan	1400.00 to 1700.00
HN 336	Lady With Rose	1500.00 to 1700.00
HN 337	Parson's Daughter	700.00
HN 338	Parson's Daughter	700.00 to 800.00
HN 339	In Grandma's Days	1200.00
HN 340	In Grandma's Days	1200.00
HN 341	Katharine	1300.00
HN 342	Lavender Woman	1600.00 to 1800.00
HN 343	Arab	1400.00 to 1750.00
HN 344	Henry Irving, Cardinal Wolsey	2000.00
HN 345	Doris Keene As Cavallini	1800.00 to 2500.00
HN 346	Tony Weller	1200.00 to 1400.00
HN 347	Guy Fawkes	1050.00 to 1200.00
HN 348	Carpet Vendor	1800.00 to 2000.00
HN 349	Fisherwomen	N.A.
HN 350	Carpet Vendor	1800.00 to 3000.00
HN 351	Picardy Peasant, Female	1500.00 to 2000.00
HN 352	Gainsborough Hat	1200.00
HN 353	Digger	900.00 to 1200.00
HN 354	Geisha	2000.00
HN 355	Dolly	1140.00
HN 356	Sir Thomas Lovell	1200.00
HN 357	Dunce	1800.00 to 2500.00
HN 358	Old King	1200.00 to 1400.00
HN 359	Fisherwomen	N.A.
HN 360	No Information Available	
HN 361	Pretty Lady	1400.00 to 1600.00
HN 362	In Grandma's Days	1000.00
HN 363	Curtsey	1500.00
HN 364	Moorish Minstrel	2200.00 to 2500.00
HN 365	Double Jester	1500.00 to 2000.00
HN 366	Mandarin	1450.00 to 1600.00
HN 367	Jester	1300.00 to 1500.00
HN 368	Tony Weller	1200.00 to 1400.00
HN 369	Cavalier	2000.00
HN 370	Henry VIII	2300.00
HN 371	Curtsey	1500.00
HN 372	Spooks	1200.00
HN 373	Boy On Crocodile	4000.00
HN 374	Lady & Blackamoor	2300.00 to 2600.00
HN 375	Lady & Blackamoor	2300.00 to 2600.00
HN 376	Geisha	2200.00
HN 377	Lady & Blackamoor	2300.00 to 2600.00
HN 378	Arab	1600.00 to 1750.00
HN 379	Ellen Terry, Queen Catherine	2100.00 to 2500.00
HN 380	Gnome	950.00
HN 381	Gnome	950.00
HN 382	Mandarin	1900.00 to 2100.00
HN 383	Gainsborough Hat	1100.00
HN 384	Pretty Lady	1400.00 to 1600.00

HN 385	St. George	4500.00 to 5000.00
HN 386	St. George	4500.00 to 5000.00
HN 387	Geisha	2000.00
HN 388	In Grandma's Days	1400.00
HN 389	Little Mother	N.A.
HN 390	Little Mother	N.A.
HN 391	Princess	2100.00 to 2400.00
HN 392	Princess	2100.00 to 2400.00
HN 393	Lady Without Bouquet	1400.00 to 1700.00
HN 394	Lady Without Bouquet	1400.00 to 1700.00
HN 395	Contentment	1500.00
HN 396	Contentment	1500.00
HN 397	Puff And Powder	1800.00 to 2000.00
HN 398	Puff And Powder	1800.00 to 2000.00
HN 399	Japanese Fan	1000.00 to 1400.00
HN 400	Puff And Powder	1800.00 to 2000.00
HN 401	Marie	1800.00 to 2000.00
HN 402	Betty	1750.00
HN 403	Betty	1750.00
HN 404	King Charles	500.00 to 850.00
HN 405	Japanese Fan	1000.00 to 1200.00
HN 406	Bouquet	120.00
HN 407	Omar Khayyam And The Beloved	2800.00 to 3000.00
HN 408	Omar Khayyam	1800.00 to 2000.00
HN 409	Omar Khayyam	1800.00 to 2000.00
HN 410	Blue Beard	2000.00 to 3000.00
HN 411	Lady Of The Elizabethan Period	1800.00 to 2000.00
HN 412	Jester	1300.00
HN 413	Crinoline	1700.00
HN 414	Bouquet	1300.00
HN 415	Moorish Minstrel	2200.00 to 2500.00
HN 416	Moorish Piper Minstrel	2000.00 to 2200.00
HN 417	Forty Thieves	1000.00
HN 418	Forty Thieves	1000.00
HN 419	Omar Khayyam And The Beloved	2800.00 to 3000.00
HN 420	Princess	2100.00 to 2400.00
HN 421	Contentment	1350.00
HN 422	Bouquet	1300.00
HN 423	Forty Thieves	300.00
HN 424	Sleep	1000.00 to 1100.00
HN 425	Goosegirl	N.A.
HN 426	Jester	1200.00
HN 427	Forty Thieves	1000.00
HN 428	Bouquet	1300.00
HN 429	Bouquet	1300.00
HN 430	Princess	2100.00 to 2400.00
HN 431	Princess	2100.00 to 2400.00
HN 432	Puff And Powder	1800.00 to 2000.00
HN 433	Puff And Powder	1800.00 to 2000.00
HN 434	Marie	1800.00 to 2000.00

HN 435	Betty	1750.00
HN 436	Goosegirl	N.A.
HN 437	Goosegirl	N.A.
HN 438	Betty	2100.00
HN 439	Japanese Fan	1400.00
HN 440	Japanese Fan	1400.00
HN 441	Parson's Daughter	650.00
HN 442	In Grandma's Days	1400.00
HN 443	Out For A Walk	2000.00 to 2200.00
HN 444	Lady Of The Georgian Period	1800.00 to 2100.00
HN 445	Guy Fawkes	1050.00 to 1200.00
HN 446	Jester	1300.00
HN 447	Lady With Shawl	2200.00
HN 448	Goosegirl	N.A.
HN 449	Fruit Gathering	2300.00
HN 450	Mandarin	1400.00 to 1500.00
HN 451	Old Man	N.A.
HN 452	No Information Available	N.A.
HN 453	Gainsborough	1100.00
HN 454	Smiling Buddha	1200.00
HN 455	Mandarin	1400.00 to 1500.00
HN 456	Welsh Girl	1900.00 to 2100.00
HN 457	Crouching Nude	475.00
HN 458	Lady With Shawl	2200.00
HN 459	Omar Khayyam And The Beloved	2800.00 to 3000.00
HN 460	Mandarin	1400.00 to 1500.00
HN 461	Mandarin	1400.00 to 1500.00
HN 462	Woman Holding Child	1500.00
HN 463	Polly Peachum	650.00
HN 464	Captain MacHeath	600.00 to 750.00
HN 465	Polly Peachum	550.00
HN 466	Tulips	1200.00 to 1400.00
HN 467	Doris Keene As Cavallini	1500.00 to 2000.00
HN 468	Contentment	1350.00
HN 469	Little Mother	1800.00 to 2000.00
HN 470	Lady & Blackamoor	2300.00 to 2600.00
HN 471	Katharine	1600.00 to 1800.00
HN 472	Spring, The Seasons	1080.00
HN 473	Summer, The Seasons	1100.00
HN 474	Autumn, The Seasons	1100.00
HN 475	Winter, The Seasons	1000.00 to 1100.00
HN 476	Fruit Gathering	2300.00
HN 477	Betty	2100.00
HN 478	Betty	2100.00
HN 479	Balloon Seller	1000.00
HN 480	Forty Thieves	1000.00
HN 481	Forty Thieves	1000.00
HN 482	Forty Thieves	1000.00
HN 483	Forty Thieves	1000.00
HN 484	Forty Thieves	1000.00

HN 485	Lucy Lockett	600.00
HN 486	Balloon Seller	1000.00 to 1200.00
HN 487	Pavlova	1200.00
HN 488	Tulips	1200.00 to 1400.00
HN 489	Polly Peachum	500.00
HN 490	Forty Thieves	1000.00
HN 491	Forty Thieves	875.00
HN 492	Forty Thieves	1000.00
HN 493	Forty Thieves	1000.00
HN 494	Forty Thieves	1000.00
HN 495	Forty Thieves	1000.00
HN 496	Forty Thieves	1000.00
HN 497	Forty Thieves	1000.00
HN 498	Forty Thieves	1000.00
HN 499	Forty Thieves	1000.00
HN 500	Forty Thieves	1000.00
HN 501	Forty Thieves	1000.00
HN 502	Marie	1800.00 to 2000.00
HN 503	Fruit Gathering	2300.00
HN 504	Marie	1800.00 to 2000.00
HN 505	Marie	1800.00 to 2000.00
HN 506	Marie	1800.00 to 2000.00
HN 507	Pussy	2500.00 to 2700.00
HN 508	Orange Vendor	950.00
HN 509	Lady Of The Fan	1400.00 to 1700.00
HN 510	Child's Grace	1500.00
HN 511	Upon Her Cheeks She Wept	1300.00
HN 512	Spook	900.00
HN 513	Picardy Peasant, Female	1600.00 to 1800.00
HN 514	Welsh Girl	1900.00 to 2100.00
HN 515	Lady With Rose	1500.00 to 1700.00
HN 516	Welsh Girl	1900.00 to 2100.00
HN 517	Lady With Rose	1500.00 to 1700.00
HN 518	Curtsey	1600.00
HN 519	Welsh Girl	1900.00 to 2100.00
HN 520	Welsh Girl	1900.00 to 2100.00
HN 521	Orange Vendor	950.00
HN 522	Upon Her Cheeks She Wept	1300.00
HN 523	Sentinel	5000.00
HN 524	Lucy Lockett	475.00 to 600.00
HN 525	Flower Seller's Children	600.00
HN 526	Beggar	495.00
HN 527	Highwayman	650.00
HN 528	Forty Thieves	1000.00
HN 529	Mr. Pickwick	60.00
HN 530	Fat Boy	60.00
HN 531	Sam Weller	60.00
HN 532	Mr. Micawber	60.00
HN 533	Sairey Gamp	60.00
HN 534	Fagin	60.00

HN 535	Pecksniff	60.00
HN 536	Stiggins	60.00
HN 537	Bill Sykes	80.00
HN 538	Buz Fuz	60.00
HN 539	Tiny Tim	60.00
HN 540	Little Nell	60.00
HN 541	Alfred Jingle	60.00
HN 542	Cobbler	900.00
HN 543	Cobbler	900.00
HN 544	Tony Weller	60.00
HN 545	Uriah Heep	60.00
HN 546	Artful Dodger	18.00 to 30.00
HN 547	Curtsey	1300.00
HN 548	Balloon Seller	600.00 to 800.00
HN 549	Polly Peachum	175.00 to 360.00
HN 550	Polly Peachum	275.00 to 480.00
HN 551	Flower Seller's Children	500.00
HN 552	Jester	1300.00
HN 553	Pecksniff	400.00
HN 554	Uriah Heep	275.00 to 400.00
HN 555	Fat Boy	300.00 to 500.00
HN 556	Mr. Pickwick	195.00 to 310.00
HN 557	Mr. Micawber	400.00
HN 558	Sairey Gamp	400.00
HN 559	Goosegirl	N.A.
HN 560	Goosegirl	N.A.
HN 561	Fruit Gathering	2300.00
HN 562	Fruit Gathering	2300.00
HN 563	Man In Tudor Costume	1400.00
HN 564	Parson's Daughter	350.00 to 425.00
HN 565	Pretty Lady	880.00
HN 566	Crinoline	1250.00
HN 567	Bouquet	1000.00
HN 568	Shy Anne	1120.00
HN 569	Lavender Woman	1300.00 to 1600.00
HN 570	Woman Holding Child	1500.00
HN 571	Falstaff	700.00
HN 572	Contentment	1400.00
HN 573	Madonna Of The Square	1400.00 to 1500.00
HN 574	No Information Available	N.A.
HN 575	Falstaff	700.00
HN 576	Madonna Of The Square	1100.00 to 1200.00
HN 577	Chelsea Pair	495.00
HN 578	Chelsea Pair	600.00
HN 579	Chelsea Pair	650.00
HN 580	Chelsea Pair	650.00
HN 581	Perfect Pair	850.00 to 950.00
HN 582	Grossmith's Tsang Thang	460.00
HN 583	Balloon Seller	300.00 to 500.00
HN 584	Lady With Rose	1500.00 to 1700.00

HN 585	Harlequinade	*750.00*
HN 586	Boy With Turban	*475.00*
HN 587	Boy With Turban	*475.00*
HN 588	Girl With Yellow Frock	1100.00
HN 589	Polly Peachum	350.00
HN 590	Captain MacHeath	*600.00 to 750.00*
HN 591	Beggar	600.00
HN 592	Highwayman	*650.00*
HN 593	Nude On Rock	*800.00*
HN 594	Madonna Of The Square	*1000.00 to 1100.00*
HN 595	Grief	*850.00*
HN 596	Despair	1400.00
HN 597	Bather	*600.00*
HN 598	Omar Khayyam And The Beloved	*2800.00 to 3000.00*
HN 599	Masquerade	*650.00*
HN 600	Masquerade	350.00
HN 601	Mandarin	*1300.00 to 1400.00*
HN 602	No Information Available.	
HN 603A	Child Study	*300.00*
HN 603B	Child Study	*300.00*
HN 604A	Child Study	*300.00*
HN 604B	Child Study	*300.00*
HN 605A	Child Study	*300.00*
HN 605B	Child Study	*300.00*
HN 606A	Child Study	*300.00*
HN 606B	Child Study	*300.00*
HN 607	No Information Available.	
HN 608	Falstaff	*700.00*
HN 609	Falstaff	*700.00*
HN 610	Henry Lytton As Jack Point	*750.00*
HN 611	Mandarin	*1300.00 to 1400.00*
HN 612	Poke Bonnet	1200.00
HN 613	Madonna Of The Square	*1000.00 to 1100.00*
HN 614	Polly Peachum	*500.00*
HN 615	Katharine	*1200.00 to 1400.00*
HN 616	Jester	*1300.00*
HN 617	Shepherd	*1600.00 to 1800.00*
HN 618	Falstaff	*700.00*
HN 619	Falstaff	*700.00*
HN 620	Polly Peachum	*450.00*
HN 621	Pan On Rock	*900.00*
HN 622	Pan On Rock	*900.00*
HN 623	Old King	*1400.00 to 1600.00*
HN 624	Lady With Rose	*1500.00 to 1700.00*
HN 625	Spook	*900.00*
HN 626	Lady With Shawl	*2200.00 to 2800.00*
HN 627	Jester	1295.00
HN 628	Crinoline	*1350.00*
HN 629	Curtsey	*1300.00*
HN 630	Jester	*1300.00*

HN 631	Fisherwomen	2400.00
HN 632	Shepherd	1600.00 to 1800.00
HN 633	Princess	2100.00 to 2400.00
HN 634	Geisha	1600.00
HN 635	Harlequinade	800.00 to 1200.00
HN 636	Masquerade	700.00
HN 637	Masquerade	700.00
HN 638	Falstaff	700.00
HN 639	Elsie Maynard	700.00
HN 640	Charley's Aunt	800.00
HN 641	Mandarin	1300.00 to 1400.00
HN 642	Pierrette	650.00
HN 643	Pierrette	650.00
HN 644	Pierrette	525.00 to 760.00
HN 645	Forty Thieves	1000.00
HN 646	Forty Thieves	1000.00
HN 647	Forty Thieves	1000.00
HN 648	Forty Thieves	1000.00
HN 649	Forty Thieves	1000.00
HN 650	Crinoline Lady	500.00
HN 651	Crinoline Lady	500.00
HN 652	Crinoline Lady	500.00
HN 653	Crinoline Lady	500.00
HN 654	Crinoline Lady	500.00
HN 655	Crinoline Lady	500.00
HN 656	Mask	500.00 to 796.00
HN 657	Mask	800.00 to 900.00
HN 658	Mam'selle	750.00
HN 659	Mam'selle	800.00
HN 660	Welsh Girl	1900.00 to 2100.00
HN 661	Boy With Turban	450.00
HN 662	Boy With Turban	450.00
HN 663	Forty Thieves	1000.00
HN 664	Forty Thieves	800.00 to 950.00
HN 665	Forty Thieves	1000.00
HN 666	Forty Thieves	940.00
HN 667	Forty Thieves	1000.00
HN 668	Welsh Girl	1900.00 to 2100.00
HN 669	Welsh Girl	1900.00 to 2100.00
HN 670	Curtsey	1300.00
HN 671	Lady Ermine	400.00 to 1600.00
HN 672	Tulips	1200.00 to 1400.00
HN 673	Henry VIII	2300.00
HN 674	Masquerade	600.00
HN 675	Gainsborough Hat	1100.00
HN 676	Pavlova	1200.00 to 1400.00
HN 677	Forty Thieves	1000.00
HN 678	Lady With Shawl	2200.00 to 2800.00
HN 679	Lady With Shawl	2200.00 to 2800.00
HN 680	Polly Peachum	600.00

HN 681	Cobbler	*550.00*
HN 682	Cobbler	*650.00*
HN 683	Masquerade	560.00
HN 684	Tony Weller	950.00
HN 685	Contentment	*1400.00*
HN 686	Contentment	*1400.00*
HN 687	Bather	675.00
HN 688	Yeoman Of The Guard	715.00 to 960.00
HN 689	Chelsea Pensioner	*1100.00*
HN 690	Lady Of The Georgian Period	*1800.00*
HN 691	Pierrette	*900.00*
HN 692	Sleep	*1000.00 to 1200.00*
HN 693	Polly Peachum	*600.00*
HN 694	Polly Peachum	*450.00*
HN 695	Lucy Lockett	*600.00*
HN 696	Lucy Lockett	*600.00*
HN 697	Balloon Seller	*600.00 to 800.00*
HN 698	Polly Peachum	340.00
HN 699	Polly Peachum	340.00
HN 700	Pretty Lady	*1300.00 to 1400.00*
HN 701	Welsh Girl	*1900.00 to 2100.00*
HN 702	Lady Of The Georgian Period	*1800.00 to 2000.00*
HN 703	Woman Holding Child	*1500.00*
HN 704	Forty Thieves	950.00
HN 705	Gainsborough Hat	1030.00
HN 706	Fruit Gathering	*2185.00*
HN 707	Fruit Gathering	*2300.00*
HN 708	Shepherdess	*550.00*
HN 709	Shepherd	*500.00*
HN 710	Sleep	*1000.00 to 1200.00*
HN 711	Harlequinade	*750.00*
HN 712	Forty Thieves	*1000.00*
HN 713	Forty Thieves	*1000.00*
HN 714	Forty Thieves	*1000.00*
HN 715	Proposal	850.00
HN 716	Proposal	*850.00*
HN 717	Lady Clown	*1000.00 to 1300.00*
HN 718	Lady Clown	*1000.00 to 1300.00*
HN 719	Butterfly	680.00
HN 720	Butterfly	*700.00*
HN 721	Pierrette	*900.00*
HN 722	Mephisto	*1200.00 to 1300.00*
HN 723	Mephisto	*1100.00 to 1300.00*
HN 724	Mam'selle	*800.00*
HN 725	Proposal	*850.00*
HN 726	Victorian Lady	380.00
HN 727	Victorian Lady	235.00 to 320.00
HN 728	Victorian Lady	250.00 to 295.00
HN 729	Mask	*800.00*
HN 730	Butterfly	*700.00*

HN 731	Pierrette	900.00
HN 732	Pierrette	925.00
HN 733	Mask	800.00
HN 734	Polly Peachum	350.00
HN 735	Shepherdess	1000.00 to 1300.00
HN 736	Victorian Lady	350.00
HN 737	No Information Available.	
HN 738	Lady Clown	1000.00 to 1300.00
HN 739	Victorian Lady	350.00
HN 740	Victorian Lady	360.00
HN 741	Geisha	2000.00
HN 742	Victorian Lady	350.00
HN 743	Woman Holding Child	1500.00
HN 744	Lavender Woman	1300.00 to 1600.00
HN 745	Victorian Lady	350.00
HN 746	Mandarin	1800.00 to 2000.00
HN 747	Tulips	1200.00 to 1400.00
HN 748	Out For A Walk	2000.00 to 2100.00
HN 749	London Cry, Strawberries	700.00
HN 750	Shepherdess	1000.00 to 1300.00
HN 751	Shepherd	1000.00 to 1300.00
HN 752	London Cry, Turnips And Carrots	650.00
HN 753	Dandy	900.00 to 1100.00
HN 754	Belle	1000.00
HN 755	Mephistopheles And Marguerite	1000.00 to 1100.00
HN 756	Modern Piper	1395.00 to 1660.00
HN 757	Polly Peachum	350.00
HN 758	Polly Peachum	350.00
HN 759	Polly Peachum	350.00
HN 760	Polly Peachum	350.00
HN 761	Polly Peachum	350.00
HN 762	Polly Peachum	350.00
HN 763	Pretty Lady	1300.00 to 1400.00
HN 764	Madonna Of The Square	1100.00 to 1200.00
HN 765	Poke Bonnet	1200.00 to 1400.00
HN 766	Irish Colleen	1300.00 to 1500.00
HN 767	Irish Colleen	1200.00
HN 768	Harlequinade Masked	1000.00 to 1200.00
HN 769	Harlequinade Masked	1000.00 to 1200.00
HN 770	Lady Clown	1000.00 to 1300.00
HN 771	London Cry, Turnips And Carrots	700.00
HN 772	London Cry, Strawberries, Potted	750.00
HN 773	Bather	700.00
HN 774	Bather	700.00
HN 775	Mephistopheles And Marguerite	880.00 to 900.00
HN 776	Belle	1050.00
HN 777	Bo-Peep	1000.00
HN 778	Captain	1200.00
HN 779	Geisha	2000.00
HN 780	Harlequinade	750.00

HN 781	Bather	650.00
HN 782	Bather	650.00
HN 783	Pretty Lady	1300.00 to 1400.00
HN 784	Pierrette	900.00
HN 785	Mask	800.00
HN 786	Mam'selle	800.00
HN 787	Mandarin	1700.00 to 1800.00
HN 788	Proposal	850.00 to 900.00
HN 789	Flower Seller	800.00
HN 790	Parson's Daughter	600.00
HN 791	Mandarin	1700.00 to 1800.00
HN 792	Welsh Girl	1900.00 to 2100.00
HN 793	Katharine	1500.00
HN 794	Bouquet	1300.00
HN 795	Pierrette	600.00
HN 796	Pierrette	600.00
HN 797	Moorish Minstrel	1500.00
HN 798	Tete-A-Tete	1150.00
HN 799	Tete-A-Tete	800.00
HN 800-1200	See Animal And Bird List, Pages 194-198.	
HN 1201	Hunts Lady	1000.00
HN 1202	Bo-Peep	900.00
HN 1203	Butterfly	700.00
HN 1204	Angela	680.00
HN 1205	Miss 1926	1600.00
HN 1206	Flower Seller's Children	500.00
HN 1207	Miss 1926	1600.00 to 1700.00
HN 1208	Victorian Lady	350.00
HN 1209	Proposal	850.00 to 900.00
HN 1210	Boy With Turban	450.00
HN 1211	Quality Street	750.00
HN 1212	Boy With Turban	385.00 to 450.00
HN 1213	Boy With Turban	450.00
HN 1214	Boy With Turban	450.00
HN 1215	Pied Piper	700.00
HN 1216	Falstaff	700.00
HN 1217	Prince Of Wales	1100.00 to 1300.00
HN 1218	Spook	900.00
HN 1219	Negligee	850.00
HN 1220	Lido Lady	700.00
HN 1221	Lady Jester	950.00 to 1100.00
HN 1222	Lady Jester	960.00
HN 1223	Geisha, Potted	825.00
HN 1224	Wandering Minstrel	620.00 to 980.00
HN 1225	Boy With Turban	450.00
HN 1226	Huntsman	1400.00
HN 1227	Bather	750.00
HN 1228	Negligee	850.00 to 950.00
HN 1229	Lido Lady	700.00
HN 1230	Baba	500.00

HN 1231	Cassim	500.00
HN 1232	Cassim	500.00
HN 1233	Susanna	900.00
HN 1234	Geisha	850.00
HN 1235	Scribe	900.00
HN 1236	Tete-A-Tete	600.00
HN 1237	Tete-A-Tete	600.00
HN 1238	Bather	750.00
HN 1239-41	See Animal And Bird List, Pages 194-198.	
HN 1242	Parson's Daughter	600.00
HN 1243	Baba	500.00
HN 1244	Baba	500.00
HN 1245	Baba	500.00
HN 1246	Baba	500.00
HN 1247	Baba	500.00
HN 1248	Baba	500.00
HN 1249	Circe	1100.00
HN 1250	Circe	1100.00
HN 1251	Cobbler	600.00
HN 1252	Kathleen	680.00
HN 1253	Kathleen	700.00
HN 1254	Circe	1100.00
HN 1255	Circe	1100.00
HN 1256	Captain MacHeath	700.00
HN 1257	Highwayman	650.00
HN 1258	Victorian Lady	350.00
HN 1259	Alchemist	1400.00
HN 1260	Carnival	1100.00
HN 1261	Sea Sprite	500.00
HN 1262	Spanish Lady	800.00
HN 1263	Lady Clown	800.00
HN 1264	Judge And Jury	2000.00 to 2500.00
HN 1265	Lady Fayre	500.00
HN 1266	Ko-Ko	700.00
HN 1267	Carmen	680.00
HN 1268	Yum-Yum	650.00
HN 1269	Scotch Girl	1000.00 to 1200.00
HN 1270	Swimmer	1000.00
HN 1271	Mask	800.00
HN 1272	Negligee	850.00
HN 1273	Negligee	850.00
HN 1274	Harlequinade Masked	900.00 to 1000.00
HN 1275	Kathleen	700.00
HN 1276	Victorian Lady	460.00
HN 1277	Victorian Lady	350.00
HN 1278	Carnival	1000.00
HN 1279	Kathleen	700.00
HN 1280	Blue Bird	500.00
HN 1281	Scotties	675.00 to 680.00
HN 1282	Alchemist	1280.00

HN 1283	Cobbler	*600.00*
HN 1284	Lady Jester	720.00
HN 1285	Lady Jester	720.00 to 900.00
HN 1286	Ko-Ko	640.00
HN 1287	Yum-Yum	640.00
HN 1288	Susanna	*900.00*
HN 1289	Midinette	*1100.00 to 1200.00*
HN 1290	Spanish Lady	*800.00*
HN 1291	Kathleen	*700.00*
HN 1292	Geisha	*800.00*
HN 1293	Spanish Lady	*800.00*
HN 1294	Spanish Lady	*800.00 to 900.00*
HN 1295	Jester	780.00
HN 1296	Columbine	*600.00*
HN 1297	Columbine	600.00 to 660.00
HN 1298	Sweet And Twenty	225.00 to 240.00
HN 1299	Susanna	*900.00*
HN 1300	Carmen	700.00
HN 1301	Gypsy Woman With Child	*1500.00 to 2000.00*
HN 1302	Gleaner	*1500.00 to 2000.00*
HN 1303	Angela	*800.00*
HN 1304	Harlequinade Masked	*900.00 to 1000.00*
HN 1305	Siesta	900.00
HN 1306	Midinette	*1000.00 to 1100.00*
HN 1307	Irishman	*1000.00*
HN 1308	Moor	*1500.00*
HN 1309	Spanish Lady	*800.00*
HN 1310	Geisha	*750.00*
HN 1311	Cassim	*600.00*
HN 1312	Cassim	*600.00*
HN 1313	Sonny	*700.00*
HN 1314	Sonny	680.00
HN 1315	Old Balloon Seller	82.00 to 175.00
HN 1316	Toys	*1500.00 to 1700.00*
HN 1317	Snake Charmer	*950.00*
HN 1318	Sweet Anne	190.00 to 220.00
HN 1319	Darling	110.00 to 160.00
HN 1320	Rosamund	*1400.00 to 1600.00*
HN 1321	Geisha	*2000.00*
HN 1322	Geisha	*2000.00*
HN 1323	Contentment	1560.00
HN 1324	Fairy	*600.00 to 800.00*
HN 1325	Orange Seller	475.00
HN 1326	Swimmer	*1000.00 to 1200.00*
HN 1327	Bo-Peep	*900.00*
HN 1328	Bo-Peep	*900.00*
HN 1329	Swimmer	*1000.00 to 1200.00*
HN 1330	Sweet Anne	*300.00*
HN 1331	Sweet Anne	300.00
HN 1332	Lady Jester	*950.00 to 1100.00*

HN 1333	Jester	*1300.00*
HN 1334	Tulips	*1200.00 to 1400.00*
HN 1335	Folly	950.00
HN 1336	Forty Thieves	*1000.00*
HN 1337	Priscilla	360.00
HN 1338	Courtier	*1100.00*
HN 1339	Covent Garden	*900.00*
HN 1340	Priscilla	250.00 to 315.00
HN 1341	Marietta	375.00
HN 1342	Flower Seller's Children	197.50 to 395.00
HN 1343	Dulcinea	*850.00*
HN 1344	Sunshine Girl	*1100.00*
HN 1345	Victorian Lady	*250.00*
HN 1346	Iona	*1500.00 to 2000.00*
HN 1347	Moira	1800.00 to 2000.00
HN 1348	Sunshine Girl	*1100.00*
HN 1349	Scotties	*650.00*
HN 1350	Forty Thieves	*1000.00*
HN 1351	Forty Thieves	1120.00
HN 1352	Forty Thieves	*1000.00*
HN 1353	Forty Thieves	*1000.00*
HN 1354	Forty Thieves	*1000.00*
HN 1355	Mendicant	*375.00*
HN 1356	Parson's Daughter	*550.00*
HN 1357	Kathleen	*700.00*
HN 1358	Rosina	*650.00*
HN 1359	Two-A-Penny	820.00
HN 1360	Sweet And Twenty	*300.00*
HN 1361	Mask Seller	250.00
HN 1362	Pantalettes	300.00 to 380.00
HN 1363	Doreen	*500.00 to 700.00*
HN 1364	Rosina	*650.00*
HN 1365	Mendicant	225.00 to 300.00
HN 1366	Moor	*1200.00 to 1300.00*
HN 1367	Kitty	*850.00*
HN 1368	Rose	37.50 to 75.00
HN 1369	Boy On Pig	*850.00*
HN 1370	Marie	45.00 to 68.00
HN 1371	Darling	*300.00*
HN 1372	Darling	*300.00*
HN 1373	Sweet Lavender	540.00 to 850.00
HN 1374	Fairy	310.00
HN 1375	Fairy	*700.00 to 800.00*
HN 1376	Fairy	*500.00 to 650.00*
HN 1377	Not Issued.	
HN 1378	Fairy	*400.00 to 550.00*
HN 1379	Fairy	*500.00 to 650.00*
HN 1380	Fairy	800.00
HN 1381-1386 Not Issued		
HN 1387	Rose	*250.00*

HN 1388	Marie	*300.00*
HN 1389	Doreen	*700.00*
HN 1390	Doreen	475.00
HN 1391	Pierrette	720.00
HN 1392	Paisley Shawl	*300.00*
HN 1393	Fairy	*450.00 to 550.00*
HN 1394	Fairy	*450.00 to 550.00*
HN 1395	Fairy	*450.00 to 550.00*
HN 1396	Fairy	*400.00 to 550.00*
HN 1397	Gretchen	500.00
HN 1398	Derrick	500.00
HN 1399	Young Widow	*1300.00*
HN 1400	Windmill Lady	320.00 to 1000.00
HN 1401	Chorus Girl	*1400.00*
HN 1402	Miss Demure	150.00 to 250.00
HN 1403	Not Issued.	
HN 1404	Betty	400.00
HN 1405	Betty	*400.00*
HN 1406	Flower Seller's Children	*500.00*
HN 1407	Winner	*2400.00 to 2600.00*
HN 1408	John Peel	2600.00
HN 1409	Hunting Squire	2250.00
HN 1410	Abdullah	920.00
HN 1411	Charley's Aunt	*1200.00*
HN 1412	Pantalettes	*350.00*
HN 1413	Margery	315.00 to 400.00
HN 1414	Patricia	400.00 to 520.00
HN 1415	No details available	
HN 1416	Rose	110.00 to 255.00
HN 1417	Marie	*300.00*
HN 1418	Little Mother	*900.00 to 1100.00*
HN 1419	Dulcinea	625.00 to 1200.00
HN 1420	Phyllis	545.00 to 575.00
HN 1421	Barbara	*600.00*
HN 1422	Joan	535.00
HN 1423	Babette	*500.00*
HN 1424	Babette	520.00
HN 1425	Moor	*1200.00*
HN 1426	Gossips	*450.00*
HN 1427	Darby	380.00
HN 1428	Calumet	1020.00
HN 1429	Gossips	440.00
HN 1430	Phyllis	*650.00*
HN 1431	Patricia	400.00 to 680.00
HN 1432	Barbara	*600.00*
HN 1433	Little Bridesmaid	125.00 to 160.00
HN 1434	Little Bridesmaid	95.00 to 200.00
HN 1435	Betty	*400.00*
HN 1436	Betty	*400.00*
HN 1437	Sweet And Twenty	250.00

HN 1438	Sweet And Twenty	300.00
HN 1439	Columbine	600.00
HN 1440	Miss Demure	300.00
HN 1441	Child Study	350.00
HN 1442	Child Study	350.00
HN 1443	Child Study	350.00
HN 1444	Pauline	400.00
HN 1445	Biddy	165.00 to 300.00
HN 1446	Marietta	600.00
HN 1447	Marigold	400.00
HN 1448	Rita	700.00
HN 1449	Little Mistress	295.00 to 460.00
HN 1450	Rita	500.00
HN 1451	Marigold	400.00
HN 1452	Victorian Lady	350.00
HN 1453	Sweet Anne	300.00
HN 1454	Negligee	850.00
HN 1455	Molly Malone	1100.00 to 1200.00
HN 1456	Butterfly	675.00
HN 1457	Fall-A-Blooming	800.00
HN 1458	Monica	200.00
HN 1459	Monica	200.00
HN 1460	Paisley Shawl	265.00 to 400.00
HN 1461	Barbara	550.00
HN 1462	Patricia	600.00
HN 1463	Miss Demure	300.00
HN 1464	Carpet Seller	200.00 to 325.00
HN 1464A	Carpet Seller	255.00
HN 1465	Lady Clare	680.00
HN 1466	All-A-Blooming	800.00
HN 1467	Monica	50.00 to 100.00
HN 1468	Pamela	495.00 to 500.00
HN 1469	Pamela	475.00
HN 1470	Chloe	280.00
HN 1471	Annette	360.00
HN 1472	Annette	400.00
HN 1473	Dreamland	1400.00
HN 1474	In The Stocks	900.00 to 1200.00
HN 1475	In The Stocks	1000.00
HN 1476	Chloe	280.00 to 285.00
HN 1477	No Information Available.	
HN 1478	Sylvia	500.00
HN 1479	Chloe	270.00
HN 1480	Newhaven Fishwife	1100.00 to 1200.00
HN 1481	Dreamland	1400.00
HN 1482	Pearly Boy	280.00
HN 1483	Pearly Girl	350.00
HN 1484	Jennifer	360.00
HN 1485	Greta	175.00 to 240.00
HN 1486	Phyllis	575.00

Buz Fuz HN 538

Uriah Heep HN 2101

Tiny Tim HN 539

Miss Muffet HN 1936

Yeoman Of The Guard HN 2122

Melanie HN 2271

Leading Lady HN 2269

Pillow Fight HN 2270

Picnic HN 2308

Lights Out HN 2262

Coralie HN 2307

Suitor HN 2132

Dancing Years HN 2235

Nanny HN 2221

Cup Of Tea HN 2322

Make Believe HN 2225

Mother's Help HN 2151

Cherie HN 2341

Golden Days HN 2274

Bunny HN 2214

Tinkle Bell HN 1677

Lily HN 1798

Easter Day HN 2039

Diana HN 1986

Marie HN 1370

Loretta HN 2337

Grace HN 2318

Heart To Heart HN 2276

Scenic Rack Plate, Giraffe, D.6482

*Historical Britain, Plate,
Anne Hathaway's Cottage,
10 In.*

*Head Rack Plate,
Mayor, D.6283, 10 In.*

Mr. Pickwick Bookend HN 1623

Sairey Gamp Bookend HN 1625

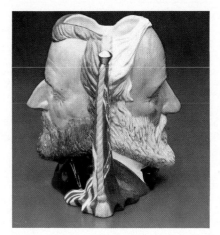

Grant And Lee, Large, D.6698

Jug, Dickens Dream

Cliff Cornell, Brown, Blue, 9 In.

Geisha HN 779

HN 1487	Suzette	300.00
HN 1488	Gloria	620.00
HN 1489	Marie	320.00
HN 1490	Dorcas	*450.00*
HN 1491	Dorcas	460.00
HN 1492	Old Lavender Seller	560.00 to 625.00
HN 1493	Potter	185.00 to 350.00
HN 1494	Gwendolen	495.00
HN 1495	Priscilla	*450.00*
HN 1496	Sweet Anne	200.00
HN 1497	Rosamund	550.00 to 975.00
HN 1498	Chloe	*300.00*
HN 1499	Miss Demure	*350.00*
HN 1500	Biddy	*300.00*
HN 1501	Priscilla	460.00
HN 1502	Lucy Ann	200.00 to 260.00
HN 1503	Gwendolen	*650.00*
HN 1504	Sweet Maid	*800.00*
HN 1505	Sweet Maid	*800.00*
HN 1506	Rose	*250.00*
HN 1507	Pantalettes	*450.00*
HN 1508	Helen	*550.00*
HN 1509	Helen	*550.00*
HN 1510	Constance	*800.00*
HN 1511	Constance	*800.00*
HN 1512	Kathleen	*700.00*
HN 1513	Biddy	150.00 to 240.00
HN 1514	Dolly Vardon	*650.00*
HN 1515	Dolly Vardon	*700.00*
HN 1516	Cicely	*800.00*
HN 1517	Veronica	265.00 to 325.00
HN 1518	Potter	550.00
HN 1519	Veronica	440.00
HN 1520	Eugene	*600.00*
HN 1521	Eugene	*600.00*
HN 1522	Potter	*400.00*
HN 1523	Lisette	*700.00 to 800.00*
HN 1524	Lisette	*700.00*
HN 1525	Clarissa	495.00 to 520.00
HN 1526	Anthea	500.00
HN 1527	Anthea	540.00
HN 1528	Bluebeard	720.00
HN 1529	Victorian Lady	*350.00*
HN 1530	Little Bridesmaid	*200.00*
HN 1531	Marie	*300.00*
HN 1532	Fairy	*400.00*
HN 1533	Fairy	*400.00*
HN 1534	Fairy	*400.00*
HN 1535	Fairy	*400.00*
HN 1536	Fairy	360.00

HN 1537	Janet	120.00
HN 1538	Janet	*300.00*
HN 1539	Saucy Nymph	*275.00*
HN 1540	Little Child Rare And Sweet	*350.00*
HN 1541	Happy Joy, Baby Boy	*300.00*
HN 1542	Little Child Rare And Sweet	320.00
HN 1543	Dancing Eyes And Sunny Hair	*300.00*
HN 1544	Do You Wonder Where	*300.00*
HN 1545	Called Love	*300.00*
HN 1546	Here A Little Child I Stand	225.00 to 320.00
HN 1547	Pearly Boy	*300.00*
HN 1548	Pearly Girl	*350.00*
HN 1549	Sweet And Twenty	*300.00*
HN 1550	Annette	295.00 to 350.00
HN 1551	Rosamund	*650.00*
HN 1552	Pinkie	*400.00*
HN 1553	Pinkie	*400.00 to 500.00*
HN 1554	Charley's Aunt	*950.00*
HN 1555	Marigold	*400.00*
HN 1556	Rosina	740.00
HN 1557	Lady Fayre	325.00 to 675.00
HN 1558	Dorcas	210.00 to 425.00
HN 1559	Priscilla	*450.00*
HN 1560	Miss Demure	*300.00*
HN 1561	Willy Won't He	*400.00*
HN 1562	Gretchen	*650.00*
HN 1563	Sweet And Twenty	*300.00*
HN 1564	Pamela	*600.00*
HN 1565	Lucy Ann	*350.00*
HN 1566	Estelle	*700.00*
HN 1567	Patricia	*650.00*
HN 1568	Charmian	*450.00*
HN 1569	Charmian	400.00 to 700.00
HN 1570	Gwendolen	*600.00*
HN 1571	Old Lavender Seller	*600.00*
HN 1572	Helen	550.00 to 560.00
HN 1573	Rhoda	*550.00*
HN 1574	Rhoda	560.00
HN 1575	Daisy	545.00
HN 1576	Tildy	400.00 to 545.00
HN 1577	Suzette	*400.00*
HN 1578	Hinged Parasol	300.00
HN 1579	Hinged Parasol	*400.00*
HN 1580	Rosebud	*600.00*
HN 1581	Rosebud	*600.00*
HN 1582	Marion	*650.00*
HN 1583	Marion	*650.00*
HN 1584	Willy Won't He	*400.00*
HN 1585	Suzette	*400.00*
HN 1586	Camille	*500.00*

HN 1587	Fleurette	395.00 to 500.00
HN 1588	Bride	*600.00*
HN 1589	Sweet And Twenty	250.00
HN 1590-1597	Wall Masks	N.A.
HN 1598	Clothilde	495.00
HN 1599	Clothilde	*500.00*
HN 1600	Bride	425.00
HN 1601-1603	Wall Masks	N.A.
HN 1604	Emir	*700.00*
HN 1605	Emir	680.00
HN 1606	Falstaff	*700.00*
HN 1607	Cerise	260.00
HN 1608-1609	Wall Masks	
HN 1610	Sweet And Twenty	250.00 to 320.00
HN 1611-1614	Wall Masks	N.A.
HN 1615	Mr. Micawber	*300.00*
HN 1616	Tony Weller, Bookend	*300.00*
HN 1617	Primroses	475.00 to 650.00
HN 1618	Maisie	375.00
HN 1619	Maisie	320.00
HN 1620	Rosabell	640.00
HN 1621	Irene	285.00 to 425.00
HN 1622	Evelyn	500.00
HN 1623	Mr. Pickwick Bookend	*300.00*
HN 1624	No Details Available	
HN 1625	Sairey Gamp Bookend	*300.00*
HN 1626	Bonnie Lassie	225.00 to 310.00
HN 1627	Curly Knob	*500.00*
HN 1628	Margot	540.00
HN 1629	Grizel	460.00
HN 1630	Wall Masks	N.A.
HN 1631	Sweet Anne	*300.00 to 400.00*
HN 1632	Gentlewoman	500.00 to 700.00
HN 1633	Clemency	*550.00*
HN 1634	Clemency	*650.00*
HN 1635	Marie	326.00
HN 1636	Margot	*600.00*
HN 1637	Evelyn	*650.00*
HN 1638	Ladybird	*750.00 to 900.00*
HN 1639	Dainty May	250.00 to 320.00
HN 1640	Ladybird	*750.00 to 900.00*
HN 1641	Little Mother	*900.00*
HN 1642	Granny's Shawl	*375.00*
HN 1643	Clemency	560.00
HN 1644	Herminia	*800.00*
HN 1645	Aileen	*650.00*
HN 1646	Herminia	620.00
HN 1647	Granny's Shawl	225.00 to 390.00
HN 1648	Camille	*475.00*
HN 1649	Sweet And Twenty	*300.00*

HN 1650	Veronica	450.00
HN 1651	Charmian	575.00
HN 1652	Janet	325.00
HN 1653	Margot	600.00
HN 1654	Rose	250.00
HN 1655	Marie	300.00
HN 1656	Dainty May	265.00
HN 1657	Moor	1300.00 to 1400.00
HN 1658-1661	Wall Masks	N.A.
HN 1662	Delicia	460.00
HN 1663	Delicia	550.00
HN 1664	Aileen	600.00
HN 1665	Miss Winsome	480.00
HN 1666	Miss Winsome	530.00
HN 1667	Blossom	600.00
HN 1668	Sibell	600.00
HN 1669	Anthea	500.00
HN 1670	Gillian	500.00
HN 1670A	Gillian	560.00
HN 1671-1676	Wall Masks	N.A.
HN 1677	Tinkle Bell	42.00 to 76.00
HN 1678	Dinky Do	33.00 to 68.00
HN 1679	Babie	75.00 to 76.00
HN 1680	Tootles	45.00 to 115.00
HN 1681	Delicia	550.00
HN 1682	Teresa	800.00
HN 1683	Teresa	800.00
HN 1684	Lisette	700.00
HN 1685	Cynthia	600.00
HN 1686	Cynthia	595.00
HN 1687	Clarissa	680.00
HN 1688	Rhoda	540.00
HN 1689	Calumet	600.00 to 880.00
HN 1690	June	400.00
HN 1691	June	300.00 to 400.00
HN 1692	Sonia	650.00
HN 1693	Virginia	600.00
HN 1694	Virginia	600.00
HN 1695	Sibell	600.00
HN 1696	Suzette	400.00
HN 1697	Irene	450.00
HN 1698	Phyllis	700.00
HN 1699	Marietta	650.00
HN 1700	Gloria	700.00
HN 1701	Sweet Anne	300.00
HN 1702	Jester	740.00
HN 1703	Charley's Aunt	750.00
HN 1704	Herminia	850.00 to 950.00
HN 1705	Cobbler	240.00 to 540.00
HN 1706	Cobbler	225.00 to 295.00

HN 1707	Paisley Shawl	540.00
HN 1708	Bather	*850.00*
HN 1709	Pantalettes	*500.00*
HN 1710	Camilla	*600.00*
HN 1711	Camilla	*600.00*
HN 1712	Daffy Down Dilly	250.00 to 350.00
HN 1713	Daffy Down Dilly	285.00
HN 1714	Millicent	960.00
HN 1715	Millicent	895.00
HN 1716	Diana	*250.00*
HN 1717	Diana	240.00
HN 1718	Kate Hardcastle	425.00 to 535.00
HN 1719	Kate Hardcastle	475.00 to 680.00
HN 1720	Frangcon	*600.00*
HN 1721	Frangcon	560.00
HN 1722	Coming Of Spring	*1100.00*
HN 1723	Coming Of Spring	*1100.00*
HN 1724	Ruby	*300.00*
HN 1725	Ruby	*300.00*
HN 1726	Celia	800.00
HN 1727	Celia	700.00 to 850.00
HN 1728	New Bonnet	*550.00*
HN 1729	Vera	460.00
HN 1730	Vera	*500.00*
HN 1731	Daydreams	85.00 to 156.00
HN 1732	Daydreams	*300.00*
HN 1733	Wall Mask	N.A.
HN 1734	Kate Hardcastle	*700.00*
HN 1735	Sibell	375.00 to 520.00
HN 1736	Camille	*550.00*
HN 1737	Janet	285.00 to 300.00
HN 1738	Sonia	*650.00*
HN 1739	Paisley Shawl	380.00
HN 1740	Gladys	*500.00*
HN 1741	Gladys	*500.00*
HN 1742	Sir Walter Raleigh	*600.00*
HN 1743	Mirabel	*650.00 to 750.00*
HN 1744	Mirabel	*650.00*
HN 1745	Rustic Swain	*1300.00 to 1400.00*
HN 1746	Rustic Swain	*1300.00 to 1400.00*
HN 1747	Afternoon Tea	175.00 to 325.00
HN 1748	Afternoon Tea	*500.00*
HN 1749	Pierrette	1080.00
HN 1750	Folly	1200.00
HN 1751	Sir Walter Raleigh	450.00 to 750.00
HN 1752	Regency	560.00
HN 1753	Eleanore	*600.00*
HN 1754	Eleanore	600.00
HN 1755	Court Shoemaker	*1000.00*
HN 1756	Lizana	*600.00*

HN 1757	Romany Sue	540.00 to 675.00
HN 1758	Romany Sue	*600.00*
HN 1759	Orange Lady	175.00 to 240.00
HN 1760	Four O'Clock	*500.00*
HN 1761	Lizana	*700.00 to 800.00*
HN 1762	Bride	495.00
HN 1763	Windflower	360.00
HN 1764	Windflower	420.00
HN 1765	Chloe	240.00 to 275.00
HN 1766	Nana	240.00
HN 1767	Nana	240.00
HN 1768	Ivy	74.00 to 80.00
HN 1769	Ivy	*300.00*
HN 1770	Maureen	170.00 to 310.00
HN 1771	Maureen	*550.00*
HN 1772	Delight	125.00 to 200.00
HN 1773	Delight	200.00
HN 1774	Spring	N.A.
HN 1775	Salome	N.A.
HN 1776	West Wind	N.A.
HN 1777	Spirit Of The Wind	4675.00
HN 1778	Beethoven	N.A.
HN 1779	Bird	N.A.
HN 1780	Lady Of The Snows	N.A.
HN 1781-1786	Wall Masks	N.A.
HN 1787-1790	No Information Available	N.A.
HN 1791	Old Balloon Seller And Bulldog	*1000.00 to 1100.00*
HN 1792	Henry VIII	*2000.00*
HN 1793	This Little Pig	37.50 to 80.00
HN 1794	This Little Pig	220.00
HN 1795	M'Lady's Maid	*1200.00 to 1300.00*
HN 1796	Hazel	*300.00*
HN 1797	Hazel	*300.00*
HN 1798	Lily	95.00 to 145.00
HN 1799	Lily	*125.00*
HN 1800	St. George	2860.00
HN 1801	Old King	N.A.
HN 1802	Estelle	*600.00*
HN 1803	Aileen	*600.00*
HN 1804	Granny	*700.00*
HN 1805	To Bed	180.00
HN 1806	To Bed	280.00
HN 1807	Spring Flowers	200.00 to 325.00
HN 1808	Cissie	220.00
HN 1809	Cissie	50.00 to 100.00
HN 1810	Bo-Peep	*250.00*
HN 1811	Bo-Peep	45.00 to 100.00
HN 1812	Forget-Me-Not	*500.00*
HN 1813	Forget-Me-Not	400.00
HN 1814	Squire	*2000.00*

HN 1815	Huntsman	3000.00
HN 1816-1817	Wall Masks	N.A.
HN 1818	Miranda	*650.00*
HN 1819	Miranda	*650.00*
HN 1820	Reflections	*850.00*
HN 1821	Reflections	*850.00*
HN 1822	M'Lady's Maid	*800.00 to 1000.00*
HN 1823-1824	Wall Masks	N.A.
HN 1825	Spirit Of The Wind	N.A.
HN 1826	West Wind	*3000.00 to 3400.00*
HN 1827	Spring	*2200.00 to 2500.00*
HN 1828	Salome	*1500.00 to 1800.00*
HN 1829	Bird	N.A.
HN 1830	Lady Of The Snows	N.A.
HN 1831	Cloud	*3000.00*
HN 1832	Granny	*700.00*
HN 1833	Top O' The Hill	145.00 to 200.00
HN 1834	Top O' The Hill	68.00 to 175.00
HN 1835	Verena	*600.00*
HN 1836	Vanessa	250.00 to 450.00
HN 1838	Vanessa	*450.00*
HN 1839	Christine	*700.00*
HN 1840	Christine	740.00
HN 1841	Bride	700.00
HN 1842	Babie	*150.00*
HN 1843	Biddy Penny Farthing	70.00 to 180.00
HN 1844	Odds And Ends	620.00 to 725.00
HN 1845	Modena	*700.00*
HN 1846	Modena	*700.00*
HN 1847	Reflections	650.00 to 800.00
HN 1848	Reflections	*750.00*
HN 1849	Top O' The Hill	175.00
HN 1850	Antoinette	*700.00*
HN 1851	Antoinette	*700.00*
HN 1852	Mirror	*750.00*
HN 1853	Mirror	*750.00*
HN 1854	Verena	600.00
HN 1855	Memories	325.00
HN 1856	Memories	*400.00*
HN 1857	Memories	*400.00*
HN 1858	Dawn	*950.00*
HN 1858A	Dawn	710.00
HN 1859	Tildy	N.A.
HN 1860	Millicent	*850.00*
HN 1861	Kate Hardcastle	475.00 to 720.00
HN 1862	Jasmine	*600.00*
HN 1863	Jasmine	*600.00*
HN 1864	Sweet And Fair	*650.00*
HN 1865	Sweet And Fair	580.00 to 940.00
HN 1866	Wedding Morn	*900.00 to 1000.00*

HN 1867	Wedding Morn	900.00 to 1000.00
HN 1868	Serena	720.00
HN 1869	Dryad Of The Pines	2300.00
HN 1870	Little Lady Make Believe	350.00
HN 1871	Annabella	400.00
HN 1872	Annabella	400.00 to 675.00
HN 1873	Granny's Heritage	450.00
HN 1874	Granny's Heritage	450.00
HN 1875	Annabella	450.00
HN 1876	Jasmine	640.00
HN 1877	Jean	275.00
HN 1878	Jean	400.00
HN 1879	Bon Jour	600.00
HN 1880	Lambeth Walk	1200.00
HN 1881	Lambeth Walk	1200.00
HN 1882	Nell Gwynn	500.00 to 650.00
HN 1883	Prudence	760.00
HN 1884	Prudence	750.00
HN 1885	Nadine	550.00
HN 1886	Nadine	480.00 to 695.00
HN 1887	Nell Gwynn	475.00 to 540.00
HN 1888	Bon Jour	540.00
HN 1889	Goody Two Shoes	250.00
HN 1890	Lambing Time	105.00 to 175.00
HN 1891	Pecksniff	350.00
HN 1892	Uriah Heep	340.00
HN 1893	Fat Boy	260.00 to 340.00
HN 1894	Mr. Pickwick	240.00
HN 1895	Mr. Micawber	350.00
HN 1896	Sairey Gamp	350.00
HN 1897	Miss Fortune	460.00
HN 1898	Miss Fortune	450.00
HN 1899	Midsummer Noon	550.00
HN 1900	Midsummer Noon	500.00
HN 1901	Penelope	265.00 to 500.00
HN 1902	Penelope	560.00
HN 1903	Rhythm	1000.00
HN 1904	Rhythm	800.00
HN 1905	Goody Two Shoes	200.00
HN 1906	Lydia	325.00
HN 1907	Lydia	325.00
HN 1908	Lydia	68.00 to 79.00
HN 1909	Honey	325.00 to 345.00
HN 1910	Honey	350.00
HN 1911	Autumn Breezes	120.00 to 260.00
HN 1912	Old Balloon Seller And Bulldog	N.A.
HN 1913	Autumn Breezes	165.00 to 250.00
HN 1914	Paisley Shawl	165.00 to 225.00
HN 1915	Veronica	300.00 to 450.00
HN 1916	Janet	150.00 to 280.00

HN 1917	Meryll	*1000.00*
HN 1918	Sweet Suzy	*600.00*
HN 1919	Kate Hardcastle	*750.00*
HN 1920	Windflower	*500.00*
HN 1921	Roseanna	*350.00*
HN 1922	Spring Morning	160.00 to 200.00
HN 1923	Spring Morning	245.00 to 400.00
HN 1924	Fiona	680.00
HN 1925	Fiona	555.00 to 585.00
HN 1926	Roseanna	250.00 to 400.00
HN 1927	Awakening	*1400.00 to 1750.00*
HN 1928	Marguerite	265.00 to 310.00
HN 1929	Marguerite	*400.00*
HN 1930	Marguerite	*400.00*
HN 1931	Meriel	760.00 to 965.00
HN 1932	Meriel	*800.00*
HN 1933	Fiona	760.00
HN 1934	Autumn Breezes	100.00 to 240.00
HN 1935	Sweeting	110.00 to 200.00
HN 1936	Miss Muffet	100.00 to 180.00
HN 1937	Miss Muffet	155.00 to 320.00
HN 1938	Sweeting	*300.00*
HN 1939	Windflower	*500.00*
HN 1940	Toinette	1000.00
HN 1941	Peggy	155.00
HN 1942	Pyjams	*300.00*
HN 1943	Veronica	*450.00*
HN 1944	Daydreams	400.00
HN 1945	Spring Flowers	600.00
HN 1946	Marguerite	*400.00*
HN 1947	June	*400.00*
HN 1948	Lady Charmian	175.00 to 200.00
HN 1949	Lady Charmian	175.00 to 240.00
HN 1950	Claribel	380.00
HN 1951	Claribel	375.00
HN 1952	Irene	*550.00*
HN 1953	Orange Lady	175.00 to 240.00
HN 1954	Balloon Man	70.00 to 180.00
HN 1955	Lavinia	90.00 to 120.00
HN 1956	Chloe	320.00
HN 1957	New Bonnet	480.00
HN 1958	Lady April	195.00 to 350.00
HN 1959	Choice	*700.00*
HN 1960	Choice	700.00 to 720.00
HN 1961	Daisy	260.00
HN 1962	Genevieve	160.00 to 240.00
HN 1963	Honey	*350.00*
HN 1964	Janet	320.00
HN 1965	Lady April	475.00
HN 1966	Orange Vendor	540.00 to 850.00

HN 1967	Lady Betty	275.00 to 375.00
HN 1968	Madonna Of The Square	*800.00*
HN 1969	Madonna Of The Square	*800.00*
HN 1970	Milady	520.00 to 700.00
HN 1971	Springtime	*700.00*
HN 1972	Regency Beau	800.00
HN 1973	Corinthian	*950.00*
HN 1974	Forty Winks	165.00 to 280.00
HN 1975	Shepherd	140.00 to 220.00
HN 1976	Easter Day	360.00 to 600.00
HN 1977	Her Ladyship	225.00 to 310.00
HN 1978	Bedtime	40.00 to 55.00
HN 1979	Gollywog	280.00
HN 1980	Gwynneth	220.00 to 300.00
HN 1981	Ermine Coat	220.00 to 320.00
HN 1982	Sabbath Morn	195.00 to 320.00
HN 1983	Rosebud	225.00 to 460.00
HN 1984	Patchwork Quilt	200.00 to 480.00
HN 1985	Darling	30.00 to 55.00
HN 1986	Diana	90.00 to 135.00
HN 1987	Paisley Shawl	200.00 to 300.00
HN 1988	Paisley Shawl	120.00 to 220.00
HN 1989	Margaret	320.00
HN 1990	Mary Jane	350.00 to 475.00
HN 1991	Market Day	215.00 to 325.00
HN 1991A	Country Lass	105.00 to 148.00
HN 1992	Christmas Morn	77.50 to 156.00
HN 1993	Griselda	335.00 to 400.00
HN 1994	Karen	350.00
HN 1995	Olivia	375.00
HN 1996	Prue	310.00 to 320.00
HN 1997	Belle O' The Ball	175.00 to 280.00
HN 1998	Collinette	420.00
HN 1999	Collinette	275.00 to 420.00
HN 2000	Jacqueline	340.00
HN 2001	Jacqueline	380.00
HN 2002	Bess	220.00 to 295.00
HN 2003	Bess	*350.00*
HN 2004	A'Courting	495.00 to 550.00
HN 2005	Henrietta Maria	450.00 to 600.00
HN 2006	Lady Anne Nevill	600.00 to 950.00
HN 2007	Mrs. Fitzherbert	520.00 to 725.00
HN 2008	Phillippa Of Hainault	480.00
HN 2009	Eleanor Of Provence	600.00 to 850.00
HN 2010	Young Miss Nightingale	520.00 to 725.00
HN 2011	Matilda	520.00 to 600.00
HN 2012	Margaret Of Anjou	475.00 to 700.00
HN 2013	Angelina	600.00
HN 2014	Jane	600.00
HN 2015	Sir Walter Raleigh	350.00 to 695.00

HN 2016	Jester	100.00 to 200.00
HN 2017	Silks And Ribbons	75.00 to 150.00
HN 2018	Parson's Daughter	400.00
HN 2019	Minuet	200.00 to 325.00
HN 2020	Deidre	275.00 to 350.00
HN 2021	Blithe Morning	140.00 to 240.00
HN 2022	Janice	285.00 to 540.00
HN 2023	Joan	300.00 to 535.00
HN 2024	Darby	225.00 to 300.00
HN 2025	Gossips	295.00 to 395.00
HN 2026	Suzette	245.00 to 300.00
HN 2027	June	340.00
HN 2028	Kate Hardcastle	580.00
HN 2029	Windflower	420.00
HN 2030	Memories	300.00 to 420.00
HN 2031	Granny's Heritage	*400.00*
HN 2032	Jean	210.00 to 340.00
HN 2033	Midsummer Noon	295.00 to 675.00
HN 2034	Madonna Of The Square	650.00 to 775.00
HN 2035	Pearly Boy	240.00
HN 2036	Pearly Girl	*250.00*
HN 2037	Goody Two Shoes	50.00 to 100.00
HN 2038	Peggy	55.00 to 90.00
HN 2039	Easter Day	235.00 to 300.00
HN 2040	Gollywog	220.00
HN 2041	Broken Lance	550.00 to 695.00
HN 2042	Owd Willum	200.00 to 280.00
HN 2043	Poacher	275.00 to 340.00
HN 2044	Mary Mary	135.00 to 160.00
HN 2045	She Loves Me Not	110.00 to 160.00
HN 2046	He Loves Me	*175.00*
HN 2047	Once Upon A Time	*200.00*
HN 2048	Mary Had A Little Lamb	50.00 to 100.00
HN 2049	Curly Locks	250.00 to 280.00
HN 2050	Wee Willie Winkie	179.00 to 375.00
HN 2051	St. George	240.00 to 475.00
HN 2052	Grandma	250.00 to 350.00
HN 2052A	Grandma	340.00
HN 2053	Gaffer	310.00 to 350.00
HN 2054	Falstaff	70.00 to 148.00
HN 2055	Leisure Hour	350.00 to 475.00
HN 2056	Susan	*375.00*
HN 2057	Jersey Milkmaid	200.00 to 325.00
HN 2057A	Milkmaid	85.00 to 150.00
HN 2058	Hermione	640.00
HN 2059	Bedtime Story	97.00 to 225.00
HN 2060	Jack	150.00 to 170.00
HN 2061	Jill	150.00 to 160.00
HN 2062	Little Boy Blue	110.00 to 160.00
HN 2063	Little Jack Horner	240.00

HN 2064	My Pretty Maid	225.00 to 300.00
HN 2065	Blithe Morning	150.00 to 225.00
HN 2066	Minuet	340.00
HN 2067	St. George	2000.00 to 2500.00
HN 2068	Calumet	480.00 to 700.00
HN 2069	Farmer's Wife	469.00 to 520.00
HN 2070	Bridget	175.00 to 300.00
HN 2071	Bernice	700.00 to 800.00
HN 2072	Rocking Horse	960.00 to 1700.00
HN 2073	Vivienne	220.00 to 300.00
HN 2074	Marianne	460.00
HN 2075	French Peasant	375.00 to 520.00
HN 2076	Promenade	1600.00
HN 2077	Rowena	455.00 to 520.00
HN 2078	Elfreda	480.00 to 645.00
HN 2079	Damaris	720.00
HN 2080	Jack Point	1350.00 to 1600.00
HN 2081	Princess Badoura	6700.00
HN 2082	Moor	798.00 to 1450.00
HN 2083	Harriette	*400.00*
HN 2084	King Charles	625.00 to 1500.00
HN 2085	Spring	400.00
HN 2086	Summer	340.00 to 400.00
HN 2087	Autumn	400.00
HN 2088	Winter	175.00 to 400.00
HN 2089	Judith	235.00 to 380.00
HN 2090	Midinette	255.00 to 325.00
HN 2091	Rosemary	295.00 to 325.00
HN 2092	Sweet Maid	460.00
HN 2093	Georgiana	400.00 to 950.00
HN 2094	Uncle Ned	320.00 to 600.00
HN 2095	Ibrahim	560.00 to 750.00
HN 2096	Fat Boy	240.00 to 320.00
HN 2097	Mr. Micawber	275.00 to 310.00
HN 2098	Pecksniff	285.00 to 350.00
HN 2099	Mr. Pickwick	225.00 to 350.00
HN 2100	Sairey Gamp	260.00 to 320.00
HN 2101	Uriah Heep	299.00 to 320.00
HN 2102	Pied Piper	225.00 to 260.00
HN 2103	Mask Seller	90.00 to 180.00
HN 2104	Abdullah	475.00 to 675.00
HN 2105	Bluebeard	365.00 to 380.00
HN 2106	Linda	120.00
HN 2107	Valerie	52.50 to 100.00
HN 2108	Baby Bunting	*250.00*
HN 2109	Wendy	75.00 to 76.00
HN 2110	Christmas Time	300.00 to 385.00
HN 2111	Betsy	340.00
HN 2112	Carolyn	250.00 to 360.00
HN 2113	Maytime	230.00 to 320.00

HN 2114	Sleepyhead	680.00 to 850.00
HN 2115	Coppelia	540.00 to 795.00
HN 2116	Ballerina	200.00 to 325.00
HN 2117	Skater	300.00 to 350.00
HN 2118	Good King Wenceslas	280.00 to 325.00
HN 2119	Town Crier	185.00 to 280.00
HN 2120	Dinky Do	46.00 to 65.00
HN 2121	Babie	52.50 to 75.00
HN 2122	Yeoman Of The Guard	600.00 to 695.00
HN 2123	Rose	45.50 to 65.00
HN 2124-2127 Not Issued		
HN 2128	River Boy	125.00 to 160.00
HN 2129-2131 Not Issued		
HN 2132	Suitor	375.00 to 400.00
HN 2133	Faraway	225.00 to 340.00
HN 2134	Old King	220.00 to 475.00
HN 2135	Gay Morning	225.00 to 300.00
HN 2136	Delphine	250.00 to 265.00
HN 2137	Lilac Time	265.00 to 280.00
HN 2138	La Sylphide	325.00 to 450.00
HN 2139	Giselle	325.00
HN 2140	Giselle, Forest Glade	352.00 to 380.00
HN 2141	Choir Boy	70.00 to 100.00
HN 2142	Rag Doll	39.00 to 76.00
HN 2143	Friar Tuck	385.00 to 550.00
HN 2144	Jovial Monk	155.00 to 240.00
HN 2145	Wardrobe Mistress	400.00 to 450.00
HN 2146	Tinsmith	460.00 to 495.00
HN 2147	Autumn Breezes	140.00 to 325.00
HN 2148	Bridesmaid	140.00 to 225.00
HN 2149	Love Letter	280.00 to 300.00
HN 2150	Willy Won't He	275.00 to 320.00
HN 2151	Mother's Help	190.00
HN 2152	Adrienne	135.00
HN 2153	One That Got Away	*250.00*
HN 2154	Child From Williamsburg	62.50 to 115.00
HN 2155	Not Issued.	
HN 2156	Polka	185.00 to 260.00
HN 2157	Gypsy Dance	400.00
HN 2158	Alice	80.00 to 110.00
HN 2159	Fortune Teller	365.00 to 475.00
HN 2160	Apple Maid	275.00 to 395.00
HN 2161	Hornpipe	560.00 to 750.00
HN 2162	Foaming Quart	82.00 to 168.00
HN 2163	In The Stocks	540.00 to 700.00
HN 2164	Not Issued.	
HN 2165	Janice	440.00 to 550.00
HN 2166	Bride	225.00 to 240.00
HN 2167	Home Again	69.00 to 125.00
HN 2168	Esmeralda	300.00 to 325.00

HN 2169	Dimity	295.00 to 320.00
HN 2170	Invitation	100.00 to 160.00
HN 2171	Fiddler	600.00 to 1100.00
HN 2172	Jolly Sailor	560.00 to 625.00
HN 2173	Organ Grinder	595.00 to 695.00
HN 2174	Tailor	600.00 to 625.00
HN 2175	Beggar	380.00 to 575.00
HN 2176	Not Issued.	N.A.
HN 2177	My Teddy	280.00
HN 2178	Enchantment	78.00 to 156.00
HN 2179	Noelle	350.00 to 385.00
HN 2180	Not Issued.	
HN 2181	Summer's Day	360.00
HN 2182	Not Issued.	
HN 2183	Boy From Williamsburg	56.50 to 115.00
HN 2184	Sunday Morning	250.00 to 280.00
HN 2185	Columbine	240.00
HN 2186	Harlequin	180.00 to 240.00
HN 2187-2190 Not Issued		
HN 2191	Sea Sprite	220.00 to 300.00
HN 2192	Wood Nymph	*300.00*
HN 2193	Fair Lady	80.00 to 156.00
HN 2194-2195 Not Issued		
HN 2196	Bridesmaid	88.00 to 115.00
HN 2197-2201 Not Issued		
HN 2202	Melody	300.00
HN 2203	Teenager	235.00 to 280.00
HN 2204	Long John Silver	420.00 to 575.00
HN 2205	Master Sweep	540.00 to 575.00
HN 2206	Sunday Best	150.00 to 295.00
HN 2207	Stayed At Home	160.00
HN 2208	Silversmith Of Williamsburg	90.00 to 200.00
HN 2209	Hostess Of Williamsburg	99.00 to 200.00
HN 2210	Debutante	300.00 to 360.00
HN 2211	Fair Maiden	51.00 to 100.00
HN 2212	Rendezvous	300.00 to 420.00
HN 2213	Contemplation	60.00 to 75.00
HN 2214	Bunny	100.00 to 160.00
HN 2215	Sweet April	275.00 to 400.00
HN 2216	Pirouette	200.00 to 260.00
HN 2217	Old King Cole	560.00 to 700.00
HN 2218	Cookie	125.00 to 160.00
HN 2219	Not Issued.	
HN 2220	Winsome	77.50 to 166.00
HN 2221	Nanny	88.00 to 180.00
HN 2222	Camellia	200.00 to 260.00
HN 2223	Schoolmarm	125.00 to 180.00
HN 2224	Not Issued.	
HN 2225	Make Believe	50.00 to 100.00
HN 2226	Cellist	335.00 to 475.00

HN 2227	Gentleman From Williamsburg	99.00 to 200.00
HN 2228	Lady From Williamsburg	99.00 to 200.00
HN 2229	Southern Belle	92.50 to 185.00
HN 2230	Gypsy Dance	245.00 to 320.00
HN 2231	Sweet Sixteen	165.00 to 300.00
HN 2232	Not Issued.	
HN 2233	Royal Governor's Cook	99.00 to 200.00
HN 2234	Michelle	77.50 to 156.00
HN 2235	Dancing Years	250.00 to 360.00
HN 2236	Affection	52.50 to 104.00
HN 2237	Celeste	200.00 to 225.00
HN 2238	My Pet	115.00 to 120.00
HN 2239	Wigmaker Of Williamsburg	95.00 to 200.00
HN 2240	Blacksmith Of Williamsburg	99.00 to 200.00
HN 2241	Contemplation	60.00 to 75.00
HN 2242	First Steps	400.00 to 450.00
HN 2243	Treasure Island	160.00 to 200.00
HN 2244	Newsboy	470.00 to 625.00
HN 2245	Basket Weaver	395.00 to 450.00
HN 2246	Cradle Song	395.00 to 400.00
HN 2247	Omar Khayyam	80.00 to 168.00
HN 2248	Tall Story	165.00 to 220.00
HN 2249	Favourite	83.00 to 165.00
HN 2250	Toymaker	350.00 to 450.00
HN 2251	Masquerade	240.00 to 395.00
HN 2252	Not Issued.	
HN 2253	Puppetmaker	425.00 to 475.00
HN 2254	Shore Leave	165.00 to 200.00
HN 2255	Teatime	82.50 to 168.00
HN 2256	Twilight	155.00 to 220.00
HN 2257	Sea Harvest	165.00 to 184.00
HN 2258	Good Catch	75.00 to 168.00
HN 2259	Masquerade	360.00
HN 2260	Captain	129.00 to 365.00
HN 2261	Marriage Of Art And Industry	N.A.
HN 2262	Lights Out	150.00 to 215.00
HN 2263	Seashore	180.00 to 250.00
HN 2264	Elegance	125.00 to 220.00
HN 2265	Sara	108.00 to 220.00
HN 2266	Ballad Seller	225.00 to 320.00
HN 2267	Rhapsody	175.00 to 245.00
HN 2268	Daphne	145.00 to 225.00
HN 2269	Leading Lady	145.00 to 200.00
HN 2270	Pillow Fight	200.00
HN 2271	Melanie	95.00 to 160.00
HN 2272	Repose	165.00 to 220.00
HN 2273	Denise	225.00 to 260.00
HN 2274	Golden Days	125.00 to 145.00
HN 2275	Sandra	78.00 to 156.00
HN 2276	Heart To Heart	300.00 to 325.00

HN 2277-2278	Not Issued	
HN 2279	Clockmaker	185.00 to 320.00
HN 2280	Mayor	380.00 to 425.00
HN 2281	Professor	160.00
HN 2282	Coachman	440.00 to 500.00
HN 2283	Dreamweaver	200.00 to 240.00
HN 2284	Craftsman	400.00
HN 2285-2286	Not Issued	
HN 2287	Symphony	340.00 to 520.00
HN 2288-2303	Not Issued	
HN 2304	Adrienne	83.00 to 156.00
HN 2305	Dulcie	92.50 to 185.00
HN 2306	Reverie	120.00 to 250.00
HN 2307	Coralie	78.00 to 156.00
HN 2308	Picnic	52.50 to 104.00
HN 2309	Buttercup	85.00 to 156.00
HN 2310	Lisa	85.00 to 172.00
HN 2311	Lorna	65.00 to 125.00
HN 2312	Soiree	85.00 to 175.00
HN 2313	Not Issued.	
HN 2314	Old Mother Hubbard	300.00
HN 2315	Last Waltz	93.00 to 185.00
HN 2316	Not Issued.	
HN 2317	Lobster Man	83.00 to 168.00
HN 2318	Grace	84.00 to 160.00
HN 2319	Bachelor	195.00 to 260.00
HN 2320	Tuppence A Bag	83.00 to 168.00
HN 2321	Family Album	325.00 to 380.00
HN 2322	Cup Of Tea	85.00 to 155.00
HN 2323	Not Issued.	
HN 2324	Matador & Bull	1150.00
HN 2325	Master	91.00 to 168.00
HN 2326	Antoinette	180.00
HN 2327	Katrina	255.00 to 295.00
HN 2328	Queen Of Sheba	525.00 to 1250.00
HN 2329	Lynne	81.00 to 172.00
HN 2330	Meditation	125.00 to 236.00
HN 2331	Cello	800.00 to 1400.00
HN 2332	Monte Carlo	195.00
HN 2333	Jacqueline	100.00 to 145.00
HN 2334	Fragrance	85.00 to 172.00
HN 2335	Hilary	96.00 to 150.00
HN 2336	Alison	155.00 to 156.00
HN 2337	Loretta	84.00 to 140.00
HN 2338	Penny	40.00 to 68.00
HN 2339	My Love	82.00 to 185.00
HN 2340	Belle	45.00 to 68.00
HN 2341	Cherie	51.00 to 100.00
HN 2342	Not Issued.	
HN 2343	Premiere	185.00

HN 2344	Deauville	195.00
HN 2345	Clarissa	125.00 to 140.00
HN 2346	Kathy	45.00 to 100.00
HN 2347	Nina	165.00 to 185.00
HN 2348	Geraldine	135.00 to 185.00
HN 2349	Flora	260.00
HN 2350-2351	Not Issued	
HN 2352	Stitch In Time	100.00 to 160.00
HN 2353-2355	Not Issued	
HN 2356	Ascot	89.00 to 185.00
HN 2357-2358	Not Issued	
HN 2359	Detective	82.50 to 168.00
HN 2360	Not Issued	
HN 2361	Laird	86.00 to 180.00
HN 2362	Wayfarer	150.00 to 200.00
HN 2363-2367	Not Issued	
HN 2366	Character From Isle Of Man	1000.00
HN 2368	Fleur	95.00 to 185.00
HN 2369	Fleur	185.00
HN 2370	Sir Edward	400.00 to 500.00
HN 2371	Sir Ralph	400.00 to 500.00
HN 2372	Sir Thomas	400.00 to 500.00
HN 2373	Joanne	67.00 to 95.00
HN 2374	Not Issued.	
HN 2375	Viking	260.00
HN 2376	Indian Brave	5200.00
HN 2377	Georgina	100.00
HN 2378	Simone	119.00 to 185.00
HN 2379	Ninette	93.00 to 185.00
HN 2380	Sweet Dreams	75.00 to 150.00
HN 2381	Kirsty	93.00 to 185.00
HN 2382	Secret Thoughts	108.00 to 220.00
HN 2383	Breton Dancer	595.00 to 850.00
HN 2384	West Indian Dancer	625.00 to 850.00
HN 2385	Debbie	100.00
HN 2386	Duke Of Edinburgh	325.00 to 700.00
HN 2387	Helen Of Troy	695.00 to 1250.00
HN 2388	Karen	105.00 to 175.00
HN 2389	Angela	67.00 to 95.00
HN 2390	Not Issued	
HN 2391	Tz'u-Hsi Empress Dowager	999.00 to 1250.00
HN 2392	Jennifer	40.00 to 150.00
HN 2393	Rosalind	200.00
HN 2394	Lisa	88.00 to 125.00
HN 2395	Catherine	210.00
HN 2396	Wistful	163.00 to 325.00
HN 2397	Margaret	67.00 to 95.00
HN 2398	Alexandra	135.00 to 220.00
HN 2399	Buttercup	98.00 to 145.00
HN 2400	Debbie	53.00 to 75.00

HN 2401	Sandra	155.00
HN 2402-2416	Not Issued	
HN 2417	Boatman	75.00 to 185.00
HN 2418-2420	Not Issued	
HN 2421	Charlotte	95.00 to 185.00
HN 2422	Francine	55.00 to 85.00
HN 2423	Not Issued	
HN 2424	Penny	45.50 to 65.00
HN 2425	Southern Belle	185.00
HN 2426	Tranquility	56.00 to 110.00
HN 2427	Virginals	*1000.00*
HN 2428	Palio	6600.00
HN 2429	Elyse	185.00
HN 2430	Romance	85.00 to 145.00
HN 2431	Lute	880.00 to 1300.00
HN 2432	Violin	720.00 to 1400.00
HN 2433	Peace	35.00 to 75.00
HN 2434	Fair Maiden	67.00 to 95.00
HN 2435	Queen Of The Ice	125.00
HN 2436	Scottish Highland Dancer	450.00 to 600.00
HN 2437	Queen Of The Dawn	125.00
HN 2438	Sonata	95.00
HN 2439	Philippine Dancer	450.00 to 650.00
HN 2440-2441	Not Issued	
HN 2442	Sailor's Holiday	125.00 to 200.00
HN 2443	Judge	225.00
HN 2443A	Judge	180.00
HN 2444	Bon Appetit	145.00 to 225.00
HN 2445	Parisian	125.00 to 225.00
HN 2446	Thanksgiving	165.00 to 225.00
HN 2447-2454	Not Issued	
HN 2455	Seafarer	200.00 to 225.00
HN 2456-2460	Not Issued	
HN 2461	Janine	170.00 to 172.00
HN 2462	Not Issued.	
HN 2463	Olga	179.00 to 200.00
HN 2464-2466	Not Issued	
HN 2467	Melissa	94.00 to 172.00
HN 2468	Not Issued	
HN 2469	Tranquility	56.00 to 110.00
HN 2470	Peace	39.00 to 75.00
HN 2471	Victoria	94.00 to 172.00
HN 2472	Not Issued.	
HN 2473	At Ease	135.00 to 200.00
HN 2474	Not Issued.	
HN 2475	Vanity	52.50 to 100.00
HN 2476	Mandy	45.00 to 65.00
HN 2477-2481	Not Issued	
HN 2482	Harp	1200.00
HN 2483	Flute	800.00 to 1300.00

HN 2484	Past Glory	150.00 to 200.00
HN 2485	Lunchtime	140.00 to 200.00
HN 2486	Not Issued.	
HN 2487	Beachcomber	135.00 to 200.00
HN 2488-2491 Not Issued		
HN 2492	Huntsman	125.00 to 200.00
HN 2493	Not Issued	
HN 2494	Old Meg	165.00 to 250.00
HN 2495-2498 Not Issued		
HN 2499	Helmsman	200.00
HN 2500-2501 Animals & Birds, See Pages 198-199.		
HN 2502	Queen Elizabeth II	1260.00
HN 2503-2519 Animals & Birds, See Page 199.		
HN 2520	Farmer's Boy	700.00 to 960.00
HN 2521-2541 Animals & Birds, See Page 199.		
HN 2542	Boudoir	300.00 to 375.00
HN 2543	Eliza	150.00 to 225.00
HN 2543A	Eliza	240.00
HN 2544	A La Mode	175.00 to 240.00
HN 2545	Carmen	159.00 to 240.00
HN 2546	Buddies	175.00 to 220.00
HN 2547	Royal Can. Mtd. Police	120.00
HN 2548-2553 Animals & Birds, See Page 199.		
HN 2554	Masque	85.00 to 180.00
HN 2555	Royal Can. Mtd. Police, 1873	40.00
HN 2555-2631 Animals & Birds, See Pages 199-200.		
HN 2632	Pheasant, Cock	229.00 to 495.00
HN 2633	Not Issued	
HN 2634	Fox, Sitting	350.00 to 750.00
HN 2635-2637 Animals & Birds, See Page 200.		
HN 2638	Leopard On Rock	1200.00 to 1650.00
HN 2639	Tiger On Rock	1200.00 to 1650.00
HN 2640	Fighting Elephant	1080.00 to 1450.00
HN 2641	Lion On Rock	907.00 to 1650.00
HN 2642-2645 Animals & Birds, See Page 200.		
HN 2646	Tiger	850.00 to 950.00
HN 2647-2670 Animals & Birds, See Pages 200-201.		
HN 2671	Good Morning	110.00 to 200.00
HN 2672-2676 Not Issued		
HN 2677	Taking Things Easy	99.00 to 220.00
HN 2678	Not Issued.	
HN 2679	Drummer Boy	246.00 to 380.00
HN 2680-2682 Not Issued		
HN 2683	Stop Press	99.00 to 180.00
HN 2684-2693 Not Issued		
HN 2694	Fiona	105.00 to 160.00
HN 2695-2698 Not Issued		
HN 2699	Cymbals	625.00 to 880.00
HN 2700	Chitarrone	725.00 to 880.00
HN 2701	Deborah	210.00

HN 2702-2703	Not Issued	
HN 2704	Pensive Moments	105.00 to 185.00
HN 2705	Julia	78.00 to 156.00
HN 2706-2708	Not Issued	
HN 2709	Regal Lady	87.00 to 172.00
HN 2710	Jean	95.00
HN 2711	Not Issued.	
HN 2712	Mantilla	250.00 to 325.00
HN 2713	Tenderness	60.00 to 75.00
HN 2714	Tenderness	60.00 to 75.00
HN 2715	Patricia	67.00 to 95.00
HN 2716	Cavalier	99.00 to 200.00
HN 2717	Private, 2nd S.C. Reg., 1781	840.00
HN 2718	Lady Pamela	110.00 to 160.00
HN 2719	Laurianne	125.00
HN 2720	Family	95.00 to 145.00
HN 2721	Family	70.00 to 145.00
HN 2722	Veneta	85.00 to 159.50
HN 2723	Grand Manner	159.00 to 236.00
HN 2724	Clarinda	115.00 to 200.00
HN 2725	Santa Claus	49.00 to 195.00
HN 2726	Centurion	150.00 to 250.00
HN 2727	Not Issued	
HN 2728	Rest Awhile	110.00 to 200.00
HN 2729	Song Of The Sea	105.00
HN 2730	Not Issued	
HN 2731	Thanks Doc	100.00 to 200.00
HN 2732	Thank You	101.50
HN 2733	Officer Of The Line	136.50
HN 2734	Sweet Seventeen	92.00 to 185.00
HN 2735	Young Love	350.00 to 695.00
HN 2736	Tracy	67.00 to 95.00
HN 2737	Harlequin	750.00
HN 2738	Columbine	750.00
HN 2739	Ann	95.00
HN 2740-2751	Not Issued	
HN 2752	Major, 3rd N.J. Reg., 1776	840.00
HN 2753	Serenade	95.00
HN 2754	Private, 3rd N.C. Reg., 1778	840.00
HN 2755	Captain, 2nd N.Y. Reg., 1775	840.00
HN 2756	Musicale	95.00
HN 2757	Lyric	95.00
HN 2758	Not Issued	
HN 2759	Private, Rhode Is. Reg., 1781	840.00
HN 2760	Private, Mass. Reg., 1778	840.00
HN 2761	Private, Delaware Reg., 1776	840.00
HN 2762	Lovers	70.00 to 145.00
HN 2763	Lovers	95.00 to 145.00
HN 2764	Not Issued.	
HN 2765	Punch And Judy Man	165.00 to 300.00

HN 2766-2769	Not Issued	
HN 2770	New Companions	110.00 to 175.00
HN 2771-2778	Not Issued	
HN 2779	Private, Ist Georgia Reg., 1777	840.00
HN 2780	Corporal, 1st N.H. Reg., 1778	840.00
HN 2781-2787	Not Issued	
HN 2788	Marjorie	83.00 to 185.00
HN 2789	Kate	98.00 to 156.00
HN 2790	Not Issued	
HN 2791	Elaine	90.00 to 185.00
HN 2792	Christine	125.00 to 250.00
HN 2793	Clare	125.00 to 250.00
HN 2794	Not Issued	
HN 2795	French Horn	725.00 to 800.00
HN 2796	Hurdy Gurdy	880.00
HN 2797	Viola D'Amore	800.00
HN 2798	Dulcimer	880.00 to 1650.00
HN 2799	Ruth	50.00 to 100.00
HN 2800	Carrie	45.00 to 105.00
HN 2801	Lori	45.00 to 100.00
HN 2802	Anna	65.00 to 100.00
HN 2803	First Dance	85.00 to 172.00
HN 2804	Not Issued.	
HN 2805	Rebecca	165.00 to 325.00
HN 2806	Jane	95.00 to 135.00
HN 2807	Stephanie	87.00 to 172.00
HN 2808	Balinese Dancer	950.00
HN 2809	North American Indian Dancer	950.00
HN 2810	Solitude	107.00 to 220.00
HN 2811	Stephanie	114.00 to 170.00
HN 2812-2813	Not Issued	
HN 2814	Eventide	81.00 to 168.00
HN 2815	Sergeant, 6th Md. Reg., 1777	840.00
HN 2816	Votes For Women	140.00 to 236.00
HN 2817	Not Issued	
HN 2818	Balloon Girl	80.00 to 125.00
HN 2819-2823	Not Issued	
HN 2824	Harmony	85.00 to 172.00
HN 2825	Lady & The Unicorn	2500.00
HN 2826	Leda & The Swan	2500.00
HN 2827-2829	Not Issued	
HN 2830	Indian Temple Dancer	560.00
HN 2831	Spanish Flamenco Dancer	560.00
HN 2832	Fair Lady	79.00 to 156.00
HN 2833	Sophie	50.00 to 100.00
HN 2834	Emma	45.00 to 100.00
HN 2835	Fair Lady	77.00 to 170.00
HN 2836	Polish Dancer	550.00 to 750.00
HN 2837	Awakening	35.00 to 75.00
HN 2838	Sympathy	56.00 to 110.00

HN 2839	Nicola	125.00 to 250.00
HN 2840	Chinese Dancer	525.00 to 750.00
HN 2841	Mother & Daughter	70.00 to 145.00
HN 2842	Innocence	80.00 to 156.00
HN 2843	Mother & Daughter	70.00 to 145.00
HN 2844	Sergeant, 1st Va. Reg., 1777	1440.00 to 1750.00
HN 2845	Private, Conn. Reg., 1777	840.00
HN 2846	Private, Pa. Rifle Bat., 1776	840.00
HN 2847-2850 Not Issued		
HN 2851	Christmas Parcels	109.50 to 220.00
HN 2852-2854 Not Issued		
HN 2855	Embroidering	100.00 to 220.00
HN 2856	St. George And The Dragon	5200.00 to 7000.00
HN 2857	Not Issued.	
HN 2858	Doctor	99.00 to 220.00
HN 2859-2860 Not Issued		
HN 2861	General Washington At Prayer	1200.00 to 1500.00
HN 2862	First Waltz	109.00 to 295.00
HN 2863	Lucy	55.00 to 100.00
HN 2864	Tom	56.00 to 100.00
HN 2865	Tess	56.00 to 100.00
HN 2866	Mexican Dancer	500.00 to 750.00
HN 2867	Kurdish Dancer	500.00 to 750.00
HN 2868	Cleopatra	895.00 to 1200.00
HN 2869	Louise	50.00 to 100.00
HN 2870	Beth	45.00 to 100.00
HN 2871	Beat You To It	150.00 to 360.00
HN 2872	Young Master	163.00 to 360.00
HN 2873	Bride	93.00 to 172.00
HN 2874	Bridesmaid	65.00 to 100.00
HN 2875	Awakening	39.00 to 75.00
HN 2876	Sympathy	56.00 to 110.00
HN 2877	Wizard	108.00 to 215.00
HN 2878	Queen Elizabeth II	520.00
HN 2879	Not Issued	
HN 2880	Paula	185.00
HN 2881	Not Issued.	
HN 2882	Queen Mother	1095.00 to 1900.00
HN 2883	Prince Of Wales	350.00 to 750.00
HN 2884	Prince Of Wales	600.00
HN 2885	Princess Of Wales	350.00 to 760.00
HN 2886	Not Issued.	
HN 2887	Princess Of Wales	600.00
HN 2888	Pope John Paul II	88.00 to 150.00
HN 2889	Captain Cook	199.00 to 380.00
HN 2890	Clown	145.00 to 300.00
HN 2891	Not Issued.	
HN 2892	Chief	95.00 to 220.00
HN 2893-2897 Not Issued		
HN 2898	Ko-Ko	300.00 to 750.00

HN 2899	Yum-Yum	760.00
HN 2900	Ruth The Pirate Maid	299.00 to 760.00
HN 2901	Pirate King	299.00 to 760.00
HN 2902	Elsie Maynard	600.00 to 750.00
HN 2903	Colonel Fairfax	435.00 to 750.00
HN 2904-2905 Not Issued		
HN 2906	Paula	180.00 to 185.00
HN 2907	Piper	125.00 to 252.00
HN 2908	Ajax	300.00 to 760.00
HN 2909	Benmore	300.00 to 760.00
HN 2910	Lalla Rookh	425.00 to 950.00
HN 2911	Gandalf	34.00 to 56.00
HN 2912	Frodo	18.00 to 40.00
HN 2913	Gollum	23.00 to 40.00
HN 2914	Bilbo	23.00 to 40.00
HN 2915	Galadriel	23.00 to 48.00
HN 2916	Aragorn	23.00 to 48.00
HN 2917	Legolas	23.00 to 48.00
HN 2918	Boromir	23.00 to 56.00
HN 2919	Rachel	102.00 to 185.00
HN 2920	Yearning	60.00 to 75.00
HN 2921	Yearning	60.00 to 75.00
HN 2922	Gimli	23.00 to 48.00
HN 2923	Barliman Butterbur	28.00 to 45.00
HN 2924	Tom Bombadil	32.00 to 50.00
HN 2925	Samwise	22.00 to 35.00
HN 2926	Tom Sawyer	32.00 to 50.00
HN 2927	Huckleberry Finn	32.00 to 50.00
HN 2928	Nelson	425.00 to 950.00
HN 2929	Chieftain	950.00
HN 2930	Pocahontas	950.00
HN 2931	Mary Queen Of Scots	950.00
HN 2932	Hibernia	950.00
HN 2933-2939 Not Issued		
HN 2940	All Aboard	110.00 to 175.00
HN 2941	Tom Brown	34.00 to 50.00
HN 2942	Prized Possessions	125.00
HN 2943	China Repairer	124.00 to 130.00
HN 2944-2945 Not Issued		
HN 2946	Elizabeth	135.00 to 225.00
HN 2947-2951 Not Issued		
HN 2952	Susan	105.00 to 185.00
HN 2953	Sleepy Darling	100.00
HN 2954	Samantha	60.00 to 95.00
HN 2955	Nancy	60.00 to 95.00
HN 2956	Heather	60.00 to 95.00
HN 2957	Edith	58.00 to 100.00
HN 2958	Amy	58.00 to 100.00
HN 2959	Save Some For Me	47.00 to 75.00
HN 2960	Laura	98.00 to 145.00

HN 2961	Carol	60.00 to 95.00
HN 2962	Barbara	60.00 to 95.00
HN 2963	It Won't Hurt	47.00 to 75.00
HN 2964	Dressing Up	47.00 to 75.00
HN 2965	Pollyanna	32.00 to 50.00
HN 2966	And So To Bed	47.00 to 75.00
HN 2967	Please Keep Still	47.00 to 75.00
HN 2968	Juliet	210.00
HN 2969	Kimberly	210.00
HN 2970	And One For You	47.00 to 75.00
HN 2971	As Good As New	47.00 to 75.00
HN 2972	Little Lord Fauntleroy	32.00 to 50.00
HN 2973	Not Issued	
HN 2974	Carolyn	108.00 to 155.00
HN 2975	Heidi	34.00 to 50.00
HN 2976	Not Issued.	
HN 2977	Magic Dragon	75.00
HN 2978	Magpie Ring	95.00
HN 2979	Fairyspell	65.00
HN 2980-2988	Not Issued	
HN 2989	Genie	57.00 to 75.00
HN 2990-3012	Not Issued	
HN 3013	James	100.00
HN 3014	Nell	100.00
HN 3015-3023	Not Issued	
HN 3024	April Shower	75.00
HN 3025	Rumpelstiltskin	125.00
HN 3026-3521	Not Issued	
HN 3522	Leap	75.00
HN 3523	Capricorn	50.00
HN 3524	Gift Of Life	175.00
HN 3525	Courtship	250.00
HN 3526	Shadowplay	75.00
HN 3527	Going Home	50.00

M List with Prices

M 1	Victorian Lady	280.00 to 295.00
M 2	Victorian Lady	*300.00*
M 3	Paisley Shawl	245.00
M 4	Paisley Shawl	215.00 to 280.00
M 5	Sweet Anne	240.00 to 280.00
M 6	Sweet Anne	255.00
M 7	Patricia	325.00
M 8	Patricia	*325.00*
M 9	Chloe	215.00 to 280.00
M 10	Chloe	280.00 to 300.00
M 11	Bridesmaid	280.00
M 12	Bridesmaid	235.00 to 280.00

M 13	Priscilla	*450.00*
M 14	Priscilla	200.00 to 300.00
M 15	Pantalettes	*275.00*
M 16	Pantalettes	250.00 to 280.00
M 17	Shepherd	280.00
M 18	Shepherdess	420.00
M 19	Shepherd	*450.00*
M 20	Shepherdess	*450.00*
M 21	Polly Peachum	275.00 to 300.00
M 22	Polly Peachum	*300.00*
M 23	Polly Peachum	*300.00*
M 24	Priscilla	280.00
M 25	Victorian Lady	*300.00*
M 26	Paisley Shawl	225.00 to 300.00
M 27	Sweet Anne	215.00 to 290.00
M 28	Patricia	225.00 to 285.00
M 29	Chloe	280.00 to 285.00
M 30	Bridesmaid	280.00 to 285.00
M 31	Pantalettes	*275.00*
M 32	Rosamund	355.00
M 33	Rosamund	325.00 to 420.00
M 34	Denise	*350.00*
M 35	Denise	*350.00*
M 36	Norma	320.00
M 37	Norma	*320.00*
M 38	Robin	*320.00*
M 39	Robin	320.00
M 40	Ermine	360.00
M 41	Mr. Pickwick	30.00 to 32.00
M 42	Mr. Micawber	30.00 to 32.00
M 43	Pecksniff	29.95 to 32.00
M 44	Fat Boy	19.00 to 32.00
M 45	Uriah Heep	29.95
M 46	Sairey Gamp	19.00 to 32.00
M 47	Tony Weller	29.95 to 32.00
M 48	Sam Weller	25.00 to 32.00
M 49	Fagin	18.00 to 32.00
M 50	Stiggins	25.00 to 32.00
M 51	Little Nell	19.00 to 32.00
M 52	Alfred Jingle	25.00 to 30.00
M 53	Buz Fuz	21.00 to 32.00
M 54	Bill Sykes	29.95
M 55	Artful Dodger	30.00 to 32.00
M 56	Tiny Tim	21.00 to 32.00
M 63	Not Issued.	
M 64	Veronica	280.00
M 65	June	*350.00*
M 66	Monica	300.00
M 67	Dainty May	275.00 to 300.00
M 68	Mirabel	*200.00 to 300.00*

M 69	Janet	320.00
M 70	Veronica	*280.00*
M 71	June	320.00 to 375.00
M 72	Monica	*300.00*
M 73	Dainty May	*350.00*
M 74	Mirabel	*200.00 to 300.00*
M 75	Janet	300.00
M 76	Bumble	19.00 to 32.00
M 77	Captain Cuttle	21.00 to 32.00
M 78	Windflower	*400.00*
M 79	Windflower	320.00 to 450.00
M 80	Goody Two Shoes	*500.00*
M 81	Goody Two Shoes	320.00 to 450.00
M 82	Bo-Peep	*500.00*
M 83	Bo-Peep	*400.00*
M 84	Maureen	300.00 to 400.00
M 85	Maureen	320.00 to 360.00
M 86	Mrs. Bardell	21.00 to 32.00
M 87	Scrooge	18.00 to 32.00
M 88	David Copperfield	18.00 to 55.00
M 89	Oliver Twist	29.95 to 32.00
M 90	Dick Swiveller	22.00 to 32.00
M 91	Trotty Veck	30.00 to 32.00

Character Jugs

The tradition of pitchers or jugs shaped like human figures dates back to the eighteenth century in England. Staffordshire potters made pitchers shaped like seated men or women. Jugs shaped like humans were made by various medieval potters.

These drinking vessels became popular and were referred to as Toby jugs. It has been said that they were probably named for a character in a 1761 song named "Toby Philpot."

This tradition was well known to Charles Noke in 1933 when he developed the Royal Doulton character jug. Pitchers or jugs were shaped like the bust of a person, and only the head and shoulders were shown. The name "Toby jug" has meant a full-figure representation to Doulton, and they have continued making character and Toby jugs.

Noke designed a series of jugs picturing famous English characters of history, literature, and song. The first jugs were of John Barleycorn, who represented the personification of whiskey, and of Old Charley, a night watchman.

A series of the character jugs was developed based on designs by Charles Noke, Leslie Harradine, Harry Fenton, Max Henk, David Brian Biggs, and others. The jugs were made in various sizes. The tiny size was temporarily discontinued in 1960. The large jugs ranged in size from 5¼ to 7 inches in height. The small ranged from 3¼ to 4 inches in height. The miniatures were made from 2¼ to 2½ inches high and the tiny was 1¼ inches or less.

In 1983 a new series of twelve tiny character jugs was made and sold by Lawleys of London. The twelve jugs included one jug depicting Charles Dickens and eleven showing characters from his novels.

A character jug is modeled, a mold made, and the clay is poured into the mold. The molded jug is made, dried, fired, and decorated, and fired several times. Character jugs were made of fine china instead of earthenware from 1968 to 1971. These jugs have a slightly different appearance because of their translucent body. Each character jug has a name that is molded into the back of the jug and printed on the bottom. A "D" number is usually found on the bottom. Some jugs are marked with the so-called A mark. There have been many stories throughout the years about the meaning of the "A" mark. Even the Royal Doulton firm has made suggestions. In 1975, a letter was received by us from the factory. It reads, "By a strange coincidence, we have recently made contact with one of our ex-employees who has been able to confirm that the mark was a factory identification symbol which was used approximately 25 years ago. Apparently, at that time we were compelled to print the words "Made in England" on the base of pieces sent out of the country, particularly to Australia and the U.S.A. Apparently, our warehouse staff experienced difficulty in identifying the pieces destined for overseas markets as the wording was extremely small. Our work's director at the time then came up with the idea to print a large "A" alongside the trademark which helped identification."

The final decision seems to be that the A mark was a factory-control mark used during production that indicated the wares to go to a certain kiln. It is found on some character jugs and also on some tablewares and series wares. It seems likely that the A mark was used between 1939 and 1955.

The words "Reg. applied for" or a single registered design number appear on the early jugs. Later jugs were marked with the printed name of the jug inside quotation marks. About 1950 the factory began using several registered design numbers with the lion and crown trademark and the D number. These registration numbers are different in different countries. Some small jugs, because of the limited space available on the bottom, are marked only with the words "Royal Doulton, Made in England." The words "Reg. in Australia" can be found on some jugs. (See the discussion of marks at the beginning of this book for further information about the Royal Doulton crown and lion mark and its changes.)

CHARACTER JUG DESIGN CHANGES

A few jugs have been made with slight changes through the years. The design was occasionally changed enough for a new D number. Dick Turpin was made from 1934 to 1960, large size, D.5485. The jug had a pistol-shaped handle and an unmasked man. From 1960 a new version of Dick Turpin was made, large size, D.6528. This version shows a masked man and a horse-shaped handle. Robin Hood had plain handles, large size, D.6205, made 1947–1960. A new version, D.6527, made 1960–present, has a quiver on the handles and oak leaves on his hat.

A few variations appear in character jugs that have not been renumbered. 'Arriet and 'Arry were first made in 1947. The color was changed in 1951, and in 1960 the jugs were withdrawn. A few jugs were made in blue or brown with pearl buttons as part of the decorations. Auld Mac has the words "Auld Mac bang went sixpence" on the back of the hat.

The printed name on the bottom was "Owd Mac" from 1938 to 1945. It was marked with the printed mark "Auld Mac" from 1946. Beefeater was made from 1947. The handle has the Royal Cypher GR for George Rex on the handle from 1947 to 1953. After 1953, the handle had the initials ER for Elizabeth Regina. Cavalier was introduced in 1940. The style of the collar was altered and the Cavalier lost his goatee. A few jugs showing Drake with no hat and with earrings were evidently made in an early version. Granny was first made in 1935 with no teeth showing in her mouth. Later versions show a single front tooth. The first John Barleycorn jug that was made in 1933 had a handle ending inside the lip. Later versions had the handle joined to the outside of the lip. A limited edition reissue of the jug was made in 1978. It is clearly marked. Monty was issued in 1946, and in 1954 it was colored a darker shade. Old King Cole was first made in 1939. The first year, a version, possibly never made in a production model, shows the figure with a yellow crown and slightly different details. The usual version has an orange-brown crown. Three jugs, Lumberjack, North American Indian, and the Trapper, were originally issued only in Canada in 1967, with the backstamp "Canadian Centennial Series 1867–1967." In 1968, the backstamp was removed and the jugs were sold in all countries. Six jugs picturing Dickens characters, Buz Fuz, Cap'n Cuttle, Fat Boy, Mr. Micawber, Mr. Pickwick, and Sam Weller, were made in a special size of 4½ inches and that was changed to a more typical small size in 1949. The size changed, but the D number did not. An extra-large version of Tony Weller was made in the early years. One jug, McCallum, was made for a liquor company to distribute and was never sold through stores. In 1983, a character jug Dewar's bottle was issued for limited distribution. The Pick-Kwik jugs were introduced in 1981.

A few prototype jugs were made that have by some means become available to the public. These jugs were made as samples and were never in production. Buffalo Bill was found in the United States a few years ago. Others pictured in the book *Royal Doulton Character and Toby Jugs,* by Desmond Eyles, include the Maori and the Baseball Player.

Discrepancies have appeared in some of the literature we used while we were gathering our information. The spelling of the name Old Charley (Charlie), of Izaak (Isaac) Walton, and of Sancho Panza (Panca) have caused us continual trouble. We have no explanation for this other than the difference between the United States and the English spellings. (The names impressed on the jugs are those given above that are not in parentheses.)

Some books say 'Arry, 'Arriet, Cavalier, and Drake had color changes; but the collectors and dealers we interviewed did not think this was true.

The dates given for some of the jugs may vary by a year in some listings. The copyright date is printed on the bottom of the jug, but the date that it was actually offered for sale was sometimes as much as twelve months later. Either date seems to be acceptable in the various lists put out by Royal Doulton and others.

Miscellaneous articles that resemble the character jugs were also made and are listed in the chapter titled Miscellaneous.

Complete Character Jug Price List

'Ard of 'earing represents a man who is partially deaf.

'ARD OF 'EARING, Large	D.6588	1964-1967	675.00 to 1200.00
'ARD OF 'EARING, Miniature	D.6594	1964-1967	900.00 to 1195.00
'ARD OF 'EARING, Small	D.6591	1964-1967	650.00 to 695.00

'Arriet is a London Cockney costermonger or street trader. A few jugs were made in either brown or blue with pearl buttons as part of the decoration. These are called Pearly Girl.

'ARRIET, see also Pearly Girl			
'ARRIET, Large	D.6208	1947-1960	145.00 to 200.00
'ARRIET, Miniature	D.6250	1947-1960	55.00 to 75.00
'ARRIET, Small	D.6236	1947-1960	65.00 to 90.00
'ARRIET, Tiny	D.6256	1947-1960	155.00 to 220.00

'Arry is a London Cockney costermonger or street trader. A few jugs were made in either brown or blue with pearl buttons as part of the decoration. These are called Pearly Boy. In 1951 the shade of yellow was changed.

'ARRY, see also Pearly Boy			
'ARRY, Large	D.6207	1947-1960	125.00 to 200.00
'ARRY, Miniature	D.6249	1947-1960	60.00 to 75.00
'ARRY, Small	D.6235	1947-1960	65.00 to 90.00
'ARRY, Small, Marked A	D.6235	1947-1960	85.00
'ARRY, Tiny	D.6255	1947-1960	165.00 to 210.00
'ARRY, Tiny, Marked A	D.6255	1947-1960	150.00

Anne Boleyn was the second wife of King Henry VIII in 1533. She had a daughter who became Queen Elizabeth I. Anne Boleyn was beheaded in 1536 and Henry VIII remarried four more times.

ANNE BOLEYN, Large	D.6644	1974-Present	48.00 to 75.00
ANNE BOLEYN, Miniature	D.6651	1980-Present	19.00 to 30.00
ANNE BOLEYN, Small	D.6650	1980-Present	29.00 to 50.00

Anne of Cleves lived from 1515 to 1557. She was the fourth wife of Henry VIII. The couple was married in 1540 but the marriage was annulled after a few months. The earliest examples had a horse head handle with raised ears. After about a year the handle was redesigned with the horse's ears lying back flat against the head.

ANNE OF CLEVES, Large   D.6653   1980-Present   48.00 to 75.00

ANTAGONISTS, see Grant and Lee

Apothecary is a character from the Williamsburg series depicting the eighteenth-century town inhabitants. The apothecary sold drugs as medicine and sometimes treated patients.

APOTHECARY, Large	D.6567	1962-Present	50.00 to 75.00
APOTHECARY, Large	D.6567	1962-Present	50.00 to 75.00
APOTHECARY, Miniature	D.6581	1962-Present	20.00 to 30.00
APOTHECARY, Small	D.6574	1962-Present	30.00 to 50.00

Aramis is one of the characters from the book "The Three Musketeers" by Alexandre Dumas.

ARAMIS, Large	D.6441	1956-Present	48.00 to 75.00
ARAMIS, Miniature	D.6508	1960-Present	30.00
ARAMIS, Small	D.6454	1956-Present	30.00 to 50.00

The character Artful Dodger, or Jack Dawkins, has long been popular with Royal Doulton. The tiny character jug depicting him was made in 1983 as part of the Dickens Collection.

ARTFUL DODGER, Tiny   1983-Present   20.00

Athos is one of the characters from the book "The Three Musketeers" by Alexandre Dumas.

ATHOS, Large	D.6439	1955-Present	48.00 to 75.00
ATHOS, Miniature	D.6509	1955-Present	20.00 to 30.00
ATHOS, Small	D.6452	1955-Present	30.00 to 50.00

Auld Mac represents a thrifty Scot. The printed name on the bottom of the jug from 1936 to 1945 was "Owd Mac." "Auld Mac" was used from 1946.

AULD MAC, Large	D.5823	1937-Present	48.00 to 75.00
AULD MAC, Large, Marked A	D.5823	1937-Present	55.00 to 65.00
AULD MAC, Miniature	D.6250	1946-Present	20.00 to 44.00
AULD MAC, Miniature, Marked A			
	D.6253	1946-Present	32.50 to 40.00
AULD MAC, Small	D.5824	1938-Present	30.00 to 50.00
AULD MAC, Small, Marked A	D.5824	1938-Present	39.00 to 45.00
AULD MAC, Tiny	D.6257	1946-1960	200.00 to 250.00

Bacchus is the ancient Greek god of wine and the grape harvest.

BACCHUS, Large	D.6499	1958-Present	48.00 to 75.00
BACCHUS, Miniature	D.6521	1958-Present	19.00 to 30.00
BACCHUS, Small	D.6505	1958-Present	29.00 to 50.00

A baseball player jug was made as an experimental model but never went into general production. The player has a red cap. The handle of the jug is a baseball and bat. It is so rare the only known example is in the Doulton museum. No estimated dollar value is possible.

Beefeater is the name for the Yeomen of the Guard, the bodyguard for the Queen. The handle of the jug had the Royal Cypher GR for George Rex from 1947 to 1953. After 1953 the handle had the initials ER for Elizabeth Regina.

BEEFEATER,	Large, ER	D.6206	1954-Present	48.00 to 75.00
BEEFEATER,	Large, GR	D.6206	1947-1953	90.00 to 110.00
BEEFEATER,	Miniature, ER	D.6251	1946-Present	20.00 to 35.00
BEEFEATER,	Miniature, GR	D.6251	1947-1953	55.00
BEEFEATER,	Small, ER	D.6233	1946-Present	30.00 to 65.00
BEEFEATER,	Small, Marked A, GR			
		D.6233	1947-1953	· 50.00

The American statesman, scientist, and philospher Benjamin Franklin lived and worked on both sides of the ocean. Franklin was born in 1706 in Boston, Massachusetts. He became a printer and publisher in Philadelphia, wrote "Poor Richard's Almanack," created the philosophy of the public library, improved the lighting of the city of Philadelphia streets, was postmaster, invented a stove, experimented with electricity, and by 1754 was elected to the state Congress. He then traveled to England as a representative of Pennsylvania. When the Revolution started he became a member of Congress, helped draft and sign the Declaration of Independence, and went to France to negotiate a treaty. He served in many other government offices before he died in 1790.

BENJAMIN FRANKLIN,	Small*	D.6995	1982-Present	28.00 to 30.00

Betsy Trotwood was a character in the novel "David Copperfield." She was the inspiration for one of the twelve tinies designed as a set in 1983.

BETSY TROTWOOD,	Tiny	1983-Present	20.00

Bill Sykes is a character in "Oliver Twist" by Charles Dickens. This is one of the twelve tinies made as part of the Charles Dickens collection in 1983.

BILL SYKES,	Tiny	1983-Present	20.00

Blacksmith is a character from the Williamsburg series depicting the eighteenth-century town inhabitants. The blacksmith was an iron worker.

BLACKSMITH,	Large	D.6571	1962-Present	48.00 to 75.00
BLACKSMITH,	Miniature	D.6585	1962-Present	20.00 to 30.00
BLACKSMITH,	Small	D.6578	1962-Present	27.50 to 50.00

Bootmaker is a character from the Williamsburg series depicting the eighteenth-century town inhabitants. The bootmaker produced shoes and boots.

BOOTMAKER,	Large	D.6572	1962-Present	48.00 to 75.00
BOOTMAKER,	Miniature	D.6586	1962-Present	20.00 to 30.00
BOOTMAKER,	Small	D.6570	1962-Present	27.50 to 50.00

Buffalo Bill, the Wild West star, was pictured in a character jug that was not put into general production. The one known jug was discovered in the United States in a private collection. No estimated value is possible.

BUZ FUZ, See Sergeant Buz Fuz

Cap'n Cuttle or Captain Edward Cuttle is a character in the book "Dombey and Son" by Charles Dickens. The jug was originally made in 4 1/2-inch size but by 1949 it was made in a more typical size.

CAP'N CUTTLE,	Small, Marked A	D.5842	1948-1960	60.00 to 95.00
CAP'N CUTTLE,	4 1/2 In.	D.5842	1938-1948	165.00

Captain Ahab is a character in the book "Moby Dick" by Herman Melville.

CAPTAIN AHAB,	Large	D.6500	1958-Present	48.00 to 75.00
CAPTAIN AHAB,	Miniature	D.6522	1958-Present	20.00 to 30.00
CAPTAIN AHAB,	Small	D.6506	1958-Present	29.00 to 50.00

Captain Hook is a pirate captain in the book "Peter Pan" by James M. Barrie.

CAPTAIN HOOK,	Large*	D.6597	1965-1971	250.00 to 400.00
CAPTAIN HOOK,	Miniature	D.6635	1965-1971	320.00 to 340.00
CAPTAIN HOOK,	Small	D.6601	1965-1971	235.00 to 250.00

Captain Hook, Large, D.6597

Cardinal represents a dignitary of the Catholic clergy. This mug may depict an actor playing the part of Cardinal Wolsey in the play "Henry VIII" by Shakespeare.

CARDINAL,	Large	D.5614	1936-1960	110.00 to 150.00
CARDINAL,	Large, Marked A	D.5614	1936-1960	100.00 to 145.00
CARDINAL,	Miniature	D.6129	1940-1960	60.00
CARDINAL,	Miniature, Marked A	D.6129	1940-1960	42.50 to 46.00
CARDINAL,	Small	D.6033	1939-1960	50.00 to 60.00
CARDINAL,	Tiny	D.6258	1947-1960	225.00 to 250.00

Catherine Howard was the fifth wife of King Henry VIII. She was beheaded.

CATHERINE HOWARD,	Large	D.6645	1978-Present	48.00 to 75.00

Catherine of Aragon was the first wife of King Henry VIII. The marriage was annulled.

CATHERINE OF ARAGON, Large D.6643		1974-Present	48.00 to 75.00
CATHERINE OF ARAGON, Miniature			
	D.6658	1981-Present	17.50 to 30.00
CATHERINE OF ARAGON, Small D.6657		1981-Present	40.00 to 50.00

Catherine Parr was born in 1512. She married twice before, as a widow, she became the sixth wife of Henry VIII. As Queen she befriended Prince Edward and the Princesses. After the King died Catherine married Sir Thomas Seymour, her husband till she died in 1548.

CATHERINE PARR, Large	D.6664	1981-Present	75.00

Cavalier represents an Englishman who fought for Charles I during the Civil War of 1642 to 1649. The style of the collar of the jug changed in 1950. At the same time the cavalier lost his goatee and the green color was changed.

CAVALIER, Large	D.6114	1940-1960	110.00 to 150.00
CAVALIER, Large, Marked A	D.6114	1940-1960	110.00
CAVALIER, Small	D.6173	1941-1960	55.00 to 70.00
CAVALIER, Small, Marked A	D.6173	1941-1960	55.00

In 1983 a new series of tiny character jugs was introduced. A set of twelve jugs was made and sold under the name "The Charles Dickens Collection." These jugs were purchased by mail from Lawleys of London as part of a subscription offer. The twelve jugs and a rack were sold for $20.00 each plus $2.50 for shipping. Each jug has a plain black handle. The twelve jugs depict the real Charles Dickens and eleven of his characters: Mrs. Bardell, David Copperfield, Bill Sikes, Uriah Heep, Betsy Trotwood, Fagin, Mr. Bumble, Artful Dodger, Scrooge, Little Nell, and Oliver Twist. Each character is listed in this book by name. Charles Dickens is, as would be expected, one of the series of jugs known as the Charles Dickens Collection. The twelve tinies made for this set were introduced in 1983.

CHARLES DICKENS, Tiny	1983-Present	20.00

Clown represents a comic from traditional Italian comedy or the circus of today.

CLOWN, Red Hair, Large	D.5610	1937-1942	
			3300.00 to 4300.00
CLOWN, White Hair, Large	D.6322	1951-1955	890.00 to 1050.00

The fictional character D'Artagnan was in the book "The Three Musketeers" by Alexandre Dumas.

D'ARTAGNAN, Large	D.6691	1982-Present	75.00

David Copperfield is the hero of the Charles Dickens novel by the same name. The jug is made only in the tiny size.

DAVID COPPERFIELD, Tiny	1983-Present	20.00

DEVIL, see Mephistopheles

Dick Turpin was an English highwayman in the eighteenth century who was convicted and hanged for his crimes. From 1934 to 1960 the jug had a pistol-shaped handle and an unmasked man. From 1960 a new version was made with a masked man and a horse-shaped handle.

DICK TURPIN, Gun Handle, Large

	D.6485	1935-1960	115.00 to 165.00

DICK TURPIN, Gun Handle, Miniature

	D.6128	1940-1960	42.50 to 55.00

DICK TURPIN, Gun Handle, Small

	D.5618	1936-1960	45.00 to 65.00

DICK TURPIN, Horse Handle, Large

	D.6528	1960-1981	49.50 to 70.00

DICK TURPIN, Horse Handle, Miniature

	D.6542	1960-1981	22.50 to 35.00

DICK TURPIN, Horse Handle, Small

	D.6535	1960-1981	35.00 to 40.00

Dick Whittington was the Lord Mayor of London in the fifteenth century. Legend says he became mayor because of his pet cat.

DICK WHITTINGTON, Large	D.6375	1953-1960	375.00 to 400.00
DICK WHITTINGTON, Large, Marked A			
	D.6375	1953-1960	300.00

Don Quixote was a character in the book "Don Quixote" by Miguel de Cervantes.

DON QUIXOTE, Large	D.6455	1956-Present	75.00
DON QUIXOTE, Miniature	D.6511	1956-Present	30.00
DON QUIXOTE, Small	D.6460	1956-Present	40.00

Drake or Sir Francis Drake was a famous British seaman. He sailed around the world in 1580. The green color became a different shade in 1950. A few jugs showing Drake with no hat and with earrings were made in an earlier version.

DRAKE, Hatless Version, Large			3520.00
DRAKE, Large	D.6115	1939-1960	110.00 to 150.00
DRAKE, Large, Marked A	D.6115	1940-1960	175.00
DRAKE, Small	D.6174	1939-1960	55.00 to 85.00

The well-known character of Fagin is reproduced in the tiny character jug that is part of the Dickens collection. Fagin is an evil old man from the novel "Oliver Twist."

FAGIN, Tiny		1983-Present	20.00

Falconer represents the trainer of birds including falcons for hunting.

FALCONER, Large	D.6533	1959-Present	48.00 to 75.00
FALCONER, Miniature	D.6547	1959-Present	20.00 to 30.00
FALCONER, Small	D.6540	1959-Present	29.00 to 50.00

Falstaff, or Sir John Falstaff, is a character in the plays "Henry IV" and "The Merry Wives of Windsor" by Shakespeare.

FALSTAFF,	Large	D.6287	1949-Present	48.00 to 95.00
FALSTAFF,	Miniature	D.6519	1960-Present	20.00 to 30.00
FALSTAFF,	Small	D.6385	1949-Present	30.00 to 50.00

Farmer John represents the English farmer.

FARMER JOHN,	Large	D.5788	1938-1960	140.00 to 175.00
FARMER JOHN,	Small	D.5789	1938-1960	60.00 to 90.00
FARMER JOHN,	Small, Marked A	D.5789	1938-1960	55.00 to 90.00

Fat Boy is a character in the book "Pickwick Papers" by Charles Dickens. The jug was originally made in 4 1/2-inch size, but by 1949 it was made in a more typical size.

FAT BOY,	Miniature	D.6139	1940-1960	45.00 to 70.00
FAT BOY,	Small	D.5840	1948-1960	75.00 to 125.00
FAT BOY,	Tiny	D.6142	1940-1960	75.00 to 110.00
FAT BOY,	4 1/2 In.	D.5840	1938-1948	165.00

Field Marshal Smuts or Jan Christian Smuts was a famous South African statesman who died in 1950.

FIELD MARSHAL SMUTS,	Large	D.6198	1946-1948
			1800.00 to 2200.00

Griffith Pottery House of Oreland, Pennsylvania, had Royal Doulton make a special character jug in 1982. The Fireman, a 7-inch jug, pictured a man with mustache and typical fireman's hat. The number one is on the hat's shield. The jug handle is a hose. The jug was issued at $75.00 plus $4.00 shipping. It was originally available only through the Griffith Pottery House.

FIREMAN,	Large*	D.6697	1982-Present	75.00

Fireman, Large, D.6697

Fortune Teller represents a gypsy.

FORTUNE TELLER, Large	D.6497	1959-1967	265.00 to 450.00
FORTUNE TELLER, Miniature	D.6523	1960-1967	275.00 to 385.00
FORTUNE TELLER, Small	D.6503	1959-1967	290.00 to 350.00

Friar Tuck was the chaplain who was a member of Robin Hood's band. He is also a character in the book "Ivanhoe" by Sir Walter Scott.

| FRIAR TUCK, Large | D.6321 | 1951-1960 | 325.00 to 400.00 |
| FRIAR TUCK, Large, Marked A | D.6321 | 1951-1960 | 300.00 |

Gaoler is a character from the Williamsburg series depicting the eighteenth-century town inhabitants. The gaoler was the jailer.

GAOLER, Large	D.6570	1962-Present	48.00 to 75.00
GAOLER, Miniature	D.6584	1962-Present	17.50 to 30.00
GAOLER, Small	D.6577	1962-Present	30.00 to 50.00

Gardener represents the man who likes to work in the garden.

GARDENER, Large	D.6630	1972-1981	59.50 to 77.00
GARDENER, Miniature	D.6638	1972-1981	23.50 to 40.00
GARDENER, Small	D.6634	1972-1981	30.00 to 46.00

The first president of the United States, George Washington, was born in Virginia in 1732. He was educated at home and became a surveyor. In 1752 he was commissioned in the army and a few years later established an outpost near Pittsburgh. He fought the French in many battles, then became a political leader and Congress member and in 1775 was elected commander of the Continental armies. When his troops won the war he again retired. In 1787 he was chosen the President of the new country. He was re-elected in 1793, refused a third term and again retired in 1797. When war threatened again in 1798 he again became commander in chief of the army. He died in 1799.

| GEORGE WASHINGTON, Large | D.6669 | 1982-Present | 55.00 to 75.00 |

Gladiator represents the fighters of the Roman days.

GLADIATOR, Large	D.6550	1961-1967	500.00 to 550.00
GLADIATOR, Miniature	D.6556	1961-1967	300.00 to 350.00
GLADIATOR, Small	D.6553	1961-1967	295.00 to 385.00

Golfer represents an Englishman dressed for his favorite game of golf.

| GOLFER, Large | D.6623 | 1973-Present | 48.00 to 75.00 |

Gondolier represents the singing boatman who propels his gondola in Venice, Italy.

GONDOLIER, Large*	D.6589	1964-1969	475.00 to 525.00
GONDOLIER, Miniature	D.6595	1964-1969	300.00 to 400.00
GONDOLIER, Small	D.6592	1964-1969	325.00 to 345.00

Gondolier, Large, D.6589   Gone Away, Large, D.6531   Granny, Large, Toothless, D.5521

Gone Away represents the huntsman dressed for a fox hunt.

GONE AWAY, Large*	D.6531	1960-1981	65.00 to 75.00
GONE AWAY, Miniature	D.6545	1960-1981	22.50 to 35.00
GONE AWAY, Small	D.6538	1960-1981	30.00 to 50.00

Granny represents the grandmother of everyone's childhood. Early jugs, probably those made the first year, show Granny with no teeth. Later versions show a single tooth.

GRANNY, Large	D.5521	1934-Present	48.00 to 100.00
GRANNY, Large, Marked A	D.5521	1934-Present	50.00 to 79.00
GRANNY, Large, Toothless*	D.5521	1934-1935	950.00
GRANNY, Miniature	D.6520	1959-Present	20.00 to 30.00
GRANNY, Small	D.6384	1952-Present	29.00 to 50.00
GRANNY, Small, Marked A	D.6384	1952-Present	75.00

In 1937 Royal Doulton made a double-faced jug called Mephistopheles. In 1982 a new series of jugs called The Antagonists was introduced, again a double design. The first of the series is the Ulysses S. Grant and Robert E. Lee jug commemorating these famous generals of the war between the North and the South. The faces of both men are shown. The handle is a double-faced flag. The series is limited to 9500 worldwide.

GRANT AND LEE, Large**	D.6698	1982-Present	57.00 to 95.00

Guardsman is a character from the Williamsburg series depicting the eighteenth-century town inhabitants.

GUARDSMAN, Large	D.6568	1962-Present	48.00 to 75.00
GUARDSMAN, Miniature	D.6582	1962-Present	20.00 to 30.00
GUARDSMAN, Small	D.6575	1962-Present	27.50 to 50.00

Gulliver is a character in the book "Gulliver's Travels" by Jonathan Swift.

GULLIVER, Large	D.6560	1962-1967	550.00
GULLIVER, Miniature	D.6566	1962-1967	350.00 to 375.00

GULLIVER, Small   D.6563   1962-1967   325.00 to 385.00

Gunsmith is a character from the Williamsburg series depicting the eighteenth-century town inhabitants.

GUNSMITH, Large   D.6573   1962-Present 48.00 to 75.00
GUNSMITH, Miniature   D.6587   1962-Present 20.00 to 30.00
GUNSMITH, Small   D.6580   1962-Present 30.00 to 50.00

Hamlet is one of a series of jugs depicting characters from Shakespeare's plays. The tragic play about Hamlet, a Prince of Denmark, was written about 1602.

HAMLET, Large   D.6672   1982-Present 48.00 to 75.00

Henry Morgan was a British buccaneer. He was born in Wales about 1635 and is said to have been kidnapped and sold as a slave at Barbados. He was commissioned by the Governor of Jamaica and captured or ravaged many cities before returning to England. He gained favor of the King and was appointed lieutenant governor of Jamaica and commander in chief. He died in 1688.

HENRY MORGAN, Large*   D.6467   1958-1981   50.00 to 77.00
HENRY MORGAN, Miniature   D.6510   1960-1981   22.50 to 40.00
HENRY MORGAN, Small   D.6467   1957-1981   35.00 to 50.00

Henry V is a character in the Shakespearean play written in 1599.

HENRY V, Large   D.6671   1982-Present 48.00 to 75.00

Henry VIII was the ruler of England from 1509 to 1547.

HENRY VIII, Large   D.6642   1975-Present 48.00 to 75.00
HENRY VIII, Miniature   D.6648   1979-Present 19.00 to 30.00
HENRY VIII, Small   D.6647   1979-Present 29.00 to 50.00

Izaak Walton was the author of many books. He first published "The Compleat Angler" in 1653. Catalogs refer to "Izaak" although the jug is spelled "Isaac."

IZAAK WALTON, Large   D.6404   1953-1981   55.00 to 75.00

Henry Morgan, Large, D.6467

Jane Seymour was the third wife of Henry VIII. She died in 1537.

JANE SEYMOUR, Large	D.6646	1979-Present	48.00 to 75.00

Jarge represents the typical country bumpkin.

JARGE, Large	D.6288	1950-1960	250.00 to 320.00
JARGE, Small	D.6295	1950-1960	150.00 to 200.00

Jester represents the minstrel of the courts in medieval days.

JESTER, Small	D.5556	1936-1960	80.00 to 110.00
JESTER, Small, Marked A	D.5556	1936-1960	95.00

Jockey represents the horseman of racetrack fame.

JOCKEY, Large	D.6625	1971-1975	125.00 to 195.00

John Barleycorn was a figure from early English ballads. He was the personification of barley used for whiskey or liquor. The first John Barleycorn jug made in 1933 had a handle ending inside the lip. Later versions had the handle joined to the outside of the lip. A clearly marked limited edition was made in 1978.

JOHN BARLEYCORN, Large, Inside Handle*			
	D.5327	1934-1960	200.00
JOHN BARLEYCORN, Large	D.5327	1934-1960	135.00 to 150.00
JOHN BARLEYCORN, Large, Marked A			
	D.5327	1934-1960	175.00
JOHN BARLEYCORN, Large, Special Exhibition Reproduction			
		1978	125.00
JOHN BARLEYCORN, Miniature	D.6041	1939-1960	60.00 to 65.00
JOHN BARLEYCORN, Small	D.5735	1937-1960	55.00 to 80.00

The Royal Doulton International Collectors Club offers a special limited edition piece each year. The first year, 1980, the club had the John Doulton character

*John Barleycorn, Inside Handle,
Large, D.5327*

jug. John Doulton was the founder of Doulton Company. The 4 1/2-inch (small) jug was availble for $50. The price included a year's membership in the club, worth $15.

JOHN DOULTON, Small   1980-1980   50.00 to 65.00

John Peel was a man who liked fox hunting and was the subject of the song "D'ye ken John Peel," written in 1866.

JOHN PEEL,	Large	D.5612	1936-1960	110.00 to 150.00
JOHN PEEL,	Large, Marked A	D.5612	1936-1960	245.00
JOHN PEEL,	Miniature	D.6130	1940-1960	40.00 to 50.00
JOHN PEEL,	Miniature, Marked A	D.6130	1940-1960	40.00 to 65.00
JOHN PEEL,	Small	D.5731	1937-1960	45.00 to 65.00
JOHN PEEL,	Small, Marked A	D.5731	1937-1960	55.00
JOHN PEEL,	Tiny	D.6259	1947-1960	200.00 to 275.00

Johnny Appleseed was the nickname of New Englander John Chapman, who traveled the midwest planting apple seeds in the early nineteenth century. The jug was made only in the large size.

JOHNNY APPLESEED, Large   D.6372   1953-1969   150.00 to 300.00

Lawyer represents the typical British lawyer who appears in court wearing a wig.

LAWYER,	Large	D.6498	1957-Present	75.00
LAWYER,	Miniature	D.6524	1957-Present	19.00 to 30.00
LAWYER,	Small	D.6504	1957-Present	29.00 to 50.00

LEE AND GRANT, see Grant and Lee

Little Nell is the nickname for Nellie Trent, a character in the Charles Dickens story "Old Curiosity Shop."

LITTLE NELL, Tiny   1983-Present   20.00

Lobster man represents the fisherman who sets the pots and traps the lobsters.

LOBSTER MAN,	Large	D.6617	1967-Present	48.00 to 75.00
LOBSTER MAN,	Miniature	D.6652	1980-Present	19.00 to 30.00
LOBSTER MAN,	Small	D.6620	1967-Present	29.00 to 50.00

Long John Silver is a character in the book "Treasure Island" by Robert Louis Stevenson.

LONG JOHN SILVER,	Large	D.6335	1951-Present	48.00 to 75.00
LONG JOHN SILVER,	Miniature	D.6512	1960-Present	19.00 to 30.00
LONG JOHN SILVER,	Small	D.6386	1951-Present	27.50 to 65.00

Lord Nelson was an English naval hero who died at the Battle of Trafalgar in 1805. The jug was made only in the large size.

LORD NELSON, Large   D.6336   1952-1969   250.00 to 325.00

Lumberjack represents the loggers of the United States and Canada. The jug was originally issued in 1967 in Canada with a special backstamp "Canadian Centennial Series." In 1968 the backstamp was removed and the jugs were sold in all countries.

LUMBERJACK, Large		D.6610	1967-1982	48.00 to 75.00
LUMBERJACK, Large, Canadian Centennial				
		D.6610	1967-1967	150.00
LUMBERJACK, Small		D.6613	1967-1982	29.00 to 50.00

Macbeth was a king of Scotland. His tragic story was told in Shakespeare's play, written in 1605.

MACBETH, Large	D.6667	1982-Present	48.00 to 75.00

Mad Hatter is a character from the book "Alice's Adventures in Wonderland" by Lewis Carroll.

MAD HATTER, Large*	D.6598	1966-Present	45.00 to 75.00
MAD HATTER, Miniature	D.6606	1964-Present	19.00 to 30.00
MAD HATTER, Small	D.6602	1964-Present	29.00 to 50.00

Mae West, the curvaceous blonde movie star, was born in 1892 and died in 1980. She wrote all of her own material, often double entendre. Her most famous movie was "My Little Chickadee," with W. C. Fields. The jug is one of a series first offered by American Express showing past stars of the screen. See also W. C. Fields.

MAE WEST, Large*	D.6688	1982-Present	52.50 to 95.00

The Maori native of New Zealand was depicted in an experimental character jug. Several versions were made but none were put into production. No estimated price is possible.

Samuel Langhorne Clemens is best known by his pseudonym, Mark Twain. Clemens lived in Hannibal, Missouri, from 1835 to 1910. He was a printer, a river pilot, a prospector, and a newspaper reporter. He is best known for his short stories and novels.

MARK TWAIN, Large*	D.6654	1980-Present	48.00 to 75.00
MARK TWAIN, Small	D.6694	1982-Present	27.50 to 50.00

The McCallum character jug was made in the 1930s with the Kingsware glaze or white glaze. It shows a Highlander. D. & J. McCallum, whiskey distillers, ordered about 1,000 of these jugs. Each has the words "The McCallum Jug" incised on the front of the base.

MCCALLUM *700.00*

Mephistopheles is a legendary character of medieval lore. He is one of the second of the fallen archangels, only Satan is more important. The more modern association for Mephistopheles is a character in the book "Faust" by Goethe.

Mad Hatter, Large, D.6598

Mark Twain, Large, D.6654, 1980-Present;
Benjamin Franklin, Small, D.6995, 1982-Present

Merlin, Large, D.6529

Mine Host, Large, D.6468

MEPHISTOPHELES, Large	D.5757	1937-1948	
			1850.00 to 2500.00
MEPHISTOPHELES, Small	D.5758	1937-1948	900.00 to 1000.00

Merlin is a legendary magician and prophet of the fifth century. He is part of the King Arthur series.

MERLIN, Large*	D.6529	1959-Present	45.00 to 75.00
MERLIN, Miniature	D.6543	1959-Present	19.00 to 30.00
MERLIN, Small	D.6536	1959-Present	29.00 to 50.00

Mikado represents the Japanese Emperor, perhaps the one famous in the Gilbert and Sullivan operetta of 1885 called "The Mikado."

MIKADO, Large	D.6501	1959-1969	300.00 to 400.00
MIKADO, Miniature	D.6525	1960-1969	265.00 to 335.00
MIKADO, Small	D.6507	1959-1969	240.00 to 385.00

Mine Host represents the typical English host of nineteenth-century England.

MINE HOST, Large*	D.6468	1958-1981	45.00 to 85.00
MINE HOST, Miniature	D.6513	1960-1981	22.50 to 34.00
MINE HOST, Small	D.6470	1958-1981	35.00 to 50.00

Monty was the nickname for Field-Marshal Montgomery who was commander of the British Forces during Allied invasion of Europe. There have been two color changes: a different shade of yellow in 1951 and a different shade of khaki in 1954.

MONTY, Large	D.6202	1946-Present	48.00 to 75.00
MONTY, Large, Marked A	D.6202	1946-Present	55.00 to 75.00
MONTY, White, Large	D.6202	1946-Present	125.00

MOTORIST, see Veteran Motorist

Mr. Bumble is one of the characters in the Charles Dickens novel "Oliver Twist." The Tiny is part of the Charles Dickens collection made for Lawleys of London.

MR. BUMBLE, Tiny	1983-Present	20.00

Mr. Micawber is a character from the book "David Copperfield" by Charles Dickens. The six Dickens jugs were originally made in a 4 1/2-inch size but in 1949 the size was changed.

MR. MICAWBER, Miniature	D.6138	1940-1960	40.00 to 59.00
MR. MICAWBER, Miniature, Marked A			
	D.6138	1940-1960	45.00 to 55.00
MR. MICAWBER, Small	D.5843	1948-1960	65.00 to 95.00
MR. MICAWBER, Small, Marked A			
	D.5843	1948-1960	72.00
MR. MICAWBER, Tiny	D.6143	1940-1960	75.00 to 110.00
MR. MICAWBER, 4 1/2 In..	D.5843	1938-1948	165.00

Mr. Pickwick is a character from the book "Pickwick Papers" by Charles Dickens. The jug was originally made in a 4 1/2-inch size but in 1949 the size was changed.

MR. PICKWICK, Large, Marked A	D.6060	1940-1960	165.00
MR. PICKWICK, Tiny	D.6260	1947-1960	180.00 to 275.00
MR. PICKWICK, 4 1/2 In.	D.5839	1938-1948	165.00

Mr. Pickwick is the first in a series of character jugs made by the Pick-Kwik Company of England, a wines and spirits firm. In 1982 the company commissioned Doulton to make a limited edition series. The first jug was Mr. Pickwick. The handle is a whiskey bottle. The words "Pick-Kwik, Derby" are on the jug. The backstamp says "First of a series, limited edition of 2,000. Made for Pick-Kwik Wines and Spirits." The jug is 4 inches high. It was given as a premium for orders and was not sold by Pick-Kwik.

MR. PICKWICK/PICK-KWIK, Small*	1982-1982	125.00 to 160.00

Mrs. Martha Bardell is a character in the "Pickwick Papers" by Charles Dickens. The Tiny is part of the Charles Dickens collection made for Lawleys of London.

MRS. BARDELL, Tiny	1983-Present	20.00

Neptune, Large, D.6548

Neptune is a Roman god of the springs and sea, later considered the god of the sea.

NEPTUNE, Large*	D.6548	1960-Present	48.00 to 75.00
NEPTUNE, Miniature	D.6555	1960-Present	19.00 to 30.00
NEPTUNE, Small	D.6552	1960-Present	29.00 to 50.00

Night Watchman is a character from the Williamsburg series depicting the eighteenth-century town inhabitants.

NIGHT WATCHMAN, Large	D.6569	1963-Present	48.00 to 75.00
NIGHT WATCHMAN, Miniature	D.6583	1963-Present	20.00 to 30.00
NIGHT WATCHMAN, Small	D.6576	1963-Present	30.00 to 50.00

North American Indian represents a chief of the Blackfoot tribe. The jug was originally issued in 1967 in Canada, with the backstamp "Canadian Centennial Series." In 1968 the backstamp was removed and the jugs were sold in all countries.

NORTH AMERICAN INDIAN, Canadian Cent.			
	D.6611	1967-Present	150.00
NORTH AMERICAN INDIAN, Large			
	D.6611	1967-Present	75.00
NORTH AMERICAN INDIAN, Small			
	D.6614	1967-Present	27.00 to 50.00

Old Charley represents the night watchman of the nineteenth century. The jug is sometimes referred to as "Old Charlie" although the name on the jug is spelled Old Charley. Small size jugs were made with a special backstamp for the Silver Jubilee and sold by Bentalls, Ltd.

OLD CHARLEY, Large	D.5420	1934-Present	48.00 to 85.00
OLD CHARLEY, Large, Marked A	D.5420	1934-Present	60.00 to 100.00
OLD CHARLEY, Miniature	D.6046	1938-Present	19.00 to 30.00
OLD CHARLEY, Miniature, Marked A			
	D.6046	1938-Present	20.00 to 65.00
OLD CHARLEY, Small	D.5527	1934-Present	30.00 to 60.00
OLD CHARLEY, Small, Marked A	D.5527	1934-Present	35.00 to 55.00
OLD CHARLEY, Tiny	D.6144	1940-1960	65.00 to 100.00

Old King Cole is the "merry old soul" of the nursery rhyme. Two versions are known.

OLD KING COLE, Large	D.6036	1939-1960	220.00 to 275.00
OLD KING COLE, Small	D.6037	1939-1960	75.00 to 110.00
OLD KING COLE, Small, Marked A			
	D.6037	1939-1960	80.00
OLD KING COLE, Small, Yellow Crown			
	D.6037	1939-1960	1000.00

Old Salt represents the aging fisherman.

OLD SALT, Large	D.6551	1960-Present	48.00 to 75.00
OLD SALT, Small	D.6554	1960-Present	30.00 to 50.00

The school boy Oliver Twist, hero of the novel named for him, was the first of the 1983 tinies in the Charles Dickens Collection. The blonde boy wears a blue shirt and black cap.

OLIVER TWIST, Tiny	1983-Present	20.00

"Othello, the Moor of Venice" was a tragic play written by Shakespeare in 1622. The jug pictures the hero of the play.

OTHELLO, Large	D.6673	1982-Present	55.00 to 75.00

Paddy represents the typical Irishman.

PADDY, Large	D.5753	1937-1960	110.00 to 160.00
PADDY, Large, Marked A	D.5753	1937-1960	110.00 to 115.00
PADDY, Miniature	D.6042	1939-1960	40.00 to 50.00
PADDY, Miniature, Marked A	D.6042	1939-1960	40.00 to 60.00
PADDY, Small	D.5768	1937-1960	50.00 to 65.00
PADDY, Tiny	D.6145	1940-1960	60.00 to 110.00

Parson Brown represents the typical Anglican parson of the nineteenth century. Small size jugs were made with a special backstamp for the Silver Jubilee and sold by Bentalls, Ltd.

PARSON BROWN, Large	D.5486	1935-1960	115.00 to 150.00
PARSON BROWN, Small	D.5529	1935-1960	50.00 to 69.00
PARSON BROWN, Small, Marked A			
	D.5529	1935-1960	55.00

'Arriet and 'Arry are character jugs, first made in 1947. A few of these jugs were made with pearl buttons as part of the decorations on the costume, a typical street trader dress of past times.

PEARLY BOY, Brown, Large	D.6207	1947-1948	850.00
PEARLY GIRL, Large	D.6208	1947-1948	*1000.00*

Pied Piper is the legendary character the Piper of Hamelin who charmed the rats and children with his music.

Pied Piper, Large, D.6403   *Poacher, Large, D.6429*

PIED PIPER, Large*	D.6403	1954-1981	45.00 to 90.00
PIED PIPER, Miniature	D.6514	1960-1981	18.00 to 40.00
PIED PIPER, Small	D.6462	1957-1981	30.00 to 45.00

Poacher represents the fish or game hunter who steals the catch illegally from private property.

POACHER, Large*	D.6429	1954-Present	48.00 to 75.00
POACHER, Miniature	D.6515	1960-Present	20.00 to 30.00
POACHER, Small	D.6464	1957-Present	30.00 to 50.00

Porthos is one of the characters from the book "The Three Musketeers" by Alexandre Dumas.

PORTHOS, Large	D.6440	1955-Present	48.00 to 75.00
PORTHOS, Miniature	D.6516	1960-Present	30.00
PORTHOS, Small	D.6453	1955-Present	30.00 to 50.00

Punch & Judy Man represents the man who gives the puppet shows still popular with English children.

PUNCH & JUDY MAN, Large*	D.6590	1964-1969	480.00 to 600.00
PUNCH & JUDY MAN, Miniature	D.6596	1964-1969	325.00 to 400.00
PUNCH & JUDY MAN, Small	D.6593	1964-1969	350.00 to 375.00

Punch & Judy Man, Large, D.6590

Regency Beau represents the fashionable, fun-loving gentleman of nineteenth-century England. Best known of this type of man was Beau Brummell whose name still indicates fashion.

REGENCY BEAU, Large	D.6559	1962-1967	500.00 to 600.00
REGENCY BEAU, Miniature	D.6565	1962-1967	325.00
REGENCY BEAU, Small	D.6562	1962-1967	350.00 to 475.00

Rip Van Winkle is a character in a story in "Sketch Book" by Washington Irving.

RIP VAN WINKLE, Large*	D.6438	1954-Present	48.00 to 75.00
RIP VAN WINKLE, Miniature	D.6517	1960-Present	20.00 to 30.00
RIP VAN WINKLE, Small	D.6463	1956-Present	30.00 to 50.00

Robin Hood is a legendary character who robbed from the rich to feed the poor. From 1947 to 1960 the jug had a plain handle. After 1960 the jug handle was shaped like a quiver and Robin's hat was decorated with oak leaves.

ROBIN HOOD, Bow Handle, Large*			
	D.6527	1960-Present	75.00
ROBIN HOOD, Bow Handle, Miniature			
	D.6541	1960-Present	30.00
ROBIN HOOD, Bow Handle, Small			
	D.6534	1960-Present	50.00 to 65.00
ROBIN HOOD, Large	D.6205	1947-1960	125.00 to 175.00
ROBIN HOOD, Miniature	D.6252	1947-1960	43.00 to 50.00
ROBIN HOOD, Small	D.6234	1947-1960	65.00

Robinson Crusoe is a character in the book "Robinson Crusoe" by Daniel Defoe.

ROBINSON CRUSOE, Large*	D.6532	1960-1982	48.00 to 75.00
ROBINSON CRUSOE, Miniature	D.6546	1961-1982	19.00 to 30.00
ROBINSON CRUSOE, Small	D.6539	1960-1982	29.00 to 50.00

Rip Van Winkle, Large, D.6438

Robinson Crusoe, Large, D.6532

Robin Hood, Bow Handle, Large, D.6527

Romeo is the hero of the Shakespeare play "Romeo and Juliet."

ROMEO, Large*   D.6670 1983-Present 45.00 to 75.00

Sairey Gamp is a character from the book "Martin Chuzzlewit" by Charles Dickens. Small size jugs were made with a special backstamp for the Silver Jubilee and sold by Bentalls, Ltd.

SAIREY GAMP, Large	D.5451	1934-Present	48.00 to 75.00
SAIREY GAMP, Large, Marked A	D.5451	1934-Present	70.00 to 79.00
SAIREY GAMP, Miniature	D.6045	1938-Present	22.50 to 35.00
SAIREY GAMP, Miniature, Marked A	D.6045	1938-Present	25.00 to 30.00
SAIREY GAMP, Small	D.5528	1934-Present	25.00 to 60.00
SAIREY GAMP, Small, Marked A	D.5528	1934-Present	35.00 to 45.00
SAIREY GAMP, Tiny	D.6146	1940-1960	90.00 to 100.00

Sam Weller is a character from the book "Pickwick Papers" by Charles Dickens. The jug was originally made in a 4 1/2-inch size but in 1949 the jug was issued in the more typical size.

SAM WELLER, Large	D.6064	1940-1960	135.00 to 160.00
SAM WELLER, Large, Marked A	D.6064	1940-1960	110.00 to 125.00
SAM WELLER, Miniature	D.6140	1940-1960	50.00
SAM WELLER, Small	D.5841	1948-1960	60.00 to 70.00
SAM WELLER, Small, Marked A	D.5841	1948-1960	75.00
SAM WELLER, Tiny	D.6147	1939-1960	90.00 to 125.00
SAM WELLER, 4 1/2 In.	D.5841	1938-1948	165.00

Samuel Johnson was the English writer who is best known for his "Dictionary of the English Language," completed in 1756.

SAMUEL JOHNSON, Large	D.6289	1950-1960	250.00 to 290.00
SAMUEL JOHNSON, Small	D.6296	1950-1960	105.00 to 175.00
SAMUEL JOHNSON, Small, Marked A	D.6296	1950-1960	165.00

Sancho Panza is a character from the book "Don Quixote" by Miguel de Cervantes. Catalogs refer to "Sancho Panca" although the name on the jug is "Sancho Panza."

SANCHO PANZA, Large	D.6456	1960-1982	48.00 to 75.00
SANCHO PANZA, Miniature	D.6518	1960-1982	20.00 to 30.00
SANCHO PANZA, Small	D.6461	1960-1982	29.00 to 50.00

The Santa Claus jug is an annual Christmas jug picturing the mythical symbol of Christmas. The first jug was made in 1981. Each year the jug is redesigned and the handle is shaped like different toys or animals.

SANTA CLAUS, Doll & Drum Handle, Large			
	D.6668	1981-1981	59.50

SANTA CLAUS, Reindeer Handle, Large

	D.6675	1982-1982	52.50 to 75.00

SANTA CLAUS, Stocking Handle, Large

	D.6690	1983-1983	75.00

Scaramouche was a character in the old Italian comedy who was a cowardly buffoon and ne'er-do-well.

SCARAMOUCHE, Large	D.6558	1962-1967	475.00 to 575.00
SCARAMOUCHE, Miniature	D.6564	1962-1967	325.00 to 400.00
SCARAMOUCHE, Small	D.6561	1962-1967	390.00 to 400.00

Few people would have trouble identifying Scrooge, the villain of Charles Dickens's tale "A Christmas Carol."

SCROOGE, Tiny		1983-Present	20.00

Sergeant Buz Fuz, Buz Fuz, or Mr. Sergeant is a barrister or trial lawyer in the book "Pickwick Papers" by Charles Dickens. The jug was originally made in a 4 1/2-inch size but was changed to the typical small size in 1949.

SERGEANT BUZ FUZ, Small	D.5838	1948-1960	80.00 to 100.00
SERGEANT BUZ FUZ, 4 1/2 In.	D.5838	1938-1948	165.00

The second character jug in the Pick-Kwik series is Sergeant Buz Fuz. The 4-inch-high jug has a Dewar's bottle handle. It was made in a limited edition of 2,000 for Pick-Kwik Wines and Spirits. The jugs are given free to customers but can be purchased on the secondary market.

SERGEANT BUZ FUZ/PICK-KWIK*		1983-1983	100.00

Simon the Cellarer was a man in charge of the wine cellar who was the subject of a popular drinking song of the nineteenth century.

SIMON THE CELLARER, Large	D.5504	1935-1960	110.00 to 165.00
SIMON THE CELLARER, Small	D.5616	1936-1960	50.00 to 65.00

Sergeant Buz Fuz/Pick-Kwik; Mr. Pickwick/
Pick-Kwik, Small

Simple Simon is a character in the well-known children's nursery rhyme about the pieman.

SIMPLE SIMON, Large	D.6374	1953-1960	465.00 to 500.00
SIMPLE SIMON, Large, Marked A	D.6374	1953-1960	500.00

SIR FRANCIS DRAKE, see Drake

Sir Winston Churchill was Prime Minister of Britain. The white jug is a tribute to his leadership in 1940 during the Battle of Britain.

SIR WINSTON CHURCHILL, Large			
	D.6170	1940-1942	4750.00

Sleuth represents a character similar to Sherlock Holmes, the fictional detective.

SLEUTH, Large	D.6631	1973-Present	48.00 to 75.00
SLEUTH, Miniature	D.6639	1973-Present	19.00 to 30.00
SLEUTH, Small	D.6635	1973-Present	29.00 to 50.00

Smuggler represents the eighteenth-century thieves who brought goods into the country without paying duty.

SMUGGLER, Large	D.6616	1968-1981	45.00 to 65.00
SMUGGLER, Small	D.6619	1968-1981	30.00 to 45.00

SMUTS, see Field Marshal Smuts

St. George is a legendary character who saved the king's daughter by slaying a dragon during the time of the crusades. There was a real St. George who died in 1303 but little is known about him.

ST. GEORGE, Large	D.6618	1968-1975	90.00 to 150.00
ST. GEORGE, Small	D.6621	1967-1974	45.00 to 75.00

Tam O'Shanter is a character in a 1790 poem by Robert Burns. He is a farmer who finds some witches and barely escapes.

TAM O'SHANTER, Large	D.6632	1973-1979	49.50 to 85.00
TAM O'SHANTER, Miniature	D.6640	1973-1979	24.50 to 35.00
TAM O'SHANTER, Small	D.6636	1973-1979	30.00 to 45.00

Toby Philpots was a character in a song in 1761 but he had been a legendary drinker before that time. The toby jug, a full figure of a man, has been called a toby jug or a Toby Philpots since the eighteenth century.

TOBY PHILPOTS, Large	D.5736	1937-1969	120.00 to 145.00
TOBY PHILPOTS, Miniature	D.6043	1939-1969	40.00 to 50.00
TOBY PHILPOTS, Small	D.5737	1937-1969	50.00 to 60.00
TOBY PHILPOTS, Small, Marked A			
	D.5737	1937-1969	55.00

Tony Weller is a character from the book "Pickwick Papers" by Charles Dickens. The jug was made in an extra large size, as well as the usual ones. Small-size jugs were made with a special backstamp for the Silver Jubilee and sold by Bentalls, Ltd.

TONY WELLER, Extra Large				200.00
TONY WELLER, Large	D.5531	1936-1960		135.00 to 145.00
TONY WELLER, Large, Marked A	D.5531	1936-1960		160.00
TONY WELLER, Miniature	D.6044	1939-1960		40.00 to 50.00
TONY WELLER, Miniature, Marked A				
	D.6044	1939-1960		35.00 to 40.00
TONY WELLER, Small	D.5530	1936-1960		40.00 to 60.00
TONY WELLER, Small, Marked A	D.5530	1936-1960		55.00

Touchstone is a character in the play "As You Like It" by Shakespeare. He is a clown.

TOUCHSTONE, Large	D.5613	1936-1960	195.00 to 225.00
TOUCHSTONE, Large, Marked A	D.5613	1936-1960	175.00 to 225.00

Town Crier represents the eighteenth-century man who called the news for the town in the days before newspapers.

TOWN CRIER, Large	D.6530	1960-1973	130.00 to 135.00
TOWN CRIER, Miniature	D.6544	1960-1973	119.00 to 125.00
TOWN CRIER, Small	D.6537	1960-1973	80.00 to 110.00

Trapper represents the North American man who trapped fur-bearing animals in the wild. The jug was originally issued in 1967 in Canada, with the backstamp "Canadian Centennial Series." In 1968 the backstamp was removed and the jugs were sold in all countries.

TRAPPER, Large	D.6609	1967-1982	48.00 to 75.00
TRAPPER, Large, Canadian Centennial			
	D.6609	1967-1967	150.00
TRAPPER, Small	D.6612	1967-1982	27.50 to 50.00

Ugly Duchess is a character in the book "Alice in Wonderland" by Lewis Carroll.

UGLY DUCHESS, Large*	D.6599	1965-1973	345.00 to 375.00
UGLY DUCHESS, Miniature	D.6607	1965-1973	250.00 to 340.00
UGLY DUCHESS, Small	D.6603	1965-1973	275.00

Ugly Duchess, Large, D.6599

Uncle Tom Cobbleigh is a character in a song from the 1800s which tells how he rode a horse to the Widdecombe Fair.

UNCLE TOM COBBLEIGH, Large D.6337   1952-1960   370.00 to 450.00

The character jug Uriah Heep was made only in the tiny size. The character, from the Dickens novel "David Copperfield," was part of the Dickens collection.

URIAH HEEP, Tiny   1983-Present   20.00

Veteran motorist represents the drivers of the motor cars of the pre-1905 period.

VETERAN MOTORIST, Large   D.6633   1973-Present   48.00 to 75.00
VETERAN MOTORIST, Miniature
                                  D.6641   1973-Present   19.00 to 30.00
VETERAN MOTORIST, Small   D.6637   1973-Present   29.00 to 50.00

Vicar of Bray is a character in an eighteenth-century song. He was a country parson.

VICAR OF BRAY, Large   D.5615   1936-1960   169.00 to 210.00
VICAR OF BRAY, Large, Marked A
                                  D.5615   1936-1960   165.00 to 190.00

Viking represents the Scandinavian seafarers of the eighth to tenth centuries.

VIKING, Large   D.6496   1959-1975   90.00 to 135.00
VIKING, Miniature   D.6526   1960-1975   107.00 to 125.00
VIKING, Small   D.6502   1959-1975   45.00 to 70.00

The famous American movie comedian W. C. Fields is pictured on a character jug first distributed by American Express. It is part of a series of movie star jugs.

W. C. FIELDS, Large*   D.6674   1982-Present   52.50 to 95.00

W. C. Fields, Large, D.6674; Mae West, Large, D.6688

Walrus & Carpenter, Large, D.6600

William Shakespeare, Large, D.6689;
Romeo, Large, D.6670

Walrus and Carpenter are characters in the book "Through the Looking Glass" by Lewis Carroll.

WALRUS & CARPENTER, Large* D.6600	1965–1979	49.50 to 135.00
WALRUS & CARPENTER, Miniature		
D.6608	1965–1979	23.50 to 40.00
WALRUS & CARPENTER, Small D.6604	1965–1979	30.00 to 50.00

The famous English playwright William Shakespeare is pictured with a quill pen handle.

WILLIAM SHAKESPEARE, Large*			
D.6689	1983–Present	45.00 to 75.00

Yachtsman represents the modern sailing man.

YACHTSMAN, Large	D.6622	1971–1979	65.00 to 95.00

Animals and Birds

Animal and bird figures have been an important part of the Royal Doulton line for many years. A few animal figures were made before 1912, but it was not until that date that Charles Noke's models were produced in great numbers. Very realistic figures of wild and domestic animals, stylized figures, and birds were made. Animal figurines were made and the same animals were used to decorate ashtrays, bookends, and other small pieces. This was done in much the same manner that the character jug designs were adapted to miscellaneous pieces.

Several special groups of animals have been made. The Championship Dog series started about 1939. They were realistic portrayals of champions of the breed and are listed in the catalogs with the abbreviation "Ch." at the beginning of each title. The HN numbers used were all between 1007 and 2667, although other types of animals are also included in these numbers. At least forty-one models have been made and many are still in production. Character dogs depict dogs playing, running, sitting, hunting, or in typical poses. Thirty-nine miniature dog, bird, cat, and rabbit models were made. Earthenware goats, calves, and deer modeled by Raoh Schorr were made in limited numbers about 1936. The Chatcull Range animals started in 1940. The Chatcull Range was named for Mr. Joe Ledger's home, Chatcull Hall. He was the artist who designed the animal figures for the series. These figures were given the HN numbers 2655 to 2666. Most of them are now out of production. A few whimsical figures were also made, such as the Huntsman Fox which depicts a fox dressed in a red hunting coat. Flambé animals and birds were made and are listed in the rouge flambé chapter. The Jefferson sculptures were designed by Robert Jefferson and produced in limited numbers after 1973.

ART SCULPTURES BY ROBERT JEFFERSON

Many of these figures are priced in the list beginning on page 202.

Figurine	HN Number	Date Issued	Edition Limit
Black-Throated Loon	3500	1974	150
Chipping Sparrow	3511	1976	200

Colorado Chipmunks	3506	1974	75
Downy Woodpecker	3509	1975	unlimited
Fledgling Bluebird	3510	1976	250
Golden-Crowned Kinglet	3504	1974	unlimited
Harbor Seals	3507	1975	75
King Eider	3502	1974	150
Puffins	2668	1974	250
Roseate Terns	3503	1974	150
Snowshoe Hares	3508	1975	75
Snowy Owl, Female	2670	1974	150
Snowy Owl, Male	2669	1974	150
White-Winged Cross Bills	3501	1974	250
Winter Wren	3505	1974	unlimited

CHATCULL RANGE

HN2655 Siamese Cat, sitting, 5½ In.
HN2656 Pine Marten, 4¼ In.
HN2657 Langur Monkey, 4⅜ In.
HN2658 White-Tailed Deer, 5⅝ In.
HN2659 Brown Bear, 4⅛ In.
HN2660 Siamese Cat, standing, 5 In.

HN2661 Mountain Sheep, 5¼ In.
HN2662 Siamese Cat, lying, 3¾ In.
HN2663 River Hog, 3½ In.
HN2664 Nyala Antelope, 5⅝ In.
HN2665 Llama, 6½ In.
HN2666 Badger, 3 In.

Numerical Model List

HN100	Fox, red frock coat	HN125	Guinea Fowl
HN101	Hare, red coat	HN126	Hare, crouching
HN102	Hare, white coat	HN127	Pekinese
HN103	Penguins, two	HN128	Puppy, sitting
HN104	Penguin	HN129	Bulldog, sitting
HN105	Alsatian, sable	HN130	Fox, sitting
HN106	Alsatian, white and sable	HN131	Kingfisher on rock
HN107	Hare, crouching	HN132	Drake on rock
HN108	Rabbit, one ear up	HN133	Penguins, two
HN109	Cat, sitting, white	HN134	Penguin
HN111	Cockerel on stand	HN135	Raven on rock
HN112	Alsatian, pale gray	HN136	Robin on rock
HN113	Penguin	HN137	Blue Tit on rock
HN114	Drake, green	HN138	Squirrel
HN115	Drake, blue	HN139	Falcon on rock
HN116	Drake, standing	HN140	Ape
HN117	Turtle Doves	HN141	Rhinoceros
HN118	Monkey	HN142	Hare, crouching
HN119	Polar Bear, sitting on green cube	HN143	Chaffinch on its back
		HN144	Wren
HN120	Cat, white	HN145	Yellow Finch, on rock, beak open
HN121	Polar Bear, sitting		
HN122	Turtle Doves, two	HN145A	Yellow Finch, on rock, beak closed
HN123	Pelican		
HN124	Cockerel, sitting	HN146	Bulldog, Old Bill, helmet and haversack
		HN147	Fox. Various models issued include model 12, Fox on rock, head down; model 14,

*Miniature
**Character
***Miniature Character

	Fox sitting, head up; model 15, Fox curled up; model 29A, Fox slinking.
HN148	Drakes, two
HN149	Swallow on rock
HN150	Duck
HN151	Rabbit
HN152	Kingfisher on rock
HN153	Bulldog, Old Bill, tammy and haversack
HN154	Cat**
HN155	Owl
HN156	Monkey, listening
HN157	Cockerel
HN158	Toucan
HN159	Toucan
HN160	Owl and Owlette
HN161	Thrush Chicks, four
HN162	Butterfly, blue and gold
HN163	Budgerigar on tree stump
HN164	Cockerel, crowing
HN165	Kingfisher on tree stump
HN166	Beagle, sitting
HN167	Tern Duck
HN168	Tern Drake
HN169	Owl
HN170	Brown Bear, Titanian Ware
HN171	Baby Birds, four
HN172	Buffalo
HN173	Owl, red cloak, ermine collar**
HN174	Unknown
HN175	Great Crested Grebe
HN176	Bloodhound
HN177	Powder bowl, small ape figure seated on lid
HN178	Cockerel, crouching
HN179	Foxes, two
HN180	Cockerel, crouching
HN181	Elephant
HN182	Monkey, green jacket**
HN183	Monkey, blue jacket**
HN184	Cockerel, crowing
HN185	Parrot on rock
HN186	Elephant
HN187	Owl, checkered shawl, ermine collar**
HN188	Duckling, yellow and brown
HN189	Duckling, black and yellow
HN190	Duckling, green and blue
HN191	Parrot, baby, blue and purple
HN192	Parrot, baby, red and orange
HN193	Tortoise
HN194	Terrier Puppy
HN195	Tern Duck

HN196	Toucan
HN197	Bird on rock
HN198	Penguin and Chick
HN199	Budgerigar on stand, green and yellow
HN200	Parrot, baby, enamel flowers
HN201	Cat, tabby, and Mouse
HN202	Cat, black, and Mouse
HN203	Cat, tortoiseshell, on pillar
HN204	Cat, tortoiseshell
HN205	Ducklings, black and white, two
HN206	Ducklings, brown and white, two
HN207	Mouse**
HN208	Toucan**
HN209	Rabbits, two, cuddling
HN210	Cat, black and white
HN211	Black-Headed Gull
HN212	Black-Headed Gull
HN213	Pigs, two
HN214	Bird and Chicks, black, pink and brown
HN215	Bird and Chicks, gray, blue and lemon
HN216	Bird and Chicks, green, blue and lemon
HN217	Rabbits, two, brown patches on faces
HN218	Rabbits, two, brown and black patches on faces
HN219	Rabbits, two, brown, black and yellow patches on faces
HN220	Bird on rock
HN221	Cat, black and white
HN222	Owl in boat**
HN223	Lion, sitting
HN224	Kingfisher on rock
HN225	Tiger, lying
HN226	Mouse, blue coat**
HN227	Cat, tabby, sleeping
HN228	Mouse, yellow coat**
HN229	Teal Duck
HN230	Not issued
HN231	St. Bernard
HN232	Puppy with bone
HN233	Kitten
HN234	Cats, two
HN235	Duckling
HN236	Baby Birds, two
HN237	Mouse with basketful of babies**
HN238	Pigs, two
HN239	Ducks, two
HN240	Bird on rock

HN241	Eagle, brown and gold
HN242	Eagle, white head and neck
HN243	Piggy Bowl
HN244	Cat, black and white, with Mouse
HN245	Cat, black, with Mouse
HN246	Pig**
HN247	Guinea Fowl
HN248	Drake, large
HN249	Mallard Drake, large
HN250	Heron
HN251	Heron
HN252	Drake, large
HN253	Ape, sitting
HN254	Apes, two
HN255	Not issued
HN256-66	Puffins and Penguins***
HN267	Cockerel, sitting
HN268	Kingfisher
HN269	Bluebird on rock
HN270	Brown Bear, sitting up
HN271	Duck
HN272	Bird with three Chicks
HN273	Rabbit
HN274	Bird, green
HN275	Birds, two, orange
HN276	Rabbit, one ear up
HN277	Wren
HN278	Birds, two, green
HN279	Bird on rock
HN280	Chicks, three
HN281	Yellow Bird on rock
HN282	Bluebird
HN283-93	Puffins and Penguins***
HN294	Toucan, black and white, red beak, large
HN295	Toucan, black and green, red beak, large
HN295A	Toucan, black and green, brown beak, large
HN296	Penguin
HN297	Penguin and Chick
HN298	Duck, sitting
HN299	Drake, lying
HN800	Pig, asleep
HN801	Pig, asleep, larger version
HN802	Pigs, two
HN803	Rabbit
HN804	Puppy, orange*
HN805	Puppy, green and purple*
HN806	Drake, white, 2⅜ in.*
HN807	Drake, green and purple, 2⅜ in.*
HN808-12	Puppies***
HN813	White Bird
HN814-15	Puppies***
HN818	Cat, Lucky, black and white**
HN819	Cat, Lucky, white***
HN820-25	Kittens*
HN826	Pup**
HN827	Cat, tortoiseshell**
HN828	Cat, tabby**
HN829	Cat, black and white**
HN830	Unknown
HN831	Beagle Puppy
HN832	Pekinese Puppy, sitting
HN833	Pekinese Puppy, standing
HN834	Pekinese Puppy, on stand, black and brown
HN835	Pekinese Puppy, on stand, light brown
HN836	Pekinese Puppy, on stand, light color
HN837	Chow, on stand, brown
HN838	Chow, on stand, light brown
HN839	Chow, on stand, white and gray
HN840-45	Ducks**
HN846	Toucan
HN847	Yellow Bird
HN848	Unknown
HN849	Ladybird and Duck
HN850	Duck, standing on rocks
HN851	Bird on tree stump
HN852	Penguin, standing on rocks
HN853	Drake, Mallard, on rocks, small
HN854	Budgerigar
HN855	Bird on tree stump
HN856	Penguin on rocks
HN857	Unknown
HN858	Kingfisher on rock
HN859	Tortoise on rocks
HN860	Bird on tree stump
HN861	Polar Bear
HN862A	Kingfisher, with primroses
HN862B	Kingfisher, with kingcups
HN863-65	Ducks, quacking**
HN866	Fox, sitting
HN867-74	Birds**
HN875	Kingfisher on tree stump

HN876	Tiger on rock
HN877	Parrot, baby
HN878	Cockerel, white
HN879	Cockerel, blue and green
HN880	Cockerel, brown and orange
HN881	Bulldog, sitting
HN882	Penguin, large
HN883	Monkeys, two
HN884	Cockatoo, blue and orange
HN885	Cockatoo, pink, purple and orange
HN886	Cockatoo, red, blue and orange
HN887	Unknown
HN888	Cockatoo, pale blue and yellow
HN889	Dog, Doberman, black and white
HN890	Dog, Doberman, brown
HN891	Elephant, gray, large
HN892-97	Pigs, clown costume**
HN898	Alsatian, head only
HN899	Alsatian, sitting
HN900	Fox Terrier, white and brown
HN901	Fox Terrier, white and black
HN902-3	Pigs**
HN904	Terrier Puppy
HN905	Frog
HN906	Spaniel Puppy, black and white
HN907	Spaniel Puppy, brown and white
HN908	Spaniel Puppy, head only
HN909	Fox Terrier, standing
HN910	Fox Terrier, sitting
HN911	Tiger, lying
HN912	Tiger, sitting
HN913-18	Toucan, bowls
HN919	Leopard, sitting
HN920	Foxes, two, brown
HN921	Alsatian, sitting, large
HN922	Hare**
HN923	Fox Terrier, standing
HN924	Fox Terrier, sitting, large
HN925	Foxes, two, gray and brown
HN926	Foxes, two*
HN927	Pekinese Dogs, two
HN928	Toucan, bowl
HN929	Terrier Puppy, sitting*
HN930	Alsatian, sitting*
HN931	Terrier Puppy*
HN932	Scottish Terrier*
HN933	Scottish Terrier*
HN934	Scottish Terrier*
HN935	Pip, Squeak and Wilfred ashtray
HN936	Teal, swimming
HN937	Alsatian, on stand
HN938	Alsatian, on stand, sitting
HN939	Brown Bears
HN940	Brown Bears, light brown
HN941	Elephant, black, large
HN942	Terrier
HN943	Terrier
HN944	Fox Terrier
HN945	Fox Terrier
HN946	Penguin Chick
HN947	Penguin Chick
HN948	Bulldog, brown, large
HN949-52	Elephants, baby
HN953	Terrier Puppy, brown and black
HN954	Terrier Puppy, dark brown and black
HN955	Brown Bear, standing
HN956	Mallard Drake, large
HN957	Spaniel, liver and white
HN958	Spaniel, black and white
HN959	Not issued
HN960	Ape with book, eyes open.** Also used for Raoh Schorr cerval.
HN961	Ape with book, eyes closed**
HN962	Terrier, head only
HN963	Fox, sitting
HN964	Scottish Terrier, black, large
HN965	Scottish Terrier, brown, large
HN966	Elephant, brown and gray, large. Also used for Raoh Schorr lynx.
HN967	Cat, tabby
HN968	Pig, black and white
HN969	Rabbits, two
HN970	Dachshund
HN971	Cat, Lucky, ashtray
HN972	Ape in dunce's cap, reading book**
HN973	Duck, orange**
HN974	Duck, lemon yellow**
HN975	Collie, silver gray
HN976	Collie, brown
HN977	Duck
HN978	Fox, lying
HN979	Hare, lying
HN980	Scottish Terrier, black
HN981	Scottish Terrier, light gray and brown

HN982	Sealyham Terrier, black patches on face
HN983	Sealyham Terrier, brown patches on face
HN984	Hare, lying, white
HN985	Hare, lying, gray
HN986	Alsatian, bowl
HN987	Bulldog, bowl
HN988	Airedale Terrier, brown
HN989	Sealyham Terrier, gray
HN990	Tiger, crouching
HN991	Tiger, crouching, smaller model
HN992	Sealyham Terrier, black
HN993	Cat, sleeping
HN994	Fox on pedestal. Also used for Raoh Schorr lamb.
HN995	Pekinese, brown. Also used for Raoh Schorr lamb.
HN996	Airedale Terrier, black, blue and brown
HN997	Terrier, seated, black and brown
HN998	Penguin and Chick
HN999	Cat, Persian, black and white
HN1000	Cocker Spaniel, Lucky Star of Ware, Champion, black, large
HN1001	Cocker Spaniel and Pheasant, 6½ in.
HN1002	Cocker Spaniel, liver and white, 6½ in.
HN1003	Pekinese
HN1004	Blue Tit
HN1005	Thrush
HN1006	Unknown
HN1007	Rough-haired Terrier, Crackley Startler, Champion
HN1008	Scottish Terrier, Albourne Arthur, Champion
HN1009	Hare and babies
HN1010	Pekinese, Biddee of Ifield, Champion, large
HN1011	Pekinese, Biddee of Ifield, Champion, medium
HN1012	Pekinese, Biddee of Ifield, Champion, 3⅛ in.
HN1013	Rough-haired Terrier, Crackley Startler, Champion, medium
HN1014	Rough-haired Terrier, Crackley Startler, Champion, 4 in.
HN1015	Scottish Terrier, Albourne Arthur, Champion, medium
HN1016	Scottish Terrier, Albourne Arthur, Champion, 3½ in.
HN1017	Scottish Terrier, sitting, black
HN1018	Scottish Terrier, sitting, black
HN1019	Scottish Terrier, sitting, black
HN1020	Cocker Spaniel, Lucky Star of Ware, Champion, black, 5 in.
HN1021	Cocker Spaniel, Lucky Star of Ware, Champion, 3½ in.
HN1022	Airedale Terrier, Cotsford Topsail, Champion, 8 in.
HN1023	Airedale Terrier, Cotsford Topsail, Champion, 5¼ in.
HN1024	Airedale Terrier, Cotsford Topsail, Champion, 3¾ in.
HN1025	Foxhound, Tring Rattler, Champion, large
HN1026	Foxhound, Tring Rattler, Champion, medium
HN1027	Foxhound, Tring Rattler, Champion, small
HN1028	Cocker Spaniel and Pheasant, liver and white, 5¼ in.
HN1029	Cocker Spaniel and Pheasant, 3¾ in.
HN1030	Sealyham, Scotia Stylist, Champion, large
HN1031	Sealyham, Scotia Stylist, Champion, medium
HN1032	Sealyham, Scotia Stylist, Champion, small
HN1033	Cairn, Charming Eyes, Champion, large
HN1034	Cairn, Charming Eyes, Champion, medium
HN1035	Cairn, Charming Eyes, Champion, 3¼ in.
HN1036	Cocker Spaniel, liver and white, 5 in.
HN1037	Cocker Spaniel, liver and white, 3½ in.
HN1038	Scottish Terrier, begging
HN1039	Pekinese, sitting, large
HN1040	Pekinese, sitting, small
HN1041	Sealyham, lying, large
HN1042	Bulldog, brindle, large
HN1043	Bulldog, brindle, medium
HN1044	Bulldog, brindle, small
HN1045	Bulldog, brown and white, large
HN1046	Bulldog, brown and white, medium
HN1047	Bulldog, brown and white, small

HN1048	West Highland Terrier, white, large
HN1049	English Setter, Maesydd Mustard, Champion, 8 in.
HN1050	English Setter, Maesydd Mustard, Champion, 5¼ in.
HN1051	English Setter, Maesydd Mustard, Champion, 3¾ in.
HN1052	Sealyham, lying, medium
HN1053	Sealyham, lying, small
HN1054	Irish Setter, 7½ in.
HN1055	Irish Setter, 5¼ in.
HN1056	Irish Setter, 3¾ in.
HN1057	Collie, Ashstead Applause, Champion, 7½ in.
HN1058	Collie, Ashstead Applause, Champion, 5 in.
HN1059	Collie, Ashstead Applause, Champion, 3½ in.
HN1060	Not issued
HN1061	Not issued
HN1062	Cocker Spaniel and Pheasant, black and white, 3¾ in.
HN1063	Cocker Spaniel and Hare, liver and white, medium
HN1064	Cocker Spaniel and Hare, liver and white, small
HN1065	Greyhound, brown, large
HN1066	Greyhound, brown, medium
HN1067	Greyhound, brown, small
HN1068	Smooth-haired Fox Terrier, large
HN1069	Smooth-haired Fox Terrier, medium
HN1070	Smooth-haired Fox Terrier, small
HN1071	Hare
HN1072	Bulldog, white, 5½ in.
HN1073	Bulldog, white, 4¾ in.
HN1074	Bulldog, white, 3 in.
HN1075	Greyhound, black and white, large
HN1076	Greyhound, black and white, medium
HN1077	Greyhound, black and white, small
HN1078	Cocker Spaniel, black and white, 3½ in.
HN1079	Gordon Setter, large
HN1080	Gordon Setter, medium
HN1081	Gordon Setter, small
HN1082	Tiger, stalking, large
HN1083	Tiger, stalking, medium
HN1084	Tiger, stalking, small
HN1085	Lion, large
HN1086	Lion, medium
HN1087-93A	Ashtrays
HN1094	Leopard
HN1095-95A	Ashtrays
HN1096	Fox with Goose, green cloak and hat**
HN1097	Dog, running with ball, 2¼ in.**
HN1098	Dog, on back**
HN1099	Dog, yawning, 4¼ in.**
HN1100	Dog, standing**
HN1101	Dog, lying down**
HN1102	Fox with Goose, red cloak and hat**
HN1103	Dog, with brown ball, 2½ in.**
HN1104	Cairn, black, large
HN1105	Cairn, black, medium
HN1106	Cairn, black, small
HN1107	Cairn, black, earthenware, large
HN1108	Cocker Spaniel, black and white, large
HN1109	Cocker Spaniel, black and white, 5 in.
HN1110	Not issued
HN1111	Dalmatian, Goworth Victor, Champion, large
HN1112	Lion, large
HN1113	Dalmatian, Goworth Victor, Champion, 5¾ in.
HN1114	Dalmatian, Goworth Victor, Champion, 5¾ in.
HN1115	Alsatian, Benign of Picardy, Champion, 8½ in.
HN1116	Alsatian, Benign of Picardy, Champion, 6¼ in.
HN1117	Alsatian, Benign of Picardy, Champion, 4¼ in.
HN1118	Tiger on rock, earthenware, large
HN1119	Lion on rock, earthenware, large
HN1120	Fighting Elephant, earthenware, large
HN1121	Elephant, large
HN1122	Elephant, large
HN1123	Elephant, medium
HN1124	Elephant, large
HN1125	Lion, on alabaster base
HN1126	Tiger, on alabaster base

HN1127	Dachshund, Shrewd Saint, Champion, large
HN1128	Dachshund, Shrewd Saint, Champion, 4 in.
HN1129	Dachshund, Shrewd Saint, Champion, 3 in.
HN1130	Fox, large
HN1131	Staffordshire Bull Terrier, large
HN1132	Staffordshire Bull Terrier, medium
HN1133	Staffordshire Bull Terrier, small
HN1134	Cocker Spaniel, liver and white, large
HN1135	Cocker Spaniel, liver and white, medium
HN1136	Cocker Spaniel, liver and white, small
HN1137	Cocker Spaniel and Pheasant, black and white, 6½ in.
HN1138	Cocker Spaniel and Pheasant, black and white, 5¼ in.
HN1139	Dachshund, large
HN1140	Dachshund, 4 in.
HN1141	Dachshund, 3 in.
HN1142	Bull Terrier, Bokus Brock, Champion, large
HN1143	Bull Terrier, Bokus Brock, Champion, medium
HN1144	Bull Terrier, Bokus Brock, Champion, small
HN1145	Moufflon, standing, green, Raoh Schorr
HN1146	Calf, sleeping, green, Raoh Schorr
HN1147	Calf, standing, green, Raoh Schorr
HN1148	Buffalo, green
HN1149	Donkey, green, small, Raoh Schorr
HN1150	Young Doe, green, Raoh Schorr
HN1151	Swiss Goat, green, Raoh Schorr
HN1152	Horse, green, Raoh Schorr
HN1153	Moufflon, lying, green, Raoh Schorr
HN1154	Goat, jumping, green, Raoh Schorr
HN1155	Donkey, green, large, Raoh Schorr
HN1156	Doe, green, Raoh Schorr
HN1157	Antelope, green, Raoh Schorr
HN1158	Dog, with plate, 3 in.**

HN1159	Dog, bone in mouth, 3¾ in.**
HN1160	Moufflon, standing, cream
HN1161	Calf, sleeping, cream
HN1162	Calf, standing, cream
HN1163	Buffalo, cream
HN1164	Donkey, cream, small
HN1165	Young Doe, cream, Raoh Schorr
HN1166	Swiss Goat, cream, Raoh Schorr
HN1167	Horse, cream, Raoh Schorr
HN1168	Moufflon, lying, cream, Raoh Schorr
HN1169	Goat, jumping, cream, Raoh Schorr
HN1170	Donkey, cream, large, Raoh Schorr
HN1171	Doe, cream, Raoh Schorr
HN1172	Antelope, cream, Raoh Schorr
HN1173	Calf, sleeping, Raoh Schorr
HN1174	Calf, standing, Raoh Schorr
HN1175	Buffalo, Raoh Schorr
HN1176	Donkey, small
HN1177	Young Doe, Raoh Schorr
HN1178	Swiss Goat, Raoh Schorr
HN1179	Moufflon, standing, Raoh Schorr
HN1180	Horse, Raoh Schorr
HN1181	Moufflon, lying, Raoh Schorr
HN1182	Goat, jumping, Raoh Schorr
HN1183	Donkey, large, Raoh Schorr
HN1184	Doe, Raoh Schorr
HN1185	Antelope, Raoh Schorr
HN1186	Cocker Spaniel, golden, large
HN1187	Cocker Spaniel, golden, 5 in.
HN1188	Cocker Spaniel, golden, small
HN1189	King Penguin, 7⅜ in.
HN1190	Penguin, 7¾ in.
HN1191	Mallard, 5½ in.
HN1192	Duck, 3½ in.
HN1193	Tern, 2½ in.
HN1194	Tern, 2½ in.
HN1195	Seagull, 3¾ in.
HN1196	Seagull, 3¾ in.
HN1197	Gannet, 6½ in.
HN1198	Drake
HN1199	Penguin
HN1200	Unknown
HN1829	Macaw
HN2500	Cerval, Raoh Schorr, also numbered 960.
HN2501	Lynx, Raoh Schorr, also numbered 966.
HN2502	Deer, green, Raoh Schorr,

also numbered 944.
HN2502 is also used for
Queen Elizabeth II.

HN2503   Lamb, white, Raoh Schorr,
also numbered 994.

HN2504   Lamb, green, Raoh Schorr,
also numbered 995.

HN2505   Lamb, white, Raoh Schorr,
also numbered 995.

HN2506   Asiatic Elephant

HN2507   Zebu Cow

HN2508   Dog, head turned**

HN2509   Dog, standing**

HN2510   Dog, running, tail up**

HN2511   Dog, standing, tail straight**

HN2512   Smooth-haired Terrier,
Chosen Dan of Notts,
Champion, large.
Also known as Don of Notts.

HN2513   Smooth-haired Terrier,
Chosen Dan of Notts,
Champion, medium. Also
known as Don of Notts.

HN2514   Smooth-haired Terrier,
Chosen Dan of Notts,
Champion, small.
Also known as Don of Notts.

HN2515   Springer Spaniel, Dry Toast,
Champion, large

HN2516   Springer Spaniel, Dry Toast,
Champion, medium

HN2517   Springer Spaniel, Dry Toast,
Champion, small

HN2518   Pride of the Shires, Mare and
Foal, brown

HN2519   Gude Gray Mare and Foal, 5
in.

HN2520   Farmer's Boy, Dappled Shire,
8½ in.

HN2521   Dapple Gray, with girl

HN2522   Chestnut Mare and Foal, 6½
in.

HN2523   Pride of the Shires, Mare and
Foal, dapple gray

HN2524   American Foxhound, large

HN2525   American Foxhound, medium

HN2526   American Foxhound, small

HN2527   Fox, sitting

HN2528   Mare and Foal, Pride of the
Shires, 9 in., replaces
HN2518.

HN2529   English Setter and Pheasant,
8 in.

HN2530   Merely a Minor, brown, 12
in.

HN2531   Merely a Minor, gray, 12 in.

HN2532   Gude Gray Mare and Foal,
medium

HN2533   Chestnut Mare and Foal,
small

HN2534   Pride of the Shires, Mare and
Foal, brown, small

HN2535   Tiger on rock

HN2536   Pride of the Shires, Mare and
Foal, gray, small

HN2537   Merely a Minor, brown,
medium

HN2538   Merely a Minor, gray,
medium

HN2539   Cat, Persian, white

HN2540   Kingfisher

HN2541   Kingfisher, 3¼ in.

HN2542   Baltimore Oriole

HN2543   Bluebird, 5¾ in. This number
was also used for Eliza.

HN2544   Drake Mallard. This number
was also used for A La
Mode.

HN2545   Pheasant. This number was
also used for Carmen.

HN2546   Yellow-Throated Warbler,
4½ in. This number was also
used for Buddies.

HN2547   Budgerigars, two

HN2548   Golden-Crested Wren

HN2549   Robin

HN2550   Chaffinch, 2¼ in.

HN2551   Bullfinch

HN2552   Thrushes, baby, two

HN2553   Robins, baby

HN2554   Cardinal. This number was
also used for Masque.

HN2555   Drake Mallard, 6 in.

HN2556   Mallard

HN2557   Welsh Corgi, Spring Robin,
Champion, large

HN2558   Welsh Corgi, Spring Robin,
Champion, medium

HN2559   Welsh Corgi, Spring Robin,
Champion, 3⅝ in.

HN2560   Great Dane, Rebeller of
Ouborough, Champion, large

HN2561   Great Dane, Rebeller of
Ouborough, Champion,
medium

HN2562   Great Dane, Rebeller of
Ouborough, Champion, small

HN2563   Pride of the Shires, brown,
large

HN2564	Pride of the Shires, brown, medium
HN2565	Chestnut Mare, 6 in.
HN2566	Chestnut Mare, small
HN2567	Merely a Minor, gray, small
HN2568	Gude Gray Mare, large
HN2569	Gude Gray Mare, medium
HN2570	Gude Gray Mare, small
HN2571	Merely a Minor, brown, small
HN2572	Drake Mallard, small
HN2573	Kingfisher, small
HN2574	Seagull, small
HN2575	Swan, small
HN2576	Pheasant, small
HN2577	Peacock
HN2578	Farmer's Boy, Dappled Shire, no boy, 8½ in.
HN2579	Kitten lying on back, 1½ in.**
HN2580	Kitten licking hind paw, 2 in.**
HN2581	Kitten sleeping, 1½ in.**
HN2582	Kitten sitting up, 2¾ in.**
HN2583	Kitten licking front paw, 2 in.**
HN2584	Kitten, crouching, 1¾ in.**
HN2585	Pup in basket, lying, 2 in.**
HN2586	Pup in basket, Cocker, chewing handle, 2½ in.**
HN2587	Pup in basket, Terrier, 3 in.**
HN2588	Puppies in basket, three Terriers, 3¼ in.**
HN2589	Cairn, begging, 4 in.**
HN2590	Cocker Spaniels, sleeping, 1¾ in.**
HN2591	Drake Mallard
HN2592	Hare**
HN2593	Hare, lying, ears alert**
HN2594	Hare, lying, feet stretched out, 1¾ in.**
HN2595-98	Lambs**
HN2599	English Setter and Pheasant
HN2600	Cocker Spaniel and Pheasant, small
HN2601	American Great Dane, large
HN2602	American Great Dane, medium
HN2603	American Great Dane, small
HN2604	Peacock Butterfly
HN2605	Camberwell Beauty Butterfly
HN2606	Swallowtail Butterfly
HN2607	Red Admiral Butterfly
HN2608	Copper Butterfly
HN2609	Tortoiseshell Butterfly
HN2610	Hen Pheasant
HN2611	Chaffinch
HN2612	Baltimore Oriole
HN2613	Golden-Crested Wren
HN2614	Bluebird
HN2615	Cardinal
HN2616	Bullfinch
HN2617	Robin
HN2618	Yellow-Throated Warbler
HN2619	Grouse
HN2620	English Setter, liver and white, large
HN2621	English Setter, liver and white, medium
HN2622	English Setter, liver and white, small
HN2623	Farmer's Boy, no boy, brown, 8½ in.
HN2624	Pointer, 5⅜ in.
HN2625	Poodle, large
HN2626	Poodle, medium
HN2627	Poodle, small
HN2628	Chow, large
HN2629	Chow, medium
HN2630	Chow, small
HN2631	French Poodle, 5¼ in.
HN2632	Cock Pheasant, Prestige Figure, 6¾ X 11 in.
HN2634	Fox sitting, Prestige Figure. Number also used for Pheasant.
HN2635	Mallard, large
HN2636	Drake, Indian Runner
HN2637	Polar Bear
HN2638	Leopard on rock, Prestige Figure
HN2639	Tiger on rock, Prestige Figure
HN2640	Fighter Elephant, Prestige Figure, 12½ in.
HN2641	Lion on rock, Prestige Figure
HN2642	Squirrel
HN2643	Boxer, Warlord of Mazelaine, Champion, 6½ in.
HN2644	Elephant, 5½ in.
HN2645	Doberman Pinscher, Rancho Dobe's Storm, 6¼ in.
HN2646	Tiger
HN2647	Drake
HN2648	Pig, lying, head up, 1¾ in.**
HN2649	Pig, standing, 1½ in.**
HN2650	Pig, lying, 1¼ in.**
HN2651	Pig, lying on side, 1 in.**
HN2652	Pig, sitting, 2 in.**
HN2653	Pig, nose down, 1½ in.**

HN2654	Dog, slipper in mouth, 3¼ in.**	HN2670	Snowy Owl, female, Jefferson Sculpture
HN2655	Siamese Cat, sitting, Chatcull Range, 5½ in.	HN3500	Black-Throated Lion, Jefferson Sculpture
HN2656	Pine Marten, Chatcull Range, 4¼ in.	HN3501	White-Winged Crossbills, Jefferson Sculpture
HN2657	Langur Monkey, Chatcull Range, 4⅜ in.	HN3502	King Eider, Jefferson Sculpture
HN2658	White-Tailed Deer, Chatcull Range, 5⅝ in.	HN3503	Roseate Terns, Jefferson Sculpture
HN2659	Brown Bear, Chatcull Range, 4⅛ in.	HN3504	Golden-Crowned Kinglet, Jefferson Sculpture
HN2660	Siamese Cat, standing, Chatcull Range, 5 in.	HN3505	Winter Wren, Jefferson Sculpture
HN2661	Mountain Sheep, Chatcull Range, 5¼ in.	HN3506	Colorado Chipmunks, Jefferson Sculpture
HN2662	Siamese Cat, lying, Chatcull Range, 3¾ in.	HN3507	Harbor Seals, Jefferson Sculpture
HN2663	River Hog, Chatcull Range, 3½ in.	HN3508	Snowshoe Hares, Jefferson Sculpture
HN2664	Nyala Antelope, Chatcull Range, 5⅝ in.	HN3509	Downy Woodpecker, Jefferson Sculpture
HN2665	Llama, Chatcull Range, 6½ in.	HN3510	Fledgling Bluebird, Jefferson Sculpture
HN2666	Badger, Chatcull Range, 3 in.	HN3511	Chipping Sparrow, Jefferson Sculpture
HN2667	Black Labrador, Bumblikite of Manserge, Champion, 5 in.	HN6448	Huntsman Fox, 1½ in.
HN2668	Puffins, Jefferson Sculpture		
HN2669	Snowy Owl, male, Jefferson Sculpture		

K numbers—Miniatures

1	Bulldog, sitting 2¼ in.	16	Welsh Corgi, standing, 2¼ in.
2	Bull Pup, sitting, 1¾ in.	17	Dachshund, standing, 2 in.
3	Sealyham, 2¾ in.	18	Scottish Terrier, sitting, 2¼ in.
4	Sealyham	19	St. Bernard, lying, 1¾ in.
5	Airedale	20	Penguin and Chick, 2¼ in.
6	Pekinese, sitting, 2 in.	21	Penguin, yellow stripe on head, wings together, 2 in.
7	Foxhound, sitting, 2½ in.		
8	Terrier, sitting, 2½ in.	22	Penguin, yellow stripe on head, head down, 1¾ in.
9	Cocker Spaniel, sitting, one paw up, 2½ in.	23	Penguin, beak nearly touching toes, 1¼ in.
10	Scottish Terrier, sitting up, 3 in.	24	Penguin, head down, one wing up, 1¾ in.
11	Cairn, sitting, 2½ in.		
12	Kitten, laughing, 2¾ in.	25	Penguin, looking to side, 2¼ in.
13	Alsatian, 3 in.		
14	Bull Terrier	26	Mallard
15	Chow Chow, standing, 2¼ in.		

27	Yellow-Throated Warbler	35	Jay
28	Cardinal Bird	36	Goldfinch
29	Baltimore Oriole	37	Hare, lying down, 1¼ in.
30	Bluebird	38	Hare, sitting up, ears down,
31	Bullfinch		2¼ in.
32	Budgerigar	39	Hare, sitting up, ears up, 2¾
33	Golden-Crested Wren		in.
34	Magpie		

Alphabetical Price List

AIREDALE	HN 1024	127.00
AIREDALE, Cotsford Topsail	HN 1023	52.00 to 95.00
ALSATIAN, Benign Of Picardy, Large	HN 1115	300.00
ALSATIAN, Benign Of Picardy, Medium*	HN 1116	95.00
ALSATIAN, Benign Of Picardy, Small	HN 1117	85.00
BALTIMORE ORIOLE, 5 X 4 In.*	HN 2542	37.00
BIRD, Yellow	HN 145	95.00
BOXER, Warlord Of Mazelaine	HN 2643	60.00 to 95.00
BROWN BEAR, Chatcull Range	HN 2659	95.00 to 195.00
BULLDOG, Brindle, Medium	HN 1043	135.00 to 175.00
BULLDOG, Brindle, Small	HN 1044	125.00
BULLDOG, Brown & White, Small	HN 1047	38.00 to 60.00
BULLDOG, White, Medium	HN 1073	225.00
BULLDOG, White, Small	HN 1074	38.00 to 60.00
CAIRN, Charming Eyes, Medium	HN 1034	150.00
CAIRN, Charming Eyes, Small	HN 1035	38.00 to 60.00
CAIRN, 2 1/2 In.	K 11	35.00
CAT, Shadowplay, Images Of Nature	HN 3526	75.00
CHARACTER CAT, Lucky	HN 818	45.00
CHARACTER DOG, Ball In Mouth	HN 1103	20.00 to 70.00
CHARACTER DOG, Eating	HN 1158	20.00 to 70.00
CHARACTER DOG, Running With Ball	HN 1099	20.00 to 35.00
CHARACTER DOG, Slipper In Mouth	HN 2654	27.00 to 35.00
CHARACTER DOG, With Bone	HN 1159	23.00 to 35.00
CHARACTER DOG, Yawning	HN 1097	23.00 to 35.00
COCKER SPANIEL	K 9	35.00
COCKER SPANIEL & PHEASANT, Large	HN 1001	180.00 to 200.00
COCKER SPANIEL & PHEASANT, Large	HN 1137	225.00
COCKER SPANIEL & PHEASANT, Medium	HN 1028	65.00 to 110.00
COCKER SPANIEL & PHEASANT, Medium	HN 1138	65.00 to 110.00
COCKER SPANIEL & PHEASANT, Small*	HN 1029	100.00
COCKER SPANIEL, Black & White, Large	HN 1108	195.00 to 275.00
COCKER SPANIEL, Black & White, Medium		
	HN 1109	60.00 to 95.00
COCKER SPANIEL, Black & White, Small	HN 1078	75.00
COCKER SPANIEL, Black, Large	HN 1000	195.00 to 225.00
COCKER SPANIEL, Light Brown, Large	HN 1186	235.00

Cocker Spaniel & Pheasant, Small, HN 1029; Alsatian, Benign Of Picardy, Medium, HN 1116

Baltimore Oriole, 5 X 4 In., HN 2542

COCKER SPANIEL,	Light Brown, Medium	HN 1187	60.00 to 95.00
COCKER SPANIEL,	Light Brown, Small	HN 1188	65.00
COCKER SPANIEL,	Liver & White, Large	HN 1002	195.00 to 250.00
COCKER SPANIEL,	Liver & White, Medium	HN 1036	60.00 to 95.00
COCKER SPANIEL,	Liver & White, Small	HN 1037	65.00 to 115.00
COCKER SPANIEL,	Lucky Pride, Small	HN 1021	65.00 to 75.00
COCKER SPANIEL,	Lucky Star Of Ware	HN 1020	60.00 to 95.00
COCKER SPANIELS,	Sleeping	HN 2590	35.00 to 50.00
COLLIE,	Ashstead Applause, Large	HN 1057	275.00
COLLIE,	Ashstead Applause, Medium	HN 1058	60.00 to 95.00
COLLIE,	Ashstead Applause, Small	HN 1059	65.00 to 95.00
DACHSHUND,	Shrewd Saint, Medium	HN 1128	39.00 to 95.00
DACHSHUND,	2 3/8 In.	K 17	18.00 to 25.00
DACHSHUND,	3 In.	HN 1141	115.00
DACHSHUND,	4 In.	HN 1140	152.00
DALMATIAN,	Goworth Victor, Medium	HN 1113	55.00 to 95.00
DALMATIAN,	Goworth Victor, Small	HN 1114	75.00 to 120.00
DOBERMAN PINSCHER,	Rancho Dobe's Storm		
		HN 2645	55.00 to 95.00

DOLPHINS, Images Of Nature	HN 3522	75.00
DRAKE, Mallard	HN 2591	50.00
DRAKE, Purple, Miniature	HN 807	25.00
DRAKE, White, Miniature	HN 806	50.00
ELEPHANT	HN 2644	50.00 to 100.00
ELEPHANT, Fighting, Prestige	HN 2640	1080.00 to 1450.00
ENGLISH SETTER & PHEASANT, 8 In.	HN 2529	187.50 to 395.00
ENGLISH SETTER, Maesydd Mustard, Large		
	HN 1049	275.00
ENGLISH SETTER, Maesydd Mustard, Medium		
	HN 1050	50.00 to 95.00
ENGLISH SETTER, Maesydd Mustard, Small		
	HN 1051	75.00 to 120.00
FLEDGLING BLUEBIRD, Jefferson, 6 In.	HN 3510	600.00
FOX ON ROCK, Brown & Tan, 4 3/4 In.	HN 147	85.00 to 135.00
FOX TERRIER, Crackley Hunter, Medium	HN 1013	135.00
FOX TERRIER, Crackley Hunter, Small*	HN 1014	25.00 to 60.00
FOX TERRIER, Smooth-Haired, Medium	HN 1069	190.00
FOX, Red Frock Coat	HN 100	200.00
FOX, Sitting, Prestige	HN 2634	350.00 to 750.00
FOXHOUND, Tring Rattler, Medium	HN 1026	225.00
FOXHOUND, 2 3/8 In.	HN 7	18.00
FRENCH POODLE	HN 2631	40.00 to 95.00
GEESE, Flying, Images Of Nature	HN 3527	50.00
GOLDEN-CRESTED WREN*	HN 2613	125.00
GOLDEN-CROWNED KINGLET, Jefferson	HN 3504	525.00
GREYHOUND, Black & White, Small	HN 1077	125.00 to 198.00
GREYHOUND, Brown, Medium	HN 1066	190.00
GREYHOUND, Brown, Small	HN 1077	325.00
GUDE GRAY MARE, Medium	HN 2569	225.00
HARBOR SEALS, Jefferson, 8 1/2 In.	HN 3507	1600.00
HARE, Lying, Small	HN 2594	25.00 to 35.00
HARE, Lying, 7 In.	HN 2593	175.00
HORSE, Merely A Minor	HN 2567	315.00
HUNTSMAN FOX	HN 6448	19.00 to 40.00
IRISH SETTER, Medium*	HN 1055	55.00 to 95.00
IRISH SETTER, Small	HN 1056	55.00 to 70.00
EIDER, Jefferson, 11 In.	HN 3502	1800.00
KINGFISHER, On Rock	HN 131	125.00
KINGFISHER, Small	HN 2573	125.00
KITTEN, Licking Front Paw	HN 2583	25.00 to 35.00
KITTEN, Licking Hind Paw	HN 2580	22.00 to 35.00
KITTEN, Lying, Licking Front Paws	HN 2579	25.00 to 35.00
KITTEN, Sitting	HN 2584	22.00 to 35.00
KITTEN, Sitting Up	HN 2582	22.00 to 35.00
KITTEN, Sleeping	HN 2581	22.00 to 35.00
LABRADOR, Bumblikite Of Manserge, Medium		
	HN 2667	55.00 to 95.00
LANGUR MONKEY, Chatcull Range, 4 3/8 In.		
	HN 2657	150.00

Golden-Crested Wren HN 2613   *Peacock HN 2577*

LEOPARD ON ROCK, Prestige	HN 2638	1200.00 to 1650.00
LION ON ROCK, Prestige	HN 2641	907.00 to 1650.00
MALLARD DRAKE, 6 In.	HN 956	195.00
MARE & FOAL, Images Of Nature	HN 3524	175.00
MOUNTAIN GOAT, Images Of Nature	HN 3523	50.00
NYALA ANTELOPE, Chatcull Range	HN 2664	125.00 to 200.00
PEACOCK*	HN 2577	80.00
PEKINESE, Biddee Of Ifield, Small	HN 1012	25.00 to 95.00
PEKINESE, Biddie Of Ifield, Medium	HN 1011	230.00
PEKINESE, 2 In.	K 6	2020.00
PENGUIN, 1 3/4 In.	K 24	140.00
PENGUIN, 2 1/4 In.	K 25	140.00
PENGUIN AND CHICK, 2 1/4 In.	K 20	140.00
PERSIAN CAT, Black & White	HN 999	33.00 to 55.00
PHEASANT	HN 2545	225.00 to 275.00
PHEASANT, Prestige Figure	HN 2632	229.00 to 495.00
PIG, Asleep, Medium	HN 800	95.00
PIG, Lying	HN 2650	45.00
PIG, Nose Down	HN 2653	45.00
POINTER	HN 2624	150.00 to 295.00
POLAR BEAR	HN 119	150.00
PRIDE OF THE SHIRES, Brown, Medium	HN 2564	200.00
PUFFINS, Jefferson, 11 In.	HN 2668	1600.00
PUPPIES IN BASKET	HN 2588	22.50 to 50.00
PUPPY IN BASKET, 2 In.	HN 2585	30.00 to 50.00
PUPPY IN BASKET, 2 1/2 In.	HN 2586	30.00 to 50.00
PUPPY IN BASKET, 3 In.	HN 2587	30.00 to 50.00
RIVER HOG, Chatcull Range	HN 2663	40.00 to 200.00
ROSEATE TERNS, Jefferson, 12 1/4 In.	HN 3503	2500.00
SCOTCH TERRIER, Albourne Arthur, Medium		
	HN 1015	150.00
SCOTCH TERRIER, Albourne Arthur, Small	HN 1016	25.00 to 60.00
SCOTCH TERRIER, 3 In.	K 10	45.00
SEAGULL	HN 2574	125.00
SEALYHAM, Scotia Stylist, Medium	HN 1031	150.00 to 165.00
SIAMESE CAT, Lying, Chatcull Range	HN 2662	42.00 to 70.00

Fox Terrier, Crackley Hunter, Small, HN 1014; Springer Spaniel, Dry Toast, Small, HN 2517; Irish Setter, Medium, HN 1055

SIAMESE CAT, Sitting, Chatcull Range	HN 2655	42.00 to 70.00
SIAMESE CAT, Standing, Chatcull Range	HN 2660	42.00 to 70.00
SNOWSHOE HARES, Jefferson, 13 In.	HN 3508	2750.00
SNOWY OWL, Female, Jefferson, 9 1/2 In.	HN 2670	215.00
SNOWY OWL, Male, Jefferson, 16 In.	HN 2669	1750.00
SPRINGER SPANIEL, Dry Toast, Medium	HN 2516	150.00
SPRINGER SPANIEL, Dry Toast, Small*	HN 2517	60.00 to 95.00
ST. BERNARD	K 19	22.00 to 77.00
TERRIER, Seated, Black & Brown	HN 997	195.00
TIGER ON ROCK, Prestige Figure	HN 2639	1200.00 to 1650.00
TIGER, Prestige Figure	HN 2646	850.00 to 950.00
WELSH CORGI	K 16	20.00
WELSH CORGI, Medium	HN 2558	110.00 to 200.00
WHITE-WINGED CROSSBILLS, Jefferson	HN 3501	1450.00
WHITE-TAILED DEER, Chatcull Range	HN 2658	175.00
WINTER WREN, Jefferson, 4 3/4 In.	HN 3505	3750.00

Limited Editions

The term "limited edition" has had a special meaning since the early 1970s when many companies including the Doulton Company began making plates and other pieces in announced limited numbers. Before this time, the Doulton factory made special commemorative jugs and presentation pieces that we would refer to as limited editions. The first of these was a jug called "Regency Coach" made in 1931 and limited to 500 pieces. Each piece was signed and numbered. The jugs were made with three-dimensional scenes picturing people and places.

Some limited edition black basalt loving cups were made during the 1970s. Limited edition busts, loving cups, and jugs were also made commemorating royal events such as weddings and coronations. Limited pieces listed in other chapters of this book include several character jugs, figurines that are listed in the figurines chapter, and Jefferson bird sculptures, listed in animals and birds.

The modern limited edition plates, tankards, and plaques were first made in 1972. They are included in the price list by title and year.

Three trial limited edition jugs have been mentioned in the records—the Jackdaw of Rheims that is known to have been made at least once, and two other possible jugs, I. T. Wigg, Broom-man, and Roger Solemel, Cobbler.

Complete Limited Editions Price List

In 1979 Royal Doulton started issuing the cherub bells, or Speech of Angels, series of bells. The series is limited to 5,000 a year.

BELL, Speech Of Angels, Glad Tidings	1980	95.00
Speech Of Angels, Glory	1983	100.00
Speech Of Angels, Joy	1982	100.00
Speech Of Angels, Peace	1981	95.00

A black basalt bust of Sir Winston Churchill was issued in 1974 to commemorate the centenary of his birth in 1874. The issue was limited to 750.

BUST, Winston Churchill   325.00 to 550.00

One hundred and fifty copies of a limited edition black basalt bust of Prince Charles were made to commemorate his investiture as Prince of Wales in 1969.

BUST, Prince Charles   625.00

A limited edition black basalt bust of Princess Anne was made in 1973 to commemorate her marriage to Captain Mark Phillips. There were 750 busts made.

BUST, Princess Anne   550.00 to 625.00

A pair of busts of Queen Elizabeth and the Duke of Edinburgh was made to commemorate the silver wedding anniversary of the royal couple on November 20, 1972. The 10 1/2-inch black basalt busts were made in a limited edition of 1,000.

BUST, Queen Elizabeth   625.00 to 1250.00
Duke Of Edinburgh   625.00

The Joy to the World nativity cup and saucer series, limited to 10,000 a year, was started in 1980.

CUP & SAUCER, Joy To World,
    Annunciation   1980   55.00
Joy To World, Bethlehem Journey   1983   60.00
Joy To World, Shepherds In Fields   1982   60.00

The egg series was started by Royal Doulton in 1979; 3,500 eggs are issued each year.

EGG, Minton Emperor's Garden   1982   95.00
Minton 19th Century*   1979   75.00
Royal Crown Derby   1981   175.00
Royal Doulton Rouge Flambe   1980   100.00

The limited edition Twelve Days of Christmas goblet series started with the Partridge in a Pear Tree in 1980; 10,000 goblets are made each year. The series will consist of a dozen goblets.

GOBLET, Twelve Days Of Christmas,
    French Hens   1982   60.00
Twelve Days Of Christmas, Partridge   1980   55.00 to 60.00
Twelve Days Of Christmas, Turtle Doves   1981   60.00
Twelve Days Of Christmas, Calling Birds   1983   60.00

Captain Arthur Phillip was a member of the British navy. He is best remembered for his work with the first penal colony in South Wales, founded in 1786. The jug shows his ship, the Sirius. On the bottom are the words "Colony New

Egg, Minton, 19th Century

Jug, Captain Phillip

South Wales Founded January 1788 Sydney." There were 350 of these jugs issued in 1938.

JUG, Captain Phillip*   1938   1800.00 to 2000.00

The Charles Dickens jug was made in 1936. The author is shown as a mask at the lip of the jug. Many characters from his novels are pictured on the sides. Raised letters on the base say "Lord Keep My Memory Green." One thousand of the 10 1/2-inch-high jugs were made.

JUG, Charles Dickens*   1936   750.00

The Dickens Dream jug was not issued as a limited edition but few were made and it is estimated that only 1,000 were produced. The jug shows Dickens daydreaming as dozens of characters from his novels appear above his head. The handle is Poor Jo. The inscription below the bust of Dickens is "Keep My Memory Green." The 10 1/2-inch jugs were issued in 1933.

JUG, Dickens Dream**   1933   700.00

Sir Francis Drake led an expedition around the world in 1577 and returned to England with treasures for the Queen. He later fought the Spanish Armada, after finishing his game of bowls because he felt there was time to finish the game and win the battle as well. The jug pictures these two events. Drake, the Queen, and other Elizabethans are pictured. Below the lip of the jug is part of a poem about Drake's Drum. Five hundred jugs were made in this 1933 limited edition.

JUG, Drake*   1933   550.00

George Washington, first President of the United States, was born in 1732. In 1932 a limited edition jug was issued honoring the bicentenary of his birth. The jug shows Washington in front of the Capitol with a group of citizens on one side. The other side pictures a view of Washington in military uniform with other soldiers. Around the base are the words "Declaration of Independence." Although 1,000 of the jugs were announced, less than that number were made.

JUG, George Washington*	1932	225.00

In 1605 Guy Fawkes was caught in a cellar under the Parliament house with a pile of gunpowder and coal. He was arrested and eventually revealed the plot to blow up Parliament. The jug, issued in 1934, commemorated the event. One side shows Guy Fawkes, the other Sir Thomas Knyvet, his captor. The 7 1/2-inch-high jug was made in a limited edition of 600.

JUG, Guy Fawkes	1934	575.00 to 650.00

A trial jug is known picturing Jackdaw of Rheims. The jug has the raised figures typical of the limited edition jugs. Around the border is written "Bishop and abbot and prior were there/And off that terrible curse he took." Do not confuse this jug with the more common Jackdaw of Rheims series ware pieces. It is not known if more than one of these jugs were made.

JUG, Jackdaw Of Rheims*		N.A.

The Master of Foxhounds Presentation Jug is one of the strangest of all Royal Doulton jugs. The spout is the head of a rooster, the jug pictures a fox dressed in a jacket hiding from a group of hounds. The 13-inch-high jug was made in 1930 in a limited edition of 500. The bottom is marked "M.F.H. Presentation Jug."

JUG, M.F.H. Presentation, 13 1/2 In.*	1930	600.00

"The Pied Piper of Hamelin" is a poem written by Robert Browning in 1845. The story is pictured on the jug with the piper leading the children from town. The jug, made in a limited edition of 600 in 1934, is 10 inches high.

JUG, Pied Piper	1934	600.00

The horse-drawn coach was the best means of travel in England during the time of the Regency, from 1811 to 1820. The jug shows the coach driving up to an inn and a lady and children near a house. The jug, 10 inches high, was made in a limited edition of 500 in 1931.

JUG, Regency Coach*	1931	420.00 to 750.00

The William Shakespeare jug pictures characters from the author's plays. Books, comedy and tragedy masks, and the words "Great Heir of Fame Dear Son of Memory" complete the design. The jug was made in 1933. One thousand of the 10 1/2-inch-high jugs were made.

JUG, Shakespeare*	1933	250.00 to 650.00

In 1933 Royal Doulton made a jug, limited to 500, depicting the Tower of London. Yeomen of the Guard are shown on one side, and a lord and lady with Yeomen on the other. The jug is 9 1/2 inches high.

Jug, M.F.H. Presentation,
13 1/2 In.

Jug, Regency Coach   *Jug, George Washington*

JUG, Tower Of London   1933   675.00 to 785.00

The Robert Louis Stevenson novel "Treasure Island" has been read since 1881.
The jug shows the pirates burying treasure and Long John Silver and Jim
Hawkins. Palm trees form the spout and handle. The 7 1/2-inch-high jug was
made in 1934 in a limited edition of 600. The bottom of the jug shows the
treasure map.

JUG, Treasure Island*   1934   600.00

"The Village Blacksmith" is a poem by Henry Wadsworth Longfellow of Maine.
The jug pictures the blacksmith and the group of children described in the
poem. The jug, limited to 600 copies, was issued in 1936. It is 7 1/2 inches high.

JUG, Village Blacksmith*   1936   550.00

The apothecary of Elizabethan times is pictured on this limited edition cup. Six
hundred were made in 1934. The 6-inch cup has a special design on the bottom
which says "The Apothecary/O True Apothecary Thy Drugs are Quick."

Jug, Treasure Island   *Jug, Drake*

LOVING CUP, Apothecary   1934   535.00

In 1933 a limited edition of 350 loving cups was issued honoring Captain James Cook. The cup commemorates Cook's landing at Botany Bay. The crew are landing in a longboat in one scene, Captain Cook is shown in another. The two handles are draped with flags. The cup is 9 1/2 inches high.

LOVING CUP, Captain Cook   1933   *3000.00*

In 1970 Royal Doulton produced a limited edition of 500 black basalt loving cups honoring Captain Cook.

LOVING CUP, Captain Cook, Basalt   285.00

A black basalt loving cup honoring Charles Dickens was made in a limited edition of 500 in 1970. It was issued at $285.

LOVING CUP, Charles Dickens, Basalt   1970   285.00

Edward VIII would have been crowned king in 1937, but he abdicated and became the Duke of Windsor. The loving cup pictures Edward and has the words "Edward VIII God Save the King." The 10-inch cup was limited to 2,000 but only 1,080 were made.

LOVING CUP, Edward VIII Coronation, Large* 1937   475.00 to 685.00

A small loving cup, made to commemorate the coronation of Edward VIII, pictures the King with a crown and Edward as the Prince of Wales. The 6 1/2-inch loving cup was made in a limited edition of 1,000, but only 454 were sold.

LOVING CUP, Edward VIII Coronation, Small*
                                               1937   *500.00*

In 1953 a limited edition of 1,000 loving cups was produced for the coronation of Elizabeth II. The 10 1/2-inch cup pictures Queen Elizabeth I on one side, Queen Elizabeth II on the other. An unlimited jug of similar design was also made.

Loving Cup, Edward VIII Coronation, Small   *Jug, Village Blacksmith*

Loving Cup, Edward VIII
Coronation, Large

LOVING CUP, Elizabeth II Coronation   1953   450.00 to 525.00

The King George VI and Queen Elizabeth loving cup was made in 1937. The design is similar to the cup made for Edward VIII because of the short notice of the change in succession. The 10 1/2-inch cup pictures the King and Queen. Two thousand cups were issued. A small, 6 1/2-inch loving cup was made for the coronation of King George VI and Queen Elizabeth. The King is shown in profile on one side, the Queen on the other. Two thousand of these cups were made in 1937.

LOVING CUP, George VI Coronation, Large   1937   500.00
    George VI Coronation, Small   1937   *500.00*

Jan Van Riebeeck was commander of the Dutch East India Company settlement at the Cape of Good Hope. The loving cup pictures Van Riebeeck planting the flag and the ships landing. The handles are three-dimensional figures of Van Riebeeck. The jug says on the base "Landing at the Cape of Good Hope 1652." Only 300 of these 10 1/4-inch cups were made in 1935.

LOVING CUP, Jan Van Riebeeck   1935   *1500.00*

Although John Peel was a real person born in 1776, he is best remembered as the hero of a famous hunting song "D'ye ken John Peel." The loving cup called John Peel pictures the man in a top hat and a group of hounds. The handles are topped with the hounds' heads. Five hundred of the 9-inch cups were made in 1933.

LOVING CUP, John Peel   1933   400.00 to 500.00

In 1935 Royal Doulton issued a limited edition of 1,000 loving cups to commemorate the silver jubilee of King George V and Queen Mary. The crowned King and Queen are shown in profile on a medallion and St. George on a horse is pictured standing in front of Windsor Castle. A version of the loving cup showing the King and Queen uncrowned is also reported.

LOVING CUP, King George & Queen Mary, Silver Jubilee*
                                         1935   500.00

Backstamp

A black basalt loving cup commemorating the ship Mayflower was made in a limited edition of 500 in 1970. It was issued at $285.

LOVING CUP, Mayflower*   300.00

Admiral Lord Nelson is shown on the limited edition loving cup at the Battle of Trafalgar. The cup handles are ropes. The 10 1/2-inch cup was issued in 1935 in an edition of 600.

LOVING CUP, Nelson   1935   900.00

In 1983 a special limited edition loving cup was offered to members of the Royal Doulton International Collectors Club. The cup shows the Exterior of the Burslem Pottery and a scene with Victorian ladies working in the Lambeth studio. The edition was limited to the number of loving cups ordered before June 30, 1983.

LOVING CUP, Pottery In The Past*   1983   75.00

In 1977 the Silver Jubilee of Queen Elizabeth was celebrated. The limited edition loving cup honoring the occasion pictures Queen Elizabeth on one side, the Royal Coat of Arms on the other. Only 250 of these 10 1/2-inch cups were made.

LOVING CUP, Queen Elizabeth Silver Jubilee*
                                         1977   475.00 to 875.00

Loving Cup, Mayflower

Loving Cup, Pottery In The Past

Loving Cup, Queen Elizabeth Silver Jubilee, 1977; Jug,
Charles Dickens, 1936

Robin Hood, who robbed the rich to give to the poor, is part of English tradition. The loving cup pictures Robin and his men shooting an arrow on one side, and Maid Marian, Friar Tuck, and Little John on the other. The 8 1/2-inch loving cup was made in a limited edition of 600 in 1938.

LOVING CUP, Robin Hood   1938   *500.00*

The Three Musketeers were heroes in the Alexandre Dumas novel. The loving cup, issued in 1936, pictures the musketeers and the Cardinal and Rochefort. The 10-inch loving cup was issued in an edition of 600.

LOVING CUP, Three Musketeers*   1936   675.00

Wandering minstrels entertained by singing in old England. The loving cup shows the minstrel on a wall and a lady and a page. The 5 1/2-inch loving cup was made in a limited edition of 600 in 1934.

LOVING CUP, Wandering Minstrel   1934   550.00

Loving Cup, Three Musketeers   *Jug, Shakespeare*

A special limited edition loving cup was issued for the wedding of the Prince of Wales and Lady Diana in 1981. They are shown on the jug in sepia portraits. Five thousand loving cups were made at the price of $125.

LOVING CUP, Wedding, Prince Of Wales, Lady Diana		
	1981	125.00

Although the William Wordsworth loving cup was issued in an unlimited edition in 1933, few were made. The cup pictures the poet on one side, his sister Dorothy on the other. The cup is 6 1/2 inches high.

LOVING CUP, Wordsworth	1933	*500.00*

Bas relief Christmas carol plaques that match the Christmas carol tankards were issued in a limited edition of 13,000 per year. The issue price for the first plaque in 1972 was $37.50.

PLAQUE, Christmas, Carolers	1972	38.00 to 40.00
Christmas, Solicitation	1973	35.00 to 40.00

All God's Children series by Lisette De Winne is limited to 10,000 each year. The first plate was issued in 1979 at $60.

PLATE, All God's Children, A Brighter Day	1979	60.00 to 75.00
All God's Children, Buddies	1982	62.00 to 85.00
All God's Children, Noble Heritage	1981	65.00 to 85.00
All God's Children, Village Children	1980	65.00

American Tapestries series by C. A. Brown is limited to 10,000 each year. The first plate was issued in 1978 for $70.

PLATE, American Tapestries, Fourth Of July	1982	95.00
American Tapestries, General Store	1981	85.00 to 95.00
American Tapestries, Pumpkin Patch*	1979	70.00
American Tapestries, Sleigh Bells	1978	37.00 to 70.00

Annual Christmas series, decorated with Victorian Era drawings, is limited to the period of issue each year. The first plate was issued in 1977.

Plate, American Tapestries,
Pumpkin Patch

Plate, Annual Christmas,
Victorian Girl

PLATE, Annual Christmas, Christmas Caroler	1981	37.50
Annual Christmas, Christmas Day	1979	25.00 to 29.95
Annual Christmas, Santa On Bicycle	1982	15.00 to 40.00
Annual Christmas, Santa's Visit	1980	25.00 to 32.95
Annual Christmas, Victorian Girl*	1978	17.50 to 27.50
Annual Christmas, Winter Fun	1977	25.00 to 55.00

Behind the Painted Masque is a series of four limited edition plates by Ben Black. Each plate pictures a clown. The series, limited to 10,000, started in 1982.

PLATE, Behind The Painted Masque, Painted Feelings*		
	1982	95.00

In 1982 a series was introduced called Celebration of Faith. Each plate is limited to 7,500. The issue price for Rosh Hashanah and Passover was $250 each.

PLATE, Celebration Of Faith, Passover	1983	250.00
Celebration Of Faith, Rosh Hashanah	1982	250.00

Character Plates are illustrated with Royal Doulton figurines. They are hand-painted, embossed and sculpted. The back of the plates has information about the figurines. The first plates were issued in 1979. Production is limited to one year.

PLATE, Character, Balloon Man*	1980	100.00
Character, Biddy Penny Farthing	1982	100.00
Character, Old Balloon Seller*	1979	50.00 to 100.00
Character, Silks And Ribbons	1981	100.00

Charing Cross Medical Research Centre issued a series of four limited edition plates as a fund-raising project. The first plate, issued in 1983, cost $50. The plates, designed by Alan Car Linford, are limited to an edition of 1,500 each.

Plate, Behind The Painted Masque,
Painted Feelings

Plate, Character, Balloon Man

Plate, Character, Old
Balloon Seller

Plates, Charing Cross, Feeding Time;
The Milking Lesson

Plate, Children Of The Pueblo,
Apple Flower

PLATE, Charing Cross, Feeding Time*   1983   50.00
  Charing Cross, The Milking Lesson*   1983   50.00

Mim Jungbluth was the artist who designed the Children of the Pueblo series, started in 1983 and limited to 10,000. The series has two matched, numbered plates each year.

PLATE, Children Of The Pueblo, Apple Flower*
                                           1983   60.00
  Children Of The Pueblo, Morning Star   1983   60.00

Christmas Around the World series was produced by Royal Doulton from 1972 to 1978 and is limited to 15,000 each year. It is sometimes called the Beswick Christmas series.

PLATE, Christmas, Christmas In America*   1978   52.00 to 55.00
  Christmas, Christmas In Bulgaria*   1974   45.00

Plate, Christmas, Christmas
In America

Plate, Christmas, Christmas
In Bulgaria

Christmas, Christmas In England	1972	48.00
Christmas, Christmas In Holland	1976	40.00 to 44.00
Christmas, Christmas In Mexico	1973	30.00 to 38.00
Christmas, Christmas In Norway	1975	48.00 to 54.00
Christmas, Christmas In Poland	1977	60.00 to 73.00

Commedia Dell' Arte series by Leroy Neiman is limited to 15,000 each year. The four-plate series was first issued in 1974 for $50. A related plate, Winning Colors, was issued in 1980. It was limited to 10,000.

PLATE, Commedia Dell' Arte, Columbine	1977	55.00 to 80.00
Commedia Dell' Arte, Harlequin	1974	96.00 to 100.00
Commedia Dell' Arte, Pierrot*	1976	84.00 to 90.00
Commedia Dell' Arte, Punchinello	1978	50.00 to 75.00
Commedia Dell' Arte, Winning Colors	1980	70.00 to 85.00

Festival Children of the World is a series of limited edition plates by Brenda Burke. The six-plate series, limited to 15,000, started in 1983. Issue price was $65.

PLATE, Festival Children Of The World, Mariani*	1983	65.00

Flower Garden series by Hahn Vidal, first issued in 1975, was limited to 15,000 each year. Issue price was $60.

PLATE, Flower Garden, Country Bouquet	1978	75.00
Flower Garden, Dreaming Lotus*	1976	90.00
Flower Garden, From Mother's Garden	1979	85.00
Flower Garden, Poet's Garden	1977	75.00
Flower Garden, Spring Harmony*	1975	80.00

I Remember America series by Eric Sloane is limited to 15,000 each year. The first plate was issued in 1977 for $70.

Plate, Commedia Dell' Arte, Pierrot

Plate, Festival Children Of The World, Mariani

Plate, Flower Garden, Dreaming Lotus

Plate, Flower Garden, Spring Harmony

Plate, I Remember America, Lovejoy Bridge

Plate, Jungle Fantasy, The Ark

PLATE, I Remember America, Four Corners	1979		75.00
I Remember America, Lovejoy Bridge*	1978		80.00
I Remember America, Marshlands	1981		95.00
I Remember America, Pennsylvania	1977		90.00

Jungle Fantasy series by Gustavo Novoa is limited to 10,000 each year. The first plate was issued in 1980 at $75. Later plates were issued at $95.

PLATE, Jungle Fantasy, Compassion	1980		75.00 to 95.00
Jungle Fantasy, Patience	1982		95.00
Jungle Fantasy, Refuge	1983		95.00
Jungle Fantasy, The Ark*	1979		75.00

Log of Dashing Wave series by John Stobart is limited to 15,000 each year. The first plate was offered in 1976 for $65.

PLATE, Log Of Dashing Wave, Bora Bora	1981		95.00
Log Of Dashing Wave, Hong Kong*	1979		75.00 to 90.00

Plate, Log Of Dashing Wave,
Hong Kong

Plate, Log Of Dashing Wave,
Sailing With Tide

Log Of Dashing Wave, Journey's End	1982	95.00
Log Of Dashing Wave, Rounding Horn	1978	70.00 to 90.00
Log Of Dashing Wave, Running Free	1977	70.00 to 143.00
Log Of Dashing Wave, Sailing With Tide*	1976	65.00 to 133.00

Mother and Child series by Edna Hibel is limited to 15,000 each year. The first plate was issued in 1973, but no new plates were offered in 1978, 1979, or 1980. The first plate cost $40.

PLATE, Mother And Child, Colette & Child	1973	495.00
Mother And Child, Kathleen & Child	1981	120.00
Mother And Child, Kristina & Child*	1975	125.00 to 135.00
Mother And Child, Lucia & Child*	1977	96.00
Mother And Child, Marilyn & Child	1976	110.00 to 125.00
Mother And Child, Sayuri & Child	1974	175.00 to 204.00

Plate, Mother And Child,
Kristina & Child

Plate, Mother And Child,
Lucia & Child

Plate, Portraits Of Innocence,
Angelica

Plate, Portraits Of Innocence,
Juliana

Plate, Ports Of Call, Paris,
Montmartre

Plate, Ports Of Call,
San Francisco

Francisco Masseria is the artist for the series Portraits of Innocence. The plates, first issued in 1980, each picture the head of a child against an abstract background. The series is limited to 15,000.

PLATE, Portraits Of Innocence, Adrien	1981	85.00 to 200.00
Portraits Of Innocence, Angelica*	1982	90.00 to 105.00
Portraits Of Innocence, Juliana*	1983	95.00
Portraits Of Innocence, Panchito	1980	75.00 to 199.00

Ports of Call series by Dong Kingman is limited to 15,000 each year. The series started in 1975 for $60.

PLATE, Ports Of Call, New Orleans	1976	80.00
Ports Of Call, Paris, Montmartre*	1978	70.00
Ports Of Call, San Francisco*	1975	75.00 to 90.00
Ports Of Call, Venice	1977	60.00 to 65.00

Plate, Reflections On China,
Imperial Palace

Plate, Valentine,
On A Swing

Reflections on China series by Chen Chi is limited to 15,000 each year. The first issue was in 1976 for $70.

PLATE, Reflections On China, Imperial Palace*	1977	80.00
Reflections On China, Lake Of Mists	1980	85.00
Reflections On China, Temple Of Heaven	1978	70.00
Reflections On China, Tranquility Garden	1976	90.00

A series called Silent Night was started in 1983. The 10-inch Christmas plates are limited to the year of issue. Issue price was $39.95.

PLATE, Silent Night, Caroler	1983	39.95

Valentine series is limited to the period of issue each year. The series started in 1976.

PLATE, Valentine, From My Heart	1982	37.50 to 40.00
Valentine, If I Loved You	1978	25.00 to 40.00
Valentine, My Sweetest Friend	1977	23.00 to 40.00
Valentine, My Valentine	1979	30.00 to 38.00
Valentine, On A Swing*	1980	33.00 to 35.00
Valentine, Sweet Music	1981	35.00 to 40.00
Valentine, To My Valentine	1983	18.00 to 40.00
Valentine, Victorian Boy & Girl*	1976	25.00 to 65.00

Sepia portraits of Prince Charles and Lady Diana decorate a plate commemorating their wedding in 1981. The ten-inch plate was made in an edition of 5,000. Issue price was $195.

PLATE, Wedding, Sepia Portraits	1981	195.00

Christmas tankards series was made from 1971 through 1973 in a limited edition of 13,000 for each year. In later years the edition was limited to 15,000. The series is sometimes called the Beswick Christmas Tankard series.

Plate, Valentine, Victorian Boy & Girl, 1976

Tankard, Christmas, Ghost Of Christmas Future

TANKARD, Christmas, Bob Cratchit	1982	39.50
Christmas, Carolers	1972	37.50 to 39.50
Christmas, Cratchit & Scrooge	1971	35.00 to 50.00
Christmas, Ghost Of Christmas Future*	1979	50.00 to 55.00
Christmas, Ghost Of Christmas Past*	1975	45.00
Christmas, Ghost Of Christmas Present, 1st	1976	50.00 to 55.00
Christmas, Ghost Of Christmas Present, 2nd	1977	50.00 to 55.00
Christmas, Ghost Of Christmas Present, 3rd	1978	50.00 to 55.00
Christmas, Going To Church	1981	60.00 to 75.00
Christmas, Scrooge Visiting Grave	1980	65.00
Christmas, Solicitation	1973	37.50
Marley's Ghost	1974	37.50

Tankard, Christmas, Ghost Of Christmas Past

Rouge Flambé

Rouge flambé is the name given to the blood red color that was found in the early Chinese glazes. Many potters have tried to duplicate the color, and during the 1890s the Doulton potters also tried. Charles J. Noke experimented with various red glazes, as did John Salter, Cuthbert Bailey, and Bernard Moore, a potter from another factory. The red glaze, a transmutation glaze, is created by the proper combination of copper oxide and other chemicals and the amount of oxygen admitted to the kiln at various times during the firing.

Doulton perfected a rouge flambé glaze and it received instant acclaim. The factory had many artists work on designs for flambé wares, and several types of the ware were made. The first of the Doulton flambé wares was shown in the St. Louis exhibition of 1904.

Experimentation continued for several years and required special kilns. Two types of decoration were selected. The veined Sung, first made about 1920, is a glazed piece that depends upon the results of the kiln to determine the exact coloring of the glaze. No two pieces were exactly alike but each had shadings of red to purple. The woodcut flambé, started in 1964, combines the red glaze and woodcut vignettes based on Thomas Bewick drawings that picture the English landscape. A special series of rouge flambé animals was also made. Some pieces in all of these lines are still being made.

Partial List of Flambé Pieces

ITEM	NUMBER	SIZE	TYPE
Bowl	1355B		Mottled flambé
Vase	770	6¼ in.	Mottled flambé
Vase	859	6 in.	Mottled flambé
Vase	920	7¼ in.	Veined Sung
Vase	925	7 in.	Veined Sung
Vase	1433	7¾ in.	Veined Sung
Vase	1441	10¼ in.	Mottled flambé
Vase	1603	7¼ in.	Veined Sung; woodcut flambé
Vase	1605	4¼ in.	Veined Sung; woodcut flambé

ITEM	NUMBER	SIZE	TYPE
Vase	1606	4¼ in.	Veined Sung; woodcut flambé
Vase	1612	8 in.	Veined Sung; woodcut flambé
Vase	1613	6½ in.	Veined Sung; woodcut flambé
Vase	1614	5¾ in.	Veined Sung; woodcut flambé
Vase	1616	8¾ in.	Veined Sung; woodcut flambé
Vase	1617	13¼ in.	Veined Sung; woodcut flambé
Vase	1618	9½ in.	Veined Sung; woodcut flambé
Vase	1619	11 in.	Veined Sung; woodcut flambé
Vase	1622	15¾ in.	Veined Sung; landscape flambé
Vase	1623	15½ in.	Veined Sung; landscape flambé
Vase	1624	16¼ in.	Veined Sung; landscape flambé
Vase	7684	6 in.	Landscape flambé
Vase	7754	7¾ in.	Landscape flambé
Vase	8362	11½ in.	Landscape flambé
Vase	8363	6 in.	Landscape flambé
Vase	8365	8¼ in.	Landscape flambé

NAME	NUMBER	SIZE	TYPE
Ape	52	2½ in.	
Bear, brown	1688	4¼ in.	Sung
Bear with Cub		13 in.	Sung & Chang
Bear with Cub		7¼ in.	Sung & Chang
Bird, fledgling, tail down		2½ in.	
Bison	1847	3 in.	
Bison		5½ in.	
Blue Tit on rock		3¾ in.	
Budgerigar	221	6 in.	
Bull		6 in.	
Bull		7 in.	
Butterfly		2 X 4 in.	
Cat, sitting	2259	11½ in.	
Cat, sitting	9	5 in.	
Cat, Mouse on tail	216	5 in.	
Cat, Persian, snarling	242	5 in.	Sung
Chicks, two		2 in.	Sung
Cockatoo on rock	68	6¼ in.	
Cockatoos, two		4½ in.	Chinese jade
Crab		2 X 4½ in.	Flambé crystalline

NAME	NUMBER	SIZE	TYPE
Dog of Fo		4¾ in.	For members of the Royal Doulton Collectors Club exclusively. Not available after June 30, 1982.
Dog, Airedale, sitting	800	5 in.	
Dog, Airedale, standing, Cotsfold Topsail		7 in.	
Dog, Alsatian		8 in.	
Dog, Alsatian	494	4 in.	
Dog, Bloodhound	48	6 in.	
Dog, Bulldog, seated	135	6 in.	
Dog, Bulldog, seated		3 in.	
Dog, Bulldog, seated, head on one side		4 in.	
Dog, Cocker Spaniel		3½ in.	
Dog, Cocker Spaniel		5¼ in.	
Dog, Collie, seated		7 in.	
Dog, Dachshund, begging		5 in.	
Dog, Hound, sitting		8 in.	
Dog, Labrador		4 in.	
Dog, Labrador, on base		4½ in.	
Dog, Pekinese, standing		2 in.	
Dog, Pekinese, standing		2 in.	Chinese jade
Dog, Pekinese, looking up	82	3½ in.	
Dog, Pekinese, sitting		2½ in.	
Dog, puppy, sitting	116	4 in.	
Dog, puppy, lying down	121	2 X 7¼ in.	
Dog, Scotch Terrier		4 in.	
Dog, Sealyham, Scotia Stylist		6½ in.	
Dog, Sealyham, head up		3 in.	
Dogs, two Pekinese		2½ in.	
Dragon	2085	7½ in.	
Duck, Drake, standing	137	6¼ in.	
Duck, Mallard	654	4 in.	
Duck, preening		3 in.	
Duck, sitting	112	1½ in.	Blue details
Duck, standing	395	2½ in.	
Duck on rock		3¼ in.	
Duck on rock		3¼ in.	Chinese jade
Duckling	3	3 in.	
Ducklings, two	97	2 X 5 in.	
Elephant, trunk raised	489B	4½ in.	
Elephant, trunk raised	489B	4½ in.	Sung
Elephant, trunk raised	489A	5½ in.	
Elephant, trunk raised	489A	5½ in.	Sung
Elephant, trunk raised	489	7 in.	
Elephant, trunk raised	489	7 in.	Sung
Elephant, trunk raised		12 in.	Sung
Elephant, trunk down		3 in.	Chinese jade
Elephant, trunk down		4 in.	
Elephant, trunk down		4 in.	Sung
Elephant, trunk down		5 in.	

NAME	NUMBER	SIZE	TYPE
Elephant, trunk down		6½ in.	
Elephant, trunk down		9 in.	
Elephant, trunk down		12 in.	
Elephant, trunk down		13 in.	
Elephant, trunk down		14 in.	
Elephant, trunk forward		11 in.	Sung
Elephant, trunk forward		13 in.	
Finch, crouching		1½ in.	
Finch, mouth open		2 in.	
Finches, three young		2 in.	
Fish		3½ X 5½ in.	Chinese jade
Fish, group of fish	682	6½ in.	
Fish, leaping Salmon	666	12 in.	
Fish, leaping Salmon		11½ in.	Chinese jade
Fox, sitting, head up	14	4 in.	
Fox, sitting, head up	102	9¼ in.	
Fox, sitting, head down	12A	3 in.	
Fox, sitting, head down	12	5 in.	Flambé & Sung
Fox, curled asleep	15	2 in.	
Fox, climbing on pillar	12	5¾ in.	
Fox, climbing on onyx thermometer stand		5½ in.	
Fox, slinking	29B	1 X 6 in.	Flambé & Sung
Fox, slinking	29A	1¾ X 9 in.	
Fox, slinking	29	2½ X 12 in.	
Foxes, one sitting, one asleep	6	3½ in.	Flambé & Sung
Foxes, two asleep	15	4 in.	
Frog	1162	1¼ X 3½ in.	
Guinea Fowl	69	3 in.	Painted details
Hare, lying down	656A	1¾ in.	
Hare, lying down	656	3¼ in.	
Hare, on haunches, ears up	1157	2¾ in.	
Hare, on haunches, ears down	119	2 in.	
Hare, standing on hind legs		5¾ in.	
Hen	357	1 X 1¼ in.	
Kingfisher on rock	44	3½ in.	
Kingfisher on tree stump	227	3½ in.	
Llama		6 in.	Flambé & Chinese jade
Lion, head on paws		2½ X 7 in.	
Monkey, seated, arms folded	53	2¾ in.	
Monkey, listening		3½ in.	
Monkey, dunce's cap		5½ in.	
Monkeys, embracing	486	5½ in.	Flambé & Sung
Mouse, on cube	1164	2½ in.	
Mouse with nut		2½ in.	
Owl, Owlet under wing		5 in.	Onyx base

NAME	NUMBER	SIZE	TYPE
Panther on rock		8½ X 9 in.	
Parrot on rock		15 in.	Sung
Parrot on pillar	45	7 in.	
Peacock on box		7¾ in.	Sung
Pelican, beak up	109	4½ in.	
Pelican, beak down	125	6¼ in.	
Penguin, Peruvian, on rock		5½ in.	
Penguin, Peruvian, on rock	585	8¾ in.	
Penguin	104	4 in.	Onyx base
Penguin	1287		
Penguin, King	84	6 in.	
Penguin, King and Chick	239	6 in.	
Penguin, double	103	6 in.	
Pig, lying down	110A	2 X 4 in.	Flambé or Sung
Pig, corpulent Sow		2½ X 5 in.	
Pig, standing		2½ in.	
Pig, head turned		2 X 4½ in.	
Pig, head turned		2½ X 5½ in.	
Pigs, two sleeping	61	4 in.	
Pigs, two sleeping	62	2 in.	
Pigs, two at trough	819	3 X 4 in.	
Pigs, three at trough		2 X 4 in.	
Pigs, three at trough		3¼ X 6½ in.	
Pigeons, two fantail	46	3¾ in.	
Pine Marten	115	4 in.	Sung
Polar Bear on cube	67	4 in.	
Polar Bear on dish		5 in.	
Polar Bear on ice floe		8 X 10 in.	
Polar Bear on haunches		3½ in.	
Polar Bears, two on ice		3¼ in.	
Rabbit, one ear up	113	2½ in.	
Rabbit, one ear up	1165	4 in.	
Rabbits, two cuddling	249	3¼ in.	
Raven on rock	43	3 in.	
Rhinoceros	615	9½ in.	
Rooster			
Squirrel	1689	2¼ in.	
Thrushes, two young		2 in.	
Thrushes, four young		2 X 5 in.	
Tiger	111		
Tiger	809	6 in.	
Tiger	1082	6 in.	
Tiger, feet to front		4 in.	
Tiger, sitting up		6½ in.	
Tiger, snarling		2½ X 9 in.	
Tortoise	101	1 X 3 in.	
Tortoise		1½ X 4½ in.	

Rouge Flambé Price List

Ashtray, Country Scene, Noke, 4 1/2 In.	35.00
Bottle, Liqueur, Floral & Leaf Design, Stopper, Signed	695.00
Bulldog, 2 3/4 In.	150.00
Cat, Sitting, No. 9, 5 In.	55.00 to 85.00
Cat, 12 In.	260.00
Child Study	230.00
Dog Of Fo, 4 3/4 In.	50.00
Dragon, 14 In.	525.00
Drake, No. 137, 6 In.	49.00 to 95.00
Duck, Rouge, No. 112, 1 1/2 In.	30.00 to 60.00
Duck, Rouge, No. 395, 2 1/2 In.	29.00 to 60.00
Elephant, No. 489a, 5 1/2 In.*	150.00 to 225.00
Elephant, 4 1/2 In.	150.00
Fox, Lying, Rouge, No. 29b	39.00 to 60.00
Fox, Sitting, Rouge, No. 14, 4 In.	52.00 to 85.00
Hare, Lying, Rouge, No. 656a	40.00 to 60.00
Hare, Sitting, Rouge, No. 1157, 2 3/4 In.	36.00 to 85.00
Owl, Flambé	350.00
Penguin, Rouge, No. 84, 6 In.	62.50 to 95.00
Rabbit, Ear Up, Rouge, No. 110, 2 1/2 In.	45.00
Rabbit, Ear Up, Rouge, No. 113	85.00
Rhinoceros, Flambé, 19 In.	395.00 to 445.00
Tiger, Rouge, No. 809, 5 1/2 In.	650.00
Tray, No. 1620, 4 In.	33.00 to 55.00
Tray, No. 1621, 6 In.	85.00
Vase, Art Deco-Shaped, Deer Design, Signed Ock, 7 In.	175.00
Vase, Bull Elk & Mate, 4 1/2 In.	175.00
Vase, Countryside Scene, Barrel-Shaped, 5 In.	85.00
Vase, Deer, 7 In.	175.00
Vase, Fish Design, Artist Signed FM, 8 1/2 In.	995.00
Vase, Harbor Scene, Sailing Vessels, 8 X 5 In.	165.00
Vase, Landscape, No. 6868	110.00
Vase, No. 1605, Veined Sung, 4 1/4 In.	41.00 to 100.00
Vase, No. 1612, Veined Sung, 8 In.	125.00

*Elephant,
No. 489a, 5 1/2 In.*

Vase, No. 1614, 5 3/4 In.   36.00 to 85.00
Vase, No. 1616, 8 3/4 In.   325.00
Vase, Pumpkin-Shaped, 7 1/2 In.   525.00
Vase, Scenic, 6 1/2 In.   62.00
Vase, Scenic, 8 1/2 In.   280.00
Vase, Veined Sung Design, Ovoid, 10 In.   235.00
Vase, Woodcut, Hunter With Rifle, 8 In.   225.00
Vase, Woodcut, No. 1603, 7 1/4 In.   36.00 to 85.00
Vase, Woodcut, No. 1606, 4 1/4 In.   65.00
Vase, Woodcut, No. 1613, 6 1/2 In.   41.00 to 100.00
Vase, Woodcut, No. 1619, 11 In.   325.00

Series Wares

Early in the 1900s, Charles J. Noke had still another idea for the Royal Doulton factory. He designed or had others design a line called series wares. The first of these seemed to be the series called Eglington Tournament, first made in 1902. Other series followed, and by 1906 advertisements for them appeared in papers throughout the United States. Many of the series pictured scenes from literary or historic events. Some were based on illustrations that had appeared in books. Several series pictured scenes or characters from Shakespearean plays. Many of the series wares had special borders and special backstamps.

The Dickens ware was probably Mr. Noke's most popular series. A huge selection of dishes for luncheon and dinner sets was made, as well as many types of serving pieces, pitchers, vases, humidors, toothbrush holders, butter pats, and match holders. There were at least thirty-six different characters pictured.

The Doulton factory made a special plate for the Dickens centennial in 1911. It had a picture of Dickens's head in the center and a border of his characters. The factory made similar-style plates, called "head rack plates," in the late 1940s. They pictured British historical and literary figures, including head portraits of celebrities. Most of them have special borders. Another series, called "scenic rack plates," pictures animals, scenery, or people and their way of life in the United Kingdom.

There is still much confusion about series wares. Most of it will never be solved because the orderly designations that are wanted by today's collector were never a part of the original thinking of the Doulton works. Their wares were made, adapted, and sold in the way to make their most popular pieces available. There was never a thought as to whether a border was part of an earlier series. Border and center designs were often used in several ways. We have included a listing on page 234 to help the collector. The D. numbers and other numbers, name of the series, and books for further information are listed in numerical order.

We will always welcome any and all comments. A great many of the pictures, marks, and designations in this edition are from readers. If you can add anything to the lists, please let us hear from you. Write to Kovel, c/o Crown Publishers, Inc., One Park Avenue, New York, New York 10016. If it is possible, please include a photograph or a photocopy of the patterns and marks.

SERIES WARE NUMBER LIST

Series wares by Royal Doulton are confusing for the collector. The company used similar themes, renamed series, used the same ceramic shapes for many series, and had no interest in keeping the type of records today's collectors need. Two books about Royal Doulton include extensive information about the series wares; but unfortunately the material is indexed by series name, not by series number. Many pieces have only a number, no name, no special backstamp; so the novice has a difficult research problem. To solve this dilemma, we computerized the information in these books and other sources. The following list includes all references to series wares in the books *Royal Doulton Series Ware* and *The Doulton Burslem Wares*, plus additions from other research sources for material *not* found in these books. The list is in numerical order by D., E., H., TC., or V. number with a key to indicate the source of the information. Sometimes the series is listed by different names in different places. The name in this list is the name used in the source. If several names are possible, we have indicated the name used in this book by putting it in parentheses. An asterisk indicates a series that is priced in this book. We welcome any additions or corrections to this list. If you have a piece of numbered series ware that is not included, please send a picture and the number to Kovel, Crown Publishers, Inc., One Park Avenue, New York, New York 10016.

Key for D. List

(1) Irvine, Louise. *Royal Doulton Series Ware,* vol. 1. Privately printed, 1980. 144 Kensington Church St., London W8 4BN, England.
(2) Eyles, Desmond. *The Doulton Burslem Wares.* London, England: Barrie & Jenkins, Ltd., 1980.
(3) Kovel, Ralph and Terry. Information obtained through research which was not found in books (1) or (2) above.

*	D. 357	Shakespeare (1)	D.1242	Eastern Figures (1)
	D. 540	Eastern Figures (1)	D.1263	Eastern Figures (1)
*	D. 914	Shakespeare (1)	D.1375	Hunting (2)
	D. 943	Eastern Figures (1)	D.1376	Hunting (2)
	D. 947	Eastern Figures (1)	* D.1385	Golfers (1)
	D.1017	Eastern Figures (1)	D.1386	Eastern Figures (1)
	D.1020	Eastern Figures (1)	* D.1395	Golfers (1)
	D.1027	Eastern Figures (1)	* D.1396	Golfers (1),(2)
	D.1036	Eastern Figures (1)	* D.1398	Golfers (1),(2)
	D.1126	Eastern Figures (1)	* D.1424	Golfers (1)
	D.1127	Eastern Figures (1)	* D.1425	Eglington Tournament (1), (2)
*	D.1132	Golfers (1)		
*	D.1165	Golfers (1)	* D.1430	Golfers (1)

D.1432	Eastern Figures (1)	
D.1440	Isthmian Games (2)	
* D.1455	Eglington Tournament (1)	
* D.1773	Shakespeare (1)	
* D.1776	Eglington Tournament (1)	
* D.1811	Nursery Rhymes (2)	
* D.1881	Dutch (3)	
* D.1884	Dutch (3)	
D.1886	Harlem (2)	
* D.1898	Old Moreton (3)	
* D.1909	Nursery Rhymes (2)	
* D.1914	Nursery Rhymes (2)	
D.1929	Birds (2)	
* D.1943	Dickens Ware (3)	
D.1978	I Say A Stoop of Wine (2)	
* D.1978	Shakespeare (1)	
* D.2039	Eglington Tournament (1)	
D.2043	Eastern Figures (1)	
D.2044	Eastern Figures (1)	
D.2051	Eastern Figures (1)	
D.2054	American Statesmen (2)	
D.2061	Eastern Figures (1)	
* D.2079	Authors and Inns (1)	
D.2091	Cattle (2)	
D.2092	Cattle (2)	
D.2104	Historic Towns, Old London (1)	
D.2105	Historic Towns, Old London (1)	
D.2105	Old London (2)	
D.2108	Cattle (2)	
D.2117	Eastern Figures (1)	
* D.2129	Shakespeare (1),(2)	
* D.2137	Shakespeare (1),(2)	
* D.2160	Old Sea Dogs (2)	
* D.2204	Flowers and Foliage (2)	
D.2204	Geometrical and Stylized Design (2)	
* D.1461	Eglington Tournament (1), (2)	
* D.1462	Eglington Tournament (1), (2)	
* D.1464	Golfers (1)	
D.1475	Eastern Figures (1)	
* D.1496	Eglington Tournament (1), (2)	
D.1501	Birds (2)	
D.1502	Birds (2)	
D.1503	Birds (2)	
D.1504	Birds (2)	
D.1505	Birds (2)	
D.1506	Children Scenes (2)	
D.1507	Children Scenes (2)	
D.1508	Children Scenes (2)	
* D.1513	Nursery Rhymes (2)	
* D.1514	Eglington Tournament (1)	
D.1515	Children Scenes (2)	
D.1516	Children Scenes (2)	
D.1517	Birds (2)	
D.1518	Birds (2)	
D.1544	Grimm's Fairy Tales (1)	
D.1545	Grimm's Fairy Tales (1)	
D.1546	Grimm's Fairy Tales (1)	
D.1564	Grimm's Fairy Tales (1)	
* D.1712	Nursery Rhymes (2)	
D.1754	Birds (2)	
D.1755	Birds (2)	
* D.1771	Shakespeare (1)	
* D.1772	Shakespeare (1)	
* D.2205	Flowers and Foliage (2)	
D.2205	Geometrical and Stylized Designs (2)	
* D.2206	Flowers and Foliage (2)	
D.2206	Geometrical and Stylized Designs (2)	
* D.2208	Flowers and Foliage (2)	
D.2214	Stag (2)	
D.2215	Hunting (2)	
* D.2220	Shakespeare (1)	
D.2227	Eastern Figures (1)	
* D.2227	Golfers (1)	
D.2232	Children Scenes (2)	
D.2233	Children Scenes (2)	
D.2268	Geometrical and Stylized Designs (2)	
D.2273	Blue Ships (2)	
D.2274	Brown Ships (2)	
* D.2312	Gallant Fishers (1)	
* D.2312	Isaac Walton (2)	
D.2351	Historic Towns, Old London (1)	
D.2351	Old London (2)	
* D.2373	Shakespeare (1)	
* D.2385	Monks (2)	
D.2391	Children Scenes (2)	
D.2394	Children Scenes (2)	
D.2395	Wedlock (2)	
D.2397	Hunting (2)	
D.2398	Hunting (2)	
D.2399	Hunting (2)	
* D.2404	Nursery Rhymes (2)	
* D.2406	Motoring (2)	
D.2408	Birds (2)	
D.2410	Stag (2)	
D.2415	Birds (2)	
D.2417	Birds (2)	
D.2420	Fisherfolk (2)	
* D.2420	Gallant Fishers (1)	
D.2433	Nursery Subjects (2)	
D.2434	Nursery Subjects (2)	

* D.2440	Sketches from Teniers (2)	
* D.2452	Landscapes (2)	
* D.2493	Shakespeare (1),(2)	
* D.2494	Shakespeare (1),(2)	
* D.2495	Shakespeare (1),(2)	
* D.2498	Souter's Cats (1)	
* D.2504	Souter's Cats (1)	
* D.2515	Nursery Rhymes (2)	
* D.2517	Gallant Fishers (1)	
* D.2532	Jackdaw of Rheims (1),(2)	
* D.2538	Landscapes (2)	
* D.2539	Nursery Rhymes (2)	
* D.2540	Nursery Rhymes (2)	
D.2541	Jessopeak Pressgang (2)	
D.2542	Jessopeak Pressgang (2)	
* D.2543	Shakespeare (1),(2)	
* D.2544	Flowers and Foliage (2)	
D.2545	Grimm's Fairy Tales (1)	
D.2545	Leda and The Swan (2)	
* D.2546	Flowers and Foliage (2)	
D.2551	Sailing Barges (2)	
* D.2553	Rip Van Winkle (1),(2)	
* D.2554	Rip Van Winkle (1)	
* D.2555	Rip Van Winkle (1)	
D.2557	Historic Towns, Old London (1)	
* D.2557	Izaak Walton, The Compleat Angler (1)	
* D.2567	Monks (2)	
* D.2591	Souter's Cats (1)	
* D.2644	Shakespeare (1),(2)	
* D.2648	Sketches from Teniers (2)	
* D.2652	Landscapes (2)	
* D.2654	Castles and Churches, Muckross Abbey (1)	
* D.2654	Cathedrals and Churches (Castles and Churches) (2)	
* D.2654	Cornfield and Churches (Castles and Churches) (2)	
* D.2654	Landscapes (2)	
* D.2666	Souter's Cats (1)	
D.2673	Witches (2)	
D.2677	Tudor Sailing Ships (2)	
* D.2678	Don Quixote (1)	
D.2679	Gulliver's Travels (1)	
* D.2682	Coaching Days (2)	
* D.2683	Landscapes (2)	
* D.2687	Don Quixote (1)	
D.2688	Gulliver's Travels (1)	
* D.2690	Don Quixote (1)	
D.2691	Gulliver's Travels (1)	
* D.2692	Don Quixote (2)	
* D.2699	Shakespeare (1)	
D.2700	Anniversary Tea(1)	
* D.2701	Flowers and Foliage (2)	
D.2701	Geometrical and Stylized Designs (2)	
* D.2702	Flowers and Foliage (2)	
D.2702	Geometrical and Stylized Designs (2)	
* D.2704	Gallant Fishers (1)	
* D.2704	Isaac Walton (2)	
D.2707	Gulliver (2)	
D.2707	Gulliver's Travels (1)	
D.2707	Washington, George (2)	
D.2708	Washington, George (2)	
* D.2709	Don Quixote (1),(2)	
* D.2710	Flowers and Foliage (2)	
D.2710	Geometrical and Stylized Designs (2)	
* D.2716	Coaching Days (2)	
D.2716	Town Crier (2)	
D.2717	Welsh Women (2)	
* D.2721	Shakespeare (1),(2)	
* D.2722	Shakespeare (1)	
D.2724	Old Bob Ye Guard (2)	
D.2735	Witches (2)	
D.2761	Jessopeak Pressgang (2)	
* D.2768	Don Quixote (2)	
D.2777	Horses (2)	
D.2778	Horses (2)	
D.2778	Hunting (2)	
* D.2779	Shakespeare (1),(2)	
D.2780	Geometrical and Stylized Designs (2)	
* D.2785	Sketches from Teniers (2)	
* D.2786	Sketches from Teniers (2)	
* D.2787	Nautical History (1)	
* D.2787	Raleigh, Sir Walter (Nautical History) (2)	
* D.2788	Nautical History (1)	
* D.2788	Rip Van Winkle (1),(2)	
* D.2789	Skating (2)	
* D.2790	Sketches from Teniers (2)	
* D.2792	Eglington Tournament (1)	
* D.2793	Eglington Tournament (1)	
* D.2794	Eglington Tournament (1)	
* D.2799	Sayings (Sayings Ware) (2)	
* D.2810	Nautical History (1)	
* D.2826	Shakespeare (1)	
* D.2846	Cathedrals and Churches (Castles and Churches) (2)	
* D.2846	Landscapes (2)	
* D.2863	Alice (Alice in Wonderland) (2)	
D.2864	All Black Cricketers (2)	
* D.2865	Skating (2)	
D.2872	Brown Ships (2)	
* D.2873	Bayeux Tapestry (1),(2)	
* D.2874	Shakespeare (Shakespeare	

	Plays) (1),(2)
* D.2875	Cavaliers (2)
* D.2876	Gnomes (2)
* D.2877	Monks (2)
D.2879	Bears (2)
D.2880	Bison (2)
* D.2881	Shakespeare (1),(2)
* D.2882	Landscapes (2)
* D.2883	Alice (Alice in Wonderland) (2)
* D.2884	Children Scenes (Blue Children) (2)
* D.2894	Rip Van Winkle (1)
D.2903	Witches (2)
* D.2921	Nursery Rhymes (2)
* D.2922	Nursery Rhymes (2)
* D.2938	Landscapes (2)
* D.2948	Castles and Churches (3)
D.2955	Children Scenes (2)
* D.2955	Blue Children (2)
* D.2956	Blue Children (2)
* D.2956	Children Scenes (Blue Children) (2)
* D.2961	King Arthur's Knights (2)
D.2964	Dickens Portrait (1)
D.2964	Robert Burns (2)
D.2965	St. George (1)
* D.2966	Cavaliers (1)
D.2969	Caldecott (1)
* D.2970	Don Quixote (1)
* D.2973	Dickens (Dickens Ware) (1),(2)
* D.2976	Monks (2)
* D.2978	Dickens (Dickens Ware) (1)
* D.2978	Don Quixote (1)
* D.2982	Proverbs (2)
D.3018	Geometrical and Stylized Designs (2)
D.3018	Urn and Flame (2)
D.3019	Geometrical and Stylized Designs (2)
D.3019	Urn and Flame (2)
* D.3020	Dickens (Dickens Ware) (1),(2)
* D.3039	Gondoliers (2)
* D.3040	Landscapes (2)
* D.3044	Hiawatha (1),(2)
D.3045	Stirrup Cup (2)
D.3046	Stirrup Cup (2)
* D.3049	Nautical History (1)
D.3051	New Cavaliers (2)
* D.3052	Nautical History (1)
* D.3053	Drake (Nautical History) (2)
* D.3053	Nautical History (1)
* D.3053	Sir Walter Raleigh (Nautical History) (2)
* D.3054	Eglington Tournament (1), (2)
* D.3055	Eglington Tournament (1), (2)
* D.3056	Flowers and Foliage (2)
D.3056	Geometrical and Stylized Designs (2)
* D.3057	Flowers and Foliage (2)
D.3057	Geometrical and Stylized Designs (2)
* D.3058	Flowers and Foliage (2)
D.3058	Geometrical and Stylized Designs (2)
D.3059	Old Salt (2)
* D.3060	Flowers and Foliage (2)
D.3060	Geometrical and Stylized Designs (2)
* D.3062	Flowers and Foliage (2)
* D.3066	Souter's Cats (1)
D.3080	Birds (2)
* D.3082	Nursery Rhymes (2)
* D.3083	Nursery Rhymes (2)
* D.3084	Cavaliers (2)
* D.3084	Monks (2)
D.3085	Old Salt (2)
* D.3086	Nautical History (1)
* D.3086	Spanish Armada (Nautical History) (2)
* D.3086	Trafalgar, Battle of (Nautical History) (2)
D.3087	Geometrical and Stylized Designs (2)
D.3088	Geometrical and Stylized Designs (2)
D.3089	The Bookworm (2)
* D.3101	Nautical History (1)
* D.3103	Cavaliers (2)
* D.3111	Diversions of Uncle Toby (1)
* D.3111	Uncle Toby, Old English Games (Diversions of Uncle Toby) (2)
D.3112	Zodiac (1),(2)
D.3117	Squire (2)
* D.3118	Old Jarvey, An (2)
* D.3119	Children Scenes (Blue Children) (2)
* D.3120	Don Quixote (1),(2)
* D.3120	King Arthur's Knights (2)
* D.3121	Diversion of Uncle Toby (1)
* D.3121	Uncle Toby, Old English Games (Diversions of Uncle

	Toby) (2)			Ladies) (2)
D.3123	Doctor Johnson (1)		* D.3368	Bobbie Burns (1)
D.3123	Doctor Johnson at the Cheshire Cheese (2)		* D.3368	Green Grow the Rushes (Bobbie Burns) (2)
* D.3127	Polar Bears (2)		* D.3368	Robert Burns (Bobbie Burns) (2)
* D.3128	Polar Bear (3)			
* D.3143	Flowers and Foliage (2)		D.3375	Washington, George (2)
D.3143	Geometrical and Stylized Designs (2)		D.3376	Washington, George (2)
			D.3382	Willow Pattern (2)
D.3149	Shakespeare Portrait (2)		* D.3385	Bobbie Burns (1)
* D.3169	Gallant Fishers (1)		D.3388	Harlem (2)
* D.3188	Canterbury Pilgrims (1),(2)		D.3389	Harlem (2)
D.3189	Doctor (2)		D.3390	Harlem (2)
* D.3190	Night Watchman (2)		D.3391	Burns Portrait (1)
* D.3191	Gleaners and Gipsies (English Old Scenes) (2)		* D.3391	Golfers (2)
* D.3191	Old English Scenes (English Old Scenes) (2)		* D.3391	Proverbs (1),(2)
			D.3392	Burns Portrait (1)
* D.3192	Desert Scenes (2)		D.3392	Robert Burns (2)
D.3193	Medallion (2)		D.3393	Willow Pattern (2)
* D.3194	Shakespeare (1)		* D.3394	Golfers (2)
* D.3195	Shakespeare (1)		* D.3395	Golfers (2)
D.3195	Shakespeare Portrait (2)		D.3397	Burns Portrait (1)
* D.3197	Diversions of Uncle Toby (1)		D.3399	Deadwood Crackle (2)
			* D.3407	Souter's Cats (1)
* D.3198	Arabian Nights (1),(2)		* D.3416	Poplar Trees, Sunset (2)
* D.3199	Shakespeare (1),(2)		* D.3418	Sir Roger de Coverley (1), (2)
D.3204	Paxton (2)			
D.3205	Aeronautical (2)		* D.3419	Egyptian (2)
D.3205	Aeronautical Scenes (1)		* D.3420	Arabian Nights (1),(2)
D.3207	William and Mary (2)		* D.3425	Castles and Churches (1)
* D.3208	Welsh Women (Welsh Ladies) (2)		* D.3425	Castles and Palaces (Castles and Churches) (2)
* D.3225	Flowers and Foliage (2)		* D.3426	Castles and Churches (1)
* D.3226	Flowers and Foliage (2)		* D.3426	Castles and Palaces (Castles and Churches) (2)
* D.3227	Flowers and Foliage (2)		* D.3427	An Open Door May Tempt A Saint (English Old Proverbs) (2)
D.3253	Shakespeare (1)			
* D.3287	Omar Khayyam (1),(2)			
* D.3288	Omar Khayyam (1),(2)		* D.3427	Old English Proverbs Illustrated (English Old Proverbs) (2)
D.3289	Omar Khayyam (1)			
* D.3300	Nursery Rhymes (2)			
* D.3301	Poplar Trees, Sunset (2)		* D.3428	Old English Proverbs Illustrated (English Old Proverbs) (2)
* D.3302	Athens (2)			
D.3303	Parson (2)			
* D.3305	Poplar Trees, Sunset (2)		* D.3429	Monks (2)
* D.3312	Nursery Rhymes (2)		* D.3429	Tomorrow Will Be Friday (Monks) (2)
* D.3323	Arabian Nights (1)			
D.3348	Mayor (2)		* D.3430	Flowers and Foliage (2)
* D.3354	Old English Proverbs Illustrated (English Old Proverbs) (2)		D.3430	Geometrical and Stylized Designs (2)
			* D.3435	Old English Proverbs Illustrated (English Old Proverbs) (2)
D.3356	Man With Scythe (2)			
D.3356	Shepherd (2)			
* D.3357	Nursery Rhymes (2)		* D.3439	Flowers and Foliage (2)
* D.3363	Welsh Women (Welsh		D.3470	Old English Scenes (2)

* D.3470	Uncle Toby, Old English Games (Diversions of Uncle Toby) (2)	
* D.3471	Castles and Churches, Battle Abbey (1)	
* D.3471	Castles and Churches, Bodiam Castle (1)	
* D.3471	Castles and Churches, Hurstmonceaux Castle (1)	
* D.3471	Castles and Palaces (Castles and Churches) (2)	
* D.3475	Athens (2)	
* D.3477	Sketches From Teniers (2)	
* D.3481	Golfers (2)	
* D.3481	Proverbs (1)	
* D.3491	Castles and Churches, Bodiam Castle (1)	
* D.3491	Castles and Palaces (Castles and Churches) (2)	
D.3514	Admiral Earl of St. Vincent (2)	
* D.3514	Admiral Lord Nelson (Nautical History) (2)	
* D.3514	Nautical History (1)	
* D.3534	Arabian Nights (2)	
* D.3538	Tunis (2)	
* D.3544	Old English Proverbs Illustrated (English Old Proverbs) (2)	
* D.3545	Old English Proverbs Illustrated (English Old Proverbs) (2)	
D.3546	Geometrical and Stylized Designs (2)	
* D.3547	Uncle Toby, Old English Games (Diversions of Uncle Toby) (2)	
D.3550	Persian (2)	
D.3569	Viking Ship (2)	
D.3570	Swans (2)	
* D.3571	Monks (2)	
D.3572	Geometrical and Stylized Designs (2)	
D.3576	Falconer (2)	
D.3577	Silhouettes (2)	
* D.3578	Tunis (2)	
* D.3579	Flowers and Foliage (2)	
D.3579	Geometrical and Stylized Designs (2)	
* D.3596	Shakespeare (Shakespeare Characters) (1),(2)	
D.3597	Sedan Chair (2)	
D.3598	Silhouettes (2)	
* D.3599	Castles and Churches, Pembroke Castle (1)	

* D.3599	Castles and Palaces (Castles and Churches) (2)
D.3601	Shepherd (2)
* D.3602	Authors and Inns (1)
* D.3603	Authors and Inns (1)
D.3606	Fairy Tales (2)
* D.3606	Nursery Rhymes (2)
D.3607	Owl (2)
D.3608	Refectory Bell (2)
* D.3610	Castles and Churches, Pembroke Castle (1)
* D.3610	Castles and Palaces (Castles and Churches) (2)
D.3611	Old English Country Fairs (2)
D.3611	Old English Scenes (2)
D.3616	Admiral Lord Nelson (2)
D.3617	Admiral Earl of St. Vincent (2)
D.3617	Cottage Door (2)
* D.3624	Authors and Inns (1)
D.3625	Willow Pattern (2)
D.3625	Willow Pattern Story (1)
* D.3634	Countryside (2)
D.3636	Hunting (2)
* D.3647	Countryside (2)
* D.3655	Jansson (King of Hearts) (1)
* D.3655	Ye Knave of Hearts (King of Hearts) (1)
* D.3657	Jansson (King of Hearts) (1)
* D.3659	Cock-A-Doodle-Doo (Nursery Rhymes) (2)
* D.3659	Nursery Rhymes (2)
* D.3660	Cock-A-Doodle-Doo (Nursery Rhymes) (2)
* D.3665	Jansson (King of Hearts) (1)
* D.3666	Shakespeare (1)
* D.3668	Landscapes (2)
* D.3671	Castles and Churches, Brundel Castle (1)
* D.3680	Gallant Fishers (1),(2)
D.3682	Town Crier (2)
* D.3683	Don Quixote (1),(2)
D.3684	Jester (2)
D.3688	Burns Portrait (1)
D.3688	Town Crier (2)
* D.3691	Castles and Churches, Bodiam Castle (1)
D.3694	Stag (2)
D.3695	Hunting (2)
* D.3696	Falconry (2)
D.3697	Moonlight Landscape (2)
D.3699	Geometrical and Stylized Designs (2)
* D.3700	Flowers and Foliage (2)

D.3700	Geometrical and Stylized Designs (2)
D.3707	Old Wellesley (2)
D.3716	Town Crier (2)
D.3717	Refectory Bell (2)
* D.3719	Sketches From Teniers (2)
D.3730	Cats (2)
* D.3746	Shakespeare (1),(2)
D.3749	Sampler (2)
* D.3751	Under the Greenwood Tree (1),(2)
D.3754	Open Door (2)
D.3755	Nineteenth Hole (2)
* D.3808	Flowers and Foliage (2)
D.3811	Wattle Frieze (2)
D.3812	Bluebell Gatherers (2)
* D.3814	Flowers and Foliage (2)
* D.3822	Old Moreton Hall (Old Moreton) (1)
D.3822	Old Moreton, 1589 (Old Moreton) (2)
D.3832	Prunus (2)
D.3833	Prunus (2)
* D.3835	Shakespeare (1),(2)
D.3838	World War I (1)
* D.3842	Old Moreton, 1589 (Old Moreton) (2)
* D.3858	Old Moreton Hall (Old Moreton) (1)
D.3866	Willow Pattern (2)
D.3867	Willow Pattern (2)
* D.3882	Shakespeare (1),(2)
* D.3884	Children Scenes (Blue Children) (2)
* D.3918	Nursery Rhymes (2)
* D.3919	Gnomes (2)
D.3930	Parson (2)
D.3931	Doctor (2)
D.3932	Squire (2)
D.3933	Mayor (2)
* D.3934	Shakespeare (2)
* D.3939	Nautical History (1)
* D.3939	Sir Walter Raleigh (Nautical History) (2)
* D.3940	Drake (Nautical History) (2)
* D.3940	Nautical History (1)
* D.3941	Explorers (Nautical History) (2)
D.3941	Nautical History (1)
D.3943	Cattle (2)
D.3945	It's A Long Way to Tipperary (2)
D.3945	World War I (1)
D.3946	Tudor Lady (2)
D.3948	Dickens Portrait (1)
* D.3953	Souter's Cats (1)
D.3969	Geometrical and Stylized Designs (2)
* D.3969	Jansson (King of Hearts) (1)
* D.3969	King of Hearts (2)
D.3990	Tudor Lady (2)
D.3991	Tudor Lady (2)
D.4006	Three Musketeers (2)
* D.4016	Nursery Rhymes (2)
D.4030	Dickens (1)
D.4031	Geometrical and Stylized Designs (2)
* D.4049	Flowers and Foliage (2)
* D.4064	Nursery Rhymes (2)
D.4069	Dickens (1)
* D.4070	Shakespeare (1)
* D.4083	Nursery Rhymes (2)
D.4119	Dickens Ware (3)
D.4149	Anne Hathaway's Cottage (2)
* D.4149	Shakespeare (1),(2)
* D.4153	Souter's Cats (1)
D.4162	Kang-He (2)
D.4174	Geometrical and Stylized Designs (2)
D.4175	Geometrical and Stylized Designs (2)
* D.4176	Flowers and Foliage (2)
D.4176	Geometrical and Stylized Designs (2)
* D.4177	Flowers and Foliage (2)
D.4177	Geometrical and Stylized Designs (2)
* D.4178	Flowers and Foliage (2)
D.4178	Geometrical and Stylized Designs (2)
* D.4179	Flowers and Foliage (2)
D.4179	Geometrical and Stylized Designs (2)
* D.4180	Flowers and Foliage (2)
D.4180	Geometrical and Stylized Designs (2)
D.4205	Kookaburra (2)
D.4206	Birds (2)
D.4206	Kookaburra (2)
* D.4210	Gaffers (2)
D.4222	Birds of Paradise (2)
D.4234	Cobbler (2)
* D.4243	Minstrels (2)
D.4251	Anemone (2)
D.4252	Anemone (2)
* D.4263	Egyptian (2)
D.4273	Watchman and Minstrel (2)
* D.4274	Poplar Trees, Sunset (2)

* D.4358   Castles and Churches,
            Fountains Abbey (1)
* D.4361   Flowers and Foliage (2)
  D.4361   Geometrical and Stylized
            Designs (2)
  D.4365   Geometrical and Stylized
            Designs (2)
* D.4368   Landscapes (2)
* D.4385   Landscapes (2)
* D.4390   Landscapes (2)
* D.4391   Castles and Churches,
            Bodiam Castle (1)
* D.4391   Castles and Palaces (Castles
            and Churches) (2)
  D.4392   Shakespeare (1)
  D.4405   Fisherfolk (2)
* D.4419   Bobbie Burns (1)
* D.4419   Robert Burns (Bobbie
            Burns) (2)
* D.4467   Kensington Gardens (2)
  D.4468   Quorn Hunt (2)
  D.4475   Hunting (2)
  D.4478   Willow Pattern (2)
  D.4478   Willow Pattern Story (1)
  D.4490   Royal Mail Coach (2)
  D.4498   Royal Mail Coach (2)
* D.4504   Castles and Churches,
            Bodiam Castle (1)
* D.4504   Castles and Palaces (Castles
            and Churches) (2)
* D.4505   Castles and Churches,
            Arundel Castle (1)
  D.4507   Hunting (2)
  D.4507   Old English Scenes (1),(2)
* D.4525   Aldin's Dogs (1)
  D.4533   Log-Hauling (2)
  D.4538   Cats (2)
* D.4546   Flowers and Foliage (2)
  D.4546   Geometrical and Stylized
            Designs (2)
* D.4547   Flowers and Foliage (2)
  D.4547   Geometrical and Stylized
            Designs (2)
* D.4548   Flowers and Foliage (2)
  D.4548   Geometrical and Stylized
            Designs (2)
* D.4549   Flowers and Foliage (2)
  D.4549   Geometrical and Stylized
            Designs (2)
* D.4550   Flowers and Foliage (2)
  D.4550   Geometrical and Stylized
            Designs (2)
* D.4551   Flowers and Foliage (2)
  D.4551   Geometrical and Stylized
            Designs (2)

  D.4586   Birds (2)
  D.4586   Game Birds (2)
* D.4601   Moorish Gateway (2)
* D.4602   Flowers and Foliage (2)
  D.4602   Geometrical and Stylized
            Designs (2)
* D.4617   Monks (2)
* D.4629   Aldin's Dogs (1),(2)
  D.4635   Wiltshire Moonrakers (2)
  D.4639   Birds (2)
* D.4643   Castles and Churches,
            Pembroke Castle (1)
* D.4643   Castles and Churches,
            Warwick Castle (1)
* D.4643   Castles and Palaces (Castles
            and Churches) (2)
  D.4644   Deer (2)
  D.4645   Surfing (2)
* D.4647   Gnomes (3)
* D.4658   Castles and Churches (1)
* D.4686   Cock-A-Doodle-Doo
            (Nursery Rhymes) (2)
* D.4686   Nursery Rhymes (2)
* D.4697   Gnomes (2)
  D.4713   Autumn Glory (2)
  D.4714   Autumn Glory (2)
  D.4723   Old English Scenes,
            Rochester Castle (1)
* D.4728   Castles and Churches (1)
* D.4728   Castles and Palaces (Castles
            and Churches) (2)
  D.4729   Highwayman (2)
  D.4741   Gugnunc (2)
* D.4742   Moorish Gateway (2)
* D.4746   Night Watchman (2)
* D.4750   Shakespeare (1)
  D.4758   Birds (2)
  D.4762   Pip, Squeak and Wilfred (2)
  D.4763   Pip, Squeak and Wilfred (2)
  D.4784   Pan (2)
  D.4785   Flower Sellers in Flemish
            Setting (2)
* D.4792   Flowers and Foliage (2)
  D.4792   Geometrical and Stylized
            Designs (2)
* D.4793   Flowers and Foliage (2)
  D.4793   Geometrical and Stylized
            Designs (2)
* D.4794   Flowers and Foliage (2)
  D.4794   Geometrical and Stylized
            Designs (2)
* D.4795   Flowers and Foliage (2)
  D.4795   Geometrical and Stylized
            Designs (2)
* D.4814   Flowers and Foliage (2)

	D.4814	Geometrical and Stylized Designs (2)		Designs (2)
*	D.4819	Flowers and Foliage (2)	D.4902	Geometrical and Stylized Designs (2)
	D.4819	Geometrical and Stylized Designs (2)	* D.4911	Castles and Churches, Pembroke Castle (1)
	D.4820	Geometrical and Stylized Designs (2)	* D.4914	Landscapes (2)
	D.4820	Urn and Flame (2)	D.4930	Maori Woman With Child (2)
	D.4828	Harlem (2)	D.4931	Maori Woman With Child (2)
	D.4832	Justice's Late Meeting (2)		
	D.4833	Highwayman (2)	D.4932	Country Garden (2)
	D.4834	Cobbler (2)	D.4934	Ploughing (2)
	D.4834	Roger Solemel, Cobbler (2)	* D.4941	Castles and Palaces (Castles and Churches) (2)
	D.4835	Broom-Man (2)		
	D.4841	Willow Pattern (2)	* D.4960	Old English Scenes (English Old Scenes) (2)
*	D.4843	Nautical History (1)		
*	D.4843	Sir Walter Raleigh (Nautical History) (2)	* D.4965	Don Quixote (1),(2)
*	D.4849	Drake (Nautical History) (2)	D.4977	Piping Down the Valleys Wild (2)
*	D.4849	Nautical History (1)	* D.4981	Gondoliers (2)
	D.4851	Willow Pattern (2)	* D.4983	Gleaners and Gipsies (English Old Scenes) (2)
	D.4851	Willow Pattern Story (1)		
*	D.4852	Explorers (Nautical History) (2)	* D.4983	Old English Scenes (English Old Scenes) (2)
*	D.4852	Nautical History (1)	* D.4984	Gleaners and Gipsies (English Old Scenes) (2)
	D.4859	Geometrical and Stylized Designs (2)		
*	D.4860	Flowers and Foliage (2)	* D.4984	Old English Scenes (English Old Scenes) (2)
	D.4860	Geometrical and Stylized Designs (2)	D.4988	Hunting (2)
*	D.4861	Flowers and Foliage (2)	D.4990	Hunting (2)
	D.4861	Geometrical and Stylized Designs (2)	D.4994	Hunting (2)
*	D.4862	Flowers and Foliage (2)	* D.5000	Sir Roger de Coverley (1)
	D.4862	Geometrical and Stylized Designs (2)	* D.5001	Sketches From Teniers (2)
*	D.4863	Flowers and Foliage (2)	* D.5003	Gleaners and Gipsies (English Old Scenes) (2)
	D.4863	Geometrical and Stylized Designs (2)	* D.5007	Landscapes (2)
*	D.4864	Flowers and Foliage (2)	* D.5008	Landscapes (2)
	D.4864	Geometrical and Stylized Designs (2)	D.5021	Italian Landscape (2)
	D.4872	Willow Pattern (2)	* D.5021	Landscapes (2)
*	D.4881	Flowers and Foliage (2)	* D.5027	Gleaners and Gipsies (English Old Scenes) (2)
	D.4881	Geometrical and Stylized Designs (2)	D.5030	Days of Chivalry (2)
*	D.4882	Flowers and Foliage (2)	D.5038	Birds (2)
	D.4882	Geometrical and Stylized Designs (2)	D.5038	Geometrical and Stylized Designs (2)
*	D.4883	Landscapes (2)	D.5039	Geometrical and Stylized Designs (2)
*	D.4900	Flowers and Foliage (2)		
	D.4900	Geometrical and Stylized Designs (2)	D.5104	Hunting (2)
	D.4901	Geometrical and Stylized	D.5106	Geometrical and Stylized Designs (2)
			* D.5107	Flowers and Foliage (2)
			D.5107	Geometrical and Stylized Designs (2)
			D.5108	St. George (1)

D.5108	St. George and The Dragon (2)
D.5109	St. George (1)
D.5109	St. George and The Dragon (2)
D.5110	St. George (1)
D.5110	St. George and The Dragon (2)
D.5111	St. George (1)
D.5111	St. George and The Dragon (2)
* D.5112	Flowers and Foliage (2)
D.5112	Geometrical and Stylized Designs (2)
* D.5113	Flowers and Foliage (2)
* D.5114	Flowers and Foliage (2)
D.5114	Geometrical and Stylized Designs (2)
D.5157	Timber Logging (2)
* D.5175	Dickens (Dickens Ware) (1)
* D.5180	Alice in Wonderland (2)
* D.5187	Alice in Wonderland (2)
D.5193	Deer (2)
D.5194	Deer (2)
D.5195	Woodley Dale (2)
D.5206	Swans (2)
D.5207	Geometrical and Stylized Designs (2)
D.5207	Waratah (2)
* D.5208	Flowers and Foliage (2)
D.5208	Geometrical and Stylized Designs (2)
* D.5209	Flowers and Foliage (2)
D.5209	Geometrical and Stylized Designs (2)
D.5210	Geometrical and Stylized Designs (2)
D.5291	Geometrical and Stylized Designs (2)
D.5292	Geometrical and Stylized Designs (2)
D.5293	Geometrical and Stylized Designs (2)
D.5295	Waratah (2)
D.5296	Waratah (2)
* D.5308	Flowers and Foliage (2)
* D.5309	Flowers and Foliage (2)
* D.5359	Flowers and Foliage (2)
* D.5360	Flowers and Foliage (2)
* D.5361	Flowers and Foliage (2)
D.5364	Log-Hauling (2)
D.5367	Timber Logging (2)
* D.5369	Poplar Trees, Sunset (2)
D.5386	Dog (2)
* D.5408	Flowers and Foliage (2)
D.5408	Geometrical and Stylized Designs (2)
* D.5409	Flowers and Foliage (2)
D.5409	Geometrical and Stylized Designs (2)
* D.5410	Flowers and Foliage (2)
D.5410	Geometrical and Stylized Designs (2)
D.5411	Geometrical and Stylized Designs (2)
* D.5412	Castles and Churches, St. Mary's Aisle, Dryburgh (2)
* D.5412	St. Mary's Aisle, Dryburgh (Castles and Churches) (2)
* D.5413	Castles and Churches, Cawder Castle (1)
* D.5413	Castles and Churches, St. Mary's Aisle, Dryburgh (1)
* D.5413	Castles and Palaces (Castles and Churches) (2)
* D.5433	Castles and Churches (1)
* D.5436	Flowers and Foliage (2)
D.5436	Geometrical and Stylized Designs (2)
* D.5437	Flowers and Foliage (2)
D.5437	Geometrical and Stylized Designs (2)
D.5439	Tea in The Garden (2)
* D.5444	Nursery Rhymes (2)
* D.5460	Flowers and Foliage (2)
D.5460	Geometrical and Stylized Designs (2)
D.5463	Jock of The Bushveld (2)
D.5464	Jock of The Bushveld (2)
D.5473	Geometrical and Stylized Designs (2)
* D.5490	Old Moreton, 1589 (Old Moreton) (2)
D.5497	French Courtiers (2)
D.5499	A Hundred Years Ago (2)
* D.5506	Landscapes (2)
D.5561	Cotswold Shepherd (2)
D.5584	Dickens, Old Curiosity Shop Jug (Miscellaneous chapter) (1)
D.5604	Nursery Subjects (2)
D.5607	Nursery Subjects (2)
D.5617	Dickens, Oliver Twist Jug (Miscellaneous chapter) (1)
D.5633	Australian Bush (2)
D.5650	Ploughing (2)
D.5652	Maple Tree (2)
D.5653	Maple Tree (2)
D.5657	Maple Tree (2)
D.5658	Maple Tree (2)

D.5659	Geometrical and Stylized Designs (2)
D.5659	Maple Tree (2)
D.5660	Maple Tree (2)
D.5661	Geometrical and Stylized Designs (2)
D.5661	Maple Tree (2)
* D.5680	Zunday Zmocks (Gaffers) (2)
* D.5694	Rustic England (2)
D.5708	Dickens, Mask Jug (Miscellaneous chapter) (1)
D.5711	Zulu Girl at Waterhole (2)
D.5712	Game at Drinking Pool (2)
* D.5713	Zulu Warrior (Scenic Rack Plates) (2)
D.5714	Van Riebeeck Statue (2)
D.5723	Lion (2)
D.5724	Lioness (2)
D.5747	Zulu Girl at Waterhole (2)
* D.5748	Zulu Warrior (Scenic Rack Plates) (2)
D.5750	Lion (2)
D.5751	Lioness (2)
D.5756	Dickens, Pickwick Papers Jug (Miscellaneous chapter) (1)
D.5759	Dog (2)
D.5759	Van Riebeeck Statue (2)
D.5769	Dog (2)
D.5770	Dog (2)
D.5781	Dog (2)
* D.5808	Under The Greenwood Tree (1),(2)
* D.5812	Treasure Island (1)
D.5813	Bateman (1),(2)
* D.5814	Sir Roger de Coverley (1), (2)
D.5815	Woodland (2)
D.5816	Scene at Lorne (2)
D.5833	Dickens (1)
D.5851	Weeping Rock Waterfall (2)
D.5852	Captain Arthur Phillip (2)
D.5852	Governor Phillip's Statue (2)
D.5862	Dickens (1)
D.5864	Dickens, White Hart Jug (1)
* D.5880	Gaffers (3)
D.5895	Scene at Lorne (2)
D.5898	Squire (2)
D.5899	Mayor (2)
D.5900	Dickens Portrait (1)
D.5901	Parson (2)

D.5902	The Admiral (2)
D.5903	Jester (2)
D.5905	The Bookworm (2)
D.5906	Doctor (2)
D.5907	Falconer (2)
D.5910	Doctor Johnson (1)
* D.5910	Shakespeare (1)
D.5910	Shakespeare Portrait (2)
D.5911	Dr. Johnson at The Cheshire Cheese (2)
D.5928	Log-Hauling (2)
* D.5940	Historic England (1),(2)
* D.5957	Famous Sailing Ships (Famous Ships) (1)
* D.5957	Famous Ships (2)
* D.5959	Gallant Fishers (1)
* D.5961	Gallant Fishers (1)
* D.5965	Hiawatha (1),(2)
* D.5966	Old Wife (2)
D.5979	Voortrekker (2)
D.5980	Voortrekker (2)
* D.5990	Flowers and Foliage (2)
D.5990	Geometrical and Stylized Designs (2)
* D.5991	Flowers and Foliage (2)
D.5991	Geometrical and Stylized Designs (2)
* D.5992	Flowers and Foliage (2)
D.5992	Geometrical and Stylized Designs (2)
* D.5993	Flowers and Foliage (2)
D.5993	Geometrical and Stylized Designs (2)
* D.5994	Flowers and Foliage (2)
D.5994	Geometrical and Stylized Designs (2)
* D.5995	Castles and Churches, Rochester Castle (1)
* D.5995	Flowers and Foliage (2)
D.5995	Geometrical and Stylized Designs (2)
* D.5996	Flowers and Foliage (2)
D.5996	Geometrical and Stylized Designs (2)
D.6058	Maori Girls (2)
* D.6072	Old English Inns (1),(2)
* D.6094	Under The Greenwood Tree (1),(2)
* D.6099	Monks (2)
* D.6112	Castles and Churches, Rochester Castle (1)
* D.6112	Castles and Palaces (Castles and Churches) (2)
D.6113	Timber Waggon (Scenic Rack Plates) (3)

* D.6118   Flowers and Foliage (2)
  D.6118   Geometrical and Stylized Designs (2)
* D.6119   Flowers and Foliage (2)
  D.6119   Geometrical and Stylized Designs (2)
* D.6123   Gleaners and Gipsies (English Old Scenes) (2)
  D.6153   African Girl and Kraal (2)
  D.6154   Giraffes (2)
  D.6155   Elephant (2)
* D.6156   Vermillion Lake and Mount Rundle, Canada (Scenic Rack Plates) (2)
  D.6156   Water Buck (2)
  D.6160   Lambeth Horseferry (2)
  D.6185   Hunting (2)
  D.6190   Tiger (2)
  D.6161   Lion (2)
  D.6201   Captain Arthur Phillip (2)
  D.6231   Hunting (2)
* D.6277   Jester (Head Rack Plates) (2)
* D.6278   The Admiral (Head Rack Plates) (2)
* D.6279   Falconer (Head Rack Plates) (2)
* D.6280   Parson (Head Rack Plates) (2)
* D.6281   Doctor (Head Rack Plates) (2)
* D.6282   Hunting Man (Head Rack Plates) (2)
* D.6283   Mayor (Head Rack Plates) (2)
* D.6284   Squire (Head Rack Plates) (2)
  D.6285   Dickens, Oliver Twist Jug (Miscellaneous chapter) (1)
  D.6286   Dickens, Oliver Twist Tankard (Miscellaneous chapter) (1)
  D.6291   Dickens, Old London Jug (Miscellaneous chapter) (1)
  D.6292   Dickens, Peggotty Jug (Miscellaneous chapter) (1)
  D.6297   Geometrical and Stylized Designs (2)
* D.6297   Rustic England (2)
* D.6298   Flowers and Foliage (2)
  D.6298   Magnella (2)
  D.6299   Chrysanthemums (2)
* D.6299   Flowers and Foliage (2)
* D.6302   Cobbler (Head Rack Plates) (2)

  D.6302   Shakespeare (1)
* D.6303   Shakespeare (Head Rack Plates) (1)
* D.6303   Shakespeare Portrait (Head Rack Plates) (2)
  D.6304   Dog (2)
* D.6305   Maori Girls (Scenic Rack Plates) (2)
* D.6306   Dickens Portrait (Head Rack Plates) (1)
  D.6307   Timber Waggon (2)
* D.6307   Queen's View, Loch Tummel (Scenic Rack Plates) (3)
* D.6308   Castles and Churches, Rochester Castle (Scenic Rack Plates) (1)
  D.6309   Gum Trees (2)
  D.6310   Scene at Lorne (2)
  D.6311   Weeping Rock Waterfall (2)
* D.6312   Flowers and Foliage (2)
  D.6313   Dog (2)
* D.6325   Flowers and Foliage (2)
  D.6326   Hunting (2)
  D.6327   Dickens (1)
* D.6341   Under The Greenwood Tree (1),(2)
  D.6342   Bermuda Scenes (2)
* D.6344   Burns Portrait (Head Rack Plates) (1)
  D.6344   Robert Burns (2)
  D.6347   Lion (2)
  D.6348   Lioness (2)
  D.6349   Game at Drinking Pool (2)
  D.6350   Van Riebeeck Statue (2)
  D.6351   Zulu Girl at Waterhole (2)
* D.6352   Zulu Warrior (Scenic Rack Plates) (2)
* D.6355   Good Morning Zulu Girl (2)
  D.6356   Lion (2)
* D.6359   Lion (Scenic Rack Plates) (2)
* D.6360   Lioness (Scenic Rack Plates) (2)
  D.6361   Game at Drinking Pool (2)
  D.6362   Van Riebeeck Statue (2)
* D.6363   Zulu Girl at Waterhole (Scenic Rack Plates) (2)
* D.6364   Zulu Warrior (Scenic Rack Plates) (2)
* D.6376   Treasure Island (1),(2)
  D.6377   Doctor Johnson (1)
* D.6378   Jackdaw of Rheims (1)

	D.6379	Rhodes Centenary (2)	
*	D.6387	Good Morning Zulu Girl (2)	
*	D.6393	Old English Coaching Scenes (2)	
	D.6394	Dickens, White Hart Jug (1)	
	D.6395	Dickens, Sairey Gamp Jug (1)	
	D.6396	Dickens, Bill Sikes Jug (1)	
	D.6397	Dickens, Tony Weller Jug (1)	
	D.6398	Dickens, Sam Weller Jug (1)	
*	D.6402	Flowers and Foliage (2)	
	D.6409	Aborigines in Corroboree (2)	
	D.6410	Aborigine With Hunting Weapons (2)	
	D.6411	Australian Aborigine (2)	
	D.6412	Mother Kangaroo With Joey (2)	
	D.6413	Koala Bears (2)	
	D.6414	Murray River Gums, Australia (2)	
	D.6415	Young Kookaburras (2)	
	D.6416	New Guinea Native (2)	
	D.6417	Mount Egmont, New Zealand (2)	
	D.6420	Aborigines in Corroboree (2)	
*	D.6421	Aborigine With Hunting Weapons (Scenic Rack Plates) (2)	
*	D.6422	Australian Aborigine (Scenic Rack Plates) (2)	
*	D.6423	Mother Kangaroo With Joey (Scenic Rack Plates) (2)	
*	D.6424	Koala Bears (Scenic Rack Plates) (2)	
*	D.6425	Murray River Gums, Australia (Scenic Rack Plates) (2)	
*	D.6426	Young Kookaburras (Scenic Rack Plates) (2)	
	D.6434	Home Waters (2)	
*	D.6436	Mount Egmont, New Zealand (Scenic Rack Plates) (2)	
*	D.6437	New Guinea Native (Scenic Rack Plates) (2)	
*	D.6471	Bow Falls, Canada (Scenic Rack Plates) (2)	
*	D.6472	Montmorency Falls, Canada	

		(Scenic Rack Plates) (2)	
	D.6473	Vermillion Lake and Mount Rundle, Canada (2)	
*	D.6474	Lake Louise and Victoria Glacier, Canada (Scenic Rack Plates) (2)	
*	D.6475	Bow Valley, Canada (Scenic Rack Plates) (2)	
*	D.6476	Niagara Falls, Canada (Scenic Rack Plates) (2)	
	D.6477	Elephant (2)	
	D.6478	Giraffes (2)	
*	D.6479	Good Morning Zulu Girl (2)	
*	D.6480	Water Buck (Scenic Rack Plates) (2)	
*	D.6481	Elephant (Scenic Rack Plates) (2)	
*	D.6482	Giraffes (Scenic Rack Plates) (2)	
*	D.6483	Good Morning Zulu Girl (2)	
	D.6484	Water Buck (2)	
*	D.6493	Maritime Provinces, Canada (Scenic Rack Plates) (2)	
*	D.7671	Castles and Churches (3)	
	E.2766	Gibson (1)	
	E.2827	Gibson (1)	
*	E.3236	Souter's Cats (1)	
*	E.3505	Jackdaw of Rheims (2)	
*	E.3793	Souter's Cats (1)	
*	E.3804	Coaching Days (2)	
*	E.3923	Gallant Fishers (1)	
*	E.4021	Alice in Wonderland, Looking-Glass (2)	
*	E.4090	Alice in Wonderland, Looking-Glass (2)	
	E.4336	All Black Cricketers (2)	
	E.5833	Dickens (1)	
	E.7211	Willow Pattern Story (1)	
*	E.7239	Castles and Churches (1)	
*	E.7239	Castles and Palaces (Castles and Churches) (2)	
	E.7267	Shakespeare (1)	
	E.7831	Willow Pattern Story (1)	
	E.7832	Willow Pattern Story (1)	
	E.8288	Dickens (1)	
	E.8289	Bobbie Burns (1)	
	H. 797	World War I (1)	
*	H.2941	Castles and Churches, Warwick Castle (1)	
*	H.2948	Castles and Churches, Windsor Castle (1)	
*	H.2948	Castles and Palaces (Castles	

and Churches) (2)

TC 10	Admiral (2)	
TC 102	Anne Hathaway's Cottage (2)	
TC 102	Clovelly (2)	
TC 102	Houses of Parliament (2)	
TC 103	Canada, Centennial Map (2)	
TC 103	Little Moreton Hall (2)	
TC 104	Doctor (2)	
TC 104	Falconry (2)	
TC 104	Jester (2)	
TC 104	Robert Burns (2)	
TC 105	Mayor (2)	
* TC 109	Castles and Palaces	

(Castles and Churches) (2)

TC 109	Loch Lomond (2)	
TC1040	Burns Portrait (1)	
TC1041	Shakespeare (1)	
TC1042	Dickens Portrait (1)	
* TC1092	Castles and Churches (1)	
* TC1093	Loch Lomond (Scenic Rack Plates) (3)	
* V.2352	Castles and Churches (1)	
* V.2352	Castles and Palaces (Castles and Churches) (2)	
* V.2352	Coaching Days (2)	
* V.2353	Old English Inns (1)	
V.2354	Shakespeare (1)	

Series Ware Alphabetical Price List

ALDIN'S DOGS

Cecil Aldin was a book illustrator whose best known character was a mongrel dog featured in several books. The humorous dog was pictured on dinnerware made from 1926 to 1946. Aldin's signature is on each piece.

Pitcher	75.00
Plate, 10 In.*	60.00
Tray, Oblong, 8 X 4 In.	45.00

Aldin's Dogs, Plate, 10 In.

ALI BABA, see Arabian Nights

ALICE IN WONDERLAND

Alice in Wonderland, produced 1906 to 1932, pictures scenes from Lewis Carroll's book "Alice in Wonderland."

Cup & Saucer, Mad Hatter   50.00

AMERICAN VIEWS

A series of blue and white plates was made in the early 1900s that pictured views of the United States. There is no special mark but the scene is named on the back of the plate.

Plate, Niagara Falls,
   10 1/2 In.   145.00
Plate, Pikes Peak, 10 1/2 In.   95.00

ARABIAN NIGHTS

Arabian Nights series is also known as The Thousand and One Nights. The plates picture Ali Baba and the Forty Thieves and other episodes from the famous stories. The series was made in 1909, given a new vine border in 1911, and discontinued in 1928. On the front of the plate there is a picture, a title for the picture, and a border, either the Japanese style or the trailing vine.

Pitcher, Ali Baba With The
   Treasure, 6 In.   250.00 to 295.00
Plate, Arrival of the Unknown
   Princess, 10 3/8 In.*   110.00

*Arabian Nights, Plate, Arrival
Of The Unknown Princess,
10 3/8 In.*

ATHENS

Ancient Greek festivals and processions are pictured on a series called Athens. It was made from 1910 to 1928. Pieces are marked D.3302. Another group of plates, D.3475, made from 1911 to 1928 also depicted Greek scenes.

Pitcher   45.00

AUTHORS AND INNS

Well known authors are pictured in front of their favorite inns in the series called Authors and Inns. The author's name is part of the design. It was first made in 1904.

Pitcher, Chaucer, Ye Tabard, Marked, 7 1/2 In.	110.00	Pitcher, Raleigh, 9 In. **110.00**

AUTUMN GLORY

Autumn Glory series was made from 1927 to 1942. Pieces are marked D.4713 and D.4714.

Plate, Square 110.00

BABES IN WOODS, see Blue Children

BAYEUX TAPESTRY

Bayeux Tapestry, 1906 to about 1928, is a famous embroidery depicting William the Conqueror's expedition to England. The tapestry is preserved at Bayeux in Normandy and is attributed to William's wife. The ware is marked with the words "The Battle of Hastings 1066 from the Bayeux Tapestry." Some have a green and brown border; others have battle scenes.

Jug, Concord, 6 In.   98.00 to 110.00

Border

Backstamp

BLUE CHILDREN

Blue Children was produced from the late 1880s until 1928. It is sometimes called Babes in Woods. It is a flow blue ware. There is no special mark.

Bowl, May Day Children's Procession, 9 In.	50.00	Vase, Lady Picking Berries, 5 1/4 In. 235.00
Bowl, Nursery Series, Girl By Seashore	38.00	Vase, Mother, 2 Girls, Dog Under Tree, 9 In. 325.00
Vase, Dog In Front Of Little Girls, 5 In.	259.00	Vase, Three Girls, Dog, Picnic Basket Under Tree 185.00
Vase, Handled, Gold Trim, 2 3/4 X 4 1/4 In.	250.00	

BOBBY BURNS

Bobby Burns was a Scottish poet who lived from 1759 to 1796. He was famous for his poem "Auld Lang Syne." The plates picture Burns and others accompanied with sayings from his poems. The series, redesigned several times, was made from 1910 to 1975.

Bowl, Home Waters, Sailing Scene, 10 1/2 X 7 3/8 In.	85.00	Plate, Green Grow The Rushes, D.3368, 6 In.	55.00
Bowl, 7 1/2 In.	135.00	Plate, 10 1/4 In.	50.00
Candlestick, I Hae A Wife, D.4419	70.00	Sauce, D.4419	20.00

BUNNYKINS

Bunnykins was produced from 1934 to the present. There are over 150 designs on children's ware including mush sets, cereal bowls, etc. Pieces are marked with three bunnies and the name, some with Barbara Vernon and some with the "A" mark. Some pieces also have a running bunny border.

Bank, Ball   8.00

Border

Backstamp

ENGLISH FINE BONE CHINA
" BUNNYKINS "

CANTERBURY PILGRIMS

Canterbury Pilgrims was produced from 1902 to the 1920s. It features scenes from the book "Canterbury Tales" by Geoffrey Chaucer. They have a decorative border with lion and bird shields. They are marked "Canterbury Pilgrims."

Pitcher, Ye Canterbury Pilgrims, Handled	115.00 to 125.00	Tea Tile	55.00
Tea Set	375.00	Tray, 7 3/4 X 17 1/2 In.	125.00

Border

Backstamp

ROYAL DOULTON
ENGLAND
CANTERBURY
PILGRIMS

CASTLES AND CHURCHES

Arundel Castle, Windsor Castle, Croydon Church, Fountains Abbey, and other buildings are pictured in the series Castles and Churches. Each plate has a different building. The series was made from 1911 through the 1950s. The design covers the entire plate, there is no border design. Pieces were made in blue and white, sepia, or natural colors. There were some pitchers, bowls, and other dishes made although most often it is a plate that is seen.

Creamer, Windsor Castle, D.5413
                                          55.00
Plate, Hurtsmonceaux Castle,
  D.3471, 10 In.   62.00
Plate, Muckrose Abbey, D.2654,
  10 1/2 In.   35.00
Plate, Pembroke Castle, D.3599,
  10 1/2 In.   35.00
Plate, Windsor Castle, D.2948,
  10 1/2 In.*   35.00
Tobacco Jar, Windsor Castle   95.00
Trivet, Arundel Castle, D.7671
                                          45.00

*Castles And Churches, Plate,
Windsor Castle, D.2948,
10 1/2 In.*

CAVALIERS

Cavaliers, sometimes called Three Musketeers, was produced from 1908 to the 1930s. The plates have a lion, cross, and shield border. There is no special mark.

Pitcher, Better So Than Worse, 8 In.
                                          75.00
Pitcher, Ever Drink Ever Dry, 7 In.
                                          60.00
Plate, 10 In.   200.00

COACHING DAYS, see also Old English Coaching Scenes; Old Jarvey

Coaching Days was made of bone china or earthenware. The early pieces (D.2716) are pastel and have no special mark. It is very similar to the Fox-Hunting series. The plates have a dark green border. The series was made from 1906 to 1945, then from 1948 to 1967.

Border

Backstamp

Ashtray, Gypsy Caravan, 4 3/4 In.	22.00
Biscuit Jar	225.00
Bowl, Vegetable	85.00
Bowl, 8 In.	85.00
Bowl, 9 1/2 In.	75.00
Cheese Dish, Covered	345.00
Cookie Jar, Covered	225.00
Creamer, 3 1/4 In.	45.00
Cup & Saucer	35.00 to 40.00
Dessert Set, 16 Piece	350.00
Dish, Round	95.00
Jar, Tea	265.00
Pitcher, 6 1/2 In.	135.00
Plate, 10 In.*	65.00
Soup, Dish, 7 1/2 In.	20.00
Sugar & Creamer	145.00
Tile, Square, 6 1/2 In.	20.00
Vase, 5 In.	85.00

Coaching Days, Plate, 10 In.

COUNTRY SIDE

Country Side is a series, including rack plates, made from 1912 to 1945. Scenic landscapes are pictured.

Plate, Thatched Cottages, D.3634, 10 In.	85.00

DAVID TENIERS, see Sketches from Teniers

DESERT SCENES

Desert scenes pictures camels, palm trees, pyramids, and Arabs. The plates are decorated with pastel colors and a yellow color sand. They are marked "Desert Scenes." The series was made from 1909 to 1929.

Plate, 9 In.	90.00
Vase, D.3192, 9 In.	85.00

Backstamp

DICKENS WARE, see also listings in Miscellaneous chapter

Dickens ware was produced from 1908 to 1931 in one version and 1931 to 1974 in another. All pieces feature characters from various stories by Charles Dickens. The early wares are marked in brown and the later wares, which are decorated in brighter colors, are marked in black. In the 1950s the series was changed again. These pieces are all numbered D.6327. This series was discontinued in 1960. There is also a line marked Australia. These are decorated with figures in relief.

Ashtray, D.4119, 4 In.	22.00
Bowl, Round, Dick Swiveller, D.2973	135.00
Cup & Saucer, Adam	35.00
Cup & Saucer, Mr.Micawber	65.00
Cup & Saucer, Sam Weller	55.00
Dish, Squire, Sairey Gamp*	95.00
Mug, Oliver Asks For More	225.00
Pitcher, Curiosity Shop, Square	150.00
Pitcher, Fagin, 7 In.	175.00
Pitcher, Mr.Pickwick, 6 1/2 In.	100.00
Pitcher, Poor Jo, D.5175	175.00
Plate, Artful Dodger, D.5175	85.00
Plate, Mr.Mantalini, D.1943, 10 1/2 In.	325.00
Plate, Sam Weller, Raised Figures, 1938, 10 1/2 In.	80.00
Plate, Sydney Carton, D.2973, 10 1/2 In.	52.00
Sauce, Fat Boy, Marked, 5 1/4 In.	45.00
Tankard, Oliver	185.00 to 200.00
Tray, Barnaby Rudge, 4 X 5 3/8 In.	40.00
Vase, Barnaby Rudge, Handled, 8 1/2 In.	165.00
Vase, Barnaby Rudge, 10 1/2 In.	250.00
Vase, Mr. Micawber, 2-Handled, 5 In.	85.00
Vase, Singing Monk, 10 1/2 In.	450.00
Vase, Sydney Carton, Handled, 3 3/4 X 7 In.	135.00
Vase, Tony Weller, Square, 4 5/8 X 8 In.	165.00

Mr. Macawber
D.6327

Backstamps

Mr. Pickwick.
D.6327.

Dickens Ware, Dish, Squire, Sairey Gamp

DIVERSIONS OF UNCLE TOBY

Diversions of Uncle Toby, or "Old English Games," is a series based on the character Uncle Toby from the novel "Tristram Shandy." Each pastime is named at the bottom of the plate, Uncle Toby is pictured at play in the center, and a ribbon band including the words "The Diversions of Uncle Toby" forms the border. There is a special backstamp.

Plate, Quoits	65.00
Plate, As A Taxophilite*	
	65.00

Backstamp

Diversions Of Uncle Toby, Plate, As A Taxophilite

DON QUIXOTE

Don Quixote is a famous character in the book "Don Quixote" by Miguel de Cervantes. The plates have a greenish gray background. Some have a tree and windmill border. The series was made from 1906 to 1928. There is some evidence that it was introduced again with the number D.4965 in 1929 and discontinued in the 1940s. There is no special mark.

Cup & Saucer	75.00
Plate, 10 In.	75.00

DUTCH

Dutch, sometimes called Holland, was produced from 1905. It pictures scenes of Dutch families and children in their surroundings. The wares are decorated with a yellow sky, green grass, sailboats, and sometimes brick walls. Some have a tulip border. There is no special mark except on a special advertising cookie jar for McVitie & Price.

Candlestick, Pair, D.1881	165.00
Candlestick, 6 In.	125.00
Cookie Jar	75.00
Teapot, D.1884	95.00
Trivet*	55.00
Vase, Miniature	45.00

Backstamp

Border

EGLINGTON TOURNAMENT

Eglington Tournament, 1902 to 1928, was held by Archibald, the 13th Earl of Eglington, in 1839. The wares picture knights on horseback, jousting, and other tournament events. Three different colorways were made: blue and white, sepia and green, and polychrome. It has no special mark.

Jug, Knights On Horses, Blue,
   5 1/2 In.   135.00

EGYPTIAN

Egyptian pictures scenes of Egypt. The plates have a brown, beige, and orange border. It was made from 1911 to 1929. There is no special mark.

Jug, Geometric Edge, Marked,
   6 3/8 In.   110.00

ENGLISH OLD PROVERBS, see also Proverbs

English Old Proverbs Illustrated and Old English Sayings are plates made between 1910 and 1925. Some are marked with the backstamp "Old English Proverbs Illustrated." These plates usually have a tree border, picture, and two proverbs. Other plates have a scroll border, a single figure, one proverb, and the title on the face of the plate.

Plate, Fine Feather   40.00
Plate, A Thing Of Beauty,
   D.3428*   40.00

Dutch, Trivet

*English Old Proverbs, Plate,
A Thing Of Beauty, D.3428*

ENGLISH OLD SCENES

English Old Scenes is divided into two series, the Gipsies and the Gleaners. The Gipsies life-style is featured in bright colors and the harvest-working people of the fields are pictured in the Gleaners. The series was made from 1909 to 1950.

Bowl, Gleaners, 6 In.	35.00	Plate, Gipsies, 9 In.*	65.00
Bowl, Gleaners, 8 In.	45.00	Platter, Gipsies, D.6123	45.00

Backstamp

English Old Scenes, Plate, Gipsies, 9 In.

FAIRY TALES

Fairy Tales was produced about 1933. The plates are decorated with characters from stories such as the Pied Piper or Rip Van Winkle. There is no special mark.

Plate, Rip Van Winkle   55.00

FALCONRY

Falconry is an early Royal Doulton-Burslem ware produced at the Nile St. factory. It pictures equestrian scenes. It has a decorative border. The mark is a prize ribbon with the word "Falconry." It was made from 1913 to 1930.

Plate, 10 In.*	47.50 to 65.00
Tray, Handled, 18 In.	95.00

Backstamp

Falconry, Plate, 10 In.

FAMOUS SHIPS

Famous Ships pictures ships in relief on a pastel background. The pieces have a special mark which includes the name of the ship and often the Australian mark. The series was made from 1938 to about 1960.

Plate, Revenge, 12 In.
          40.00 to 50.00
Vase, Golden Hind, Australia,
D.5957*   50.00

Backstamps

*Famous Ships, Vase, Golden
Hind, Australia, D.5957*

FLOWER-SELLERS IN FLEMISH
SETTING

Flower-Sellers in Flemish Setting is a series made from 1928 to 1945. The
number D.4785 appears on the pieces. The design shows ladies selling flowers
while seated on a cobblestone street. There is no special backstamp.

Plate, 10 In.   60.00

FLOWERS AND FOLIAGE

Flowers and Foliage is the name for a large number of rack plates that picture
leaves and blossoms. Various designs were made from 1905 to 1967.

Plate, Lake With Trees, D.6312,
   10 1/2 In.   110.00

FOX-HUNTING

Fox-Hunting, made from 1931 to 1950, is similar to Coaching Days. It has a
scalloped edge and a dark green border. The words Fox-Hunting are the special
mark. There have been several other hunting series.

Creamer	45.00	
Demitasse Set, 7 Piece	450.00	*Backstamp*
Pitcher, Green, Gold Trim, Signed		
R.Gough	200.00	
Pitcher, 4 In.	70.00	

"FOX-HUNTING"
D. 5104

GAFFERS

Gaffers, 1921 to 1949, pictures elderly country men and printed sayings. The
plates are decorated in bright colors. They are marked with a crossed umbrella
and cane and the word Gaffers. Pieces without the mark are sometimes called
Zunday Zmocks.

Bowl, I Be All The Way From		
Zummerset, 10 1/2 In.	88.00	*Backstamp*
Bowl, Oval, 11 In.	95.00	
Creamer, 4 1/2 In.	75.00 to 80.00	
Dish, Square, 4 In.	40.00	

ROYAL DOULTON
MADE IN ENGLAND
D 4210

Pitcher, Zunday Zmocks, 7 In.
165.00
Plate, Zunday Zmocks, D.5880
100.00
Sauce, D.4210   30.00
Sugar Shaker   125.00
Tobacco Jar, D.4210, 5 1/4 In.*
125.00
Tray, D.4210, 10 In.   115.00
Tray, 12 In.   125.00
Vase, 2-Handled, 5 1/4 In.   85.00

*Gaffers, Tobacco Jar,
D.4210, 5 1/4 In.*

GALLANT FISHERS, see also Isaac Walton

Gallant Fishers is one of the three series based on the scenes and sayings from Isaac Walton's book "The Compleat Angler." Gallant Fishers was made from 1913 to 1936. It often has a special mark showing a hanging fish marked "The Gallant Fishers." The center scene shows men fishing and often there is a motto on the plate. The border is of willow trees. An earlier version, made from 1901, had the same center characters, no motto, and a Jedo border. Another similar series is marked with the special Isaac Walton backstamp and is listed under that name.

Plate, Jedo Border, 10 In.*   65.00

Backstamp

*Gallant Fishers, Plate, Jedo
Border, 10 In.*

GEORGE BOWMAN

A series of blue and white or red and white plates were made that are marked "The Geo. M. Bowman Co./Sole Importers/Cleveland." Known views include Martha Washington, George Washington, Mt. Vernon, Washington Mansion, the U.S. Capitol, and the Congressional Library. The plates date from the early 1900s.

Plate, Mt.Vernon, Blue On White,
10 In.   48.00

Backstamp

GIBSON GIRL

Gibson Girl plates were made in the early 1900s. Twenty-four 10 1/2 inch plates picture in black and white episodes from the book "A Widow and Her Friends" by artist Charles Dana Gibson. There is no special mark. Other series were made picturing the girl. One blue and white set of 12 plates pictures just the head of the girl. The border is a series of bows and hearts. Another series, 1904 and after, pictures Gibson Girls golfing.

Plate, A Quiet Dinner With
   Dr.Bottles   85.00
Plate, Day After Arriving Journey's
   End   65.00 to 80.00
Plate, Failing To Find Rest In
   Country   85.00 to 90.00
Plate, Message From The Outside
   World   65.00
Plate, Miss Babbles Brings Paper
                75.00

Border

Plate, Miss Babbles The Authoress,
   Calls & Reads Aloud   65.00
Plate, Mr.Waddles Arrives Late
                85.00
Plate, Mrs.Diggs Is Alarmed   85.00
Plate, Remained In Retirement Too
   Long   65.00
Plate, She Becomes A Trained Nurse
                75.00
Plate, She Contemplates The
   Cloister   65.00 to 85.00
Plate, She Decides To Die   65.00
Plate, She Finds Consolation In Her
   Mirror   85.00
Plate, She Finds Exercise Does Not
   Improve Spirit   85.00
Plate, She Goes Into Colors   85.00
Plate, She Goes To The Fancy Dress
   Ball   65.00 to 95.00
Plate, She Is Disturbed By A Vision
                85.00

*Gibson Girl, Plate, She
Longs For Seclusion*

Plate, She Is The Subject Of Hostile
   Criticism   75.00
Plate, She Longs For Seclusion*
                80.00
Plate, She Looks For Relief Among
   The Old Ones   50.00 to 75.00
Plate, They All Go Skating   85.00
Plate, They Go Fishing   90.00
Plate, They Take A Morning Run
                90.00

Plate, Winning New Friends   85.00
Plate, 10 1/2 In., Set Of 24
          1800.00 to 2280.00

GNOMES

Gnomes is a series made with blues, maroons, and golds, resembling Fairyland luster or in just plain underglaze blue. The set, made from 1907 to 1950, pictures gnomes.

Ashtray	45.00	Plate, D.4647, 10 In.	140.00
Bowl, 6 In.	190.00	Plate, 8 1/2 In.	225.00
Bowl, 8 In.	60.00 to 65.00	Sugar & Creamer	145.00 to 175.00

GOLFERS

Golfers, about 1911 to 1932, pictures men golfing with sayings printed around the plate. It has no special mark. Other golf inspired plates were also made.

Pitcher, Baggy Trousered Golfers, 7 In.	300.00

GONDOLIERS

Gondoliers are the singing boatmen of Venice. The plates are decorated in bright colors and have no special mark. The series was made from 1930 to 1945.

Plate, 10 In.	50.00

GOOD MORNING ZULU GIRL

A series of plates with photographic scenes of Africa as decorations has the words "Good Morning Zulu Girl" and a special border.

Plate, Zebras, Animal Border, 14 In.	95.00
Plate, Zulu Girl Border, 10 In.	145.00

HEAD RACK PLATES

Head Rack Plates feature prominent characters of England, such as The Admiral, The Mayor, and The Doctor. The borders on the plates vary. Each is marked with the character's name. They were produced at three different times in earthenware or china. Charles Dickens and William Shakespeare were made in flow blue.

Admiral, D.6278, 10 In.*	55.00 to 65.00
Cobbler, 10 In.	70.00
Doctor, 10 In.	55.00 to 60.00
Falconer, 10 In.	30.00 to 65.00
Jester, D.6277, 10 In.*	45.00 to 65.00
Jousting, 10 In.	30.00
Mayor, D.6283, 10 In.**	50.00 to 65.00
Parson, 10 In.	42.00 to 65.00
Squire, D.6284, 10 In.	40.00 to 65.00

Head Rack Plate, Admiral, D.6278, 10 In.

Head Rack Plate, Jester, D.6277, 10 In.

HIAWATHA

Hiawatha is a series made from 1908 to 1930, then from 1938 to 1949. North American Indians' heads are pictured in the center of the plate. The border has teepees. A quotation from the poem "Hiawatha" by H. W. Longfellow completes the border.

Plate, Wampum Belt, 10 In.   75.00

Backstamp

HISTORIC ENGLAND

Historic England features famous people and places of England. The plates are beige with multicolored scenes. They are marked with a castle, tree, title, and the Australian mark. The series was made from 1938 to 1952.

Bowl, Dr. Johnson At Temple
  Bar, Australian Mark   35.00
Plate, Plymouth Hoe, 9 In.   45.00

Backstamp

HISTORICAL BRITAIN

Historical Britain features famous places in Britain. The plates are made of translucent china. There are five plates in the series decorated with photographic views. It has no special mark. The series was introduced in 1967.

Plate, Anne Hathaway's Cottage,
   10 In.**   25.00
Plate, Clovelly, North Devon,
   10 In.*   45.00
Plate, Tudor Mansion, 10 In.* 60.00

Historical Britain, Plate, Clovelly, North Devon, 10 In.

Historical Britain, Plate, Tudor Mansion, 10 In.

HOLLAND, see Dutch

HOME WATERS

Home Waters is a series made from 1954 to 1967. The plates picture the sea, shore, and boats drawn by W. E. Grace who has signed the front of the plate.

Plate, D.6434, 10 In.   35.00

Backstamp

HOME WATERS
MADE IN ENGLAND
D.8434

HUNTING, see Fox-Hunting

ISAAC WALTON, see also Gallant Fishers

Isaac Walton, 1906 to the 1930s, is based on the same theme as Gallant Fishers. The pieces are decorated in greens and browns; some have a saying on the plate. The plates have a willow tree border. There is a special backstamp. There is a pitcher, D.2557, that pictures Isaac Walton and a town view. It is part of the Old London series of people and places in historic towns.

Chamber Stick*   125.00
Flower Bowl   95.00

Isaac Walton, Chamber Stick

Border

Backstamp

JACKDAW OF RHEIMS

Jackdaw of Rheims, 1905 to 1930, is the chief character in a poem from "The Ingoldsby Legends." The lower half of the plate pictures a brick wall with ivy, the upper half, a scene and a line from the poem. Some have a bird border. Pieces with the same design were made in 1949. There is no special mark.

Jug, Cardinal & Monk, Words,	
5 1/4 In.	125.00
Mug, D.2532	65.00
Plate, Ruffled Edge, 9 1/2 In.	65.00
Plate, 9 1/2 In.*	65.00
Tumbler, 4 1/4 In.	125.00
Vase, 6 In.	98.00

Jackdaw Of Rheims, Plate, 9 1/2 In.

JANSSON, see King Of Hearts

KATE GREENAWAY

Kate Greenaway Almanack series was introduced in 1978. The twelve plates illustrate the astrological signs, one for each month.

Plate, Aquarius, January	25.00	Plate, Pisces, February	25.00
Plate, Aries, March	25.00	Plate, Sagittarius, November	25.00
Plate, Cancer, June	25.00	Plate, Scorpio, October	25.00
Plate, Capricorn, December	25.00	Plate, Taurus, April	25.00
Plate, Gemini, May	25.00	Plate, Virgo, August	25.00
Plate, Libra, September	25.00		

KENSINGTON GARDENS

Kensington Gardens is a series made from 1924 to 1942. The pieces are numbered D.4467. The series shows a yellow background with silhouettes of horses, trees, and carriages.

Plate, 8 In.   35.00

KING ARTHUR'S KNIGHTS

King Arthur's Knights, about 1908 to 1930, pictures scenes from "The Knights of the Round Table."

Plate, 10 In.   35.00

KING OF HEARTS

King of Hearts is an easily identified pattern. Playing card figures are shown on each piece. Some plates have a stylized flute and flower border. The plates were made from 1913 to about 1932. There is no special backstamp. Because the design was by Augustus L. Jansson, a Massachusetts artist, the pattern is sometimes called Jansson.

Plate, All Fools Are Not Knaves, All
  Knaves Are Fools   42.00
Plate, D.3665, 10 1/2 In.*   125.00

King Of Hearts, Plate, D.3665, 10 1/2 In.

LANDSCAPES

There are pictures of landscapes on many different Royal Doulton pieces. There is one series named Landscapes. These pieces were decorated in shades of orange and brown as if the landscape is pictured just at the time of sunset. D.2538 was the mark from 1906 to 1928, D.2846 from 1907 to 1928, and D.3668 from 1913 to 1940. A brown and white series of landscapes is known as Moonlight Landscapes.

Plate, D.2846, 10 1/2 In.*   65.00
Vase, 6 In., Pair   135.00

Landscapes, Plate, D.2846, 10 1/2 In.

MAY DAY CHILDREN

May Day Children pictures scenes of children carrying baskets of flowers or dancing around the maypole celebrating the European holiday. It has no special mark.

Sugar   45.00

MINSTRELS

Minstrels is a series made from 1923 to about 1940. Plates are numbered D.4243.

Plate, 10 In.   55.00

MONKS

Monks were produced in three different series. Humorous monks pictures monks enjoying such activities as fishing and includes a saying. The other two series were produced in two color combinations: blue and tan or green and tan. The various pieces were made from 1906 to 1950. They have no special mark.

Creamer, Octagonal, 6 1/4 In.
                                     125.00
Creamer, Square, 7 1/4 In.   110.00
Pitcher, 7 1/2 In.   250.00
Plate, Fishing, Tomorrow Will Be
    Friday, Signed   42.00 to 45.00
Plate, Green And Tan, 10 In.*   55.00
Teapot, Blue & White   175.00

*Monks, Plate, Green And
Tan, 10 In.*

MOORISH SCENE

Moorish Gateway, 1926 to 1945, has raised decorations showing a Moorish scene. Pieces are numbered D.4601 but there is no special backstamp.

Plate, 10 In.   60.00

MOTORING

Motoring was produced from 1905 to 1928. Nine different motorcar scenes are pictured in shades of greens and browns. It has a scenic border of trees, hills, and clouds. It has no special mark.

Plate, Deaf, 10 In.   75.00
Plate, Itch Yer On Guvenor,
    9 1/4 In.   175.00
Plate, Room For One,
    10 In.*   110.00

Motoring, Plate, Room For
One, 10 In.

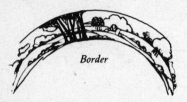

Border

MUNCHKINS, see Gnomes

NAUTICAL HISTORY

Many views of naval heroes, ships, and battles are pictured on the series known collectively as Nautical History, or Explorers. Some have a special border of ships, some have a view that covers the full plate.

Plate, Spanish Armada, 10 1/2 In.*
            40.00 to 50.00

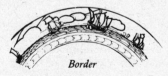

Border

Nautical History, Plate, Spanish
Armada, 10 1/2 In.

NIGHT WATCHMAN

Night Watchman pictures the night watchman performing his nightly duties. It was made from 1901 to 1928. Another series picturing watchman, marked D.4746, was made from 1928 to 1945. There is no special mark.

Pitcher, Tankard Shape, 8 1/2 In.
                            120.00
Pitcher, 8 In.*   98.00

Night Watchman, Pitcher, 8 In.

NURSERY RHYMES

Nursery Rhymes was produced in 1903 in earthenware and 1917 to about 1925 in creamware. Little Bo Peep and Mary Had A Little Lamb are still in production. They are decorated with scenes and a verse from the rhyme. Some are marked "Nursery Rhymes."

Cup & Saucer, Mother Goose   22.00
Plate, Old Mother Hubbard, 7 In.
                            35.00
Tumbler   110.00

OLD ENGLISH COACHING SCENES, see also Coaching Days

Old English Coaching Scenes was made from 1953 to 1967. Some pieces are marked with a special backstamp, some pieces were signed "Grace."

Pitcher, Old Bob, 8 3/4 In.*   125.00
Scenes, Plate, Old Bob, 10 In.   55.00

Old English Coaching Scenes, Pitcher, Old Bob, 8 3/4 In.

Border

Backstamp

OLD ENGLISH GAMES, see Diversions Of Uncle Toby

OLD ENGLISH INNS

Old English Inns pictures well-known taverns of England. It has a special mark of a tavern, the words "Old English Inns," and the Australian mark. The series was made from 1939 to 1955. Another series, 1939 to 1958, showing inns, had an oak leaf border.

Plate, Australia, D.6072   25.00

OLD ENGLISH SCENES, see English Old Scenes

OLD JARVEY, see also Coaching Days

The words "An Old Jarvey" appear on a series made from 1909 to 1928. The pieces, numbered D.3118, show an old coachman at work.

Bowl, 8 In.*   95.00

Old Jarvey, Bowl, 8 In.

OLD MORETON

Old Moreton, 1915 to 1925, pictures Elizabethan court scenes and says "Queen Elizabeth at Old Moreton 1589." The plates have an architectural border or an acanthus leaf border. They have a special backstamp. The series was made in blue and white, sepia, or polychrome.

Mug, D.1898   130.00
Plate, 10 In.*   75.00

Old Moreton, Plate, 10 In.

Backstamp

Border

OLD SEA DOGS

Old Sea Dogs illustrates the life of Jack, a typical sailor. The mark is a sailboat with the words "Old Sea Dogs."

Pitcher, Jack's The Boy For Play,
   6 In.   95.00
Pitcher, Jack's The Lad For Work,
   Water   175.00

OLD WIFE

Old Wife is a series picturing raised designs of tropical fish. It was made from 1938 to 1955. There is a special backstamp. Pieces are numbered D.5966.

Charger   125.00

Backstamp

OMAR KHAYYAM

Omar Khayyam is a series illustrating excerpts from "The Rubaiyat of Omar Khayyam." A view of the character's face and upper torso fills all of the plate except the border where the verse is written. The design was made from 1910 to 1928.

Plate, The Moving Finger, 10 In.
                         65.00 to 75.00

POLAR BEAR

Polar Bear pieces are decorated with a border of polar bears in blues, grays, and greens. It was first made in 1909. It has a crackle glaze and no special mark.

Pitcher, D.3128   110.00

POPLAR TREES

Poplar Trees is a series with rack plates. There are trees pictured on the plate. The numbers D.3301, D.3305, and D.3416 were used. The series was made from 1923 to 1929.

Pitcher, 5 In., D.3416   85.00 to 90.00
Plate, D.3416   40.00

PROVERBS

Proverbs are very similar to English Old Proverbs. Each plate is decorated with a grapevine border, a picture, and two printed proverbs. The series was made from 1911 to 1928. A similar series showed golfers and appropriate proverbs. There is no special mark.

Plate, Fine Feathers Make Fine
   Birds, 10 In.*   40.00
Plate, Hope Springs Eternal In The
   Human Breast, 10 In.   39.00

Proverbs, Plate, Fine Feathers Make Fine Birds, 10 In.

QUEEN ELIZABETH AT OLD MORETON HALL,   see Old Moreton

REYNARD THE FOX

Reynard the Fox was produced in a bone china and made only in coffee wares. A picture of a fox and a yellow border is on each piece.

Teapot   95.00

RIP VAN WINKLE

Rip Van Winkle is a story retold by Washington Irving as part of "The Sketch Book" in 1819. The story was illustrated by Arthur Rackham in 1904 and the drawings were used on the Royal Doulton series first made in 1906. The pieces are decorated with a drawing and a banner with the words of the story.

Jug, 7 In.*   195.00

Rip Van Winkle, Jug, 7 In.

ROBERT BURNS, see Bobby Burns

ROBIN HOOD, see Under The Greenwood Tree

ROGER SALEM EL COBLER, see Head Rack Plates

RUSTIC ENGLAND

Rustic England (D.5694) pictures country scenes and homes. They are marked with the Australian mark and the words Rustic England. They were made from 1949 to 1960.

Plate, D.5694, 10 In.*   75.00

Backstamp

RUSTIC ENGLAND
D 5694
REG9. AUSTRALIA 16308/7/8

Rustic England, Plate, D.5694, 10 In.

SAYINGS WARE

Sayings Ware, 1907 to 1930, pictures old ladies drinking tea, some with sayings such as "The Cup That Cheers." The sayings are written in gray and black letters. There is a brown border picturing hanging teacups. It has no special mark.

Cup & Saucer   70.00
Plate, 9 In.*   25.00

Sayings Ware, Plate, 9 In.

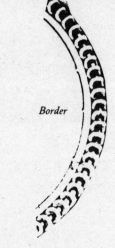

Border

SCENIC RACK PLATES

Scenic Rack Plates picture photographic scenes of animals and scenic places around the world, such as Koala Bears, Vermillion Lake, and Bow Valley. The plates are 10 inches in diameter. They are marked with a title on the back.

Bow Valley, 10 In.*   30.00
Giraffe, D.6482**   30.00
Koala Bears, 10 In.*   35.00
New Guinea Native, D.6437   28.00

Scenic Rack Plates, Bow Valley, 10 In.; Koala Bears, 10 In.

SHAKESPEARE CHARACTERS

There were many series called Shakespeare Characters. One series, made from 1912 to 1930, had pastel or sepia plates with no border design. The character's name is on the back of the plate. There is another Shakespeare Characters series with a green and brown cobblestone back ground, made from 1904 to 1928.

Pitcher, Romeo, C.1914, 4 1/2 In.
    55.00
Plate, Anne Page, 7 1/2 In.   47.50
Plate, Cardinal Wolsey, 10 In.*
    80.00
Plate, Falstaff, Brown & Green,
  10 In.*   50.00
Plate, Falstaff, Pastel, 10 In.*
    80.00
Plate, Katharine & Wolsey,
  D.3596, 10 In.   80.00
Plate, Portia, 8 In.   30.00
Plate, Romeo & Juliet, D.3596,
  10 In.   80.00
Tray, Katharine, 15 1/2 In.   80.00

Shakespeare Characters, Plate, Cardinal Wolsey, 10 In.

Shakespeare Characters, Plate, Falstaff, Brown & Green, 10 In.

Shakespeare Characters, Plate, Falstaff, Pastel, 10 In.

SHAKESPEARE PLAYS

Several series called Shakespeare Plays were made from 1903 to the 1940s. One pictures scenes from nine of Shakespeare's plays. They have a geometric border. They are marked with the act, scene, and title of a play. Other series have borders with flowers and scrolls, garland and baskets, or urns, swags, and flowers. One series was made in flow blue about 1925.

Plate, Falstaff and Dame
    Quickly, 10 In.*   55.00
Plate, Midsummer Night's Dream,
    D.2874, 10 In.   55.00

Shakespeare Plays, Plate, Falstaff and Dame Quickly, 10 In.

Backstamp

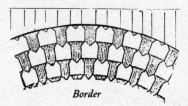

Border

SIR ROGER DE COVERLEY

Sir Roger De Coverley was a character created by Addison and Steele for "The Spectator," published 1711 to 1712. He represented a well-mannered and culti-vated country gentleman of the eighteenth century. The name was originally from an old country tune. The mark is a fox head with a crop and trumpet. The series was made from 1912 to 1949.

Plate, D.5814, 10 In.   95.00
Plate, Sir Roger Dancing With
    The Widow, 10 In.   60.00

Backstamp

SKATING

The Skating series shows a boy and others skating. The border is a Greek Key design. The pieces, made from 1907 to 1928, are numbered D. 2789 and D.2865.

Creamer, D.2789*	60.00
Plate, 9 In.	85.00
Trivet, "Pryde Goeth Before Fall"	
	50.00

Skating, Creamer, D.2789

SKETCHES FROM TENIERS

Sketches from Teniers pictures paintings by David Teniers II, a Flemish artist who lived from 1610 to 1690. The wares are decorated with deep colors. Pieces were made from 1905 to about 1942.

Jardiniere, Highways & Byways	Sugar, Highways & Byways	45.00
285.00		
Plate, The Village Fete, 10 1/2 In.		
55.00		

SOUTER'S CATS

David Souter, the cartoonist, designed a series of wares for Royal Doulton featuring his famous cartoon cats. The designs are black and white. An Art Nouveau border, the cat, and a saying appear on each piece. The plates were made from 1906 to 1939.

Plate, 6 In.*	50.00

Souter's Cats, Plate, 6 In.

THOUSAND AND ONE NIGHTS, see Arabian Nights

TREASURE ISLAND

Robert Louis Stevenson wrote "Treasure Island" in 1881. The series was sold from 1937, slightly modified in 1950. Some pieces are marked D.5812 or D.6376.

Chop Plate, D.6376   115.00

TUNIS

Tunis (D.3538) is a series made from 1912 to 1940. It pictures scenes of Arab activities.

Plate, 10 In.   55.00

Backstamp

UNCLE TOBY, see Diversions Of Uncle Toby

UNDER THE GREENWOOD TREE

Under The Greenwood Tree, 1914 to 1967, pictures the adventures of Robin Hood and his merry men. The scalloped plates are marked in a circle with a tree and the words "Under The Greenwood Tree."

Bowl, Robin Hood & Friar Tuck,
  7 3/4 In.   55.00
Cup & Saucer   75.00
Plaque, Cream Ground,
  15 1/4 In.   225.00
Plate, 10 1/2 In.*   50.00
Plate, Chop, Maid Marian, Friar
  Tuck, 13 3/8 In.   165.00
Tray, 5 X 11 In.   85.00

Backstamp

Under The Greenwood Tree,
Plate, 10 1/2 In.

WELSH LADIES

Welsh Ladies pictures four or five ladies in their native country dress: black hats and long black dresses. They have no special mark.

Vase, 3 1/4 In.   95.00

ZUNDAY ZMOCKS, see Gaffers

Toby Jugs

Jugs shaped like human figures became popular in England during the eighteenth century, and they were possibly inspired by the medieval and ancient jugs of similar form. The vessel often pictured a seated man holding a drink. The name "Toby" was in common use by the 1770s, probably referring to a character in a song of 1761 named "Toby Phillpot."

The tradition of the Toby jug was continued when the first of the Royal Doulton Tobies were offered in 1939. Sixteen were made for sale to the general market. These include The Best Is None Too Good, Cap'n Cuttle, Double XX, Falstaff, Fat Boy, Happy John, Honest Measure, Huntsman, Jolly Toby, Mr. Micawber, Mr. Pickwick, Old Charley, Sairey Gamp, Sam Weller, Sir Winston Churchill, and Squire. The Tobies were made in a variety of sizes.

Several other Toby jugs were made as advertising premiums for various companies. The Charrington Tobies, several versions of similar jugs, were made after 1954 for a brewery. The Cliff Cornell jugs were made in at least two sizes and three colors for the Cleveland Flux Company of Cleveland, Ohio. Brown, tan, and blue examples are known, but there may have been a few gray Tobies made. A special mark was used. The Hoare Toby jug was made in the 1930s, a George Robey jug was made in about 1910, and a Charlie Chaplin Toby was also produced. A prototype Toby of John Wesley is also known.

Sherlock Holmes and Sir Francis Drake were two new Toby jugs issued in 1981.

Royal Doulton created the imaginary city of Doultonville in 1983. This English town has many colorful characters that are pictured in a series of new Toby jugs. They include Reverend Cassock, Miss Nostrum the nurse, Mr. Furrow the farmer, and Mr. Litigate the lawyer. Each character was designed by William K. Harper and is four inches high. The issue price was $40.00.

Complete Toby Jug Price List

This short, squat, 4-inch-high toby pictures a smiling man holding a cup and pipe. The words "The Best Is None Too Good" are on the front of the base.

BEST IS NONE TOO GOOD*   D.6107 1939-1960   325.00

Cap'n Cuttle, or Captain Edward Cuttle, is a character in the book "Dombey and Son" by Charles Dickens.

CAP'N CUTTLE, 4 1/2 In.*   D.6266 1948-1960   150.00 to 195.00

The Charlie Chaplin toby was just a rumor to collectors until 1980. At least five are now known and in collections. The 10 1/2-inch jug pictures the English-born star of American movies. Charlie Chaplin is similar in style to the George Robey jug. The comedian carries a cane and his famous bowler hat is the cover. It has the registry number 668,948, which dates the introduction to 1918.

CHARLIE CHAPLIN   **N.A.**

There are at least two varieties of Charrington toby. These jugs, made after 1954, were 9 1/4 inches high. A man in a tricorn hat holding a jug in one hand and a mug in the other is pictured. One variety says "Toby Ales" on the base. The other says "One Toby Leads To Another." The jugs were advertisements for Charrington Brewers of England.

CHARRINGTON, Toby, Ales   300.00 to 400.00

Cliff Cornell was a Cleveland, Ohio, businessman who ordered special toby jugs in 1956 to give to friends for Christmas. The jug is a portrait of Mr. Cornell. The jug was made in brown, blue, or tan. It was made in two sizes.

CLIFF CORNELL, Blue, 5 1/2 In.	1956	299.00 to 325.00
CLIFF CORNELL, Blue, 9 In.* **	1956	235.00 to 249.00
CLIFF CORNELL, Brown, 9 In.* **	1956	245.00 to 299.00
CLIFF CORNELL, Tan, 5 1/2 In.	1956	750.00
CLIFF CORNELL, Tan, 9 In.	1956	300.00

Cliff Cornell, Blue, Brown, 9 In., 1956

Double XX, a 6 1/2-inch toby, is sometimes called the Man on the Barrel. The man, holding a mug of beer, is astride a barrel marked "XX" for "extra strong." He wears a maroon coat, black breeches and a tricorn hat.

DOUBLE XX *   D.6088 1939-1969   200.00 to 300.00

Falstaff, or Sir John Falstaff, is a character in the plays "Henry IV" and "The Merry Wives of Windsor" by Shakespeare.

FALSTAFF, 5 1/4 In.*   D.6063 1939-Present   26.50 to 60.00
FALSTAFF, 8 1/2 In.   D.6062 1939-Present   52.50 to 95.00

Fat Boy is a character in the book "Pickwick Papers" by Charles Dickens.

FAT BOY, 4 1/2 In.*   D.6264 1948-1960   195.00

Best Is None Too Good,
4 In., D.6107

Cap'n Cuttle, 4 1/2 In.,
D.6266

Double XX Or Man On
The Barrel, D.6088

Falstaff, 5 1/4 In.,
D.6063, 1939-Present

Fat Boy, 4 1/2 In.,
D.6264

Happy John, 9 In., D.6031,
1939-Present

George Robey was a famous English vaudeville performer about 1910. Some 10 1/2-inch toby jugs were made picturing him in a wrinkled suit. His flat hat was the cover. The jug seems to have been continued in production during the 1920s.

GEORGE ROBEY   3000.00

Happy John, designed by Harry Fenton, was inspired by the eighteenth-century toby jugs. A figure of a seated man is shown holding a jug in one hand, a mug of ale in the other. Happy John, 9 inches high, wears tan pants, a gray coat, yellow ascot, and black hat.

HAPPY JOHN, 5 1/2 In.   D.6070 1939-Present   26.50 to 45.00
HAPPY JOHN, 9 In.*   D.6031 1939-Present   52.50 to 95.00

It is reported that a jug shaped like a seated drinker was made in 1930s with the name of Hoare Ale at the base. No recent sale reports are available. Honest Measure is a 4 1/2-inch toby jug depicting a portly gentleman in a maroon tricorn hat, green jacket, red pants, and yellow vest. The front of the base is inscribed "Honest Measure Drink at Leisure."

HONEST MEASURE, 4 1/2 In.*   D.6108 1939-Present   26.50 to 60.00
HONEST MEASURE, 4 1/2 In.,
   Marked A   D.6108 1939-Present   60.00

The gray-haired man shown on the Huntsman toby holds a whip in one hand. He is dressed in appropriate riding clothes. The jug is 7 1/2 inches high.

HUNTSMAN, 7 1/2 In.*   D.6320 1950-Present   47.00 to 95.00

Jolly Toby, a 6 1/2-inch jug, shows a happy man holding a mug of ale and a whip. He wears a yellow vest and cream-colored trousers.

JOLLY TOBY, 6 1/2 In.*   D.6109 1939-Present   37.50 to 75.00

Honest Measure,	*Huntsman,*	*Jolly Toby,*
4 1/2 In., D.6108	*7 1/2 In., D.6320*	*6 1/2 In., D.6109*

Doultonville Toby Jugs: **Miss Nostrum, Mr. Furrow, Reverend Cassock, Mr. Litigate**

Miss Nostrum is the chubby nurse of the imaginary town of Doultonville. The series of four 4-inch toby jugs was introduced in 1983.

MISS NOSTRUM*   D.6700 1983-Present   28.00 to 40.00

Mr. Furrow, a 4-inch toby, represents the farmer in the imaginary town of Doultonville.

MR. FURROW*   D.6701 1983-Present   28.00 to 40.00

Mr. Litigate is the lawyer in the imaginary town of Doultonville. He is 4 inches high.

MR. LITIGATE*   D.6699 1983-Present   28.00 to 40.00

Mr. Micawber, 4 1/2 In., D.6262; Mr. Pickwick, 4 1/2 In., D.6261; Old Charley, 5 1/2 In., D.6069; Sairey Gamp, 4 1/2 In., D.6263

Mr. Micawber is a character from the book "David Copperfield" by Charles Dickens.

MR. MICAWBER, 4 1/2 In.* D.6262 1948-1960 180.00 to 200.00

Mr. Pickwick is a character from the book "Pickwick Papers" by Charles Dickens.

MR. PICKWICK, 4 1/2 In.* D.6261 1948-1960   195.00

Old Charley represents the night watchman of the nineteenth century.

OLD CHARLEY, 5 1/2 In.* D.6069 1939-1960 70.00 to 135.00
OLD CHARLEY, 8 3/4 In. D.6030 1939-1960 100.00 to 195.00

The clergyman of the imaginary town of Doultonville is named Reverend Cassock. This 4-inch toby was introduced in 1983.

REVEREND CASSOCK* D.6702 1983-Present 28.00 to 40.00

Sairey Gamp is a character from the book "Martin Chuzzlewit" by Charles Dickens.

SAIREY GAMP* D.6263 1948-1960   200.00

Sam Weller is a character from the book "Pickwick Papers" by Charles Dickens.

SAM WELLER, 4 1/2 In.* D.6265 1948-1960 125.00 to 195.00

In 1981, on the fifteenth anniversary of the death of Sir Arthur Conan Doyle, the Sherlock Holmes toby jug was made. It pictures the famous fictional character created by Sir Arthur.

SHERLOCK HOLMES, 8 3/4 In. D.6661 1981-Present 52.00 to 95.00

Sir Francis Drake led an expedition around the world in 1577, then returned to England with treasures for the Queen. He later fought the Spanish Armada, after finishing his game of bowls because he felt there was time to finish the

*Sam Weller, 4 1/2 In.,
D.6265*

Squire, 6 In., D.6319

game and win the battle as well. The toby shows Sir Francis kneeling with the bowling ball. It commemorates the 400th anniversary of the event.

SIR FRANCIS DRAKE, 9 In.   D.6660 1981-   52.50 to 95.00

Sir Winston Churchill was Prime Minister of Britain. The jug is a tribute to his leadership in 1940 during the Battle of Britain. Early jugs had a special back-stamp.

SIR WINSTON CHURCHILL, 4 In.   D.6175 1941-Present 22.00 to 45.00
SIR WINSTON CHURCHILL, 5 1/2 In.
                                    D.6172 1941-Present 32.00 to 65.00
SIR WINSTON CHURCHILL, 9 In.   D.6171 1941-Present 52.50 to 95.00

WINSTON CHUPCHILL
PRIME MINISTER
OF GREAT BRITAIN
— 1940 —

The Squire jug shows an unsmiling gentleman in a long green jacket and tan vest and pants. The 6-inch toby was designed by Harry Fenton.

SQUIRE*   D.6319 1950-1969   200.00 to 250.00

Dolls

Since the 1850s, doll heads have been made at some of the factories that are now part of the Royal Doulton group. Although the German and French doll heads were the most successful, the British made some. British doll heads were of a lesser quality and larger price until World War I. The English potters were not able to make a finish that compared with European doll heads. When the war cut off the supply of imported dolls, the British potteries began to make more heads. The dolls were modeled from the German and the heads were made of clay and decorated and glazed. The bodies were of cloth. Only a few of these dolls had china hands and feet. Doll manufacturing in England was successful until the war ended, when the less expensive German dolls became available again. Some English potteries continued making doll heads until World War II. Plastic doll heads became more common and only a few china doll heads are now being made for the mass market.

The House of Nisbet and Royal Doulton began making dolls in 1981. The first two series were the Victorian Birthday Dolls and the Kate Greenaway Portrait Dolls. In 1982 a special Royal Baby Doll was issued to commemorate the birth of Prince William of Wales. All of these dolls are made of English bone china with tinted faces. The doll body and the clothes are marked "Royal Doulton and Nisbet."

Complete Doll Price List

A series of annual Christmas dolls started in 1980. Each doll is limited to 3,500. Issue price was $195.

ANNUAL CHRISTMAS DOLL, 1983, Red Dress, Cap   195.00

The Edwardian Social Season dolls were first offered in 1983. The set of four dolls is dressed in the clothes popular in the early 1900s. The series is limited to 3500.

Edwardian Social Season, Ascot, Presentation At Court, Lords, Henley Regatta

EDWARDIAN SOCIAL SEASON,	Ascot*	195.00
EDWARDIAN SOCIAL SEASON,	Henley Regatta*	195.00
EDWARDIAN SOCIAL SEASON,	Lords*	195.00
EDWARDIAN SOCIAL SEASON,	Presentation At Court*	195.00

Firstborn is an unlimited doll made first in 1982. The doll is 12 inches long, has blue eyes and bone china head, hands, and legs. The doll is dressed in a christening gown and is in a lace-trimmed basket crib. It sold at retail for $175.

FIRSTBORN, 1982	106.00 to 175.00

Kate Greenaway portrait dolls were made by Eric Griffiths. Five different dolls, each limited to 5000, were made in Volume I, introduced in 1981. Five more dolls were included in Volume II. Small Sister retailed for $125, the other four 12-inch dolls of Volume I were issued at $175. The Volume II dolls were retailed at $195. The dolls were made with bone china heads and hands and cloth bodies. The clothing was marked with a label saying "Worldwide Edition of 5000." A certificate of authentication accompanied each doll.

KATE GREENAWAY,	Big Sister	175.00
KATE GREENAWAY,	Little Model	106.00 to 175.00
KATE GREENAWAY,	Muff	195.00
KATE GREENAWAY,	Pink Sash	92.00 to 150.00
KATE GREENAWAY,	Small Sister	78.00 to 125.00
KATE GREENAWAY,	Swans Down*	117.00 to 195.00
KATE GREENAWAY,	Vera	175.00
KATE GREENAWAY,	Waiting	195.00
KATE GREENAWAY,	Winter	106.00 to 175.00

Kate Greenaway, Swans Down

Another unlimited doll by Royal Doulton is called Little Bridesmaid. This 1982 doll was offered for $175.

LITTLE BRIDESMAID, 1982   106.00 to 175.00

The Princess of Wales doll was issued in 1983. It is limited to 3,500. Issue price was $250.

PRINCESS OF WALES, 1983   250.00

To commemorate the birth of Prince William, the Royal Doulton limited edition Royal Baby Doll was made in 1982. The doll is dressed in a gown inspired by the traditional royal family christening dress. It is in a lace-trimmed crib. The edition is limited to 2,500. Issue price is $295.

ROYAL BABY DOLL*   295.00

Victorian Birthday dolls were inspired by the nursery rhyme "Monday's Child is fair of face . . . " There will be fourteen dolls in the completed series, seven boys and seven girls. The series is not limited. Original price was $145 for the girl doll, $125 for the boy doll.

VICTORIAN BIRTHDAY,	Friday, Boy	125.00
VICTORIAN BIRTHDAY,	Friday, Girl	78.00 to 145.00
VICTORIAN BIRTHDAY,	Monday, Boy	125.00
VICTORIAN BIRTHDAY,	Monday, Girl	78.00 to 145.00
VICTORIAN BIRTHDAY,	Saturday, Boy	125.00
VICTORIAN BIRTHDAY,	Saturday, Girl	145.00
VICTORIAN BIRTHDAY,	Sunday, Boy	125.00

Royal Baby Doll

VICTORIAN BIRTHDAY, Sunday, Girl	145.00
VICTORIAN BIRTHDAY, Thursday, Boy	125.00
VICTORIAN BIRTHDAY, Thursday, Girl	145.00
VICTORIAN BIRTHDAY, Tuesday, Boy	125.00
VICTORIAN BIRTHDAY, Tuesday, Girl	145.00
VICTORIAN BIRTHDAY, Wednesday, Boy	125.00
VICTORIAN BIRTHDAY, Wednesday, Girl	145.00

An unlimited 14-inch doll known as Wedding Day was offered for the first time in 1982. The doll represents a young brunette lady in an ivory wedding dress. She carries a bouquet of yellow, orange, and white flowers.

WEDDING DAY, 1982   225.00

Miscellaneous

Royal Doulton made a variety of wares that resemble the character jugs. Some of them seem to have been made in the molds that were used for the character jugs but slightly adapted for other uses. Most of the miscellaneous "character" pieces were based on Dickens' characters. Ash pots were made in at least six styles during the years from 1938 to 1960. The tops of the bowls had indentations for a cigarette to rest. Ashtrays with ash pots were made during the same years in at least four styles. The pot had an open top and probably held wooden matches. The English call them "match stands." Several tobacco jars, figural teapots, small busts, sugar bowls, wall vases, toothpick holders, and a set of napkin rings were made. They were all discontinued by the 1960s. A group of fourteen table cigarette lighters was made from 1958 to 1973 (see list below). Musical jugs were made from about 1938 to 1948. Some special stoppered bottles were made in the character jug shapes for liquor companies during the 1960s. A new one was released in 1983. A paper Bols liquor label can be found on many of the bottles.

A series of six embossed jugs and a tankard were made from 1935 to 1960. The pieces pictured scenes from Dickens' stories. Other miscellaneous wares included in this chapter are such items as the "Zorro" bottle that held Sandeman sherry, lamps made from mounted figurines, wall masks, advertising pieces, etc. Bookends are listed under Figurines.

Table cigarette lighter and years of production:

Bacchus, 1964–1973
Beefeater, 1958–1973
Buz Fuz, 1958 only
Captain Ahab, 1964–1973
Cap'n Cuttle, 1958 only
Falstaff, 1958–1973
Lawyer, 1962–1973

Long John Silver, 1958–1973
Mr. Micawber, 1958 only
Mr. Pickwick, 1958–1961
Musketeer (Porthos), 1958 only
Old Charley, 1959–1973
Poacher, 1958–1973
Rip van Winkle, 1958 only

Miscellaneous Price List

Six different ash pots or ash bowls were made. Old Charley and Paddy were introduced in 1938. Auld Mac, Farmer John, Parson Brown and Sairey Gamp were introduced in 1939. All were withdrawn in 1960.

Ash Pot, Auld Mac, D.6006, A Mark	85.00 to 145.00
Ash Pot, Farmer John, D.6007	125.00 to 145.00
Ash Pot, Old Charley, D.5925	100.00 to 145.00
Ash Pot, Old Charley, D.5925, A Mark	85.00 to 145.00
Ash Pot, Paddy, D.5926	135.00 to 145.00
Ash Pot, Paddy, D.5926, A Mark	85.00 to 145.00
Ash Pot, Parson Brown, D.6008	120.00 to 145.00
Ash Pot, Sairey Gamp, D.6009	95.00 to 145.00

Ashtrays with open figural match-holders in the center were made from 1936 to 1960. The figures included John Barleycorn, Parson Brown, Dick Turpin and Old Charley.

Ashtray, John Barleycorn, D.5602	75.00
Ashtray, Old Charley, D.5599	75.00
Beaker, Wedding, A Princess For Wales, 1981	25.00
Bols Liqueur, Falstaff, 6 1/4 In.	45.00
Bols Liqueur, Poacher, 6 1/4 In.	60.00
Bols Liqueur, Rip Van Winkle, 6 1/4 In.	60.00
Bottle, Whiskey, Highland	70.00
Bottle, Whiskey, Old Crow	90.00
Bottle, Zorro, A Mark, 10 1/2 In.	50.00
Bottle, Zorro, Red, 4 In.	35.00
Bottle, Zorro, Yellow	39.00

A set of busts was made from 1939 to 1960. These included Sairey Gamp, Buz Fuz, Mr. Pickwick, Mr. Micawber, Tony Weller, and Sam Weller. Four larger busts had been made with HN numbers in 1934. They were Sairey Gamp, Pickwick, Micawber, and Tony Weller. These larger busts had been mounted as bookends and are included in the figurine section of this book.

Bust, Mr. Micawber, D.6050	70.00
Bust, Mr. Pickwick, D.6049	79.00
Bust, Sairey Gamp, D.6047	70.00 to 85.00
Bust, Sam Weller, D.6052	70.00 to 85.00
Bust, Sergeant Buz Fuz, D.6048	79.00 to 85.00
Bust, Tony Weller, D.6051	75.00
Crow, Advertising Figure	175.00
Dr. Scholl's Sign	295.00
Dr. Scholl's Toe Flex Display	295.00

A small number of musical character jugs were made with music boxes set in the base. These were made from 1937 to 1948. Each of the five jugs had the appropriate tune. Old Charley played "Here's a health unto His Majesty." Paddy played "Irish Jig." Tony Weller played "Come, Landlord, fill the flowing bowl." "The Campbells are coming" was the tune for Owd Mac and "Old King Cole" was the song by the expected Old King Cole–shaped jug.

Jug, Musical, Old Charley, D.5858	375.00
Jug, Musical, Old King Cole, D.6014	650.00
Jug, Musical, Owd Mac, D.5889	375.00
Jug, Musical, Paddy, D.5887	395.00
Jug, Musical, Tony Weller, D.5888	375.00

A series of six special jugs with raised figures and a related tankard was made from 1935 to 1960. The first jug, The Old Curiosity Shop, was introduced in 1935, Oliver Twist in 1936, Pickwick Papers in 1937, the others in 1949.

Jug, Raised Figures, Old Curiosity Shop, D.5584	150.00 to 155.00
Jug, Raised Figures, Old London, D.6291	210.00 to 250.00
Jug, Raised Figures, Oliver Asks For More, D.6285	185.00
Jug, Raised Figures, Oliver Twist, D.5617	150.00 to 200.00
Jug, Raised Figures, Peggotty, D.6292	225.00
Jug, Raised Figures, Pickwick Papers, D.5756	160.00 to 175.00
Lamp, Chelsea, Pair	1000.00

A group of small-sized character jugs was made into table cigarette lighters from 1958 to 1973. Some were made as special gifts, others sold only in the United States for $13.50 to $20.00. The lighters, made by Doulton, fit exactly into the top hole. Another company in the United States made lighters by filling jugs with plaster and setting a slightly smaller jug inside. These were discontinued in 1957. The original list of Royal Doulton–made lighters and the years of manufacture are included in the introduction to this chapter.

Lighter, Beefeater*	95.00
Lighter, Long John Silver*	67.50
Lighter, Poacher*	75.00 to 100.00
Lighter, Sergeant Buz Fuz*	125.00

Lighter, Beefeater   *Lighter, Long John Silver*

Lighter, Poacher

Lighter, Sergeant Buz Fuz

Match Holder, Mr. Squeers, 2 In.	**70.00 to 95.00**
Match Holder, Sam Weller, 3 In.	**70.00**

A set of six napkin rings was made from 1939 to 1960. These included Mr. Pickwick, Mr. Micawber, Fat Boy, Tony Weller, Sam Weller, and Sairey Gamp. Originally the six were sold only as a set but collectors today will buy the single ring.

Napkin Ring, Mr. Micawber, M.58	**485.00**

The Oliver Twist Tankard is part of a special group of jugs and tankards made from 1935 to 1960.

Tankard, Oliver Twist, Raised Figures, D.6286	**150.00 to 175.00**
Teapot, Old Charley	**600.00**
Teapot, Sairey Gamp	**575.00 to 600.00**
Teapot, Tony Weller	**600.00 to 695.00**
Wall Mask, Jester	**500.00 to 575.00**
Wall Mask, Sweet Anne, HN1590	**425.00**

OTHER KOVELS' ILLUSTRATED PRICE GUIDES

The Kovels' Bottle Price List
Sixth Edition

Over 10,000 current prices for hundreds of types of bottles —more than any other bottle price list on the market. More than 500 illustrations in full color and black and white. Includes old and new bottles, bitters, figurals, flasks, Avons, Beams, and a host of others. Notes on styles and manufacturers, lists of bottle magazines and clubs, and an extensive bibliography. The most definitive listing of current prices available.

54587-X $10.95 paper

The Kovels' Illustrated Price Guide to Depression Glass and American Dinnerware
Second Edition

The most up-to-date book ever published about Depression glass and American dinnerware. Two books in one, with current prices of more than 6,000 pieces, each listed by manufacturer; with dates, descriptions, and pottery marks. Over 250 illustrations in color and black and white. Pocket-size for easy reference.

54974-3 $10.95 paper

The Kovels' Antiques & Collectibles Price List
Sixteenth Edition

America's best-selling antiques price list. Current prices of over 45,000 antiques and collectibles for the 1983–1984 market. Over 500 illustrations with 75 full-color plates. Based on a comprehensive survey of sales, catalogs, auctions, and other reliable sources. All prices are actual reports, not estimates.

55028-8 $9.95 paper

MORE KOVELS' COLLECTORS' BOOKS

American Country Furniture
1780–1875

Over 700 close-up photographs identify styles, construction, woods, finishes, hardware, and other details. All the information you need to be an expert on American country furniture. Special sections on Pennsylvania, Shaker furniture, spool furniture, and furniture construction, plus an illustrated glossary of accessories and terms.

54668-X $8.95 paper
09737-0 $15.95 hardcover

The Kovels' Collectors' Source Book

A comprehensive A to Z directory of resources for collectors, with more than 250 black-and-white photographs and line drawings. Everything you need to know to keep your collection alive, secure, and growing. Listings of clubs and publications, how-to-repair books, price guides, parts and repair services, buying by mail, auctions and auction houses, matching services, display services, booksellers, conservators, restoration sources, preservation supplies, and much more. An absolute necessity for collectors, museums, shops, clubs, organizations, and schools.

54791-0   **$13.95 paper**
54846-1   **$24.95 hardcover**

Kovels' Know Your Antiques

Revised and Updated

The best general guide for antiques collectors in print today. Illustrated with more than 300 photographs and line drawings. Written for the novice or beginning collector, it contains information about recognizing and determining the value of virtually every type of antique. Makes identification of objects a breeze.

54501-2   **$13.95 hardcover**

Kovels' Know Your Collectibles

With more than 1,000 illustrations, this up-to-date guide to the latest collecting trends focuses on silver, glass, furniture, and other objects that are not old enough to be designated "antiques" but which are rapidly increasing in value and represent the collecting patterns of the future. Contains information about value, origin, availability, storage, and buying and selling.

53608-0   **$16.95 hardcover**

A Directory of American Silver, Pewter and Silver Plate

Hardcover

Thousands of marks of American silver, pewter, and silver plate, listed and illustrated for easy identification.

50636-X   **$9.95 hardcover**

The Kovels' Collector's Guide to American Art Pottery

Covers all manufacturers of art pottery and is arranged alphabetically by manufacturer. Eighty full-color plates and over 1,500 photographs and line drawings.

51676-4   **$17.95 hardcover**
54980-8   **$10.95 paper**

SEND ORDERS & INQUIRIES TO:
Crown Publishers, Inc.
One Park Avenue, New York, N.Y. 10016
ATT: SALES DEPT.

THE KOVELS

SALES & TITLE INFORMATION
1-800-526-4264

NAME

ADDRESS

CITY & STATE

ZIP

PLEASE SEND ME THE FOLLOWING BOOKS:

ITEM NO.	QTY.	TITLE & UNIT PRICE			TOTAL
549743	_____	The Kovels' Illustrated Price Guide to Depression Glass and American Dinnerware—2nd Edition	PAPER	$10.95	_____
550288	_____	The Kovels' Antiques & Collectibles Price List—16th Edition	PAPER	$ 9.95	_____
547910	_____	The Kovels' Collectors' Source Book	PAPER	$13.95	_____
548461	_____	The Kovels' Collectors' Source Book	HARDCOVER	$24.95	_____
54668X	_____	American Country Furniture: 1780–1875	PAPER	$ 8.95	_____
097370	_____	American Country Furniture: 1780–1875	HARDCOVER	$15.95	_____
549808	_____	The Kovels' Collector's Guide to American Art Pottery	PAPER	$10.95	_____
516764	_____	The Kovels' Collector's Guide to American Art Pottery	HARDCOVER	$17.95	_____
50636X	_____	A Directory of American Silver, Pewter and Silver Plate	HARDCOVER	$ 9.95	_____
54587X	_____	The Kovels' Bottle Price List—6th Edition	PAPER	$10.95	_____
545012	_____	Kovels' Know Your Antiques—Revised and Updated	HARDCOVER	$13.95	_____
536080	_____	Kovels' Know Your Collectibles	HARDCOVER	$16.95	_____

_____ TOTAL ITEMS   Total Retail Value _____

CHECK OR MONEY ORDER ENCLOSED MADE
PAYABLE TO CROWN PUBLISHERS, INC.
(No cash or stamps, please)

Shipping & Handling Charge **$1.40**
for one book; 60¢ for
each additional book _____

Charge: Master Card   Visa   American Express   Card
Account Number (include all digits)   Expires   MO.   YR.

TOTAL AMOUNT DUE _____

PRICES SUBJECT TO CHANGE
WITHOUT NOTICE

Signature _____

Thank you for your order